DISCOURSES OF EMPIRE

Society of Biblical Literature

Semeia Studies

Gerald O. West, General Editor

Editorial Board:
Pablo Andiñach
Fiona Black
Denise K. Buell
Gay L. Byron
Jione Havea
Jennifer L. Koosed
Jeremy Punt
Yak-Hwee Tan

Number 71
Board Editor: Jeremy Punt

DISCOURSES OF EMPIRE
The Gospel of Mark from a Postcolonial Perspective

DISCOURSES OF EMPIRE

THE GOSPEL OF MARK FROM A POSTCOLONIAL PERSPECTIVE

Hans Leander

Society of Biblical Literature
Atlanta

DISCOURSES OF EMPIRE
The Gospel of Mark from a Postcolonial Perspective

Copyright © 2013 by the Society of Biblical Literature

All rights reserved. No part of this work may be reproduced or transmitted in any form or by any means, electronic or mechanical, including photocopying and recording, or by means of any information storage or retrieval system, except as may be expressly permitted by the 1976 Copyright Act or in writing from the publisher. Requests for permission should be addressed in writing to the Rights and Permissions Office, Society of Biblical Literature, 825 Houston Mill Road, Atlanta, GA 30329 USA.

Library of Congress Cataloging-in-Publication Data

Leander, Hans.
  Discourses of empire : the gospel of Mark from a postcolonial perspective / Hans Leander.
     p. cm. — (Society of Biblical Literature. Semeia studies ; no. 4)
  Includes bibliographical references.
  ISBN 978-1-58983-889-5 (paper binding : alk. paper) — ISBN 978-1-58983-890-1 (electronic format) — ISBN 978-1-58983-891-8 (hardcover binding : alk. paper)
  1. Bible. Mark—Postcolonial criticism. I. Title.
  BS2585.52.L43 2013
  226.3'06—dc23   2013024345

Printed on acid-free, recycled paper conforming to
ANSI/NISO Z39.48-1992 (R1997) and ISO 9706:1994
standards for paper permanence.

Contents

Preface..vii
Acknowledgments..xiii

1. Introduction..1

Part 1: Postcolonial Theory and the Bible

2. Postcolonial Theory..27

3. Postcolonial Criticism in Biblical Studies................................49

Part 2: Mark in European Colonialism

4. Modern Biblical Studies and Empire..75

5. The Semitic and the Greek (1:1)...87

6. Between Man and Brute (5:1–20)..95

7. Submissive Heathen and Superior Greek (7:24–30)............109

8. The Embarrassing Parousia (8:31–9:1)...................................117

9. "Only Absolutely Spiritual" (11:1–11)....................................123

10. An Irish Cat among the Pigeons (12:13–17).......................131

11. The Centurion between East and West (15:39)..................139

12. Conclusion: Mark and European Colonialism...................145

Part 3: Mark in the Roman Empire

13. Mark Begins to Circulate..151

14. An Oppositional Beginning (1:1) 185

15. Imperial Satire (5:1–20)..201

16. Entering a Narrative Crisis (7:24–30)..221

17. The Parousia as *Pharmakon* (8:31–9:1) 239

18. With Bhabha at the Jerusalem City Gates (11:1–22).........................255

19. The Emperor Breaks the Surface (12:13–17) 269

20. The Secrecy Complex as a Third Space (15:39)................................285

21. How Mark Destabilizes Empire...295

Part 4: Uninheriting a Colonial Heritage

22. Different Marks in Different Empires..307

Bibliography..323
Index of Ancient Sources..371
Index of Subjects...381
Index of Authors...385

Preface

As I began work on this study in the fall of 2005, the global phenomenon known as the return of religion had fueled a debate regarding the relation between religion and politics. Although scholars today more often refer to a *new visibility* rather than a *return* of religion, the debate is ongoing.[1] Apart from the threatening rise of religious fundamentalism, religion also permeates contemporary Continental philosophy, the arts, and the media, as well as the rhetoric of international politics. For better or worse, this new visibility of religion has increasingly challenged two central tenets of the West: first, the assumption that modernization entails secularization and the disappearance of religion; and second, that religion and politics should be kept in strictly separate spheres. Hence several contemporary scholars describe the present condition as *postsecular* (Sigurdson 2009; Boeve 2008).

Here in Sweden the debate also concerns the role of our national church, whose relation with the state has been redefined by a January 2000 law.[2] In the Swedish media the debate concerns (among other things) whether the church ought to be involved in "politics." As indicated by an editorial headline in Gothenburg's largest morning paper (Göteborgsposten 2004), "Don't Pursue Politics in the Name of the Church," the rhetoric typically centers upon modernity's division between politics

---

1. Since *return* implies a simple reemergence of something that has been in decline, scholars today more often refer to a *new visibility* of religion (Hoelzl and Ward 2008).

2. Gaining legal force on January 1, 2000, this law basically declared the Church of Sweden to be a faith community among other faith communities (i.e., free churches, Roman Catholics, Jews, Muslims, etc.), all of which were given equal opportunities to register with the state in order to have their dues collected from their members by the state along with the income tax. It should also be acknowledged, however, that the law reserved a particular role for the Church of Sweden as compared to other religious communities, not least in terms of funeral services.

and religion, which defines religious faith as a private matter and political commitments as not genuinely rooted in Christian faith, and hence secondary to the church's true vocation. Similar sentiments have been found among Swedes in recent surveys about religious congregations and sociopolitical engagement (Lundqvist 2011).

To some extent, the questions posed in this book about Mark's Gospel address these debates. Even if modernity's definition of religion is in some sense legitimate, it can be asked whether a division of human reality into religious and political spheres, or "kingdoms" as Luther would have it, prevents us from hearing Mark's Gospel as its primary premodern audience heard it. For instance, Mark's stunning use of ὁ σταυρός (the cross) as a concept metaphor can hardly be heard with this division intact. In order not to be bereaved of significant dimensions of the gospel message, then, the argument here moves beyond the hotly debated division between religion and politics and conceptualizes the religio-political setting in which Mark was initially circulated: the ancient imperial culture of Rome. And although one might consider such a move to be fraught with difficulties and dangers, it is nevertheless a crucial journey on which to embark in a postsecular condition.

But why "postcolonial"? As will be seen, postcolonial criticism has often implied a secularist stance. Applying a postcolonial perspective on a biblical text is thus a way to challenge the secularism of postcolonial thinking, thereby connecting it with the postsecular. Postcolonial criticism, as understood here, has much in common with the more recent postsecular trajectory, not least by being critical of certain aspects of modernity and the Enlightenment. Nevertheless, since Sweden can hardly qualify as a nation with a colonial history of its own, one might ask why a Swede would find postcolonial criticism a helpful perspective for biblical interpretation. Despite major attempts to become an empire during the seventeenth century, *empire* remains somewhat foreign as a concept in Swedish. Unlike in the English-speaking world, where *empire* is used quite extensively, the Swedish term *imperium* tends to be avoided. The exception would be the movie *Star Wars*, which, of course, tends to give the concept a fictive character. Not even the Romans had an empire, if Swedish would be the norm, the Swedish term being *Romarriket*.

The postcolonial perspective used here, however, implies that empire—for better or for worse—has affected the present condition in far more ways than we would perhaps like to admit. This includes Swedish society and its contemporary mixture of cultures and religions. It is therefore an important topic, an exciting one at that, in order to understand and engage with the present. As argued by the Swedish postcolonial biblical scholar Anna Runesson (2006, 123–24), since the term *global village* tends to hide the power relations that stem from European colonialism, *postcolonial* is a better term to describe our present circumstance—even in Sweden.

Hence, even if Sweden's résumé as an actual colonizer is comparably short—the Sami people need to be mentioned here[3]—this study emphasizes the extent to which the Swedish society has been intertwined with European colonial history by promoting colonial expansion, being culturally defined by it, gaining from it economically, as well as helping to resist it. As an indication of this complex historical affiliation, there are rave debates over how to deal with racist and colonial stereotypes in Swedish popular culture. Most recently, when a children's book had been criticized for reproducing a racial stereotype known as the pickaninny, the author decided to withdraw the book.[4]

The complex ways in which Swedes have interacted with European colonialism can also be seen in Protestant mission. Reporting from a missionary meeting in London, a Swedish missionary magazine proposed that "the Englishmen are, with all their mistakes, of all nations on earth, the one that has the power and means that are required to prepare the way for Christianity and … protect its tender sprout among the heathens" (Tottie 1884, 118). The attitude was ambivalent; Protestant mission from Sweden supported as well as resisted the colonial expansion.[5] Nevertheless, the missionary magazines that grew in numbers during the latter part of the nineteenth century engaged a large number of Swedes in the project often referred to as "the white man's burden."

Also, as represented by such writers as Henning Mankell and Per Wästberg, as well as the rise of solidarity movements during the anticolonial struggles of the 1960s, the issue of colonialism has a more recent history in Sweden. Economically, Sweden was a leading supporter of the liberation movements. In 1994 the African National Congress in South

---

3. For a critical discussion on the Swedish treatment of the Sami people, see Claesson 2003.
4. Söderling 2012. The debate has been especially passionate during November and December 2012 in various media, i.e., the Internet, radio, and newspapers.
5. For a recent study of missionary magazines in relation to European colonialism, see Odén 2012.

Africa and South West Africa People's Organization (SWAPO) in Namibia had received a total of 1.6 billion SEK (Swedish kronor), which is more than the combined contributions of the socialist countries in Europe (Palmberg 2009, 36). In line with this, Fairtrade has become prominent in Sweden, not least in the churches. Promoting what used to be called "colonial products" (i.e., coffee, tea, and chocolate), albeit produced under decent working conditions, Fairtrade makes visible how a colonial heritage continues to play a role in the Swedish society.

In addition, I have personal reasons for my interest in the postcolonial research field. My grandfather worked for the Svenska tändsticks AB (now Swedish Match), and his employment in British India as a sales manager during the 1930s had a considerable influence on his self-understanding. In relation to a colonial history that also runs in the family, so to speak, I have been intrigued by postcolonial criticism, especially by its focus on the subjectification that is made possible through stereotypical discourse.

Further, the postcolonial perspective is connected to my specific social location in Hammarkullen, a suburb north of Gothenburg where 82 percent of the population is of foreign background.[6] The location's affinity with what Stuart Hall (1996, 242) describes as "the notion of post-colonial times" can be illustrated by the following anecdote. Before the initiation of the Second Gulf War in March 2003, I had participated in several large peace marches in central Gothenburg.[7] Returning home after one such march, I encountered some Iraqi neighbors who had recently escaped Saddam's brutal regime. Having ascertained the event from which I was returning, they engaged me in a lengthy discussion. I attempted to argue that democracy cannot be imposed by foreign military intervention, and they vigorously attempted to dissuade me from what they regarded as my "misguided" conduct. Eventually, since neither the attempt to stop the war nor the war itself was successful, a friendship developed between us that was beautifully represented when, during the celebration of my fortieth birthday, one of my friends, a musician, sang a mixture of Iraqi-Swedish songs accompanied by a lute.

---

6. See Göteborgs stads stadsledningskontor 2010. *Foreign background* is defined as born abroad or with both parents born abroad. Compared to 29 percent in Gothenburg as a whole, Hammarkullen clearly sticks out.

7. Hall (1996, 244) describes the First Gulf War with its colonial history and ambiguous complexity as "a classic post-colonial event."

Beyond this, my background as a peace activist, with its experiences of empowerment and disillusionment, also attracts me to the issues of the (im)possible, of agency, and of being caught up in reproductions of binary divisions, all of which are prominent in postcolonial criticism. As such, the interest with which I approach Mark's Gospel is fraught with ambiguity and a keen awareness of the risks regarding what Gayatri Spivak (1988a, 290) has called "dangerous utopianism," and what my former teacher Lennart Thörn would refer to as "an over-realized eschatology." I take this awareness as representing what Hall (1996, 247) describes as the "serialized or staggered transition to the 'post-colonial,'" which implies a transition "from difference to *différance*"—from an identification against the other to an identification with the fragmented nature of self as well as other.

Acknowledgments

This book is a revision of my doctoral dissertation (University of Gothenburg, 2011), which was made possible by a generous scholarship from the Church of Sweden Research Council that financed my employment as a doctoral student at the Department of Literature, History of Ideas and Religion.

I wish to thank my supervisor, Samuel Byrskog, who has played a key role in this project from its start. Without his initial enthusiasm as well as his thoughtful, intelligent advice and support throughout the various impasses and difficulties, this study would not have been written. I have also received significant benefit from the input of other scholars. Hanna Stenström has, on several occasions, given sharp and encouraging feedback on texts; and Stephen Moore, whose essay on Mark and empire (2004) was an eye-opener for the project during its primary phase, invited me to Drew University, where I spent six exciting weeks as a visiting scholar during the fall of 2008, participating in classes on The Bible after Postmodernism as well as in the Biblical Colloquium.

The study received a significant boost from Magnus Zetterholm's incisive reactions to an early version of the manuscript as well as from the expert comments of Klas Grinell and Mikela Lundahl on the chapter on postcolonial theory. Tommy Wasserman has given valuable feedback on the issues of textual criticism, and Stefan Arvidsson has contributed significantly to the analysis of nineteenth-century scholarship.

Drafts of my manuscripts have been discussed at several seminars at the department where I am employed as well as in Lund, Oslo, and various Society of Biblical Literature meetings. The feedback received on these occasions has been important, particularly from Halvor Moxnes, Lone Fatum, Christina Petterson, Anna Runesson, Nils Aksel Røsæg, Hans Kvalbein, Stellan Vinthagen, Ched Myers, Lasse Berndes, Elisabet Gerle, Tobias Hägerland, Göran Larsson, Staffan Olofsson, Kerstin von Brömsen, Erik Alvstad, and Daniel Enstedt.

Generous scholarships have been granted from Filosofiska fakulteternas gemensamma donationsfond, Knut och Alice Wallenbergs stiftelse, Adlerbertska Stipendiestiftelsen, and Wilhelm och Martina Lundgrens vetenskapsfond. These funds have stimulated the work by making possible the participation in international meetings and seminars. Helge Ax:son Johnsons stiftelse kindly contributed to the proofreading, and Kungliga och Hvitfeldtska stiftelsen financed the last six months of my doctoral studies.

Lastly, all support from friends and family is inestimable. But I would especially like to acknowledge how Fredrik Ivarsson and Henrik Frykberg from the beginning of this project have greatly helped by offering comments and by being dear reliable friends.

1
Introduction

> What we make of the Bible is important politically because it affects what the Bible makes of us.
> —Tat-siong Benny Liew (1999a, 21)

That such an ambiguous story as the Gospel of Mark is proclaimed as the "good news" of Jesus Christ (Mark 1:1) has been a question for many biblical interpreters and theologians through the centuries. Considering that both Matthew and Luke probably intended their Gospels to replace Mark, it is not even clear how it survived as a Gospel.[1] As illustrated by Augustine's (*Cons.* 1.2.4) well-known treatment of Mark as Matthew's "attendant," Mark became a neglected canonical Gospel for a long time—a circumstance that Brenda Schildgen (1999, 35–37) has tellingly designated: "present but absent."

As the hypothesis of Markan priority became accepted during the nineteenth century, Mark left its shadowy existence and became considerably more attractive as a scholarly object. Although this new interest mainly regarded Mark as a window through which to study the historical Jesus, or with the twentieth-century development of source and form criticism to search for the fragments and oral sources behind the Gospels, the shift was still radical. In the 1950s moreover, with the rise of redaction criticism (Marxsen 1969), Mark also began to be appreciated as a theological composition in its own right. From here, the step was not far to narrative criticism, an approach that has drawn deeply on New Criticism in literary studies, resulting in readings of Mark as a unified narrative (Rhoads and

---

1. Graham Stanton (1997, 341–42) argues that Matthew and Luke wrote to replace Mark. A common explanation for Mark's survival is its connection to the apostle Peter, which will be discussed below. Joanna Dewey (2004) has also suggested that its popularity as an oral story during the first century is an important factor.

Michie 1982; Kelber 1979). Furthermore, since an ongoing development in the field of hermeneutics has been to relocate the meaning of texts from the author's intention to the reader, the ambiguity and unfinished character of Mark's Gospel has begun to appear more attractive to contemporary scholars. With its lack of a birth narrative, paratactic style, hectic pace, and enigmatic ending, Mark has become increasingly appreciated by readers who find fascinating what appears to be ambiguous, unfinished, and in the making. Again, Schildgen (1999, 21) puts it well: "Like the gospel's empty tomb, its ambiguities, paradoxes, and 'open-endedness' prove to be precisely what interests contemporary commentators." This interest constitutes one of the premises of the current project.

Biblical Scholarship in Transition

The way in which I conduct this study of Mark's Gospel also connects to a development in biblical scholarship that, for theoretical as well as empirical reasons, emphasizes the significance of the scholar's location, interest, and perspective. Whereas the theoretical development has mainly taken place in the fields of hermeneutics and poststructuralist theory, the empirical aspects concern an actual widening and decentering of the geopolitical location of biblical scholarship and its effects on biblical interpretation.[2] Kwok Pui-lan, a Chinese American biblical scholar who prominently represents this development, regards historical-critical research, with its claims of objectivity and impartiality, as being embedded in the episteme of nineteenth-century Europe and "decisively influenced by the colonial and empire-building impulses of Europe."[3] Since historical-critical research has dominated modern biblical studies, not least the Swedish context in which I received my scholarly training, Kwok's trenchant postcolonial critique intriguingly challenges our self-understanding as biblical scholars. In this study therefore I deal with this critique in a rather careful manner.

---

2. For introductions to and overviews of hermeneutics and poststructuralist theory, and its implications for biblical interpretation, see Moore 1994; Aichele et al. 1995; Adam 2000; and Thiselton 1992; 2009.

3. Kwok 1998a, 80. As seen in the edited volumes of Sugirtharajah (1991; 2008) and Segovia and Tolbert (1995b; 1995a), this critique against what is seen as a historical-critical paradigm is widespread in the field of postcolonial biblical criticism.

1. INTRODUCTION

In one sense, however, pointing out the contingent character of biblical research is battering at an open door. Already in 1906, Albert Schweitzer famously criticized nineteenth-century scholarship on the historical Jesus for imposing its own liberal and modern notions on the ancient sources.[4] Historical-critical scholars of today therefore generally accept the impossibility of pure objectivity. The consequence of such acceptance, on the other hand, is typically seen as being of limited importance. Of course, no one can be objective (one can admit with a shrug of the shoulders), but to be as objective as possible is nevertheless upheld as the desirable ideal. Rather than to increase the level of critical academic self-consciousness, Schweitzer's critique is then taken as a call to intensify what Daniel Patte has called an anticontextual approach and to fortify the ideals of objectivity.[5] To a limited extent, however, the postmodern and postcolonial take on historiography has given rise to metacritical discussions among scholars with a historical-critical orientation, about the epistemological presumptions as well as the political and ethical nature of biblical research (cf. Via 2002; J. Collins 2005). Also, the increasingly heterogeneous character of biblical scholarship from the 1970s onward has undermined the notion of a one and only scientific approach.[6] Thus Schweitzer's critique now seems ripe for the harvesting of its metacritical potentials.[7]

I here need to point out that the postcolonial critique of biblical research, as I understand it, is not a criticism of historical investigations per se. It seems pointless to deny that historical inquiries about a text's date, provenance, authorship, genre, primary audience, and so on, as well as careful analyses of the text itself, significantly contribute to discussions

---

4. See Schweitzer 2000, which is based on the second German edition, originally published in 1913.

5. Daniel Patte (2011, 198–200) describes North Atlantic academia as denying its contextual character, hence as "anti-contextual." As for my situation, since the scholarly context is divided, it is difficult to speak in the singular about a European, or even a Nordic, research environment. Whereas some uphold the anticontextual approach, others are more prone to regard biblical research as intertwined with political, cultural, and ecclesial discourses. Cf. Segovia 2000, 11, who critiques historical criticism for its low degree of critical self-consciousness, either of itself as a paradigm or of its relationship to other modes of interpretation.

6. This heterogeneity is particularly represented by the plurality of "criticisms" that have developed in biblical studies since the 1970s—narrative criticism, structural criticism, social scientific criticism, ideological criticism, deconstructive criticism, etc.

7. For a similar interpretation of Schweitzer, see Moxnes 2012.

about a text's meaning. The critique is rather to be seen as a questioning of the epistemological premises and truth claims of biblical exegesis. When a notion of a stable original meaning is upheld, along with the possibility of extracting that meaning via a scientific methodology, biblical scholarship produces notions of biblical authority that are problematic, to put it mildly. This problem was illustrated in 1951, when Swedish biblical scholars made a common public statement known as *Exegetdeklarationen* (the exegetical declaration) that addressed the disputed issue of female ministers in the Church of Sweden. The statement was concise:

> The undersigned professors and assistant professors in New Testament exegesis at the nations' two universities hereby declare, based on careful research, as our firm opinion that the appointment of so-called female ministers in the church would be inconsistent with New Testament beliefs and would entail a departure from the fidelity to Holy Scriptures. Jesus' choice of apostles as well as Paul's words about the position of the woman in the congregation have a principal meaning and are independent of contingent conditions and opinions. The present proposition about granting women admission to ministry in the Church of Sweden must therefore be said to encounter serious exegetical obstacles.[8]

The New Testament texts, according to this declaration, have a fixed and timeless meaning that the academically trained exegete can extract and that the church is bound to follow in order to show scriptural fidelity. And while the Church of Sweden eventually granted women admission to the ministry in 1958, the exegetical declaration helped to form extant notions regarding biblical exegesis and authority that continue to fuel resistance against female ministers in a number of ecclesial circles. In other words, to claim scientific or exegetical objectivity when studying the meaning of a biblical text can be a highly political move. Indeed, the irony of the role played by these Swedish scholars is not to be missed. In the late eighteenth century, when modern biblical scholarship emerged, the claims of a strict, historical, scientific objectivity represented a critical and socially progressive position that paved the way for establishing an academic scholarship in partial opposition to church authority and dogma.[9] As I will argue in chapter 3, the rise of modern biblical scholar-

---

8. My translation. The Swedish text is published in Sjöberg 1953, 29.
9. Since historical-critical research was not accepted in the Catholic Church until

ship was a complex and paradoxical development, far from ethically and politically disinterested.

As pointed out by John Barton (1990), despite a common critique of the exegesis/eisegesis dichotomy, the notion of a text's original and stable meaning still holds sway in wide segments of biblical scholarship. The task of the exegete, it seems, is to "draw out" the true original meaning of the biblical text.

For my purposes, it is interesting that scholars with traditional exegetical training are increasingly questioning this strict division between exegesis and eisegesis. An illuminating example is Birger Olsson, a professor emeritus known in Sweden for authoring two commentaries in the Kommentar till Nya testamentet series. In an interesting response to Annika Borg's (2004) feminist critique of his commentary on 1 Peter, Olsson (2006, 156–59) refers to a development in biblical studies where a particular time has its particular "type of interpretation" (*tolkningstyp*). The type of interpretation Borg criticizes him for *not* conducting (i.e., feminist critique), he argues, was inconceivable during the late 1970s, when he was working on his commentary. He concludes his response by discussing the division between critical/exegetical and creative/theological approaches to biblical texts. Although trained in the necessity of a strict division, he is now expressing skepticism toward the possibility, and even the desirability, of such a separation:

> I am increasingly skeptical about completely leaving the one task to exegetes and the other to theologians. We both need to show our exegetical and theological premises. In the present situation I would like to see more theological discourses in the Kommentar till Nya testamentet as well as more interpretive alternatives. The reader needs to realize the lack of absolute interpretations. We must find ways to live with several simultaneous interpretations. (Olsson 2006, 159, my trans.)

Showing one's exegetical and theological premises, Olsson here implies, is not tantamount to the dutiful declaration of one's gender, ethnicity, sexual orientation, confessional belonging, geographical location, and so on, simply as a means of putting them aside as interfering elements when beginning with the "real" task of objective historical inquiry. Rather, he

---

1965, the claims of objectivity in Catholic settings can thus appear more radical as compared to Protestant contexts.

seems to suggest that such premises ought to be allowed to openly interact with the historical-critical interpretation, thereby avoiding false claims of an absolute interpretation and highlighting how different presumptions, interests, and perspectives can lead to different interpretive alternatives.

Rather than regretting the impossibility of objectivity or disinterest, then, I situate this investigation in one of the ongoing transitions of biblical scholarship and employ a type of exegesis that, in addition to inquiries about the text's historical meaning, includes metacritical analyses of the relation between the discursive location of the interpreter and the interpretation itself—an exegesis that strives to be more reflective of its presuppositions.

How to Read This Book

I address two interrelated questions in this work. The first one, which is treated in part 3, is of primary character and can be phrased in a straightforward manner: What is the stance of Mark's Gospel vis-à-vis Rome's empire? Mark has more to say about Rome than the single, highly ambiguous episode about imperial tribute (Mark 12:13–17). Being composed and initially circulated during the heyday of Flavian Rome, with its story enacted in an unruly region on the eastern outskirts of Rome's empire—then known as Palestine or Judea—the Gospel of Mark has empire inscribed in its fibers.[10] Analyzing the manner in which these fibers are interwoven, reproduced, negotiated, modified, and subverted constitutes my primary task in this book.

If the question of Mark and Rome was posed to biblical scholars today, the answers would most likely show a significant variation, ranging from pro-Roman apology to anti-Roman opposition.[11] Not so long ago, however, scholars fairly widely agreed, typically based on the tribute episode, that there was no conflict between the demands of God and the demands

---

10. How to designate the land in which the Gospel stories take place is a matter of debate. This study follows Pliny (*Nat.* 5.66–70), who seems to reflect the common linguistic usage at the time of Mark's writing. Pliny referred to the area as "Palestine" and "Judea" interchangeably, and regarded Galilee as part of Judea. See also Jacobson 1999. I will deal with the provenance and primary audience of Mark's Gospel in ch. 13.

11. These contrasting suggestions have been made by Roskam 2004 and R. Horsley 2001, respectively. See also the research overview in this chapter.

of Caesar, and that the relation therefore was quite harmonious and free of tensions.

How to understand such a scholarly shift brings us to the second question, which I deal with in part 2. My suspicion for the present study is that since the question about Mark and Rome is posed in a location that is also affected by empire, the answer will inevitably be related to that location. In other words, empire is not only part of the past but also part of the present.[12] Similarly, Mark's Gospel not only belongs to ancient bygone days, but is also part of the present. In order to catch sight of these admittedly complex correlations of the past-present, the second question is directed toward a modern time period—the second half of the nineteenth century—generally referred to as the age of empire, when modern biblical scholarship had been firmly established as an academic field. The second question can thus be phrased: How were nineteenth-century scholarly interpretations of Mark related to European colonialism? In other words, the second question dealt with in part 2 studies the relation between Markan scholarship and its nineteenth-century social context.

Purporting these two questions to be interrelated, I allow them to interact with each other, especially in the last part of the book. For both questions, moreover, the issues of location and self-understanding are important. Being the earliest written story about Jesus, the way in which Mark relates to Rome's empire had a considerable formative effect on the first-century Jesus followers.[13] Similarly, the way in which Mark's Gospel was interpreted in nineteenth-century Europe was related to how Europeans understood themselves at this time, located (as most of them were) in the center of empire. The two questions thus involve two parallel analyses of two different kinds of material—whereas the first reads Mark, the second reads Markan commentaries. In both cases, however, the material is approached from a postcolonial perspective and located in its respective imperial context. *Discourses of Empire*, the title of this book, thus refers to these two questions and the parallel analysis that I conduct of Mark in the empires of Rome and Europe, respectively.

An important motivation for the double analysis conducted here is the role played by the Bible in European colonialism. Being one of the

---

12. Cf. Webster's (1996, 8) statement regarding scholarship on the Roman Empire: "the interpretation of Roman imperialism has always, and in very complex ways, involved analogy between past and present."

13. The significance of Mark as the first written Gospel will be discussed in ch. 13.

key source documents for European expansion from the fifteenth to the twentieth century, the Bible has been deeply enmeshed in the forming of European colonial identities. To simplify, the relation has been twofold: the Bible was one of the reasons for the expansion, and the expansion also gave the Bible a particular meaning. Even if European colonialism has now formally ended, postcolonial critics typically contend that its effects are still very much present, economically as well as culturally, in both the former colonies and the increasingly heterogeneous Western societies. One can argue that these effects also have implications for biblical interpretation. Indeed, when a European such as myself poses a question about a biblical text in relation to Rome's empire, it is difficult *not* to deal with the ways in which this biblical text interplayed with the European empires, especially during its most triumphant years. Being informed by Edward Said's *Orientalism*, as well as its critics, in this investigation I set out from an initial suspicion that biblical scholarship and European colonialism were in some sense related, and that these interconnections constitute a heritage that contemporary biblical scholars need to acknowledge so as not to reproduce.

Designing the study in this parallel way, further, challenges the ideological criticism of Dube (2000, 125–55) and Liew (1999a), which tends to regard biblical texts as in themselves imperializing. This is exemplified by Dube's (2000, 129) suggestion of four criteria that are intended to establish whether a biblical text is imperializing. Since texts can hardly be said to have such fixed meanings, I remain unconvinced that the use of criteria could result in clear-cut answers. Taken as heuristic questions, however, the criteria can help to increase the sensitivity to issues of imperial domination. I propose, moreover, that similar questions could be directed to the *interpretations* of a biblical text—hence the dual analysis applied here.

The parallel approach is also connected to the discussion, mentioned above, about biblical scholarship as an academic discipline. The recent decades' development raises questions about how new approaches are related to the historical-critical paradigm that has been dominating biblical scholarship since the late eighteenth century. In part 1 of this book I therefore engage in these metacritical discussions and offer a suggestion of how to understand postcolonial biblical criticism in relation to the discipline's Enlightenment origins.

The parallel investigations in parts 2 and 3 focus on seven Markan episodes that I have selected so as to benefit the analysis in part 3. Reading Mark as a representation of an identity position for early Christ followers,

I probe in part 3 the various ways in which it related to Roman imperial discourse, the dominant social order of its time. This analysis helps to conceptualize how Mark's Gospel formed a collective identity at the time of its initial circulation among communities of Christ followers on the fringes of Roman imperial culture. Two considerations have guided the choice of the Markan passages. First, the passages have special relevance to the way in which Mark relates to Rome's imperial discourse. Second, the passages cover the three main narrative sections in Mark's Gospel—Galilee (1:14–8:21), on the way (8:22–10:52), and Jerusalem (11:1–16:8).[14] More particular reasons for the choice of each passage will be provided as the study proceeds. The passages are presented in table 1.

Table 1. The Markan Passages Included in This Study

1:1	The Incipit
5:1–20	The Gerasene Demoniac
7:24–30	The Syrophoenician Woman
8:31–9:1	The Parousia
11:1–11	The Entry into Jerusalem
12:13–17	The Question of Tax
15:39	The Roman Centurion

I can now briefly describe the basic structure of the project. Like a triple jump in track and field, the work is constituted by three parts of increasing length. After this introduction, which frames the purpose, in part 1 I delineate postcolonial criticism and discourse theory as the project's theoretical and heuristic perspective. I also explore some metacritical intersections between postcolonial criticism and biblical studies. In part 2 I conduct a nine-chapter investigation of how scholarly interpretations of Mark were related to European colonialism. These chapters deal with the passages displayed in table 1. The aim here is to analyze the complex and subtle ways in which commentators on Mark's Gospel interplayed with European colonial identity formations. Besides being itself an interesting

---

14. For the structure of Mark's narrative see ch. 17.

task, this investigation seeks to achieve a sharper postcolonial interpretive optic when approaching part 3. Corresponding to these nine chapters, part 3 then probes the primary issue: how Mark in its initial circulation relates to Rome's order. In this part, I read Mark as a collective representation that forms an identity in the outskirts of Roman imperial culture. Finally, in part 4 I conclude by locating the findings in the contemporary debates on religion and politics, the postsecular condition, and offer some parting reflections on the investigation as a whole.

Discourse, Power, and the Subject

The postcolonial perspective, which I will delineate in chapter 2, belongs to, or is closely related to, a research field known as discourse theory or discourse analysis (Loomba 2005, 22–90). However, since these terms can have different meanings, there is a risk of confusion.[15] Here I employ *discourse* with the meaning that stems from Michel Foucault's use of it in his critique of the Marxist concept of ideology, and is closely related to his understanding of knowledge, power, and the subject (McHoul and Grace 1995). Foucault's critique has been developed in the post-Marxism of Laclau and Mouffe (1987; 2001) and refined into a social scientific methodology that is outlined in textbooks such as the one by Jørgensen and Phillips (2002, 1–59). Applying this methodology, I use *discourse* to denote a system of statements and social practices within which the world becomes known and subjects are formed.

According to Laclau (1990, 100), a discourse includes linguistic as well as extralinguistic aspects, which he explains by the following simplified example of building a brick wall. One of the workers asks his colleague to hand him a brick. As soon as he gets it, he secures it in its place. Whereas the first act (asking for the brick) is linguistic, the second act (securing it in its place) is extralinguistic. Despite their different characters, both acts are included in the building of the wall. The building of the wall is thus seen as a totality—a discourse—that includes linguistic as well as extralinguistic acts, both of which signify meaning and communicate a message as part of the discursive practice of building the wall.

---

15. In NT studies, Stanley Porter and Jeffrey Reed (1999) present discourse analysis as a form of text linguistics, which implies a different approach than the one applied herein. Further, as is evident in Jørgensen and Phillips 2002, there are other variants of discourse analysis as well.

Colonial discourse, a term that figures prominently in postcolonial criticism, therefore denotes a totality that includes the material and social practices of ruling distant territories as well as the linguistic patterns of thought, attitudes, and values that make this rule appear natural and self-evident. The two sets of discourse analyses conducted in part 2 and part 3 will be introduced further in chapter 4 and chapter 13, respectively.

Discourse analysis, as used here, bears some resemblance to social-scientific approaches in biblical studies, perhaps most closely to the sociorhetorical criticism developed by Vernon Robbins (1996).[16] But whereas social scientific approaches (unlike Robbins's) usually regard the social context of a biblical text as an objective material reality that is possible to access, discourse analysis regards social history as being textually mediated.[17] This difference is seen in Bengt Holmberg's (1990, 2) introduction to sociological criticism in New Testament studies, when he points out "the serious methodological mistake of confusing phenomena with the descriptions of them." Even accepting that Holmberg has here made a significant argument against idealism, it is nonetheless important to note that discourse theory rests on the linguistic turn in poststructuralist philosophy and alleges the impossibility of having access to phenomena (or reality) apart from their discursive representations.

As do all approaches, discourse analysis has strengths and weaknesses. For example, if one were interested in ascertaining the number of Herod the Great's wives, this approach would not be the most suitable choice. On the other hand, if one were interested in the cultural, religious, and political meaning of Herod's marriages, a discourse-theoretical approach would be of great benefit.

INTERPELLATION AND REPRESENTATION

Given the significance of the conception of identity for this study, I will briefly delineate how discourse theory understands group identity. Beginning with the individual level, the subject in discourse theory is understood as formed by *interpellation*, a term that stems from Foucault's

---

16. When working with a NT text, Robbins suggests analyzing different kinds of textures that include material as well as linguistic aspects, i.e., inner texture, intertexture, social and cultural texture, and ideological texture.

17. I develop this further in ch. 3, under the heading "Decentering the Historical-critical Paradigm."

teacher, Louis Althusser. As a Marxist, Althusser (2001, 115–20) regarded interpellation in a negative light, as a function of ideology that conceals the true interest of the subject given by the economic conditions. In discourse theory, however, such economic determinism is not accepted, and hence the notion of an authentic subjectivity that is hidden by ideology is rejected. Nonetheless, the subject is still seen as formed by interpellation. By regarding the interpellation as being conducted by *discourse* rather than *ideology*, however, this approach indicates that the subject is continuously formed in cultural processes of identification. Rather than seeing the subject as a preexistent autonomous user of language, then, discourse theory sees it as formed by processes of identification with subject positions given via language and culture.

A particular discourse offers certain positions that interpellate subjects. For instance, in a classroom the positions "teacher" and "student" are specified and attached with certain expectations about how to act, what to say, and what not to say. Further, since discourse theory generally purports the existence of several discourses that compete to structure social reality, different interpellations occur simultaneously, establishing a fragmented subject. In one sense, these interpellations can coexist—for example, the positions *Christian*, *basketball player*, and *father* usually do not interfere with one another. On the other hand, there are often competing discourses that give contradictory meanings to a particular position, in which case the subject becomes overdetermined. In discourse theory, overdetermination is the default situation in social reality. Should a subject position appear to be free of conflicts, it is seen as being the result of hegemonic processes that exclude other possible articulations, making a particular discourse to appear natural and objectively true.

When it comes to collective identity, moreover, a similar understanding is applied (Jørgensen and Phillips 2002, 43–47). Rather than seeing a group (e.g., all Swedes) as bearing a particular character or essence that could be represented in a more or less accurate way, discourse theory regards group formation as the result of discursive closures that exclude certain characteristics while upholding others. According to Laclau (1993, 289–92), representation has a constituting effect on the group. Group identities are therefore not seen as existing a priori but rather as being formed in discourse by processes of collective identification with particular positions. Since groups are formed in discourse, a crucial aspect of group formation is representation; the speaking or writing about, or on behalf of, a group thus has a formative effect on the group.

1. INTRODUCTION

Of course, a representation does not always function in a constitutive way: a group may not identify itself with a particular representation, or, in other words, become interpellated. Since the purpose of this work is to analyze Mark's Gospel as a collective representation, this circumstance becomes especially significant. Given that it was the first written Gospel, and that both Matthew and Luke seem to have used it as their main source, we can assume that it did function as a representation, at least to some degree. This notwithstanding, the reception of the Gospel by its primary receivers remains unknown, and thus it will not be possible for me to analyze either the extent to which or the manner in which Mark actually managed to interpellate its audience. In view of this uncertainty, I limit the investigation in part 3 to analyzing the text's interpellative *force* and its *potential* as a collective representation—not its actual effect on the audience.

The Question of Anachronism

The analysis in part 3 of a premodern context from a postcolonial approach and by use of discourse theory might raise questions about anachronism. Considering the weight this study places on how the past tends to become caught up in the present, the issue is surely delicate.

As David Jobling has noted, the modes of production in ancient and modern societies differ considerably, and he is therefore critical of drawing direct parallels between ancient and modern empires: "Simple links between biblical and current situations, whether they leave the Bible looking good or bad, convey no lasting benefit" (in Broadbent et al. 1999, 117–19). Surely, we ought to acknowledge the differences. Whereas European imperialism during the nineteenth and twentieth centuries was fueled by a capitalist economy, the Roman Empire was based on an agrarian economy. Rome did not exploit natural resources for economic gain, nor did Romans have access to gunpowder. However, in a discourse-theoretical approach, the mode of production is given less weight than it is in a traditional Marxist analysis. Also, as I will argue more carefully in part 3, both Roman imperial power and European colonialism can be similarly seen as a totality of combined economic, military, and cultural elements. Although their technologies and economies may have been different, both the ancient and the modern empires were upheld by cultural notions that construed relations of domination and subordination. Their different modes of production need to be recognized; but this differential itself does not seem to preclude a postcolonial analysis of an ancient empire.

Fernando Segovia (2005, 71–74) thus points out the lack of a comparative analysis of empires in different times and places, and describes this as a "lacuna" in postcolonial studies that he finds "at once frustrating and challenging." Segovia helpfully describes empires as long-standing and widespread phenomena, with enough similarities to be compared over different historical periods and cultural contexts. Ancient as well as modern empires, he contends, are grounded on two basic interrelated dynamics. First, there is a fundamental structure of center and periphery, where the center is symbolized by a city or metropolis and the peripheral societies are culturally subordinated to the center. Second, this basic structure is enforced by certain hierarchical dichotomies—Greek/barbarian, civilized/primitive, scientific/superstitious, developed/underdeveloped, Christian/heathen, and so on. Considering the magnitude of these sociocultural structures, one can expect artistic and literary production in the center as well as at the margins to be highly affected by them and are fruitfully studied in their light.

Another, more theoretical, objection to the analysis in part 3 might be that postcolonial analysis and discourse theory rely rather heavily on Foucault's understanding of power, which, in turn, partly rests upon a distinction between modern and premodern societies. His argument was based on the transition in European societies, from the Middle Ages, characterized by *repressive* power, to the modern period, characterized by *productive* power. In the premodern society, according to Foucault, power was upheld by spectacular punishments that served to restore the honor of an offended ruler. In modern societies, on the other hand, discipline has been internalized such that the subject has more become its own guardian and only indirectly controlled by institutions such as prisons and mental hospitals. As ancient empires were premodern and rested primarily on repressive power, one can question whether Foucaultian discourse theory is applicable.

Interestingly, however, as Ania Loomba (2005, 49–50) points out, the same critique has been directed against the application of discourse theory to modern European colonialism. According to some critics, colonies were much more like medieval societies in their use of brute force to uphold their power. They were not modern in the European sense, and hence Foucault is far too Eurocentric to be used without adjustment in the study of modern colonialism. Then again, as Loomba (50–53) has also shown, the colonial discourse analyses of these same critics to some extent bear the markings of Foucault's influence. Colonial power is then understood as both repressive and productive—as resting upon material and economical aspects as well as on cultural and linguistic ones. Furthermore, physical brutality is seen not only as repressive, but also as producing cultural notions and relations of power that far outweigh the power of the physical brutality itself. From this appropriation of Foucault among postcolonial critics, the step is not far for postcolonial critics to engage with ancient Rome.[18]

Indeed, the step has already been taken. In *Ritual and Power*, Simon Price (1984) offers a prominent example of a Foucault-inspired study of the Roman Empire. "The rule of Rome was represented in marble," Price (3) states, pointing at the widespread imperial temples, statues, and communal celebrations that upheld the presence of the emperor in Asia Minor, even though he was physically absent. Surely, brute force also played an important role in terms of upholding Roman power; but the army could only manage so much. More important for understanding Roman power, Price (239–48) contends, are the social processes that created and defined the relation between subject and ruler. These social processes included political (administration, diplomacy, taxation, etc.) as well as cultural (rituals, statues, texts, etc.) aspects. Hence Price seems to be describing Roman imperial power as occurring in a totality of the cultural and the political. This totality, of course, can with Foucault be called a discourse.

Addressing the issue of anachronism, I think it is important to also acknowledge that all biblical interpretation involves anachronism. As I will further argue in chapter 3, the past is not accessible on its own terms. The mere act of translating a text written in a premodern society entails an anachronistic element. Therefore, although there are differences between ancient and modern empires, as long as one recognizes those differences, there does not seem to be anything that prevents a postcolonial analysis like the one conducted here. To the contrary, there is a lacuna, as Segovia said, at once frustrating and challenging, that needs to be filled.

---

18. Cf. Moore-Gilbert 1997, 12, who argues that, like feminism, postcolonial criticism can be fruitfully applied to ancient as well as modern empires.

Mark and Empire: An Orientation

As has become evident, this work contains two major analyses: (1) a reception-oriented, metacritical analysis of nineteenth-century interpretations of Mark in European colonialism; and (2) a reading of Mark in its ancient imperial setting. In what follows, I will give a brief overview of the two academic fields with which these two analyses interact.

Biblical Interpretation and European Colonialism

The delimited question of how interpretations of Mark were related to nineteenth-century European colonialism has not received particular attention by biblical scholars. A case in point is the interesting work by Brenda Deen Schildgen (1999) on the reception of Mark from the second century until today. But even if Schildgen shows how the interpretations of Mark in history have been deeply affected by different social and cultural situations, she refrains from addressing the issue of European colonialism.

As for the somewhat wider issue of biblical interpretation in relation to modern European colonialism, there are three areas of research. The first area addresses the emergence of modern biblical scholarship and can be illustrated by Shawn Kelley (2002). Focusing especially on issues of race, Kelley contends that modern biblical scholarship, represented not least by the nineteenth-century Tübingen school, was deeply enmeshed in the construction of the orientals as the Europeans' racial Other. Also, the incisive article by Jonathan Hess (2000) locates the pioneering biblical scholar Johann David Michaelis in the eighteenth-century European anti-Jewish and colonial context.

A second area focuses on the nineteenth-century quest for the historical Jesus. In a brief analysis, Kwok Pui-lan (1998a, 75–81) argues that this quest was affiliated with colonial discourse, especially in its construction of the natives. In a more recent work, Halvor Moxnes (2011) has made this area significantly wider. In dialogue with Albert Schweitzer, Moxnes analyzes how writings on the historical Jesus helped form various kinds of national identities in nineteenth-century Europe. Although Moxnes's interest primarily involves nationalism, his work includes a considerable portion of colonial discourse analysis as well.

A third area concerns biblical commentaries. John Townsend (1986) has shown how the commentators' interpretations of Acts as depicting three planned missionary journeys by Paul—often uncritically accepted in contemporary scholarship—was an eighteenth-century invention. Since premodern biblical interpreters had not found this missionary pattern in Acts, Townsend contends that it was related to the rise of modern missionary societies in eighteenth- and nineteenth-century Europe. Also, Ralph Broadbent (1998) has examined British New Testament commentaries as ideological writings. Analyzing commentaries from the late nineteenth century to the present, he concludes that the concerns of the rich and powerful have been given prominence and the concerns of the poor have been spiritualized or ignored (55). Finally, R. S. Sugirtharajah (1999b) has investigated the Indian Church Commentaries, produced during the imperial period in India. Noting that myths of race, nationality, and English superiority were integral to the commentarial interpretation, he argues that such myths were closely intertwined with the imperial cause.

As for the yet wider question concerning the complicity of academic (biblical as well as extrabiblical) scholarship on the attitudes and values underpinning the process of European expansion, a significantly greater amount of research has been performed, especially since Said's *Orientalism* (1979).[19] Of particular interest in this regard is a work by Suzanne Marchand (2009), *German Orientalism in the Age of Empire*. Although Marchand shares Said's interest in the connections between orientalist scholarship and colonial politics, her approach also parts from Said by allowing a greater complexity in Europe's way of studying the Orient. When we examine the connections between Markan interpretation and European colonialism in part 2, both these works will be important to consider.

MARK IN ITS ANCIENT IMPERIAL SETTING

Several works on the question of Mark's stance vis-à-vis Rome have been written since the late 1960s. Although categorizing here constitutes a risky task, I have nevertheless divided them into four groups: (1) Mark as a Roman apology; (2) Mark as an anti-imperial Gospel; (3) Mark as an imperial Gospel; and (4) Mark as a combined reproduction of and resistance against imperial ideology. For reasons of space, this overview only

---

19. For overviews of this research, see Moore-Gilbert 1997, 5–11; Loomba 2005, 42–62; Sardar 1999; and Macfie 2002. If the scope is further widened to include how colonialism has been related to knowledge and cultural production, the number of works dramatically increases. For overviews see Loomba 2005, 62–82; and Moore-Gilbert 1997, 5–11.

includes books, but several crucial articles and book sections written on this topic will be discussed as the project unfolds.

Mark as a Roman Apology

Giving voice to the revolutionary romantics of the 1960s, S. G. F. Brandon (1967, xi) initiated his influential study of the historical Jesus and the Zealots by asking why "the Roman governor of Judaea decide to execute Jesus for sedition." Similar to the iconoclastic work by Hermann Samuel Reimarus (1778), Brandon held that the historical Jesus was a political revolutionary who took sides with his Jewish compatriots, supported their cause against the Roman rule of Judea, and endorsed their strategy of armed struggle. The Gospel of Mark, however, presented a different picture—and it is here that we begin to see the relevance of Brandon's work for the present study. Mark's Gospel, Brandon argued, was written in Rome in the aftermath of the Jewish War as an *Apologia ad Christianos Romanos*. As part of this strategy, Brandon continued, Mark dissociated Jesus from the Jewish nationalists, the Zealots, and presented him as being cooperative with the Roman government in Judea, and as being "studiously neutral to the political issues" (Brandon 1967, 220–21). Even though Brandon's main focus was on the historical Jesus rather than on Mark's Gospel, his reading is significant for placing the question of Rome's empire on the agenda of Markan scholarship.[20]

Hendrika Roskam (2004) has made a similar suggestion. Taking Mark as being primarily written for Christ followers who were persecuted by both Jews and Romans, Roskam (238) contends that the political dimension of Jesus—his identity as Christ and as an executed rebel—is eliminated by Mark's way of depicting Jesus' ministry and death. In his Gospel, Roskam (238) notes, "Mark stresses that Jesus was not an anti-Roman rebel who intended to assume political power over an earthly Israel." Roskam, however, diverges from Brandon in two important ways: first, she argues that Mark was written in Galilee; second, she does not share Brandon's view of the historical Jesus as a political revolutionary.

---

20. As shown by the responses to his work, Brandon's claims were taken quite seriously. See Cullmann 1970; Hengel 1971; and Bammel and Moule 1984. For a more complete list, see Borg 1998, 25. Neill and Wright (1988, 388–90) regarded his work as one of the two initiators of the third quest for the historical Jesus.

Mark as an Anti-imperial Gospel

As compared to the differences between Brandon and Roskam, the works in this group are considerably more diverse, making the task of demarcation all the more difficult.[21] The works included in this category are Belo (1981), Myers (1988), Waetjen (1989), and Horsley (2001).

In 1974, while living as a Portuguese exile in France, Fernando Belo's book *Lecture matérialiste de l'évangile de Marc* was published. Translated into English in 1981, his impressive work sets out to bridge the gap between liberation theology and biblical exegesis.[22] Combining a semiotic theory developed by Roland Barthes and Julia Kristeva with the structuralist Marxism of Althusser, Belo analyzes structural oppositions in Mark's text and points out how the powerless classes are set against the local and Roman elite. Like the Zealots, the Markan Jesus has an anti-Roman perspective; but unlike them, he is nonviolent and his strategy includes all peoples. Emphasizing what he calls a messianic practice, where the Markan Jesus moves out to the poor and outcasts and is concerned with the needs of humans, Belo represents a classic liberationist reading.

Combining sociological exegesis with insights from literary criticism, Ched Myers (1988, 31–33) applies what he calls a "socio-literary reading strategy" to Mark's Gospel. Inspired by and yet critical of Belo's materialist exegesis, Myers (36–37) demurs from the Marxist tradition in certain ways and is careful not to call his method materialist. Instead, he (42–45) makes use of a sociological model developed by John Elliott (1986) that, unlike the structural-functionalist school, affirms a conflict-based theory of sociology. Of similar importance to his reading strategy, moreover, is his use of Gandhian nonviolence as a hermeneutical key (Myers 1988, 47, 472). According to Myers's reading, Mark's Gospel was written around 69 C.E. for a particular community in Galilee that was in close proximity to the war. As such, Mark was addressed to a community that was facing pressure from Jewish insurgents to join the armed resistance and from Roman troops to willingly cooperate with their rule. In this pressured situation,

---

21. The work by Hamerton-Kelly (1994) is a case in point. Focusing on the issue of violence through the lens of the thinking of René Girard, his work has some bearing on the purpose of this project. But since he refrains from discussing Mark's relation to imperial Rome, this work falls outside the scope of this overview.

22. Since Belo's work was somewhat demanding, due largely to his particular use of abbreviations, Clévenot (1985) rendered a shorter, more accessible interpretation.

Mark wrote a Gospel that was "alienative, confrontative, and non-aligned" (Myers 1988, 85–87).

Being published almost simultaneously and making use of a combined social scientific and literary approach, the work by Herman Waetjen (1989, x) is in some ways similar to that of Myers. The particular models chosen, however, are different. Waetjen (xiii–xiv) applies insights from the anthropology of Mircea Eliade, the sociological analysis of millenarian movements by Kenelm Burridge, and reader-response criticism as developed by Wolfgang Iser. The result is a Markan Jesus who represents a reordering of power under the eschatological rule of God.

Richard Horsley's work on Mark benefits from his other works on the sociopolitical context of Jesus and Paul. Like Myers and Waetjen, Horsley (2001) combines narrative criticism with sociopolitical analysis. Purporting that Mark had been composed for existing Jewish village communities, Horsley reads the story as representing a renewal movement among a subjugated people. The Markan Jesus, Horsley thus suggests, spearheads a popular rural movement in the villages of Galilee in direct opposition to the rulers and ruling institutions of Judea and Jerusalem that represent the Roman Empire.

Mark as an Imperial Gospel

Adam Winn (2008) is the only work of which I am aware that explicitly reads Mark as advancing the imperialism of God in clear-cut opposition to the imperialism of Rome. His stance thereby places him in a category that is quite distinct from the other readings. Even if Winn sees Mark as standing in opposition to the claims of the Roman emperor (a claim with which the second group would agree), he also regards Mark as in itself an imperial text.

Hence Winn's reading is based on assumptions that differ from those of the works in the previous category. Whereas the readings in the second group are based on an identification with the plight of the dominated (albeit differently understood), and therefore driven by a critique of imperial domination, Winn (2008, 40) regards imperial power as benign and unproblematic (cf. Carter 2010). In response to Horsley, Winn states that "Mark is not anti-imperial, but he is advancing the imperialism of both God's kingdom and the one who bears it, Jesus." Since imperialism, as we saw above, entails the exercise of various combinations of economic, military, and religious control, Winn's equating of it with God's kingdom is noteworthy and reflects unawareness of what Sugirtharajah (2006, 5) describes as the *receiving* end of imperialism. Consequently, imperial duplication is a nonissue in Winn's work, and one may then ask how God's imperial rule differs from the imperial rule that popular movements in the so-called third world have been struggling to free themselves from during the past century.

Mark as Combined Reproduction of and Resistance against Imperial Discourse

Whereas the works discussed thus far have tended to read Mark's story in a more or less straightforward way, the scholars in this group, Tat-siong Benny Liew (1999a) and Simon Samuel (2007), find Mark to be more complex and contradictory.

Informed by poststructuralist theory, Liew (1999a, 64) examines how Mark constructs colonial subjects and finds both resistance to and reproduction of imperial discourse. Mark resists imperial discourse, Liew (149) argues, by depicting Jesus as being tragically murdered for his constant questioning of authority and for exposing the wickedness of the collaborative scheme of the Jewish and Roman leaders. At the same time, however, in depicting a second coming of Jesus in power, Mark produces a contradictory politics (149). By promising the utter destruction of both Jewish and Roman authorities upon Jesus' eschatological return, the Markan Parousia is "in the final analysis no different from [a] 'might-is-right' ideology" (107); rather, it "duplicates the authoritarian, exclusionary, and coercive politics of his colonizers" (149). Taken in itself, this contention places Liew in the third category (Mark as an imperial Gospel). But since he is careful to point out ways in which Mark also resists imperial discourse, his work has a higher complexity and belongs to the fourth category.

But is Liew complex enough? His provocative suggestion has been debated and will be further discussed in chapters 8 and 17. Its paradoxical character, however, is not to be missed. As is evident from the initial quote above, Liew evinces awareness that the Bible, rather than being a fixed entity, is a document that can be given different meanings—which, in turn, has political consequences. Given the complex nature of Mark's Parousia, why then would Liew make it a message of "might-is-right" in his final analysis?

The last work to be mentioned in this overview, Samuel's (2007) postcolonial reading, reads Mark as negotiating a space between Roman imperial power and the relatively dominant Jewish nationalism. Inspired by Bhabha, Samuel (4–5) contends that Mark is neither procolonial nor anticolonial, but rather an ambivalent and hybrid discourse that affiliates and disrupts both internal and external colonial discourses. Unlike the present project, however, in which Mark is read as a collective representation that interpellates the Christ followers as a group, Samuel (4–5, 158) seems to regard Mark as the product of an already existing community.

Compared to the works that have been previously described, the postcolonial perspective applied by Samuel offers more nuances in terms of understanding how Mark relates to its imperial situation. However, Samuel's attempt to cover a wide range of texts and issues makes his work somewhat sweeping and cursory—hardly thirty pages are devoted to the analysis of Mark's Gospel story (1:12–16:8). As such, several motives and passages that would be significant to analyze from a postcolonial perspective are only hinted at, while others remain entirely unnoticed.

In summary, contemporary scholarship exhibits an exciting range of positions regarding the manner in which Mark relates to Roman imperial power. Considering the highly ambiguous character of the only passage in Mark (12:13–17) that explicitly deals with this issue, such an outcome should come as no surprise. Except for the last group, the mentioned readings tend to present Mark in a rather clear-cut fashion. In this sense, in this project I stand closer to Liew and Samuel in that I purport Mark to be more ambiguous and double-edged in relation to Rome.

One can also note that issues of gender are altogether absent in this admittedly limited overview.[23] Considering that gender is a prominent topic in postcolonial criticism (Loomba 2005, 128–45, 180–92) as well as a prominent motif in Roman imperial discourse (see ch. 13), this absence is dubious. In order to somewhat redress this deficiency, I here intend to press Mark's account of Jesus on this issue (see especially ch. 16).

Besides interacting with these works, in the present study I will also address the multidimensional way in which Mark interacts with empire. Not only does the initial circulation of Mark take place in an imperial setting, but Mark has also been read and used in various imperial settings ever since—not least in nineteenth-century Europe, which the analysis in part 2 will help to illuminate. Such a combination of analyses of Mark in

---

23. One exception is Liew 1999a, 133–48, who argues that Mark reproduces Greco-Roman patriarchal discourse and suppresses female subjectivity.

different empires that is undertaken here has not been undertaken before. I hope that this wider grip on the trope of Mark and empire will enable us to formulate, in a postsecular and postcolonial world, how we might perceive Mark addressing empire today.

PART 1
POSTCOLONIAL THEORY AND THE BIBLE

And what is the significance of the Bible? Who knows?
—Homi Bhabha (2004, 173)

2
Postcolonial Theory

Notwithstanding the problem of allowing a single image to represent such a heterogenic field as postcolonial biblical criticism, the cover image of *Allegories of Empire* by Jenny Sharpe (1993) is here selected to introduce this chapter on theory. Sharpe's cover (fig. 1) has an image of a woman aiming a pistol. Somewhat enigmatically, there is also an image of the Holy Bible at the lower left corner. Looking inside Sharpe's book (84), it is evident that the front-page image has been produced by cutting and pasting from the larger original—Charles Ball's 1858 *History of the Indian Mutiny*—in which the Bible is seen lying on the floor, having fallen down as the woman defends herself against Indian rebels who are attacking her with their swords (fig. 2). This image of a white European woman shooting at brown Indian insurgents highlights the complex relations of race and gender in European colonial discourse. Reminiscent of Delacroix's *Liberty Leading the People*, the woman depicted with a pistol could be taken as signaling female agency and emancipation. At the same time she is a European colonizer who represses an anticolonial rebellion. Which category is most important here—race or gender? As a woman she is the subjugated who fights against oppression and patriarchy; as a white European she is the dominant who subdues the dominated. Typically, postcolonial critics are keenly interested in examining such issues, as in the case of Sharpe's study, which focuses on how representations of dark Indian men raping white European women during India's Sepoy rebellion created a crisis in British colonial identity in the mid-nineteenth century.

Interestingly, the cover image also indicates an area that is *not* studied by Sharpe: the role played by the Bible. As I will argue below, her work represents a tendency in postcolonial criticism to overlook issues of religion. The Bible in Ball's painting seems to send several signals: innocence, the benign intentions of colonial rule, and its divine justification. Several suggestions

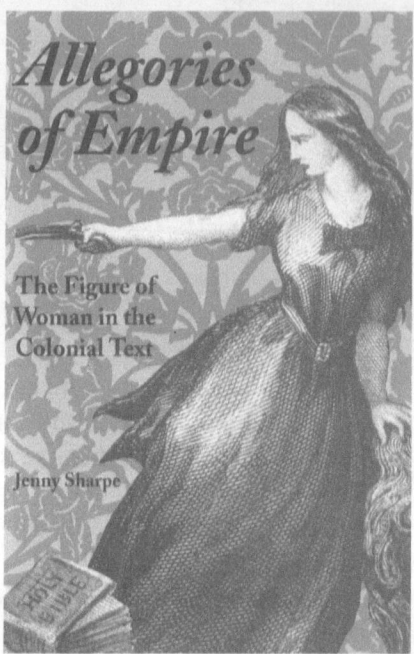

Figure 1. The cover of Sharpe (1993).

Figure 2. Charles Ball's *History of the Indian Mutiny* (1858).

seem plausible, but one will look in vain for an answer in the book, which is noteworthy considering that the Bible must have been pasted into the cover page. My point here, however, is not to fault Sharpe, nor to search for an accurate interpretation of the cover image. Rather, I take the cover as pointing intriguingly toward questions about the Bible and colonialism—questions that extrabiblical postcolonial critics rarely pose. This remarkable pasting of the Bible into the cover, as well as Bhabha's unanswered question above, calls our attention to the intersections between postcolonial criticism and biblical studies. By exploring some of these intersections, I delineate in this chapter the present work's theoretical basis.

If the cover of Sharpe's book points at the complex role played by the Bible in European colonialism, a postcolonial perspective also sheds new light on the contested issue of how biblical texts relate to their ancient imperial settings, and most pertinently how the New Testament writings relate to Rome. More interestingly, as is evident from an oft-quoted passage in Conrad's *Heart of Darkness* (1985, 31–32) comparing the Roman and the British empires, these two issues cannot be completely separated.[1] Certain notions about ancient Rome as well as early Christianity formed crucial parts of nineteenth-century European identity—and they continue to do so today.[2] In other words, mapping these intersections brings us into a field with excitingly large time spans, ranging from ancient Rome to the Enlightenment to contemporary postmodernity.

---

1. The quote is from Marlow, who sits in "the pose of a Buddha preaching in European clothes" and says: "[The Romans] were no colonists … they were conquerors, and for that you want only brute force—nothing to boast of, when you have it, since your strength is just an accident arising from the weakness of others. They grabbed what they could get for the sake of what was to be got. It was just robbery with violence, aggravated murder on a great scale, and men going at it blind—as is very proper for those who tackle a darkness. The conquest of the earth, which mostly means the taking it away from those who have a different complexion or slightly flatter noses than ourselves, is not a pretty thing when you look into it too much. What redeems it is the idea only. An idea at the back of it; not a sentimental pretense but an idea; and an unselfish belief in the idea—something you can set up, and bow down before, and offer a sacrifice to. …" The quote is partly rendered at the beginning of Said's *Culture and Imperialism* (1993, vii).

2. For a discussion on how the study of the Roman Empire became important for British imperialism during the late nineteenth and early twentieth century, see Webster 1996; Freeman 1996; Hingley 1996; and Mattingly 1996.

Part 1 is divided into two chapters. In chapter 1 I delineate how postcolonial criticism emerged as a wide and contested research field in literary studies during the 1980s and early 1990s. Chiseling out heuristic concepts from three influential postcolonial critics—Said, Spivak, and Bhabha—we will be well equipped for the subsequent analyses in parts 2 and 3. In chapter 2, in turn, I map the developing field of postcolonial biblical criticism and explore how postcolonial critique and biblical scholarship reciprocally challenge each other. These challenges bring forth a final section, in which I relate postcolonial biblical criticism to the origin of modern biblical scholarship and the dominating historical-critical paradigm.

The "Post" in "Postcolonial"

According to the *Oxford English Dictionary*, s.v., although the term *postcolonial* (with a hyphen) appears as an entry in the 1934 edition of *Webster's Dictionary*, its first factual usage is noticed in a 1959 *Daily Telegraph* article, where it refers to the condition of India after independence. During the 1960s and 1970s, the term began to be widely used in political science to designate the nations that had thrown off the yoke of the European colonizers, or as a more general reference to the period after the colonial era.

As I use the term, however, *postcolonial criticism* has been largely developed in literary studies, although, as noted by Moore-Gilbert (1997, 5–11), it arrived somewhat belatedly to the field. Despite the many attempts to redefine the discipline of literary studies during the 1970s and 1980s, the term *post(-)colonial* did not begin to gain currency in literary studies until the late 1980s with the work *The Empire Writes Back: Theory and Practice in Post-colonial Literatures* (Ashcroft et al. 1989). However, there is also a rather extensive prehistory of postcolonial criticism that stretches back to the early twentieth century and involves scholars and activists from different parts of the world.[3] Also, the work generally regarded as having

---

3. Moore-Gilbert (1997, 5) offers the following genealogy of postcolonial criticism *avant la lettre*: W. E. B. Du Bois (1868–1963, U.S.A.), Sol Plaatje (1876–1932, South Africa), the Harlem Renaissance of World War I, the *négritude* movement (1940s and 1950s), C. L. R. James (1901–1989, Trinidad), Frantz Fanon (1925–1961, Martinique/Algeria/France), Chinua Achebe (1930–, Nigeria), Anta Diop (1923–1986, Senegal), Ranajit Guha (1922–, India), Latin American criticism, "Commonwealth" literary studies (1960s and 1970s), and different kinds of aesthetic theories in non-European languages.

inaugurated the field (Said 1979) conducted postcolonial criticism *avant la lettre*. Despite its late arrival to the humanistic academy, however, it has had a major impact on the field.

As it entered literary studies, moreover, the meaning of *postcolonial* came to be significantly modified. From merely designating the period *after* the ending of colonialism, the term's meaning was fundamentally transformed to designate instead a *critical inquiry into the nature of colonial and imperial domination*. Ashcroft, Griffiths, and Tiffin (1989, 2) use the term to "cover all the culture affected by the imperial process from the moment of colonization to the present day." According to them, what makes the literatures of all these cultures postcolonial is "that they emerged from the experience of colonization and asserted themselves by foregrounding the tension with the imperial power, and by emphasizing their differences from the assumptions of the imperial center." More specifically, by highlighting the interconnections between issues of race, nation, empire, gender, migration, ethnicity, and the matter of cultural production, postcolonial criticism began to trace and untie the often labyrinthian orders and affiliations of the colonial heritage that continues to haunt our present.

As an indication of the contested nature of the academic field, there has been a debate over the hyphen in *post(-)colonial* (Appiah 1991; Ashcroft 1996). As the term has gained currency in literary studies, critics have begun to use the unhyphenated compound. This switch, I argue, accentuates the shift in the term's meaning from a supersessionist and chronological *after* to a more critical *beyond*, which is crucial for the utility of the term as a critical concept.[4] When I use "post-colonial," it refers to the situation after the formal ending of colonization.

A Contested Field of Research

Considering that postcolonial criticism from the start has been a disputed field of research, Stephen Moore's (2006, 4) characterizing the field as being "highly contested" seems accurate. As seen in two important introductions to postcolonial criticism, one of the major objects of dispute concerns the question of theory.[5] Bart Moore-Gilbert (1997) sets out

---

4. For a similar usage of these terms, see Sugirtharajah 1999a, 3; Segovia 2005, 64–65; and Liew 2008, 212–13.

5. This is evident from critical voices such as Aijaz Ahmad (1994) and Stephen Slemon and Helen Tiffin (1989a).

to discuss the differences and tensions between what he sees as a more narrow "postcolonial *theory*" and the broader field of "postcolonial *criticism*" (italics added). By theory he (1) means "French 'high' theory" represented by poststructuralist thinkers such as Jacques Derrida, Jacques Lacan, and Michel Foucault. He then insightfully presents the three postcolonial critics who have been mostly associated with the use of theory—Said, Spivak, and Bhabha—somewhat ironically referred to as the "Holy Trinity." After showing their contributions as well as the weaknesses in their work, he ends up contending that the separation between theory and criticism is artificial and that the field is far too diverse and heterogeneous to allow any such neat division.

A similar position is taken by Ania Loomba (2005, 22–23) when she delineates how postcolonial criticism has been formed by two interconnected revolutions: first, the history of decolonization and the ongoing struggle to overcome the colonial legacy; and second, the conceptual innovations in areas of language, ideology, power, identity, and culture (what Moore-Gilbert refers to as theory). As Loomba elegantly notes, these two contexts ought not to be seen as contradictory, but rather as jointly forming the field of postcolonial criticism. To introduce the field, then, I will look briefly at these two revolutions.

The primary incitement for the development of postcolonial criticism has been the various anticolonial struggles that have brought about formal independence from colonial rule. Even if postcolonial scholars are often critical of certain aspects of these struggles (i.e., nationalism and essentialism), the impact of the revolutions in the former colonies cannot be overstated. As is evident from the maps in the *Third World Atlas* (Thomas et al. 1994, 44–45), the scope and range of such struggles are vast. One of their decisive elements was the role played by anticolonial writers and intellectuals, several of whom I mentioned in the introduction. These writers and the various struggles in which they participated emblemize the immense power problems inherent in colonial rule as well as the remarkable determination of the dominated to shake off the colonial yoke.

Two writers can be singled out as having been especially important: Gandhi and Fanon. However, whereas Fanon is widely discussed among postcolonial critics, Gandhi is conspicuous by his absence; he is not even mentioned in Moore-Gilbert's list (cited above).[6] Fanon's prominence

---

6. Two exceptions that prove the rule are Leela Gandhi (1998, 17–22) and Gyan

should come as no surprise considering that his work *Wretched of the Earth* came to be viewed as the Bible of the third world. The absence of Gandhi, however, is truly remarkable. As Robert Young (2001, 321) points out in his substantial introduction to postcolonial criticism, "no anticolonial leader identified himself more publicly and absolutely with the wretched of the earth than Gandhi." Young relates the neglect of Gandhi by postcolonial critics to his focus on nonviolence (*ahimsa*), which makes it difficult to place him in the category of other anticolonial protagonists, who tended to use more of a Marxist vocabulary. In addition, Gandhi's use of religious principles (*ahimsa* is a Hindu concept) in the struggle for independence has given him a somewhat sanctified aura, and thus the writings on him have tended to be devotional rather than critical.[7] Furthermore, Young (338) regards Gandhi's absence as indicating "the degree to which [postcolonial criticism] is distinguished by an unmediated secularism" that tends to oppose and exclude the religious traditions that have fueled resistance to Western dominance. Although Young primarily refers to Islam and Hinduism, I will argue that the secularist tendency among postcolonial critics is also reflected in a general neglect of the ambiguous role played by Christianity.

The second revolution in postcolonial criticism referred to by Loomba might come as a surprise to some. With a reputation for being inaccessible and opaque, poststructuralist theory represents a more disputed development. With its focus on the nature of power, agency, and subjectivity, however, the debate on theory is actually closer to the struggle for social change than might initially be expected. In postcolonial theory, the discussion has especially converged upon different ways of understanding the relation between material socioeconomic processes on the one hand and texts, knowledge, culture, and ideology on the other—a debate summarized by expressions such as "culture and politics," and "knowledge and power." There are two interrelated issues involved in these theoretical debates: the linguistic turn and a critique

---

Prakash (1995, 6–9), both of whom make illuminating comparisons between Gandhi and Fanon. It may be of some relevance to note that Leela Gandhi is the granddaughter of Gandhi himself.

7. Young (2001, 337–38) here fails to acknowledge, however, that there are significant political readings of Gandhi, such as Naess 1974; Sharp 1979; and Bondurant 1988.

of Marxism, both of which can be viewed as belonging under the wider umbrella of poststructuralism.[8]

These intertwined theoretical developments have enabled postcolonial critics to conceptualize how colonial power is not merely a question of economic and military strength, but also concerns cultural representations, notions about identity, and what Gramsci has called an organization of consent. In partial opposition to Marxism, it then became possible to explain how ideologies can transcend classes and, conversely, how there can be different ideologies in one class. Further, since ideology and culture (known in Marxism as the superstructure) are not seen as being determined by the economic base, postcolonial critics have given more weight to analyses of linguistic and cultural representations in order to better understand colonial power. With the help of Foucault's understanding of discourse, the field has been opened for (colonial) discourse analysis, which, in turn, brings us to Edward Said and his way of understanding orientalism. As will be seen, his work largely revolves around the theoretical debate on culture and politics.

Europe and the Orient

Said's renowned critique of nineteenth-century academia will be further discussed in the subsequent examination of the nineteenth-century Markan commentaries. The focus here is on the theoretical premises. As is evident from the following quote from *Culture and Imperialism*, Said (1993, 57) challenges traditional understandings of the relation between culture and politics:

> We have on the one hand an isolated cultural sphere, believed to be freely and unconditionally available to weightless theoretical speculation and investigation, and, on the other, a debased political sphere, where the real struggle between interests is supposed to occur. To the professional student of culture—the humanist, the critic, the scholar—only one sphere is relevant, and, more to the point, it is accepted that the

---

8. Loomba (2005, 22–90) outlines and maps these theoretical developments and discusses their significance for postcolonial criticism. For an introduction to what I here refer to as the linguistic turn, see Moore 1994, 13–41. For a summary of the critique against Marxism, mostly conducted by Laclau and Mouffe, see Jørgensen and Phillips 2002, 30–33.

two spheres are separated, whereas the two are not only connected but ultimately the same.

Said's proposition that culture and politics are to be seen not as two separate spheres but as "ultimately the same" is an essential part of his oeuvre. His way of relating linguistic representations to colonial power, however, had been initiated fifteen years earlier in *Orientalism*, Said's (1979) famous analysis of Western notions of the Orient. Even if this work is generally seen as having inaugurated postcolonial criticism, it did not explicitly employ the term *postcolonial*; nor has Said's perspective escaped criticism. Nonetheless, as Moore-Gilbert (1997, 35) noted, "it is Said who so often sets up the terms of reference of subsequent debate in the postcolonial field."

In terms of theory, then, Said's (1979, 6–16) analysis of Western representations of the Orient is based on Gramsci and Foucault. Whereas Gramsci is important for his understanding of *hegemony* as the organization of consent,[9] Foucault is significant for his thinking on power and knowledge, and his particular use of the term *discourse*.[10] Unlike previous studies of European colonialism that tend to focus more on economic and military aspects, Said realized that Foucault and Gramsci make possible a different kind of analysis than a traditional Marxist separation between base and superstructure.

In Foucault's view, power does not belong to certain people or agents such as the state, the leader, the capitalists, and other such entities. Rather, power is seen as permeating all social life, creating limits as well as possibilities, discipline as well as pleasure. Power for Foucault is not something certain people *have*, but is rather understood as fibers that permeate the social, imbue social practices with meaning, distinguish objects from one another, and form knowledge, truth, subjects, and bodies. Foucault's influence can be seen when Said (1979, 15) describes that his interest in

---

9. As pointed out by Moore-Gilbert (1997, 160), Said's use of Gramsci has been criticized. Said did not study how colonial power was upheld by Gramscian hegemony (consent) in the colonies but rather how European identity was formed. It therefore seems as if Gramsci was important to Said for his way of destabilizing the division between base and superstructure.

10. Said, however, is not in total agreement with Foucault; he explains (1979, 23): "Unlike Foucault, I do believe in the determining imprint of individual writers upon the otherwise anonymous collective body of texts constituting a discursive formation like Orientalism."

the nineteenth-century orientalist scholars "is not the (to him) indisputable truth that Occidentals are superior to Orientals, but the profoundly worked over and modulated evidence of his detailed work within the very wide space opened up by that truth."

From this understanding of power, Said analyzes cultural and epistemic productions, not as belonging to a separate sphere, but as part of a totality constituted together with nineteenth-century economic and military expansion. The following quote aptly captures his Foucaultian approach: "An unbroken arch of knowledge and power connects the European or Western statesman and the Western Orientalist. ... The scope of Orientalism exactly matched the scope of empire" (Said 1979, 104). This way of understanding European colonialism as a totality or discourse that involves knowledge production as well as economic and military expansion was applied by Said to his material; and I will, in a modified manner, apply it in parts 2 and 3.

Despite (or perhaps because of) the immense influence of *Orientalism*, it has been debated and criticized—sometimes harshly.[11] First, since *Orientalism* says nothing about the self-representations of the colonized, it creates the impression that colonial discourse was completely controlled by the colonizer, with no room for negotiation or resistance.[12] Also, according to a recurrent critique of the work, it is one-sided and homogenizing in its description of orientalist discourse as unilaterally expressing a Western will to power. Ignored thereby, the critics argue, is the complexity of Western self-understandings in relation to non-Europeans as well as the complex role of oriental scholarship in relation to European colonialism. For instance, when discussing German orientalism, Suzanne Marchand (2009, xxii) rejects the idea of a unified German understanding of the Orient. As will be seen, however, this is not tantamount to denying the connections between orientalist scholarship and colonialism.

Although this criticism undoubtedly targets serious flaws in Said's project, it does not question the need to study academic discourses in relation to imperial expansion. As Marchand (2009, xx) states in the intro-

---

11. For a discussion on the critique against orientalism, see Moore-Gilbert 1997, 40–61; and Loomba 2005, 46–48. Said (1994; 1996) has also responded to some of the critiques.

12. In relation to this last point, Said (1993, 191–281) tried to compensate for this shortcoming in *Culture and Imperialism* by including a chapter on resistance and opposition.

duction to her illuminating work on German orientalism, it would not be desirable to return to a pre-Saidian way of writing uncritical histories that denies the politics of orientalist scholarship. Rather, she calls for a critical scholarship that scrutinizes orientalism's contribution to imperialism, racism, and anti-Semitism, but at the same time acknowledges how orientalism has given rise to academic discourses from which imperialism can be criticized.

Notwithstanding its shortcomings and one-sidedness, however, *Orientalism* managed to open up a field of research with a common, yet heterogeneous, interest in overcoming the legacy of colonialism. This pertinent interest is spelled out by Said (1979, 45) in the form of a critical question: "Can one divide human reality, as indeed human reality seems to be genuinely divided, into clearly different cultures, histories, traditions, societies, even races, and survive the consequences humanly?" Said's partisan, yet theoretically sophisticated, approach has generated the debate from which postcolonial criticism has emerged. Two of the most important voices in this regard have been Spivak and Bhabha, both of whom stand in critical continuity with Said. Let us begin with Spivak, who has addressed one of the neglected areas in *Orientalism*: the self-representation of the colonized.

Can the Subaltern Speak?

Gayatri Spivak's influence in postcolonial criticism has been wide (Moore-Gilbert 1997, 74–75), and some biblical scholars have found her work appealing.[13] For purposes of this work, her use of the concepts of subaltern, catachresis, and *pharmakon* are of great significance.

In her influential essay "Can the Subaltern Speak?" Spivak (1988a) probes the question of whether the colonized or marginalized can be represented in a unified way, especially the oppressed female, or the "sexed subaltern."[14] Focusing on issues of representation, subjectivity, and agency, in the essay she critiques the notion of a universal, transparent, unified subject that represents itself and that is capable of achieving liberation and revolution. Although hardly original in the poststructuralist field where

---

13. References to Spivak are very common in postcolonial biblical criticism; see especially Dube and Staley 2002; and Donaldson 2005.

14. Spivak 1988a, 307. The definition of *subaltern* in the *Penguin Dictionary of Critical Theory* (Macey 2000, s.v.) is "of inferior rank." Spivak follows Gramsci, who used the term to refer to suppressed groups that were not united.

Spivak is located, it is her specific twist that has attracted interest. The main targets of her critique are Foucault and Deleuze, which might be somewhat surprising. Foucault and Deleuze are generally seen as propagating a nonessentialist understanding of the subject.

Spivak (1988a, 272) acknowledges this general understanding of Foucault and Deleuze: "[their] chief presuppositions [are] the critique of the sovereign subject." But this critique is based on an economy of desire that results in "an unquestioned valorization of the subject" (Spivak, 274). Further, Spivak (291) argues, Foucault's understanding of power is blind to imperialism and European ethnocentrism. Spivak here refers to Foucault's notion of power as impregnating social life on the microlevel, which she sees as implying a neglect of global capitalism and macroeconomic aspects of power.

Here, however, there is the potential risk of overstating Spivak's critique of Foucault. She (290) does acknowledge that Foucault can be seen as delivering an admirable program of localized resistance; and although she finds this program lacking a theory of ideology, which in turn "can lead to dangerous utopianism," her deep influence from Derrida would point to a significantly modified "theory of ideology." Indeed, it is difficult to see how a traditional Marxist understanding of ideology, with its separation between a material base and a linguistic superstructure, can be squeezed into a Derridean framework, where such separations are routinely deconstructed.

This leads us to the more positive side of the essay. Whereas Spivak faults Foucault's sole focus on Europe, she has quite the opposite view of Derrida. Spivak defends Derrida against the accusations, not least from Said, about being inaccessible, esoteric, and textualistic. As Spivak recognizes, Said's reading of Derrida rests on a duality between text and reality and hence betrays a profound misapprehension of the notion of textuality. As implied in Spivak's critique of Said, Derrida's work significantly destabilizes this duality.

One of Spivak's (1988a, 292) main points, then, is to defend the political usefulness of Derrida for people outside the first world. Somewhat paradoxically, she (293) seems to mean that Derrida's usefulness for non-Europeans lies in his focus on Europe: "as a European philosopher he articulates the *European* Subject's tendency to constitute the Other as marginal to ethnocentrism. ... *Not* a general problem, but a *European* problem" (emphasis original). As we saw, Spivak (292) criticized Foucault for having a European focus in his texts; but, unlike Derrida, Foucault has an *unacknowledged* Western subject that "presides by disavowal."

As Spivak (292) reads him, Derrida is searching for a subject that is not constructed in relation to an Other: "The question [raised by Derrida] is how to keep the ethnocentric Subject from establishing itself by selectively defining an Other." Spivak (294) here refers to Derrida's distinction between the *self-consolidating other* and the *quite-other* (*tout-autre*). This quite-other is typically not written in the text, but, as Spivak (294) phrases it, "is, if blank, still *in the text*" (emphasis original), which implies reading strategies that attempt to listen to voices not represented in the text. This, for Spivak (294), is what Western-based postcolonial critics ought to be focusing on: "That inaccessible blankness ... is what a postcolonial critic of imperialism would like to see developed within the European enclosure as the place of *the* production of theory" (emphasis original). The postcolonial critic, in Spivak's (293) view, ought to show a high degree of self-reflectivity and self-criticism in claims of subjectivity and agency: "a vigilance precisely against too great a claim for transparency."

Spivak's stance is highlighted by a recurring, highly relevant question: "Can the subaltern speak" (294, 296)? As an illustration, she refers to the Hindu rite of widow sacrifice, in which a widow apparently places herself on her husband's funeral pyre to be immolated. The British prohibition of this rite Spivak (297) interprets as "white men saving brown women from brown men." Searching the archives, Spivak (297) also found the Indian nativist argument that she sees as "a parody of the nostalgia of lost origins: 'The women actually wanted to die.'" Not found in the archives, however, was the voice of the subaltern woman herself: "One never encounters the testimony of the women's voice-consciousness." Such a testimony, Spivak (297) is careful to point out, "would not be ideology-transcendent or 'fully' subjective, of course, but it would have constituted the ingredients for producing a countersentence."

On the one hand, the essay could be seen as ending on a negative note. The question finally receives the disappointing answer that "the subaltern cannot speak" (308)—there is no space from which the sexed subaltern can be heard or represented. Although implying a certain pessimism with regard to the possibilities of social change and emancipation, she also highlights the intellectual's responsibility—perhaps inspired by Gramsci's maxim, "pessimism of the intellect, optimism of the will"—to strive to represent the subaltern. This call for a reading approach that listens to the marginalized and questions which voices are heard and which are silent is enforced by Spivak's (308) reference to Derrida: "Derrida marks radical critique with the danger of appropriating the other by assimilation.

He reads catachresis at the origin." Enigmatic as it stands, it points to the particular use Spivak has made of catachresis.

Catachresis and *Pharmakon*

Spivak's use of the term *catachresis* is interesting for its way of detecting subtle forms of resistance to colonialism. As I will contend in part 3, it can illuminate several instances of Mark's peculiar use of terms and phrases. It is also a term with which Spivak has been specifically connected (Kumar 1997). Her way of using it differs somewhat from ordinary use. As a literary term, *catachresis* refers to a misapplication or incorrect usage of a word and serves as an explanation of how language develops and changes. For instance, the phrase "table legs" was, from the beginning, a catachresis. Since tables do not have legs, it originated from a misuse of the word *leg*. In Spivak's writing, however, catachresis receives more of a political meaning in colonial and post-colonial contexts. Regarding it as "a concept-metaphor without an adequate referent," Spivak (1990, 225) typically applies it to concepts such as nationhood, constitutionality, citizenship, and democracy, all of which are coded within the legacy of imperialism, and hence lack adequate referents in a non-Western context. But they are "reclaimed, indeed claimed, as concept-metaphors for which no historically adequate referent may be advanced from postcolonial space." Spivak therefore sees catachresis as a local, tactical maneuver that involves wrenching particular images, ideas, or rhetorical practices out of their place within a particular discourse and using them to open up new arenas of meaning, often in direct contrast to their conventionally understood meanings and functions. Catachresis is an admission of a reality that is inevitable and yet unfair. It involves the postcolonial space as a whole, which Spivak (1990, 225–28) describes as "a space that one cannot not want to inhabit and yet must criticize."

Spivak's ambiguous understanding of Western modernity is aptly captured in the Greek term *pharmakon,* which she borrows from Derrida. In his elaboration on the oppositional dynamics between speech and writing in Plato's *Phaedrus,* Derrida (1981, 70–84, 95–134) points out how the term is used to indicate the ambiguous nature of writing as both medicine and poison. In Spivak's writings, Western domination is therefore understood as *pharmakon*. Depending on how it is applied and dealt with, it can either liberate or oppress, either illuminate or darken.[15]

---

15. In a similar manner, Spivak (1999, 83) also sees capitalism as the *pharmakon*

As such, postcolonial criticism in Spivak's understanding has a basic affirmative direction in that it sees colonial discourse as in some sense enabling. Postcolonial discourse then stands in a catachrestic relation to Western domination: it is neither inside nor outside, but rather stands in "tangential" relation to it (cf. Prakash 1992, 8; Moore-Gilbert 1997, 84).

Spivak's use of *catachresis* and *pharmakon* places her in an ambivalent relation to anticolonial struggles and discourses. Although she sees the anticolonial reversal as a necessary stage (as do Said and Fanon), she also maintains that the reversal needs to be modified by a displacement of the terms in opposition: "Without this supplementary distancing, a position and its counter-position ... will keep legitimizing each other" (Spivak 1988b, 250). For Spivak, then, directly counterhegemonic discourse is more liable to cancellation or even reappropriation by the dominant than the "tangential" mode of engagement, which is epitomized by *pharmakon* and catachresis. Her approach can be seen as suggesting modes of negotiation and criticism that unsettle the dominant from within.

Identity as Identification

The third postcolonial critic to be introduced here, Homi Bhabha, has introduced several concepts that have proven useful to interpret how biblical texts relate to their imperial settings.[16] Drawing on a psychoanalytical perspective, Bhabha's approach focuses on the colonizer-colonized relation and its complex impact on collective identity and culture. For my reading of Mark here as a collective representation in its imperial setting, the concepts of colonial ambivalence, mimicry, hybridity, and third space, as well as the pedagogical/performative distinction, will be especially useful. Before presenting Bhabha's thoughts on identity formation, however, I will begin with the more contested issue of theory with which Bhabha is associated.

---

of Marxism. It makes possible the dialectical development of socialism, but if left unregulated, it can just as well obstruct that development.

16. Biblical scholars that have made use of Bhabha include Runions 2001a; Han 2005; Moore 2005; and Carter 2007.

The Question of Theory

Bhabha's use of theory has been celebrated as well as criticized.[17] As argued by Slemon and Tiffin (1989, xvi), Bhabha's theory stands in an ironic relation to the oppositional activities of the colonized and therefore implies a retreat from the political and becomes instead a part of the neocolonial apparatus. The irony that Slemon and Tiffin detect in Bhabha's writing is relevant. Although not the only trope, it is certainly one of Bhabha's interests. But even though the irony partly undermines anticolonial nationalisms, its primary target is rather to point at the inherent contradictions and impossibilities of colonial universality and hegemony. Hence Bhabha (2004, 252) describes his use of theory as an

> attempt to represent a certain defeat, or even an impossibility, of the "West" in its authorization of the "idea" of colonization. Driven by the subaltern history of the margins of modernity—rather than by the failures of logocentrism—I have tried, in some small measure, to revise the known, to rename the postmodern from the position of the postcolonial.

Postcolonial theory for Bhabha is thus a way to criticize how modernity is entangled with European colonialism. He explicitly discusses his use of theory in the first essay of *The Location of Culture* (a collection of his most important works).[18] With reference to the critique of his use of theory as a kind of neocolonialism, Bhabha (2004, 30–31) asks: "Are the interests of 'Western' theory necessarily collusive with the hegemonic role of the West as a power block? Is the language of theory merely another power ploy of the culturally privileged Western elite to produce a discourse of the Other that reinforces its own power-knowledge equation?" Although he seems somewhat double-edged—he points at the risks of "institutional containment"—it is his estimation of theory's "revisionary force" that is typically epitomized by his work (47).

Various Marxist scholars are also critical of Bhabha for what they regard as his retreat from the political. Biblical scholar Richard Horsley

---

17. For a more detailed discussion of the critique against Bhabha, see Moore-Gilbert 1997, 130–40; and Loomba 2005, 148–53.

18. Published in 1994, *The Location of Culture* is Bhabha's most widely read work. It is a collection of separate texts, most of which were previously published in different journals and books.

(2003b, 99), for example, regards postcolonial theory's rejection of Marxism as a historical scheme as "a serious lack of attention to how capitalism continues to consolidate its power as it establishes its own global empire." Although Horsley is correct in that postcolonial critics do tend to reject historical materialism and the Marxist separation between base and superstructure, I would question whether this necessarily implies a neglect of economic aspects of power.

Bhabha, for one, would affirm the impact of capitalism. As he spells it out, "economic and political domination has a profound hegemonic influence on the information orders of the Western world" (2004, 30). What Bhabha would deny, however, is the privileging of the material mode of production and the unique role given to class struggle. Although this might be taken as a retreat from a particular kind of revolutionary position (38), it is certainly not a retreat from the political. While avoiding affiliation with a particular political alliance such as the third world, the working class, or the feminist struggle, Bhabha sees his work on theory as "committed to progressive political change" (32). The recognition that activism and theory exist side by side "like the recto and verso of a sheet of paper" is, for Bhabha, a matter of political maturity (32). Rather than retreating, then, Bhabha (33–34) suggests what appears to be a reformulation of the political from the poststructural:

> the dynamics of writing and textuality require us to rethink the logics of causality and determinacy through which we recognize the "political" as a form of calculation and strategic action dedicated to social transformation. "What is to be done?" must acknowledge the force of writing, its metaphoricity and its rhetorical discourse, as a productive matrix which defines the "social" and makes it available as an objective of and for, action.

Bhabha's understanding of the "political" involves moving beyond Marxism and its division between base and superstructure as well as its Hegelian scheme of historical development. In this sense, his position is rather similar to Laclau and Mouffe and their development of post-Marxism and discourse theory.[19] Although it appears that Bhabha has

---

19. Laclau and Mouffe (2001, ix) define post-Marxism "as the process of reappropriation of an intellectual tradition, as well as the process of going beyond it." See also idem 1987.

not explicitly identified himself with post-Marxism, his preference for *negotiation* (rather than *negation*) as "a dialectic without the emergence of a teleological or transcendent history" (37) resonates rather well with this school of thought.

Colonial Ambivalence and Mimicry

One prominent trajectory in Bhabha's work is a rereading of Frantz Fanon. While Fanon's Manichaean perspective has been generally regarded as a source of inspiration for the anticolonial struggle, and as championing a rather clear sense of agency for the colonized, Bhabha finds another trajectory in his more complex discussions on human desire and psyche, represented by such questions as, "What does a *black* man want?" (Bhabha 2004, 73). By focusing on these psychological aspects, Bhabha (63) suggests that Fanon "reveals the deep psychic uncertainty of the colonial relation itself." Questioning the Hegelian scheme of progression by thesis and antithesis, Bhabha finds colonial discourse to be fraught with ambivalence and anxiety. For Bhabha, the more unified understanding of the colonized subject, which is also present in Fanon's work, is too much in conformity with the model of the heroic sovereign humanist subject, which Bhabha sees as being part of a colonial epistemology.

By applying Lacanian psychoanalysis and Derridean deconstructionism, Bhabha reads against the grain of Fanon's texts, taking them as an illustration of how colonial discourse fluctuates between self-confident universalism and the anxiety of being imitated and mocked. Probing the slippery and rupturing processes of identification that he argues typically arose in the interstitial in-between space, Bhabha (121, 183–98) designates the unstable and unsettling relation between colonizer and colonized with the term *colonial ambivalence*.

Phrased from the European perspective as "the white man's burden" and from the colonized perspective as "turn white or disappear" (Fanon 1967, 100), the confident authoritative aspect rests upon the notion of the universality and superiority of colonial culture and presupposes that the colonized learn from and imitate the colonial culture—or, in other words, "become civilized." But for Bhabha this is only one side of the coin. Whereas Fanon regards imitative behavior as a pure negative—the sign of an inferiority complex—Bhabha (2004, 121–31, 172) strips it of its essence and sees it instead as *mimicry*, which he understands as being profoundly subversive. By imitating the colonizers, by becoming almost like them, the division that upholds colonial power is undermined. Bhabha further contends that rather than being a complete harmonization, imitation is more often a form of metonymical resemblance—a repetition with a difference—or, as he repeatedly states, "almost the same *but not quite*" (123, italics original), meaning that mimicry tends to teeter on the brink of mockery, parody, and menace. Hence Bhabha argues that colonial discourse is double-edged and ambivalent, "split between its appearance as original and authoritative and its articulation as repetition and difference."[20]

The subversive effect of mimicry on colonial rule, then, is not primarily a consciously applied counterimperial strategy, but rather an elusive effect of the colonial discourse itself. On the other hand, by highlighting its subversive effects and associating it with "camouflage," "civil disobedience," and "signs of spectacular resistance," Bhabha (172) also points at the political potential of mimicry as a strategy that could be used consciously to undermine colonialism.

Also of significance to my examination of Mark as a collective representation is that Bhabha does not limit himself to an investigation of the colonizer-colonized relation, but examines the more general matter of collective identities as well. In *Nation and Narration* (1990b, 294), he points at an ambivalence that resides within the nation itself, enacted in a continuous fluctuation between what he calls the pedagogical and the performative: "In the production of the nation as narration," he suggests, "there is a split between the continuist, accumulative temporality of the pedagogical, and the repetitious, recursive strategy of the performative" (297). Whereas the *pedagogical* discourse signifies the people (or any group) as an a priori historical presence, constituted by a historical origin or event, the *performative* construes the group in repeated enunciations of the traditional discourse that both adds to and substitutes its meaning (294–306). Although Bhabha is here primarily discussing modern nations, his explicit focus on narration (rather than organizational aspects) as forming collective identities is of far wider significance.[21] Since Mark's Gospel was written at a time when the Jesus followers began to acquire the identity of a *tertium genos*, the concept of "nation" is not as distant from Mark as it might initially

---

20. Bhabha 2004, 145–74, quote from 153. See also Huddart 2006, 58–61.
21. For an argument that nationalism is applicable to antiquity, and in particular Jewish nationalism, see Goodblatt 2006.

seem.²² Bhabha's distinction between a pedagogical and a performative mode of narrating a collective self-understanding, therefore, constitutes a valuable tool for the analysis in part 3, especially for conceptualizing Mark's way of rearticulating a Jewish tradition (see ch. 18).

Hybridity and Third Space

Since this study to a high extent has been framed by Bhabha's understanding of culture and human subjectivity, I need to clarify that understanding a little more closely. Bhabha questions the common understanding of cultures and identities as stable entities. Popular terms such as *cultural diversity* and *multiculturalism* are criticized for resting on essential notions of cultures, and for leading, at best, to an appreciation of cultures as something that can be collected in museums and, at worst, to racism, xenophobia, and ethnocentrism (1990a, 208; 2004, 47–56). Bhabha's challenging of the long-standing tradition of essentialism is based primarily on the psychoanalytic critic Jacques Lacan and his understanding of the human subject.²³

Lacan makes a distinction between the ego and the subject. Whereas he regards the ego as an illusory experience of wholeness and completeness that results from imaginary identifications, he regards the subject as an incomplete structure that constantly strives to become a whole. Unlike the ego, the subject never experiences the notion of personal completeness and is therefore characterized by a sense of alienation and lack. In addition, as mentioned in the introduction, the culture typically supplies an excess of identity positions, making the subject overdetermined. For Lacan, since there is no real solution to this disparity between ego and subject, there is no other alternative but to accept the subject's experience of disunity and fragmentation—or, in more psychoanalytic terms, to accept the fact of one's own castration.

It is this notion of the subject as alienated, split, and disunified that Bhabha and other critical theorists have used to suggest nonessentialist

---

22. Although the phrase "third race" does not occur until Aristides of Athens (*Apology* 2), the notion of the Christ followers as a "race" is already present in the NT (1 Pet 2:9; Acts 17:29). Räisänen (2010, 283) claims that the idea is already present in 1 Cor 10:32. See also Buell 2005.

23. For good introductions to Lacan's understanding of the subject, see Macey 2000, s.v. "Lacan, Jacques"; Moore 1994, 74–81; and Bowie 1995.

understandings of identity and culture.[24] Although Lacan was primarily interested in the individual psyche, critical theorists have found his theories applicable to collective identities as well. Lacan's understanding of the subject is clearly echoed in Bhabha's (1990a, 210) discussion on cultural identities: "cultures are symbol-forming and subject-constituting, interpellative practices." And since symbol forming is a linguistic enterprise, and since for Bhabha (as for Lacan) the relation between signifier and signified is inherently unstable, Bhabha (210) can argue that a culture's "symbol-forming activity, its own interpellation in the process of representation ... and meaning-making always underscores the claim to an originary, holistic organic identity."

Bhabha (1990a, 207–13; 2004, 47–56, 303–37) consequently regards all cultures as being caught up in processes of *hybridity, negotiation,* and *translation.* He uses these words in a somewhat transferred and analogical sense; "hybridity," for example, does not imply the mixing of two original entities, as it does in typical biological and/or racial discourse. Rather, it implies the formation of a "'third space' which enables other positions to emerge" (1990a, 211). In this *third space,* which typically emerges when two or more cultures intermingle, histories and positions are displaced by new structures of authority and new initiatives that would not have been possible to delineate to previous traditions or cultures. In this way, hybridity and the third space are said to carry a certain innovative energy (2004, 315–19).

When asked if the third space could be seen as "an identity as such," Lacan is unmistakably echoed in Bhabha's (1990a, 211) answer:

> No, not so much identity as identification (in the psychoanalytic sense). I try to talk about hybridity through a psychoanalytic analogy, so that identification is a process of identifying with and through another object, an object of otherness, at which point the agency of identification—the subject—is itself always ambivalent, because of the intervention of that otherness. But the importance of hybridity is that it bears the traces of those feelings and practices which inform it, just like a translation, so that hybridity puts together the traces of certain other meanings or discourses.

---

24. Among the most notable critical theorists who make use of Lacan are Louis Althusser, Slavoj Žižek, Judith Butler, and Ernesto Laclau.

The third space is here closely associated with hybridity and described as an act of identification that emerges in a heterogeneous, perhaps antagonistic, context of multiple discourses. The subjectivity (or agency) that is thereby generated carries traces of previously distinguishable discourses and is therefore ambivalent. As already mentioned, otherness for Bhabha is not so much a negation as a negotiation; and along similar lines, hybridity designates not so much a final result as the continuous process of negotiation and translation that takes place in this third space.

Since Bhabha establishes his understanding of culture upon a non-sovereign notion of the subject, one can ask where such an understanding might lead in terms of social change. As Bhabha admits, his theory risks implying a pure anarchic liberalism or voluntarism that is devoid of any political relevance. As a response, he (1990a, 213) nevertheless upholds the importance of alienation in one's self and in one's culture as a basis for establishing different forms of political solidarity. In a saying that curiously echoes the exhortative speech given by the Markan Jesus (Mark 8:35), Bhabha (213) emphasizes that "it is only by losing the sovereignty of the self that you can gain the freedom of a politics that is open to the non-assimilationist claims of cultural difference." As I hope to show, given Mark's open-ended narrative and its subtle ambivalences, Bhabha's non-sovereign understanding of subjectivity will be especially appropriate for the task of this study.

Having rendered the theoretical premises for the subsequent inquiries, it is now time to proceed. While the examination of Mark during the nineteenth century (part 2) will primarily engage with Said's work, the principal analysis of Mark in its ancient setting (part 3) will be largely informed by the thought of Spivak and Bhabha. First, however, I will delineate how postcolonial criticism and biblical scholarship have begun to amalgamate into the contested field of postcolonial biblical criticism.

3
POSTCOLONIAL CRITICISM IN BIBLICAL STUDIES

Considering the prominent, yet highly dubious, role of the Bible in European colonialism, one could perhaps be surprised that biblical scholars were not engaging in postcolonial criticism when it appeared on the academic scene during the 1980s. If postcolonial criticism, as Moore-Gilbert (1997, 6) argues, arrived late in literary studies, its entrance into biblical studies is even more belated. A significant step was taken in 1996 by the experimental journal *Semeia*, with an issue entitled *Postcolonialism and Scriptural Reading* under the expert direction of Laura Donaldson (1996b).[1] Shortly thereafter, Sheffield Academic Press launched the series *The Bible and Postcolonialism*, publishing its first volume in 1998, edited by R. S. Sugirtharajah (1998a). Since then the field has grown considerably, with several introductory works as well as various postcolonial interpretations of particular biblical texts—extensive enough, indeed, to require a map.

MODIFYING A DISINTEGRATING MAP

Mapping the multifaceted terrain of postcolonial biblical criticism, Stephen Moore and Fernando Segovia (2005, 5–10; cf. Moore 2006, 14–23) delineate three main "clusters with highly permeable boarders." As they attest, mapping is a complex task—deciding where postcolonial biblical criticism begins and ends is difficult. Although their mapping has been extremely helpful in my own orientation in this field's terrain, I have also found the task to be somewhat problematic, not least regarding what the

---

1. Two years earlier, a volume edited by the literary critic Susan V. Gallagher (1994a) was published. This work, however, has been less influential among biblical scholars.

map depicts—whether it consists of postcolonial biblical criticism per se or a wider range of works representing an academic field from which postcolonial biblical criticism has emerged. But first let me briefly render the Moore-Segovia map.

The first cluster of works is a development from a certain kind of liberation hermeneutics known alternatively as contextual hermeneutics, vernacular hermeneutics, or cultural studies. One of this area's pioneering works is *Voices from the Margin*, edited by Sugirtharajah (1991).[2] In addition, the two-volume *Reading from This Place* by Segovia and Tolbert (1995) highlights the importance of the social location of the biblical interpreter. The interest in cultural and local contingency also involves a critique of the (often Marxist driven) focus on the poor or the workers as a universal category. As evident from the recently launched Texts @ Contexts series (Duran et al. 2011), this is a cluster of great vitality.

If the first cluster to some extent engages in what Moore and Segovia term "extra-biblical postcolonial studies," the second cluster typically refrains from such endeavors, undertaking more of a social-historical approach instead. As this group of works shares an interest in using empire as an exegetical lens, Moore and Segovia (2005, 8) suggest the term "'X and Empire' cluster." However, since such a title seems somewhat awkward, it is probably best to follow Moore (2006, 19), who in a later revision of this map suggests the label "Empire studies." Among the more prominent works in this cluster are those by Richard Horsley (1997; 2003a) on Paul and on the Jesus traditions as well as those by Neil Elliott (1995), Wes Howard-Brook and Anthony Gwyther (1999), and Warren Carter (2001; 2008).

If the previous two clusters are more or less straightforwardly defined, the third is a bit more amorphous. Moore and Segovia (2005, 8–9) describe this group of works as "leakage" from the wider field of extrabiblical postcolonial studies. The *Semeia* issue edited by Donaldson (1996b) belongs to this group, as does Gallagher (1994a). This cluster also consists of works by biblical scholars who are familiar with poststructuralist theory, including Erin Runions (2001b), Roland Boer (2001), and Tat-siong Benny Liew (1999a). In addition, as exemplified by Liew (1999a) and Musa Dube

---

2. As a token of its significance, the work was followed by the volume *Still at the Margins: Biblical Scholarship Fifteen Years after Voices from the Margin*, also edited by Sugirtharajah (2008).

(2000), this cluster also involves ideological criticism—a critique and questioning of the morality of the biblical texts.

As Moore and Segovia (2005, 8) have conceded, their tricluster map has severe design problems—something they appear to take a certain delight in. Considering cartography's largely unfortunate connotation in the history of colonialism, they state, "a map of postcolonial biblical criticism that disintegrates even as it is being drawn is not altogether inappropriate." Although I appreciate the comparison, I also see the need to rewrite, or at least modify, the map. While acknowledging that an alternative map is as doomed to disintegration as the original one, I nevertheless will venture to offer the following four remarks.

To begin with a minor issue regarding the first cluster, it seems somewhat misleading to describe Michael Prior's *Bible and Colonialism* (1997) as "straightforwardly rooted in liberation theology" (Moore and Segovia 2005, 7). Prior's work primarily deals with the Deuteronomic traditions on land; but whereas liberation theology typically reads these biblical traditions as stories about liberation from oppressive rule, Prior shows how these stories have been used in different colonial endeavors. His book ends with a call for morally responsible biblical scholarship, in which he (279–80) criticizes Gustavo Gutiérrez (one of the founders of liberation theology) for excluding the references in the exodus narrative to the indigenous inhabitants in Canaan. In this sense, his work can be more accurately regarded as ideological criticism, thus placing it in the third cluster instead.

Second, since the three clusters are presented as being of a more or less equivalent size, a greater problem emerges. True, the map does not claim to include all works. But to my knowledge, the second cluster seems severely underrepresented. First, if the criterion is to have *empire* in the title, Crossan and Reed's (2004) work on Paul ought to have qualified. More importantly, since Moore and Segovia (2005, 7) include other works with a similar "thematic focus and/or the name of Richard Horsley," the problem of boundary drawing becomes more urgent. From the 1980s, Horsley has written widely and seminally on the New Testament and its ancient sociopolitical context—works that are not included in the cluster. Further, Moore and Segovia's map gives the impression that Horsley is the sole pioneer in this cluster. While not denying his importance, one also needs to point out that other scholars have made significant contributions as well. Without claiming to being exhaustive, the following authors reformulate how Jesus and early Christianity related to their Roman imperial context and challenge a modern division between religion and politics: Brandon (1967),[3] Yoder (1972), Theissen (1978), Cassidy (1978), Myers (1988), Wink (1984; 1986; 1992b), Borg (1998), Malina (2001), and Crossan (1992; 2007). Although there are likely several other works that could qualify, I think the case has been clearly made: the second cluster is considerably larger than Moore and Segovia have indicated.

As already mentioned, I am somewhat troubled by the ambiguity with which Moore and Segovia define their cartographic task. This becomes a third area of critique: is it a map of postcolonial biblical criticism proper or of the terrain out of which it has emerged? Whereas their description of the first and second cluster leans heavily toward the latter view, the third cluster tilts far more toward the former. In terms of the revisionary critique undertaken here, I myself am clearly tending toward the latter—a mapping of the terrain from which postcolonial biblical criticism has emerged. As to Moore and Segovia's apparent vagueness on this matter, it may have resulted from a benign intention to define postcolonial biblical criticism in the broadest of terms. Indeed, it seems as if they went a bit too far in this regard, since even they acknowledge that some of the scholars in the second cluster have avoided using the term *postcolonial* in their works, thus signaling a possible reluctance to engage or be associated with this perspective.[4]

This leads to a fourth point of critique. As the revised map offered here depicts the terrain and trajectories from which postcolonial biblical criticism has emerged, there is at least one important cluster missing: feminist criticism. Although Moore and Segovia do mention the works of Dube and Donaldson, the absence of feminist criticism as a cluster in its own right is a rather severe flaw. Indeed, without a feminist cluster in the map, it is difficult to make sense of more recent works that use a combined postcolonial and gender-critical optic in New Testament interpretation—for example, Dube (2000), Donaldson and Kwok (2002; 2005), Vander Stichele and Penner (2005a; 2007), Schüssler Fiorenza (2007), Punt (2008), Lopez (2008), and Marchal (2006; 2008).[5]

---

3. Since Brandon had been inspired by Hermann Samuel Reimarus (1778; ET: 1970), this cluster can be seen, somewhat intriguingly, as going back to the early formation of modern biblical scholarship.

4. Of course, this can only be valid for the works that were written after the entrance of postcolonial criticism in biblical studies.

5. The works by Schüssler Fiorenza and Lopez can be only partly categorized as postcolonial biblical criticism. Most pointedly, Schüssler Fiorenza's (2007) relation to

3. POSTCOLONIAL CRITICISM IN BIBLICAL STUDIES   53

Based upon the above critique, I would first suggest a substitution of the third cluster in the map. What Moore and Segovia regard as leakage from extrabiblical postcolonial studies (their third cluster), I would instead regard as examples of postcolonial biblical criticism proper. Then I would relabel the third cluster "feminist criticism," and include within this category the works of Tolbert (1983), Schüssler Fiorenza (1983), Bird et al. (1997), and Kwok (1995). Although the list of such works can be made longer, those already mentioned should suffice as grounds for the relabeling of the third cluster.

Second, in order to make the map accurate, I also need to add a fourth rather obvious entity that also has helped to form postcolonial biblical criticism: the extrabiblical field of postcolonial criticism. The revised map could be drawn as seen in figure 3. In order to distinguish the relatively small clusters of biblical scholarship (feminist criticism, empire studies, and vernacular hermeneutics) from the wide field of extrabiblical postcolonial criticism, I have used ellipses and a rectangle, respectively.

I would like to underline, as did Moore and Segovia, that these clusters do have highly permeable boarders. Hence Kwok's work could be just easily placed in the first cluster. Further, having added a cluster for feminist criticism, I am not denying that there have been tensions between feminist (taken as a Western phenomenon) and postcolonial biblical scholars. Dube (2000, 29–30), for instance, criticizes Schüssler Fiorenza's (1983) reconstruction of Christian origins for leaving out the imperial culture of domination and for enforcing dualistic boundaries between believers and unbelievers, Christians and non-Christians. Schüssler Fiorenza (2007, 11), for her part, faults Dube and others for conducting a "dual systems analysis" as though issues of gender and colonialism were independent of each other. Schüssler Fiorenza introduces instead the term *kyriarchy* as an attempt to conceptualize power structures that include both gender and empire. Despite such tensions, the inclusion of feminist criticism in the map seems reasonable, not least due to the recent works that explore the intertwinements of gender and empire.

With this modified map, postcolonial biblical criticism becomes somewhat more narrowly defined—it only includes works that explicitly

---

postcolonial criticism can be characterized as ambivalent. Although the book is dedicated to three of the leading figures in postcolonial biblical criticism (Kwok, Segovia, and Sugirtharajah), she finds that postcolonial biblical criticism is part of "malestream studies" (2–3) and "inscribes the elite male as the generic human being" (11).

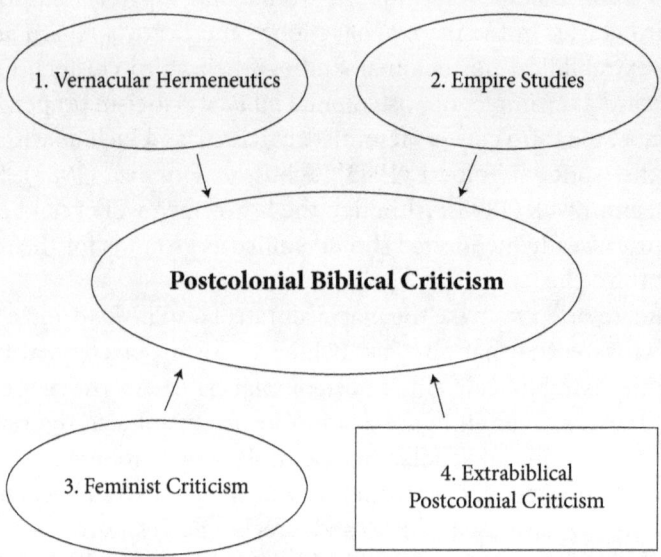

Figure 3. Map of postcolonial biblical criticism.

engage with postcolonial criticism. On the other hand, it also widens the academic terrain in biblical studies from which postcolonial biblical criticism has emerged and with which it remains closely affiliated. Further, my more narrow definition of postcolonial biblical criticism should not be taken as implying a homogeneous direction. Just as extrabiblical postcolonial criticism is highly diverse, so is its counterpart in biblical studies.

Reciprocal Challenges

Since the perspective applied in this study consists of a merging of two rather divergent academic fields, some issues need to be addressed. The merging seems to imply a critique in two directions: from biblical studies to postcolonial criticism and vice versa. Beginning with the first direction, a problem in postcolonial criticism that becomes evident from a biblical studies perspective is what has been referred to above as "unmediated secularism." Why would a biblical scholar apply a perspective that appears to presuppose that religion is a generally backward, superstitious, or reactionary phenomenon? Since secularism is becoming increasingly questioned as an ideology, however, I will here argue that scholars of religion can help challenge this tendency in postcolonial criticism. As to the critique in the opposite direction, I have already touched upon the postcolonial questioning of the historical-critical paradigm. The aim in discussing these mutual criticisms is to clarify the perspective applied in this study as well as to stimulate a critical, and potentially fruitful, dialogue between postcolonial criticism and biblical studies. Curiously enough, this dialogue can be seen as emerging from what is often seen as the founding work of postcolonial criticism: Said's *Orientalism*.

In the introduction to *Orientalism*, Said (1979, 15–19) describes how he proceeded to demarcate his material. Since a study of "the European idea of the Orient" would involve an amount of material that was far too vast to investigate, he needed to draw some limits. For a biblical scholar, one of his demarcations is particularly interesting. Said somewhat highlights in his account (17) that he refrained from studying "one of the important impulses toward the study of the Orient," namely the revolution in biblical studies that took place in Germany at the end of the eighteenth century. As Said identifies scholars whom he sees as "variously interesting pioneers," but that he nevertheless leaves out—Bishop Robert Lowth (1710–1787), Johann Gottfried Eichhorn (1753–1827), Johann Gottfried von Herder (1744–1803), and Johann David Michaelis (1717–1791)—a rather striking lacuna is made visible.

This Saidian lacuna raises two important discussions, which I will subsequently deal with. First, if postcolonial criticism has a secularist tendency, is Said's demarcation then "innocent" in the sense that it simply establishes reasonable limits for an investigation? Or is it part of a typical postcolonial privileging of secular discourses and a marginalization of religion? Second, Said's lacuna can also be taken as an invitation for biblical scholars to engage critically in our own field. Beginning with the first question, I will examine what reasons Said gives for the demarcation of his material.

The Secularism of Postcolonial Criticism

Said defends his evasion of biblical scholarship by a reference to a work by Shaffer (1975) that Said says "amply" makes up for his "failings" (1979, 18). But although Shaffer's work helpfully illuminates how some German biblical scholars (including Michaelis) became important for British romanticism, it does not—and this is also acknowledged by Said—spell out how these writings were related to a European colonial mind-set. The reference to Shaffer being a rather weak explanation, Said also contends that oriental studies were first and foremost initiated by British and French scholars. Since German oriental scholarship was elaborating on an already existing trajectory, Said seems to claim, they have only a secondary importance and can therefore be left out. In addition, as Said argues, whereas Britain and France had colonial interests in the Orient, Germany had not yet become a colonial power.

Said's rationalizations can, however, be questioned. One might interrogate, first, whether Germany's lack of colonies during the late eighteenth century ought to imply that its biblical and oriental scholarship has developed in isolation from European colonialism. True, the German context differed in important ways from that of the British and the French. But even so, Michaelis and Eichhorn, for example, were international scholars who participated in a pan-European quest for knowledge. This is seen not least in that many texts and artifacts from the Orient were kept in England, inducing numerous German scholars to spend a considerable part of their time there. Michaelis, for example, spent many years in Oxford—years that he considered to have been some of the happiest in his life (W. Baird 1992, 128). According to Marchand (2009, 104, 498), German orientalism was part of a European "imperial hubris" that presumed that Eastern cultures were "something to master and own, not an ongoing living set of traditions into which one entered as a guest."

Second, as noted by one of his early reviewers (Beckingham 1979, 562), Said's description of the British and French oriental scholars as being ahead of the Germans is highly questionable. When making his claim of French priority, Said (1979, 18) refers to the fact that Franz Bopp, German founder of comparative linguistics, had the French Arabist Silvestre de Sacy (1758–1838) as his teacher. Said fails to acknowledge, however, that several German scholars predate Sacy.

That biblical studies at an early stage began to stimulate the growth of orientalist studies is perhaps most clearly seen in Michaelis's arranging for a scientific expedition to the Orient. Driven by a keen interest in Hebrew and Arabic, Michaelis organized the first expedition of its kind to what was called *Arabia Felix* (happy Arabia). Supported by the Danish king, the expedition sailed from Copenhagen in 1761, loaded with five scholars from different disciplines and countries.[6] Although the expedition was

---

6. Hansen (2000, 9–47) describes the discussions that eventually led to the inclusion of these scholars: Professor Friderich Christian von Haven, a Danish philologist and orientalist; Professor Peter Forsskål, a Swedish botanist and expert in natural

in some ways a tragedy—four of the scholars died—it nevertheless had a major impact on the European understanding of and interest in the Orient, not least through the writings by the expedition's sole surviving scholar, Carsten Niebuhr (1772; 1774–1778), whose works spread widely and were translated into different languages. As argued in Jonathan Hess's (2000, 78) illuminating article, the voyage thereby "decisively shaped Europeans' vision of the Arab world in the latter half of the eighteenth century." As indicated by the international character of this expedition, the academic study of the Orient was hardly confined within national borders, and Said's depiction of German biblical and oriental scholarship as secondary and isolated is therefore flawed.

Also, even if Germany as a nation was not involved in colonial expansion until the second half of the nineteenth century, the Bible certainly was. Typically seen as the colonizers' book, it was a pronounced part of the European expansion, epitomized by the growing intensity of the Protestant mission (which included German missionary societies) during the nineteenth century. Seen in that light, to pass over a revolution in the academic field of biblical studies—even if it is initiated in Germany—is rather remarkable. It becomes even more bewildering if we also add *Culture and Imperialism*, Said's (1993) follow-up to *Orientalism*, which is similarly devoid of an analysis of the Bible, biblical studies, or Christian mission. As Said tends to omit religion from his studies of culture and imperialism, his works seems to rest on a rather circumscribed understanding of "culture."

True, Said (1979, 100) mentions in passing that Britain "as a Christian power" regarded itself as having legitimate colonial interests. But he refrains from discussing the churches, mission, or other Christian discourses that had contributed to the forming of European colonial identity since the fifteenth century, continuing to do so in the nineteenth century as well. Instead Said (1979, 113–23) seems to regard Christian discourses as having been somehow superseded during the nineteenth century by the development of "secular religion," of which orientalism was a crucial part. In these currents, the long-standing Christians/heathen distinction was "overwhelmed" by systematically multiplied classifications of humankind based on "race, color, origin, temperament, character, and types" (Said,

---

history who had been trained by Linnaeus; Lieutenant Carsten Niebuhr, a German mathematician and engineer who had been trained in Göttingen; Mr. Georg Wilhelm Baurenfeind, a German painter and engraver; and Doctor Christian Carl Cramer, a Danish physician.

120). If we judge from the biblical commentaries to be analyzed in part 2, however, and from the increasingly wider circulation of missionary magazines in European countries during the second half of the nineteenth century, Said's description is far too categorical and seems to be caught in a Hegelian scheme of development. Even if multiple classifications did develop in secular scientific discourse during the nineteenth century, it is not necessary to consider them as having replaced or overwhelmed the division between Christian and heathen (or, for that matter, between the Occident and the Orient); on the contrary, these various categorizations continued to exist side by side.

Apart from being a disinterested demarcation of the material, then, Said's evasion of the revolution in biblical studies also seems to be part of a secularist tendency, and a rather paradoxical one at that. While he strenuously strives to overcome the division between an economic-political and a linguistic-cultural realm, he seems just as eager to uphold the division between the secular and the religious—an eagerness that he shares with the very orientalists he criticizes. This is seen in Said's description of the French secular avant-garde, which he sees as having emerged in the aftermath of the Enlightenment denunciation of church authority. The avant-garde is epitomized by the orientalist scholar, who regarded himself as "a secular creator, a man who made new worlds as God had once made the old" (Said 1979, 121). As the church is being pushed to the margin in France, the orientalist emerges as "a spiritual hero, a knight-errant bringing back to Europe a sense of the holy mission it had now lost" (115). Although they adopted a Christian vocabulary of death, rebirth, and new creation, the orientalists nevertheless regarded any sense of religious faith or practice as belonging to the past. Hence the legitimacy of orientalist knowledge during the nineteenth century did not stem from religious authority, as had been the case before the Enlightenment, but from what Said (176) calls "the restorative citation of antecedent authority." It seems as if Said, despite his harsh critique of the orientalist discourse, writes himself into their notion of secular religion.

Said's secularism, moreover, is not his own invention, but can rather be seen as being part of a wider academic current revolving around what is known as the secularization theory. Stemming from the Enlightenment and represented by social theorists such as Karl Marx, Sigmund Freud, Max Weber, and Émile Durkheim, it basically proposed that modernization invariably leads to a decline in religion, both in society and in the minds of individuals. According to sociologist Peter Berger (1999, 3), this proposition is "in principle value free," meaning that it is descriptive and can be regarded either positively or negatively. But, as he also attests, since most Enlightenment thinkers generally regarded religion as backward, superstitious, and reactionary, they tended to have quite an outspoken interest in the development that their theory predicted. The secularization theory, then, despite its claims to being descriptive and value free, was often proposed as part of a secularist ideology; and judging from Berger, it probably remains so today.

Like most other sociologists of religion during the 1950s and 1960s, Berger predicted the universal secularization of the world. And although Berger (1999, 2) now admits that the secularization theory "is essentially mistaken" since the predicted general decline of religion did not occur, there appears to be at least one category of individuals to which the theory can be accurately applied: Western intellectuals (10). In this academic subculture, secularization seems to have taken place and progressive values seem to have become dominant. For scholars in this context, as Berger (11) ironically points out, the secularization theory remains plausible. For all they know, society is quite secular and progressive. What this group fails to see, Berger (10, italics original) argues, is that they constitute a highly influential "globalized *elite* culture" that poorly reflects the significance of religion in the world.

Said's understanding of "culture" as not including religion seems helplessly caught up in this global elite culture that pledges allegiance to the secularization theory. Whereas the secularist tendency in *Orientalism* and *Culture and Imperialism* is somewhat subtle, it is more clearly articulated in an interview in which Said (1996, 78) defends a secularist approach by referring to Gramsci:

> He [Gramsci] wrote a letter, I think it was in 1921, where he says that the great achievement of his generation ... was that they were involved in the conquest of civil society, taking it away from mythological ideas of one sort or another: he called it the secular conquest of civil society. What interested me was that he also makes the point that the conquest is never over. You keep having to reappropriate as much as possible, which is otherwise going to be taken back. It's a constant re-excavation of public space.

Perhaps one ought not be surprised at Gramsci's use of colonial rhetoric such as "secular conquest." Located as he was in Italy in the 1920s, Gramsci is known to have regarded the conflict between ecclesial authority and modernity in extremely harsh terms. More startling is that Said in the

1990s seems to be affirming the validity of this Manichaean image, thereby reinforcing and perpetuating the Enlightenment opposition between religion and modernity ("the conquest is never over").

From an ecclesial perspective, however, the secularist tendency in *Orientalism* and *Culture and Imperialism* can also be seen in more appreciative terms. Typically for the 1960s and 1970s, Christian mission was seen as an agent of imperialism. Also, consider how Christian crusaders often serve as archetypes of violent expansion and coercive conversion. Secular culture (academia as well as literary production), on the other hand, had not been criticized in the same way but was rather seen as standing in opposition to an intolerant and obsolete Christianity with prescientific dogmas and beliefs. Said's important contribution was to show how secular humanism—a humanism that he embraces—was deeply enmeshed in European colonialism. In a paradoxical, unintended way, therefore, Said can be seen as disconnecting nineteenth-century colonialism from Christian discourse, thereby absolving Christianity from its colonial collaborations.

Decentering the Historical-Critical Paradigm

As mentioned above, Said's lacuna can also be taken as an invitation to biblical scholars to engage critically in our field. Considering that more than thirty years have passed since *Orientalism* was first published, one may notice that this invitation has passed largely unnoticed among biblical scholars.[7] Standard depictions of the history of modern biblical scholarship typically have little to say about the discipline's relation to European colonialism.[8] The assertion of Sugirtharajah (2002, 74) therefore seems rather accurate in this context: "There is a remarkable reluctance among biblical scholars to speak of imperialism as shaping the contours of biblical texts and their interpretation." Nevertheless, some scholars have challenged this reluctance.

---

7. But see Donaldson 1996a, 1–2. As seen in the research overview above, a few works have engaged in this issue.

8. Although highly valuable and informative, overviews of the development of modern biblical scholarship (Kümmel 1972; Hidal 1979; Neill and Wright 1988; W. Baird 1992, 2003; Riches 1993) typically focus on the scholarly production without relating it to its wider cultural and social contexts.

3. POSTCOLONIAL CRITICISM IN BIBLICAL STUDIES

In an interview on "color-coding Jesus," Kwok (1998b, 178) suggests that the first quest for the historical Jesus was part of forming a European colonial identity. When asked whether this historical quest had been a scientific and objective study of the Bible that challenged the doctrinal authority of the church, she answers: "For a long time I was taught to read the historical quest in that way. But I have come to see that that was basically a European script. Where in the Third World did you see people using the historical quest to challenge the church?"

Placing the quest for the historical Jesus in a contingent European context, Kwok provincializes biblical scholarship. As Anna Runesson (2011, 82–86) points out, Kwok's critique represents a major current in postcolonial biblical interpretation that can be described as a decentering of the historical-critical paradigm. The critique is connected to the rise of different kinds of vernacular hermeneutics as well as to the development of postmodernism, which is taken as having facilitated the critique of a colonial heritage. For example, the Indian biblical scholar George Soares-Prabhu (1994, 264) argues that "postmodern influence [has] 'liberated' [biblical studies] from the straight-jacket of the historical critical method to which it was, since its origins, tightly confined; and it is this liberation which has made an Asian interpretation of the Bible possible." Although this short but vigorous statement can be disputed, and I will return to that, it still highlights two interrelated developments: first, a general theoretical shift represented by "postmodern influence"; and second, a geopolitical decentering of biblical scholarship. In what follows, I will discuss these two interrelated developments.

In his widely read introduction to history as an academic discipline, John Tosh (2002, 7) describes its development during the early nineteenth century in the academic wing of European romanticism. A leading figure here, Tosh points out, was the German scholar Leopold von Ranke (1795–1886), who, in an often quoted preface to his work from 1824 on the history of Latin and German nations, stated that the historian's task is "to show how it actually was" (*wie es eigentlich gewesen*). Ranke's focus on rigorous source criticism has been highly influential, and although he was mainly interested in modern history, his approach became prominent in biblical studies as well. According to Tosh (185), however, history as a discipline has recently been deeply challenged by the linguistic turn.

On the one hand, Tosh opposes this challenge and defends more of a traditional social-historian approach. The historian's task is still, Tosh (196) claims, to "look beyond discourse to the material and social world in which the texts were created." As he sees it, and contrary to poststructuralist theory, "historians can distinguish between what happened in history and the discourse in which it is represented." At the same time, however, although describing it in negative terms such as "attacks" and "assaults," Tosh (291) also acknowledges the impact of poststructuralism. In a gesture of what seems like resignation, then, he notices that culture "is now seen as a construction, rather than a reflection of reality," leaving as the only task of the historian "the study of representation—of how meanings are constructed, not what people in the past did." Although this description of the poststructuralist critique is somewhat tendentious, Tosh's way of reluctantly admitting the impact of poststructuralism on the discipline of history highlights the increasingly contested nature of history as an academic field. Even if Tosh somewhat distances himself from this development, he evidently includes it in his introduction to the field.

From this more defensive approach, let us continue by looking at a scholar who seems to run more happily with the baton of poststructuralism. In her work *History, Theory, Text: Historians and the Linguistic Turn*, Elisabeth Clark (2004, ix–x) expresses the rather modest objective "to convince historians that partisans of theory need not be branded as disciplinary insurrectionaries." As she continues to clarify what she means by *theory*, however, her objective becomes a little less modest—and more interesting. By *theory* she means the paradigm shift introduced by poststructuralism, whereby the study of language, literature, and culture becomes "obliged to attend to the semiotic operations involved in the production of meanings, meanings that can no longer be assumed to be natural" (x). Her objective, then, is to let this paradigm shift, epitomized by the linguistic turn, renew the discipline of history. Although her work primarily concerns late ancient Christianity (or patristics), she specifically calls upon scholars of premodernity to consider how poststructuralist theory can illuminate their work.

The objectivist creed and the noble dream of disinterested scholarship established by Ranke's famous dictum are thus fundamentally challenged by the linguistic turn (Clark 2004, 9–17). As an alternative, Clark (156) suggests a reformulation of the historian's task that involves a more dynamic relation between past and present. According to Clark, the past was never there on its own terms or for its own sake. The historian's disciplinary operation in the present is conducted from the questions posed by the historian, and it is not possible to completely detach the historian from the material she or he is studying. The past, according to Clark, is therefore continuously caught up in the present. I will return to this discussion about the past-present in chapter 22.

Poststructuralist historiography is sometimes charged with epistemological relativism. All interpretations of historical artifacts, the critique goes, would be considered equally valid since there would be no firm ground from which to offer critique. Clark (23) points out, however, that this is a rather unsophisticated critique that rests on a caricature of poststructuralism. Epistemological skepticism is not the same as epistemological relativism. As she (157) states, the linguistic turn does not imply that "everyone's opinion is equally good," but rather that all historiography is contingent, has a provincial quality, and is sociopolitically situated.

In her last chapter, Clark offers some case studies to show how historical inquiries informed by poststructuralism could be conducted.[9] I find it interesting, in terms of this study, that Clark (181–85) ends her study by discussing postcolonial criticism, which she sees as illustrating how the work of ancient historians can be instructively marked by issues of the present. Her final estimate of postcolonial criticism resonates closely with the approach undertaken here. By appropriating the heuristic tools of postcolonial criticism, Clark (185) argues, scholars in premodern studies "join the wider academy as contributors to, not just recipients of, a refurbished intellectual history."

As for the second development referred to above (the geopolitical decentering of biblical scholarship), its importance for postcolonial criticism has already been mentioned. Represented by scholars such as Kwok (1995), Sugirtharajah (1999c), Segovia (2000), and Dube (2000), the critique against the paradigmatic role of historical criticism in biblical studies is connected to their upbringings in China, India, Latin America, and Botswana, respectively. Seen from their various non-Western locations, the scientific ideal of objectivity in biblical studies conceals its provincial and androcentric character. But even so, one can question how radical of a break their critique implies when it comes to actual interpretations of biblical texts. Have historical matters then become irrelevant, as Soares-Prabhu seems to imply? How much of a break with historical criticism does their critique actually entail?

---

9. One example is the work by Averil Cameron (1991), which studies how sixth-century Christian discourse related to Roman imperialism.

As Kwok (2006, 46) points out, the critique is not to be taken as a rejection of the insights generated by historical criticism. Historical critics have contributed "to the understanding of the 'worldliness' of the text." Rather than a rejection of historical criticism per se, then, the critique upholds the impossibility of epistemological premises and calls for interculturally and interreligiously engaged forms of interpretation.

I have described two interrelated developments—a geopolitical decentering and a theoretical critique—as challenging the presuppositions of historical criticism and as suggesting a shift in the field of biblical studies. According to some scholars, however, this would not be a shift into something new, but rather a return to the radical currents that helped form modern biblical studies in the first place. Bearing in mind the postcolonial critique, let us then pursue the quest for a critical past that might have been lost.

A Revival of the Discipline's Lost Origin?

In their account of the radical origin of historical criticism, Caroline Vander Stichele and Todd Penner (2005b, 27) have delivered an interesting response to the postcolonial critique of the historical-critical paradigm. This critique, they argue, stands in continuity with the founding of the discipline; there is a direct relationship between modern and postmodern scholarship. This correlation is often lost, repressed, or easily passed over "in the rhetoric of self-identification that is necessary for defining a 'new' task and theory." Here we are offered an important warning against formulating too much of a break with the discipline's episteme.

Adopting a similar position, Heikki Räisänen (2000a; 2000b) affirms the postcolonial or postmodern call for ethically responsible biblical scholarship in a global context, but disagrees with the critics' negative description of historical-critical research, arguing instead that it ought to be seen as an "ally of the liberationist enterprise" (2000a, 11). In his view (2000b, 233), since "[t]he ethical critique is really not so new," it does not confront biblical studies with a paradigm shift. Highlighting what the Germans call *Sachkritik*, which he views as a kind of moral critique of the Bible, Räisänen argues that historical-critical research, despite its upholding of a value-free and objective approach, has in fact not been disinterested. This *Sachkritik*, he admits, was directed against "oppressive church structures rather than global injustice … ; a truly global vision has not yet emerged" (2000a, 21). Indeed, if a "truly global vision" implies an egalitarian decolonized world, such a global vision had not emerged. But since European powers expanded considerably during the nineteenth century, the question—unaddressed by Räisänen—is what *kind* of "global vision" biblical scholarship encompassed. I will return to this below.

There is also a more recent work that has entered this debate over how to understand the relation between postmodern critique and historical criticism. In the wake of the "after theory" debates in literary studies, Moore and Sherwood (2011) investigate the status (or nonstatus) of poststructuralist theory in biblical scholarship. In a playful and yet thought-provoking way, they contend that the more recent developments of postcolonial and ideological criticism represent a revival of a lost heritage of biblical studies. But unlike Vander Stichele and Penner and Räisänen, they trace this lost heritage to the period that immediately precedes the establishment of historical criticism as a dominant paradigm.

Early Moral Critique of the Bible

As Moore and Sherwood (2011, 46–49) point out, the birth of biblical studies in the late eighteenth century can be understood as an instance of what Foucault has called an "epistemic break." According to them, an often ignored key ingredient in this break was a moral critique of the Bible. On the basis of Immanuel Kant's proposition that reason should set limits on religion, Moore and Sherwood highlight the new possibility of a moral imperative *not* to adhere to certain biblical beliefs. Also, referring to French and British philosophers as well as Deists, Moore and Sherwood (49–58) detect a quest for a moral core—a universally true religion—that implied a questioning, or even sacrificing, of certain biblical texts. An often-neglected feature of the first modern biblical scholarship, they thus maintain, was that it contained a moral critique of the Bible.

This moral critique, they further argue, began to decline as soon as historical criticism became prominent. Epitomized by the quest for the historical and moral Jesus, the moral critique faded away. As they (64–65) phrase it, "the wound opened up by the early modern incision—the assault on the morality of the biblical God—is surreptitiously sutured, perhaps even without the cognizance of the historical Jesus questers themselves."

From this modified depiction of modern biblical studies, Moore and Sherwood (69) find the recent developments in the discipline, represented by various kinds of ideological criticism, as a resurfacing of the early Enlightenment critique that held the Bible accountable to an extrabiblical ethical standard. Hence they claim that the recent development in biblical scholarship actually amounts to a return to its "early Enlightenment moorings." Although this argument in some sense supports the position taken by Vander Stichele and Penner and Räisänen, it also challenges it. Whereas the latter scholars locate the source of recent postmodern developments in historical criticism itself, Moore and Sherwood locate it in an earlier forgotten aspect of the modern epistemic break.

A Fractured Continuity

Although "epistemic break" is an apt description of what took place in biblical studies at this time, Moore and Sherwood avoid discussing the scholars who are usually described as founders of the discipline.[10] As is evident from standard introductory works (Neill and Wright 1988; Kümmel 1972), descriptions of this epistemic break in biblical studies—although the word *episteme* is seldom used—typically begin with German scholars such as Johann Salomo Semler and Johann David Michaelis, who are seen as having initiated the historical-critical trajectory. One can then ask if these scholars, as implied by Moore and Sherwood, ought to be regarded as having replaced the moral critique with a scientific value-free approach.

Kümmel's introduction to New Testament studies is interesting since his overview of the discipline's history begins further back than most others. After the ancient and medieval "prehistory," he discusses the English Deists and their moral critique of the Bible that Moore and Sherwood highlighted. According to Kümmel, however, this critique was only a decisive stimulus that eventually led to "genuine" historical criticism. As Kümmel (1972, 57–58) phrases it:

> All these ideas of the Deists were the result, not of a historical approach to the New Testament, but of a rationalistic critique of traditional Christianity. However, the freedom with which the biblical text was treated—a characteristic of that critique—strengthened tendencies in the direction of a genuinely historical investigation of the Church's Scriptures.

---

10. Moore and Sherwood (2011, 60) do mention Julius Wellhausen (1844–1918), who they see as covertly dealing with moral problems in the Bible. But he is too late to be regarded as having participated in the epistemic break.

3. POSTCOLONIAL CRITICISM IN BIBLICAL STUDIES

By distinguishing the moral critique of the Bible from a historical-critical approach, and by regarding the former as an inferior precursor to the latter, Kümmel's description of the discipline's history serves as an example of what Sherwood and Moore (2011, 48) call "the temptation to compose histories of biblical criticism as aetiological sagas."[11] As they argue, such a description of modern biblical studies leaves out or downplays an important aspect of the epistemic break. Further, as I will show in part 2, what Kümmel describes as "genuine historical investigation" is a highly questionable term for the complex field of biblical studies that emerges in the nineteenth century. Kümmel ought to be given credit, however, for his lengthy quotations from eighteenth-century sources, which facilitate the scrutinizing of his reading of the German pioneers.

Let us then look at his interpretation of the role played by Semler, whom Kümmel firmly places among the initiators of the historical approach. One of the long quotes from Semler states:

> If a reader ... finds the tone of the Apocalypse unpleasant and repulsive when it speaks of the extermination of the heathen, and so forth; how can such a one find in this book nothing but divine, all-inclusive love and charity for the restoration of men ... ? It must remain open to many people, then, who have begun to experience the salutary power of truth, to pass judgment in light of their own knowledge both on individual books and on certain parts of many books, with reference to their moral and generally beneficial value. (Kümmel 1972, 63–64)

Contrary to the expectations established by Moore and Sherwood, the quote from Semler shows an interest in morality that is similar to that of the French and British philosophers and Deists. As Kümmel renders a three-page series of quotes from Semler, this resemblance is strengthened. Since the Bible, as Semler sees it, contains morally questionable parts that are not essential for Christian belief, he authorizes Christian believers to critically examine and question the moral validity of biblical texts. Interestingly enough, historical criticism here plays an important role. As Kümmel (65) indicates, Semler's studying of texts in their ancient settings offered a way of handling the moral critique of the Deists. What Kümmel

---

11. Of course, Sherwood and Moore can also be seen as composing an etiological saga since their description of the epistemic break is not neutral or value-free. This notwithstanding, their critique is significant and opens an important discussion about what constitutes modern biblical studies as a discipline.

(65) describes as Semler's "rigorously historical perspective" is therefore closely connected to a moral questioning of the Bible.

A similar pattern is found in Michaelis, with whom we have already made acquaintance. Generally seen as a founder of the field, he is often remembered for his insistence on Arabic for a historically correct understanding of the Hebrew Scriptures (Neill and Wright 1988, 5–6). Typically avoided in depictions of Michaelis, however, is how his historical interest was related to his effort to reformulate how Europe ought to relate to the Hebrew Scriptures. Even though Michaelis upheld the importance of disinterest and objectiveness when making historical investigations, he also regarded the Hebrew Scriptures as being only valid for a certain people at a certain time, which implies a rather outspoken moral and political agenda. As is evident in *Mosaisches Recht*, Michaelis (1793, 2–3) is divided in his understanding of the Mosaic law. On the one hand, since it was by far the oldest collection of preserved laws, he saw it as being "remarkable" (*merkwürdig*). On the other hand, he also regarded it as belonging to an inferior and less developed people: the Mosaic law belonged to "the childhood of nations" (*der Kindheit der Völker*) and hence was not relevant to his present time. Michaelis regarded his work as an attempt to help Europe develop into maturity, which meant removing the relics (*überbleibsel*) of the ancient Hebrews.[12] And since Europe was about to take a step into adulthood (for better or for worse), Michaelis reasoned that it was time to leave these texts behind and not allow them influence the present. As Jonathan Hess (2000, 67) expresses it, "Michaelis claims in this way an enormous importance for his own work, casting *Mosaisches Recht* as the intervention necessary to 'help' history realize its teleological goal of allowing modern Europe to arrive at definitive adulthood." For Michaelis, although the Hebrew Scriptures were highly interesting as historical sources from which to delineate a genealogy of legal systems, they were morally relevant only for the ancient Israelites. Michaelis therefore shares with Semler an outspoken moral and political agenda that is connected to the Deists.[13]

Since two main German founders of modern biblical studies, Semler and Michaelis, regarded their historical work on the Bible as being closely

---

12. This is evident from the very beginning of *Mosaisches Recht*, where Michaelis dedicates the book to Olaus Rabenius, professor of law at Uppsala. Cf. Hess 2000, 65–68.

13. Michaelis (1793, 7–8) explicitly refers to the moral critique of the Deist Thomas Morgan.

connected to questions of morality, it seems as if the claims discussed above about continuity between contemporary ideological criticisms and the early founders of the discipline are supported. But as soon as we begin to scrutinize the morality of these early scholars, the continuity seems strained, to put it mildly. Located as they were in the European Enlightenment with its interconnections with the colonial discourse, their moral critique was plagued by prejudice and notions of European superiority.

Beginning with Semler, his moral critique was connected to a distinction between Palestinian Jewish Christians and Pauline Christians: "The way of thinking of the Palestinian Jewish-Christians is ... too simply and too much accustomed to all sorts of local ideas and insignificant concepts, for other Christians who do not dwell among these natives to be able to accept this kind of teaching for themselves as though it were for their advantage" (Kümmel 1972, 67). Semler here questions the validity of those parts of the New Testament that reflect the teachings of the Palestinian Jewish Christians. Labeling this group as "natives," he distinguishes them from "other Christians." Since "other Christians" seems to simultaneously refer to ancient non-Jews as well as modern Europeans, Semler's moral critique of the New Testament problematically rests on modern colonial discourse with its binary division between enlightened Christian Europeans and primitive natives.

As for Michaelis, a similar problem emerges when his writings are juxtaposed with colonial discourse. Drawing on Montesquieu's theories about the correlation between climate, humanity, and society, Michaelis (1793, 2) argues that the Hebrew legal system was formed "in a climate distant from us." As seen in relation to the question of Jewish emancipation, this difference in climate becomes a means of racializing Jews in Michaelis's writings (cf. Hess 2000, 57–60). Addressing proposals intended to grant Jews civil rights, Michaelis adopted a negative stance. Contending that the Jewish people did not really belong in Europe, he suggested a rather radical solution. Even if the Jews could perhaps be of use for the Europeans through agriculture and manufacturing, the best option, Michaelis (1782, 12) states, would be "if we had sugar islands that at times could depopulate the European fatherlands." Although these islands bring wealth, Michaelis maintains, they also have "an unhealthy climate."

Apart from being an example of a long tradition of European anti-Jewish sentiments, Michaelis's suggestion is marked by European colonial discourse. The idea of relocating Jews to "sugar islands" where the climate would make them economically useful is conceivable only in relation to European colonial expansion. With its construal of southern and hot climes as implying inferior and stagnant societies, colonial discourse here reproduces itself in Michaelis's suggestion of a mass transplantation. It was not so much a specific hatred of Jews as it was a lumping together of Jews, orientals, and other so-called inferiors, who were regarded as having been formed in unhealthy climes. Hence, as Hess (2000, 59) argues, Michaelis's perspective "epitomizes a mode of colonialist discourse that is central to his scholarly work in the emergent field of Oriental studies."

In summary, Vander Stichele and Penner, Räisänen, and Moore and Sherwood have, in their different ways, suggested that postcolonial criticism stands in continuity with the discipline's origins. The argument made here both affirms and criticizes their assertions. In addition to Moore and Sherwood's important discussions on the Deists' moral critique of the Bible, one needs to note that the early historical-critical German scholars were part of this moral critique as well. Furthermore, since the moral critique was problematically intertwined with the colonial discourse, one can also question the notion of a smooth continuity. It is not a coincidence that many of the early biblical scholars were Hegelians who regarded themselves as standing at the culmination of a history that had been developing from one stage to the next. This was a time when the Bible was beginning to be seen as belonging to a lower and superseded level of historical development.

If we are to see postcolonial criticism and moral critique of the Bible as a revival of a lost heritage, as these scholars contend, it seems important to acknowledge the colonial aspects of the Enlightenment critique. In extension, it also seems essential to inquire as to the position from which one might conduct such a returning moral critique. According to Moore and Sherwood (2010, 107), most of the moral critique of the Bible is today conducted from a position that is somehow outside the Bible. The question is, of course, whether one can speak in terms of an "inside" and "outside" position relative to a text that has played such a prominent role in the development of Western civilization. Perhaps one ought to consider other factors than a dichotomous inside/outside division when conducting a moral critique of the Bible. Indeed, as exemplified by works such as Liew (1999a), Neville (2007), Dube (2000), Pippin (2005), and Stenström (2005), moral critique can be variously conducted from either inside or outside the Bible.

My main point here, however, is to somehow displace the image of a harmonic continuity between early Enlightenment critique and contemporary ideological criticism, and instead suggest a kind of fractured relation. For one thing, as Hanna Stenström (2005, 42–45) argues, historical criticism is highly diverse and can be used for emancipation as well as oppression. Thus a depiction that only stresses the emancipative aspects always runs the risk of hiding the problems. Surely, as historical criticism was emerging, it came in conflict with ecclesial dominance—a conflict that can be described in emancipative terms. Then again, since the formation of modern biblical studies was part of a much wider European current, described not least by Said, it seems somewhat inaccurate to describe it, as Vander Stichele and Penner (2005b, 27 n. 95) do, as having emerged "from the margins." On the contrary, it was part of a reformulation of European colonial identity; and as such it was a development that clearly occurred in the center.

This disagreement notwithstanding, I do find highly suggestive what I take as the vision of Vander Stichele and Penner for biblical studies. The future, they seem to think (2005b, 27–28), lies not in the continued uncritical use of the tools of traditional scholarship, nor in their outright rejection, but in engaging "the dominant discourses and creat[ing] counter-discourses and communities, reconfiguring and reconstituting traditional tools, methods and aims in alternative directions and contexts." In this way, they continue, "voices within and without of the guild find each other, and those at the center and the margins can establish (some) common cause." I hope they will be proven right.

Summary

In this study, the attention that I devote to matters of theory reflects the heterogeneous nature of contemporary biblical scholarship. Since the implications of a scholarly treatment of Mark's relation to empire cannot be taken for granted, it has been necessary to take the time and space to delineate the work's theoretical presumptions.

I divided part 1 into two chapters. In chapter 2 I introduced postcolonial criticism as a form of discourse theory that, in the aftermath of European colonialism, studies texts and cultural artifacts as being part of the social structures of imperial domination. Since the Bible played an important role in European expansion, and since it is typically avoided as a topic among postcolonial critics, the relevancy of approaching biblical texts from a postcolonial perspective was upheld. By discussing the contributions of three important postcolonial critics (Said, Spivak, and Bhabha),

I delineated postcolonial theory as applied in this study. Based on the linguistic turn, postcolonial criticism is here taken to involve an interest in how subjectivities are formed as superior and inferior by various interrelated dichotomic divisions and how they are also unstable and threatening to the imperial order.

As will be seen in the unfolding investigations, in three main ways postcolonial theory influences my pondering of the Mark-and-empire trajectory. First, the dual focus on Mark in nineteenth-century Europe and in imperial Rome stems from an aspiration to uninherit a colonial heritage. Second, the analysis of the Markan commentaries in part 2 both follows and critiques Said's analysis of the academic field of orientalism. Third, when Mark's stance vis-à-vis Rome is scrutinized in part 3, I employ the heuristic postcolonial concepts introduced in this chapter—catachresis, *pharmakon*, mimicry, colonial ambivalence, hybridity, third space, the pedagogical, and the performative.

In chapter 3 I mapped the wider academic terrain that has been established as biblical scholars have been engaging with postcolonial criticism since the mid-1990s. By discussing reciprocal challenges between postcolonial criticism and biblical scholarship, I have made visible the perspective used in this work. Whereas postcolonial criticism was criticized for its secularist tendency, biblical studies was criticized for neglecting the manner in which an allegedly objective and neutral approach is factually connected to European modernity and colonialism. Moreover, since a postcolonial framework challenges the epistemological premises of modern biblical studies, I explored the counterintuitive suggestion upheld by various biblical scholars that postcolonial criticism represents a return of the discipline's more radical Enlightenment origins. The postcolonial approach, I conclude, stands in fractured and critical continuity with modern biblical scholarship.

Part 2
Mark in European Colonialism

If, as once said by high authority, it be the mission of English men and women to "teach all nations," surely it ought to be one of their first duties to teach themselves, and especially to gain correct notions as to the nature of the religion which they would impart to others.
—David F. Strauss (1879, 1:xix)

PART 2
MARK LETTRONI AND GENEALOGY

4
MODERN BIBLICAL STUDIES AND EMPIRE

One of the most influential and controversial works in nineteenth-century biblical studies was *Leben Jesu* by David Friedrich Strauss. In 1835, as a 27-year-old scholar in Tübingen, Strauss composed this highly provocative work in which he argued that the Gospel stories should be largely understood as myths. As the work was translated into French (1840), Dutch (1840), Swedish (1841), Danish (1843), and English (1841–1843), it became famous, or rather infamous, in far wider contexts than Germany.

The above quote is from the translator's preface to an English edition of a popularized version of Strauss's work.[1] In a slight tone of irony, indicated not least by the quotation marks, the translator refers to the civilizing mission of English men and women to "teach all nations." Although he does not seem totally convinced that they have been given such an imperial mission, he seems to mean that if they have, at least they ought to be enlightened enough to spread the *correct* understanding of Christianity. Ambiguous as it stands, it points enigmatically to the complex interconnections between modern biblical studies, Christian mission, and European colonialism, interconnections that constitute the background of the investigation conducted in part 2.

Protestantism during this time can be divided into three strands: modernist, pietist, and orthodox. Strauss represented the first, and it is quite clear that both the translator and his contemporary readers were aware that the work posed a radical challenge to prevailing notions about the nature of Christianity and biblical revelation. As mentioned in the previous chapter, modern biblical scholarship emerged as part of the attempt to

---

1. After a lengthy absence from theology, Strauss wrote a popularized version entitled *Das Leben Jesu für die Deutsche Volk* that appeared 1864 (ET: Strauss 1879). The translator was anonymous, probably due to the controversies with which Strauss's first work was associated.

form a more enlightened understanding of Christianity, which in turn was related to the nineteenth-century reformulation of European colonial self-understandings. The debate surrounding Strauss's work reflects this general transition in Europe. Strauss represented a modern way of studying the Bible, and his work epitomized the conflict of this new approach with ecclesial discourses that resisted this development. The pietists (including nonconformity churches and evangelical Protestant mission), for instance, were largely uninterested in the modernist project of reading the Bible in a critical way. The orthodox theologians, on the other hand, typically had academic positions from which they outspokenly criticized what they regarded as modern attacks and assaults on the Holy Scriptures. The modern scholars, for their part, defended historical-critical ideals, often referring to what they regarded as a rational and scientific quest for truth.

In this nineteenth-century turmoil, Christianity continued to play an important role for most Europeans. One can debate the extent to which nineteenth-century industrialization and secularization were involved in the diminishment of Christianity's importance to European identities. As argued above (contra Said), European self-understandings during the nineteenth century were to a high degree continuously formed around Christianity.[2]

The aim of part 2, then, is not to study the Gospel of Mark itself, but rather to analyze how various nineteenth-century scholarly interpretations of Mark interplayed with colonial discourse, thereby illuminating what presumably constitutes a colonial heritage in biblical scholarship. More specifically, I will study sixteen biblical commentaries (see table 1), written during the latter half of the nineteenth century, and analyze them in relation to colonial discourse, involved as it was in a reformulation of European colonial identities. Apart from being an interesting project on its own terms, scrutinizing how modern biblical scholarship on Mark was interplaying with its colonial context aims at achieving a sharper postcolonial interpretive optic that will be useful in part 3, where I engage in Mark's story itself.

In order to clarify the aims for the analysis in part 2, I will first discuss some presuppositions. As explained in the introduction, the term *dis-*

---

2. For a discussion on the situation in England, see Comaroff and Comaroff 1991, 75–80. Also, as is evident from Griffiths's (2005) work on the missionary press, it is quite clear that ecclesial discourses continued to be influential during the nineteenth and twentieth centuries.

course in this study entails the understanding that the world is not simply "there" as a meaningful entity. A discourse constitutes a system of statements, social practices, and institutions within which the world becomes known and subjectivity becomes possible. *European colonial discourse* is then used as a designation for the ensemble of cultural production, academic knowledge, and social practices that, together with military and economic expansion, made European colonialism possible. A colonial discourse analysis typically involves studying writings by well-known figures like Defoe, Conrad, or Kipling. But it could also be applied to texts such as biblical commentaries that are not traditionally conceived of as having an obvious connection to imperial rule (Moore-Gilbert 1997, 8).

To say that a colonial discourse generates meaning and forms subjects is not to imply that it easily changes or that it is somehow lightly weighted. To the contrary, the effects of the nineteenth-century discourse appeared natural and self-evident. Statements that contradicted these natural notions could thus not be made without incurring punishment or making the individual who made the statement appear eccentric and abnormal.[3] Considering the powerful character of the colonial discourse, then, we can expect it to be visible in the production of various types of cultural and academic texts. It should therefore come as no surprise if one can detect the colonial discourse in nineteenth-century biblical scholarship.

Since this investigation also takes into account the critics of Said, European colonial discourse is not presumed to be a homogeneous entity. True, significant facets of the colonial discourse did have a pan-European character, the most crucial of which was the establishment of a set of interconnected binary divisions (civilized/primitive, masculine/feminine, cultured/savage, Christian/heathen, progressive/stagnant, etc.) that construed the colonizer's culture as superior and established a duty for the Europeans to administrate and educate the colonized for cultural and moral improvement. But there were important variations between the different European imperial powers and the ways in which these binaries were construed. There also existed other national and local discourses that were crucial for the self-understandings of nineteenth-century Europeans. Thus, although the colonial discourse here is taken as a powerful entity, it is not presumed to be of a total or hegemonic character. As Said's critics have pointed out, Europeans were a diverse population, and at some

---

3. For a similar definition of colonial discourse, see Ashcroft et al. 2000, 41–43.

locations colonial discourse was probably less important to the self-understanding (cf. Marchand 2009, xxi–xxii). Also, even at places where colonial discourse was dominant, surely some individuals resisted being elevated to a superior position.

Since this analysis of how the scholarly interpretations of Mark's Gospel related to European colonial discourse involves a kind of comparison, there is a need for further clarification. Hypothetically, I could have conducted a genetic comparison. An example would be if a biblical commentary was quoted in a missionary magazine, or conversely, if a commentary referred explicitly to a missionary discourse. Given the genre of biblical commentaries, as well as the nature of this study, however, such direct or causal connections have not been primary targets in the inquiry. Rather, I have juxtaposed the scholarly interpretations of Mark's Gospel with prominent facets of European colonial discourse with the aim of searching for shared rhetorical strategies and tropes that contributed to the forming of Europeans as superior rulers on the global arena. In this sense, the analysis makes use of, and somewhat develops, the research on intertextuality (Barsky 1993; Godard 1993).

Biblical Studies between Church and Enlightenment in the Age of Empire

In order to further introduce this study of nineteenth-century scholarship on Mark, it is necessary to situate biblical scholarship as a whole in its nineteenth-century setting. As mentioned in the previous chapter, the historical-critical approach that has dominated modern biblical studies emerged in Germany during the latter half of the eighteenth century in the fields of theology and orientalism (cf. Smend 1987). I will here discuss the nascent biblical scholarship in connection to three interrelated and conflict-laden developments: Protestant Christianity, the Enlightenment, and the European economic and political expansion on the global arena.

The birth of modern biblical scholarship was connected to the Reformation. The Lutheran credo of *sola scriptura* invited a closer study of the biblical texts, partly with a critical edge against the authority of ecclesial tradition. The relation of modern biblical scholarship to church tradition thus contains continuity as well as opposition. As Suzanne Marchand (2009, 30–31) pointed out, the Reformers were heirs of Renaissance humanism and its growing interest in humanist philology. Luther's call for the necessity of studying Hebrew, not only Greek and Latin, was one important background for the eighteenth-century founders of modern biblical scholarship.

But the modern scholars went further than Luther on the critical trajectory. Even if Luther, for theological reasons, did put parentheses around certain biblical texts (such as James), he did not question the Textus Receptus or the canon as such, as did Semler (W. Baird 2003, 120–24). Neither did he suggest the study of Arabic in order to better understand the Hebrew Bible, as did Michaelis (Neill and Wright 1988, 5–6). Also, these scholars went far beyond Luther in questioning whether the Bible as a whole could be taken as God's infallible words; especially the Hebrew Bible they regarded as representing a primitive or oriental level of morality and religion.

Naturally, the critical approach created conflicts with Protestant orthodoxy and ecclesial authorities, who at this time had considerable influence over the universities' theological departments. The positions of scholars such as Michaelis and Semler were therefore dependent on protection from Prussian state bureaucracy.[4] Indeed, the iconoclastic scholars in biblical and oriental studies would not have gotten any positions in the universities unless protected by the state. The relations between enlightened state officials and ecclesial authority, however, become more complicated when seen against the background of the imperial mentality that characterized Europe at this time.

As modern biblical scholarship was being formed, Europe entered the second of its two main phases of colonialism. Whereas Spain and Portugal had played leading roles during the first phase (1492–1789), the second phase (1789–1945) predominantly saw the rise of the English, French, Dutch, and eventually German empires. The transition to the second phase involved both economic and cultural aspects. Economically, the second phase was connected to a transition to a capitalist economy and the Industrial Revolution. Culturally, it went hand in hand with the Enlightenment and an increasing quest for knowledge in several areas, not least in the East.

---

4. Marchand (2009, 33–38) specifically notes that it was Frederick the Great becoming king of Prussia in 1740 that made a more critical biblical scholarship possible. Marchand (36) also shows that Michaelis's position was specifically protected by his insistence on being made professor of philosophy rather than theology—an insistence that was accepted by the administration of the University of Göttingen.

Imperial expansion made it possible for Europeans to travel in an unprecedented way. Missionaries, scientific expeditions, and explorers of different kinds brought back non-European texts and artifacts to Europe for scholarly analysis. The desire to study these distant cultures was connected to the increasing European consumption of oriental commodities such as coffee, tea, chocolate, opium, and porcelain. Consequently, orientalism developed into a scholarly field far wider than, and yet closely affiliated with, biblical studies.[5]

The development of more sophisticated categorizations of people was one significant result of this research and constitutes a main aspect of the second phase of European colonialism. The new classifications were developed in a range of academic discourses, most notably biology and anthropology, but also in linguistics. Whereas comparative anatomists such as Petrus Camper (1722–1789) and Georges Cuvier (1769–1832) made taxonomies of races based upon the so-called facial angle, comparative linguists or orientalists such as Franz Bopp (1791–1876) and Ernest Renan (1823–1892) based their categorization of human races on differences in language. Even if the focus here is on orientalism rather than anatomy or biology, it is important to point out their interconnected significance to colonial discourse. The popular nature of these new scientifically based classifications of different peoples is indicated by the wall charts used in education, on which different categories of peoples were displayed in a hierarchical way (Comaroff and Comaroff 1991, 98–108; McClintock 1995, 36–39). The academic quest for pure origins and races, then, contributed to the constructions of elevated European self-images.[6]

---

5. Marchand (2009, 1–6, 38–52, 102–18, 252–70) describes how German orientalism was closely connected to the theological departments.

6. With regard to the racializing tendencies of nineteenth-century modern biblical scholarship, see Kelley 2002, 1–88. Regarding the significance of race in the wider nineteenth-century academic discourses, see Bernal's (1991) controversial work *Black Athena*, in which he argues that the "Ancient Model" by which to understand Greek civilization was replaced during the nineteenth century by the "Aryan (or European) Model." Whereas the former model regarded Greek culture as heavily influenced by Egypt and Phoenicia, the latter model saw Greek as essentially Indo-European. Although Bernal overstated his case regarding the use of particular "models," the response from Lefkowitz and Rogers (1996, xi) is similarly exaggerated in that it entirely denies that racial and/or religious prejudice existed among scholars of the eighteenth and nineteenth centuries. However, as seen in Rogers (1996, 431), this view is not representative of all the contributions in the volume.

4. MODERN BIBLICAL STUDIES AND EMPIRE 81

Of course, the extent to which academic discourses interplayed directly with the colonial expansion can be debated. That there could have been direct connections is most clearly illustrated by the Napoleonic expedition to Egypt in 1798–1801, which Said (1979, 122) regarded as a "first enabling experience for modern orientalism," where 54,000 soldiers were accompanied by 167 savants of various specialization (Alder 2002, 254). As for German orientalism, the relations were more complex, not least due to the late arrival of Germany as a colonial power. The above-mentioned travel expedition initiated by Michaelis is a case in point. As Hess (2000, 79–80) argued, Michaelis's expedition was driven by a notion of disinterest in and independence from imperial interests. Indeed, when compared to the Napoleon expedition, Michaelis's initiative appears rather humble and innocent in intent, especially in light of the expedition's tragic outcome. As Pratt (1992, 38–39) argued, however, the innocent character of scientific travel expeditions could nevertheless contribute in a paradoxical way to the legitimization of European supremacy.

True, formal connections between imperial governments and oriental studies are not always prevalent. And as Marchand (2009, 43, 98) points out, there were orientalist scholars who despised the dirty business of imperial expansion. Nevertheless, certain ways of thinking in nineteenth-century orientalist scholarship still connected it to European colonialism. Hence, despite being critical of Said, Marchand (2009, 92–93) verifies the enabling character of colonialism for oriental studies (including German scholarship): "What enabled the forming of new canons of scholarship and ultimately though gradually the breaking with traditional authorities and texts was unquestionably Europe's new economic and political status in the world." This is discourse theory. The contention, then, that orientalist scholarship was part of European colonial discourse does not depend on formal connections between scholars and imperial governments.

Thus far I have discussed how modern biblical scholarship was related to the Reformation, Protestant orthodoxy, and a more "enlightened" colonialism. A presentation of these interconnections, however, would be severely inadequate unless Protestant mission and pietism were also taken into account. As Sugirtharajah (1998b, 95–103) and Segovia (2006, 39–40) contend, the two phases of European colonialism correspond to the two major phases of the European missionary movement—the Catholic phase during the years 1492–1792 and the Protestant phase from 1792 onward. Indications of the arrival of the Protestant phase were a work by William Carey, *On the Obligations for Christians to Convert the Heathen* (1792), and the subsequent forming of a large number of Protestant missionary societies in England, Scotland, North America, Germany, Holland, France, Scandinavia, and Finland (Warneck 1884, 65–105). As a rule, each society had its own missionary magazine and raised considerable amounts of money that were employed in the foreign mission. As the Comaroffs (1991, 78–79) point out, since this increase in Protestant mission took place when the established churches were losing their hegemonic position in European countries, there was a sense of relocating the proclamation of Jesus Christ to the fringes of the imperial world. Furthermore, even if Protestant evangelism and pietism were driven by a strong sense of newness and criticism of the ecclesial establishment, it tended to be similarly critical of modernity and secularity.

Discussing the relation between Protestant mission and European colonialism, however, brings us into a minefield of conflicting opinions, although few would question the assumption that they are *somehow* related.[7] The approach taken here concurs with the wording of the literary critic Christopher Hodgkins (2002, 2): Protestant Christianity gave the British Empire "its main paradigms for dominion and possession but also, ironically, its chief languages of anti-imperial dissent." In other words, the study does regard Protestant mission as interplaying closely with colonial discourse, although this interaction could also involve certain tensions. To clarify, in the present study I do not discuss the complex effects of mission in the colonies. My focus is rather on its interaction with European colonial discourse "at home." Therefore, we can leave aside the disputed issue of the role of the missionaries in the colonies.

Looking at the explosion of missionary magazines in the late nineteenth century, it is evident that Christian mission was a popular topic in Europe.[8] Although missionaries were relatively few in number, missionary magazines made their work widely known to the European populations and could therefore be seen as representations of how Protestant Europeans understood themselves in relation to the non-European world.

---

7. Scholars have viewed missionaries of this period from three primary perspectives: (1) as agents of colonialism (Majeke 1952); (2) as independent of colonialism (Christensen and Hutchison 1982); and (3) as revitalizing indigenous cultures often in opposition to colonialism (Sanneh 1989).

8. Griffiths 2005. See also the doctoral thesis by Robert Odén (2012) on the importance of missionary magazines for how Swedes related to the non-European world.

The complexity of Protestant self-understandings is not to be overlooked. On the one hand, Protestant mission was influenced by nonconformity ecclesial movements that were critical of the modern way of studying the Bible and ambivalent toward the "light of liberal progress." At the same time, however, the notion of progressing from darkness to light was also important for the Protestant subjectivities: proclaiming the gospel to the heathen was seen as a way of spreading Christian light in the wretched lands of heathendom.

In summary, biblical scholarship during the nineteenth century was torn between conflicting developments in churches, academia, and the global European expansion. There were mainly three important positions that were pulling in divergent directions: the rationalist (sometimes called critical, modern, or liberal), the orthodox, and the nonconformity pietist. Interestingly, despite their irreconcilable ideals, both the rationalists (by their affiliation with the Enlightenment) and the pietists were carried by a strong sense of mission to bring light to the world and were therefore crucial for the second phase of European colonialism. The pietists, however, unlike the orthodox, typically refrained from engaging in modern biblical scholarship. Nevertheless, biblical scholars were aware that their works were read not only by scientifically minded academics, but also by believing Christians, including pietists.[9] As it is now time to approach the Markan commentaries, this conflict-laden, nineteenth-century discursive terrain will be important to bear in mind.

Demarcating the Material

Before entering the world of nineteenth-century exegetes, I ought to say something regarding the demarcation of the material. Since the scholarly interpretations of Mark's Gospel in Europe are far too numerous to be analyzed here, I concentrate on an English-German nexus. As far as Germany is concerned, it hardly needs an explanation since modern biblical studies

---

9. Strauss (1860, 4–5) illuminates this awareness in the preface to his *Life of Jesus*. On the one hand, he regarded his work as independent of Christian faith and directs himself to scientifically trained theologians and explicitly warns that the book is not written for the nontheologian or the unlearned. At the same time, however, he states that if nonacademic believers, despite his warnings, are to read the book from curiosity or with an aim to denounce it, "they will have to bear the punishment in their conscience."

primarily developed there. England is also an obvious choice, not only because of its dominant role in the colonial scene, but also because English biblical scholars became highly influential, particularly the so-called Cambridge three.[10] Of course, important scholarship also existed in countries such as France, Italy, Switzerland, Holland, and Sweden. However, since this particular examination constitutes only a portion of my study, the space that can be devoted to it is limited.

But even with the focus on an English-German nexus, I still needed a way to choose what commentaries to study. In order to further delimit the material, then, I consulted a Markan commentary written by Cambridge scholar Henry Barclay Swete (1898) that is of general high repute (Neill and Wright 1988, 101). In this work, Swete includes a selected list of twenty-two Markan commentaries, mostly in German and English,[11] some of which were written in the United States.[12] I selected fifteen of these, following two basic criteria: (1) they had been written in the latter half of the nineteenth century (between 1849 and 1901 to be exact); and (2) they were Protestant commentaries (due to my focus on the second

---

10. The term "the Cambridge three" comes from Neill and Wright (1988, 35–103) and refers to J. B. Lightfoot (1825–1901), B. F. Westcott (1828–1889), and F. J. A. Hort (1828–1892).

11. Swete 1898, cvi–cix. In the 3rd edition of the commentary, the list is significantly longer (Swete 1909, cxvii–cxviii).

12. Scholars from the United States began exerting more of an influence on the European scene from the late nineteenth century onward. That American and European biblical scholarship were closely connected can be seen most clearly in the career of Philip Schaff, who was born in Switzerland (1819), educated in Germany at the University of Tübingen, and spent the latter part of his career in the United States. As shown by W. Baird (2003, 43–52), Schaff continuously worked in relation to European scholarship, as can be most notably seen in his supervision of the translation of J. P. Lange's multivolume *Bibelwerk* (included in this study). That Swete (1909, cxvii) included the work by Riddle (simultaneously published in Edinburgh and New York) is probably related to its connection to Schaff, something that can be seen in Swete's referring to this work as "Riddle, M. R.: in Schaff's *Popular Commentary*. ..." Gould's work, moreover, was one of the early volumes of the International Critical Commentary series, published simultaneously in Edinburgh and New York. As stated in the editor's preface (no page), the series has British as well as American contributors and can be quite naturally included in this examination of how biblical studies relates to European colonialism. Lastly, J. A. Alexander has been included for no other reason than his being mentioned by Swete.

phase of European colonialism).[13] In addition to these considerations, issues of a practical nature as well as the work's genre came into play.[14] Adding Swete's work to the fifteen selected commentaries makes for a total of sixteen, all of which are displayed in table 2.

The table gives some indication of the variety of the commentaries included in the study. If a commentary is part of a series, this fact is indicated in the second column. The third column provides the location of the author at the time of writing the commentary. This location generally appears in the preface of the work, but in some instances it is provided on the title page. Whereas the fourth column shows the length of the work, the fifth specifies the language in which the biblical text is rendered in the commentary.

Even if all commentaries have been analyzed relative to the chosen passages, I will not systematically recount the interpretation of each commentary. Needless to say, the commentaries can be read in different ways and from different angles. My investigation focuses on terms, patterns of thought, and binary divisions that connect in various ways to colonial discourse. In order to discuss these connections, I will sometimes need to explore the wider cultural and academic debates to which the commentators allude. Recurring detours will therefore be interspersed within the analysis.

Table 2. Nineteenth-Century Commentators				
Commentary	**Series**	**Location**	**Pages**	**NT Text**
J. A. Alexander (1858)[d]		Princeton	xxiii, 444	English
Alford (1849)[d]	The Greek Testament	Cambridge	76[a]	Greek
Bruce (1897)[d]	Expositor's Greek Testament	Glasgow	116[a]	Greek
Chadwick (1887)[d]	Expositor's Bible	Armagh (Ireland)	446	English

---

13. Schanz (1881) is the only example of an explicitly Catholic commentary that was excluded.

14. Since Luckock (1902) is not a commentary and since Morrison (1873) was too difficult to access, I excluded them.

F. C. Cook (1878)[e]	Speaker's Commentary[b]	Exeter (SW England)	109[a]	English
Gould (1896)[d]	International Critical Commentary	Philadelphia	lvii, 317	Greek
Holtzmann (1892)[e]	Hand-Commentar zum N.T.	Strasburg	xv, 304[c]	None
Klostermann (1867)[d]		Göttingen	383	None
J. P. Lange (1858)[e]	Theologisch-homiletisches Bibelwerk	Bonn	173	German
Maclear (1883)[e]	Cambridge Greek Testament	Cambridge	xxxix, 228	Greek
Menzies (1901)[e]		St. Andrews (Scotland)	306	Greek, English
Meyer (1867; 1884)[e]	Kritisch-exegetischer Kommentar über das N.T.	Hannover	221[a]	None
Plumptre (1879)[e]	N.T. Commentary for English Readers	Gloucester and Bristol	47[a]	English
Riddle (1879)[e]	Popular Commentary on the N.T.	Hartford (USA)	90[a]	English
Swete (1898)		Cambridge	434	Greek
Weiss (1872)[d]		Kiel	515	Greek

a. The commentary interprets several Gospels, and the small amount of pages devoted to Mark can be partly explained by references to what the commentator writes of other Gospels, most often Matthew.

b. Although it is not used on the title page, "Speaker's Commentary" is the designation used in the preface (F. Cook 1878, iii), and Swete also uses it.

c. The commentary interprets the three Synoptic Gospels simultaneously.

d. Mentioned in first and third editions of Swete (1898, 1909).

e. Mentioned in third edition of Swete (1909).

5
THE SEMITIC AND THE GREEK (1:1)

As a beginning, I will analyze the interpretations of Mark's incipit (1:1), or more precisely the phrase υἱοῦ θεοῦ (Son of God) with which Jesus is titled. As will be seen in part 3, "Son of God" is a debated topic in Markan scholarship; and since it will constitute an important aspect of my postcolonial reading, it serves well as a starting point in this investigation. As will be seen, this dense phrase brings us straight into one of the main binary divisions of orientalist scholarship, the one between Semites and Greeks.

Considering that the incipit is such a pregnant sentence, one would perhaps expect the commentators to be rather wordy in their discussion of it. Typically, however, the interpretations are brief. Due to this brevity, I have in some instances seen a need to include what the commentators have written regarding other passages in Mark where Jesus is described as "Son of God" (1:11, 24; 3:11; 5:9; 9:7). In some instances, the commentary's brevity indicates less of a critical approach and implies an interpretation that corresponds with an orthodox ecclesial understanding. One such example is E. H. Plumptre (1897, 192), who makes the following comment on the phrase:

> He [Jesus], of whom he [Mark] speaks, was not a prophet or righteous man only, but was, in the highest sense which could be attached to the words, the Son of God. If we think of St. Mark as reproducing St. Peter's teaching, we cannot fail to connect the words, thus placed, as they are, in the very title of his Gospel, with the Apostle's confession in Matt. xvi.16.

Plumptre's presupposition that the author of Mark has a connection to Peter is not necessarily a sign of an orthodox position. But his way of allowing a saying by Peter from Matthew's Gospel to determine the meaning of Mark 1:1 is built upon a notion of Gospel harmony. Plumptre seems to assume that there is one specific Christian understanding of the title that is reflected in Matthew as well as in Mark. Since critical scholars were beginning to question this notion at this time, it signals an orthodox rather than a critical approach (cf. Plumptre 1897, xxxiv–xxxvii).

On a similar note, Joseph Addison Alexander (1858, 2) argues that "Son of God" is to be taken "in the highest sense of a divine person, a partaker of the Godhead, and sustaining the relation of eternal Sonship to the Father." By itself, Alexander states, the title "Son of God" would be more appropriate for John's Gospel. He refers to other interpreters who therefore regard Mark as being different from Matthew and Luke. But since "Son of God" is to be taken together with the previous title (Jesus Christ), Alexander finds that Mark presents "our Lord as the Messiah and the Saviour no less than Luke and Matthew, although not precisely in the same form." What distinguishes Mark's way of presenting Jesus as Son of God, however, is not stated, and Alexander (2) instead seems to understand the Markan title "Son of God" along ecclesial lines: as "a divine deliverer of his people from their sins."

If Alexander was skeptical of those who made far-reaching comparisons between the Gospels of Mark and John, no such inhibitions can be found in the work by Matthew Riddle (1879, 247), who plainly states that the meaning of "Son of God" in Mark 1:1 is explained in full in the prologue of John's Gospel. Furthermore, when commenting on the baptism of Jesus and the divine heavenly voice that then calls Jesus "my beloved son" (Mark 1:11), Riddle (46) finds that "the Divine nature and eternal Sonship of Christ are obviously implied." In what seems to be the peak of orthodox propensity, Riddle also sees in the story of Jesus' baptism a manifestation of the Godhead as "Father, Son and Holy Ghost," or, in other words, as a revelation of the ecclesial dogma of the Trinity.

My aim here, however, is not to criticize commentators for being orthodox rather than critical, especially not when the confessional character, as in Riddle's case, is explicitly stated in the preface. What is more noteworthy, at least among the English commentators, is the blurred character of the border between confessional and critical approaches. The situation was rather different in Germany, shown not least by Johann Peter Lange's (1858; ET: 1866) commentary, which attempts to uphold this border by following a three-part structure for each passage: (1) Exegetical and Critical (*Exegetische Erläuterungen*); (2) Doctrinal and Ethical (*Dogmatisch-christologische Grundgedanken*); and (3) Homiletical and Practical (*Homiletische Andeutungen*).[1]

---

1. Lange edited the series *Theologisch-homiletisches Bibelwerk*, which included

5. THE SEMITIC AND THE GREEK (1:1)

Standing with a foot in each camp, then, Lange helps us to switch focus to the more critical commentators. In the exegetical and critical section, Lange (1858, 13; 1866, 16) makes one highly dense comment in relation to Mark's use of the title "Son of God": "Matthew: the Son of David. In Mark, the theocratic relation of Jesus recedes, as he wrote especially for Gentile Christians." Brief as it stands, it presupposes acquaintance with what Lange has previously written on the title "Son of God" in Matthew's Gospel. Lange (1857, 400; 1865, 494) there says, under the heading of "Doctrinal and Ethical," that "most Jews at that time, understood that title (Son of God) as only referring to the Messianic kingship of Jesus, without connecting with it the idea of eternal [*ewigen*] and essential [*wesentlichen*] Sonship." These comments by Lange seem to presuppose that the title "Son of God" could be understood in either a Jewish or a "Gentile" (*heidnisch*) way. Evidently, what Lange calls a "theocratic relation" designates an allegedly Jewish understanding. The Gentile conception of the title, on the other hand, implies "eternal and essential Sonship." Lange, however, is far from alone in making these assumptions. These two understandings of "Son of God," often referred to as Jewish and Greek, respectively, were part of a prominent debate among biblical scholars of this time. This debate, in turn, brings us into the nineteenth-century orientalism with its racializing tendencies.

Echoes of Orientalism

Let us then look at the distinction between Jews and Greeks in some of the critical-oriented commentaries. Commenting on Mark's incipit, Heinrich August Wilhelm Meyer (1867, 17; 1880, 18–19; italics original) states that the title Son of God "is used in the believing consciousness [*Glaubensbewusstsein*] of the *metaphysical* [*metaphysischen*] sonship of God ..., and that in the Pauline and Petrine sense." What Meyer here calls the metaphysical sonship is connected to a "believing consciousness" and therefore denotes a Christian belief. This belief, in turn, is connected to the non-Jewish readers that he suggests Mark is addressing. In order to verify this reading of Meyer, I looked at how he interpreted the baptism of Jesus (Mark 1:11). Here he refers to his commentary on Matt 3:13–17, where he states:

---

commentaries on all biblical texts (see Lange 1857, 1858). The series was translated into English under the supervision of Philip Schaff and given the series title, *A Commentary on the Holy Scriptures: Critical, Doctrinal and Homiletical* (see Lange 1865, 1866).

> The divine voice solemnly proclaims Jesus to be the Messiah, ὁ υἱός μου; which designation of Messiah, derived from Ps 2.7 and Is 42.1, is in the Christian consciousness not merely the name of an office [*Amtsname*], but has at the same time a metaphysical [*metaphysischen*] meaning, designating ... the divine origin of Jesus in accordance with his spiritual essence [*pneumatischen Wesen*]. (Meyer 1858, 104; cf. 1881, 124)

A similar dichotomy is here reproduced. With reference to the divine origin of Jesus, Meyer argues that the Markan and Matthean designations "Son of God" are to be understood in a Christian metaphysical way, designating a spiritual essence. As for the Jewish understanding, Meyers contends that "Son of God" is merely an official term.

A similar division is made by Ezra Gould (1896, 3–4), who contends that in extracanonical Jewish literature "Son of God" is applied to the messianic king and that its use "is purely theocratic and official, corresponding to the O.T. use to denote any whose office especially represents God among men, such as kings and judges." Gould (4) departs from his colleagues, however, when he states that "its application to Jesus' metaphysical relation to God is *not* found in the Synoptics" (italics added). As we have seen, "the metaphysical" is often a synonym for the Greek understanding. As Gould (4) sees it, the reason that this Greek notion is not found in the Synoptics is that "the term is applied by Jesus to himself in his discourse without any explanation, whereas it would require explanation if it was intended to convey any other meaning than the historical sense with which the people were familiar."

Even if it is unclear who "the people" refers to—Mark's audience or the people depicted in Mark's Gospel—it is clear that Gould presupposes that Jews in general had a certain understanding of "Son of God" that differed from the Greek understanding. Since Jesus was a Jew and since the Synoptics depict him in a Jewish milieu, Gould argues, Mark presents him as a Son of God in the Jewish sense—in a theocratic and official sense. Compared to his European colleagues, Gould expresses an opposite position on the meaning of "Son of God" in Mark 1:1. Nevertheless, he applies the same notions of Jews and Greeks.

A similar distinction between Jews and Greeks is made in the commentary of Allan Menzies (1901), one of the English works that has more of a critical character. In relation to the Markan incipit, Menzies (57) states:

> [T]hese words [Son of God] must be understood, like all the terms in this verse, in the Pauline sense. In the body of the Gospel ... the phrase

5. THE SEMITIC AND THE GREEK (1:1)

is an official Messianic title, denoting the representative of God who is empowered, like David of old, to execute divine purposes. It implies no doctrine as to his extraction or essential nature. In Paul, on the other hand, the Son of God is a heavenly figure, Rom. i. 4, Gal iv. 4, who was with God before he appeared in the world, and has now been exalted to still higher honours than he enjoyed before. In this verse [Mark 1:1] the words must express the writer's own view of Christ's nature, and as he writes for Gentiles, only the latter, metaphysical sense of the phrase can be thought of. The doctrine of the Son of God could not arise on Jewish soil, but to Greek speaking people it presented little difficulty.

According to Menzies, the two different understandings of "Son of God"—the Jewish and the Greek—are both present in Mark's Gospel. The author has a Greek understanding, and so does the audience. Indeed, since the audience is "Gentile" and "Greek speaking," the metaphysical conception is the *only* possibility. But in the body of Mark's Gospel the title has a Jewish meaning; "Son of God" there designates an official position that, "like David of old," executes divine purposes. The connection made between "Jewish soil" and an inability to develop a metaphysical concept is striking and requires scrutiny.

In support of his argument, Menzies (1901, 57) refers to *Die Worte Jesu* (ET: *The Words of Jesus*), by the influential scholar Gustaf Dalman. *Die Worte Jesu* is based on Dalman's previous study of Aramaic grammar and aims at investigating the words of Jesus in Aramaic. Among several Jewish phrases, Dalman (1909, 268–89) studies the title "Son of God," and this is what Menzies refers to for support. Jewish usage of the title often referred to King David or to the Jewish people, but, as Dalman (272) argues, "divine nature [*gottheitliches Wesen*] in the Son is never deduced from such expressions." Divine essence, for Dalman (272), implies a notion of giving birth, and even if the phrase for Jews expresses a singular or "special" (*eigenartige*) relation to God, it is "by no means any sort of procreation [*Zeugung*] in the literal sense of the word." The Jewish understanding is figurative, according to Dalman, and connected to royal power rather than divine essence. Procreation, as is well known, figures prominently in Matthew and Luke. Hence Dalman (288–89) regards these as representing the Greek rather than the Semitic understanding of "Son of God."

Dalman's construal of the Greek/Semitic division, however, is not made without noticeable strain. He mentions in passing that the Egyptians believed their kings to be of divine origin in a "procreational" sense (272–73). But a more conspicuous obstacle to his clear-cut division is seen in his discussion about the Roman worship of their emperors as υἱός θεοῦ. Here Dalman has to contradict the suggestion by Adolf Deissmann, who had questioned whether the Christian philosophical or metaphysical understanding of "Son of God" was the way in which ordinary Greek-speaking people during the first century would have heard and understood the phrase. Based on newly discovered papyri, Deissmann had argued that from the time of Augustus, υἱός θεοῦ was used as a title of emperors. According to Deissmann (1901, 166–67), this was the meaning that would have been primarily stamped on the minds of Greek-speaking people when used as a title for Christ. Since Menzies (1901, 57) builds his interpretation on Dalman, over against Deissmann, it is interesting to see how Dalman (1909, 273) writes Deissmann off:

> Augustus, it is true, called himself "Divi filius," θεοῦ υἱός; but that has nothing really to do with divine sonship. It was a term due to his modesty [*Bescheidenheit*], which prompted him to be known as merely "son of one who was transferred to a place among the gods," his father by adoption being Caesar, now taken to be a Divus. Hence no assistance can be derived from this designation in determining the Greek conception of the term ὁ υἱὸς τοῦ θεοῦ used by Jesus.

One part of Dalman's argument here seems to rest on the use of a definite article. Whereas the Roman emperor was called (a) son of (a) god, Jesus was called *the* Son of *the* God. But more than mere grammar, his argument is first and foremost a defense of *Greek* as a master signifier, and its connection to what was seen as the essence of Christian faith. Whereas for Dalman the phrase ὁ υἱὸς τοῦ θεοῦ (used of Jesus) represents the Greek conception, the phrase θεοῦ υἱός (used of the emperor) was not Greek. Dalman seems to mean that when the emperor was worshipped by Greek-speaking people as θεοῦ υἱός, this did not represent a "Greek understanding" of divine sonship. His position thus seems to rest on an axiomatic notion that defines the Greek conception as Christian, metaphysical, and essential.

Dalman concludes his investigation by discussing how the phrase is used in the Synoptics. Ending by ascertaining that "[t]he mode of thought in their [the Synoptics] case is Greek; that of Jesus is Semitic" (1909, 289), the Jew/Greek division comes forth as his main point. Indeed, as Dalman's study of the *Aramaic* sayings of Jesus gives such prominent weight to the *Greek* understanding, one gets the impression that, for him, the Aramaic or Jewish is largely constituted by that which is *not* Greek. Hence

5. THE SEMITIC AND THE GREEK (1:1)

Dalman (288) contends that "the Greek, unlike the Hebrew, does not use the term 'son' to denote an extensive circle of relationships. He will always be inclined [*geneigt*] to understand ὁ υἱὸς τοῦ θεοῦ in the most exact literal sense, whereas the Israelite would only accept this idea through the constraint of some special reason." The Jew/Greek division—assumed by previously mentioned scholars—is here endowed with mental dispositions whereby "the Greek" and "the Hebrew" signify different types of people who are "inclined" to understand in different ways.

The way in which Dalman divides humankind into different categories based upon linguistic differences reminds one of the writings of a leading orientalist who was also a biblical scholar: Ernest Renan (1823–1892). As is well known, Renan was one of Said's main targets in *Orientalism*. Similar to Dalman, Renan describes the Semitic race as that which is *not* Indo-European or Aryan.[2] Whereas the Indo-Europeans are capable of reflexive thinking, of philosophy and science, of progress and development, the Semitic people are characterized by a lack of such traits. Renan (1958, 144–45) finds only one area for which the Semites have "a special sense" or "a superior instinct": religion. The Indo-Europeans are longing to know the truth, and are independent, curious, and highly serious relative to this quest. The Semites, on the other hand, are satisfied with their psalms and prophecy, their enigmatic wisdom, hymns, and revelatory books. In a vigorous expression, echoing the brief statements in the Markan commentaries, Renan (145) therefore calls them "the theocratic race of the Semites" (*la race théocratique des Sémites*).

As was common among orientalists at this time, Renan presumed a connection between language, religion, and mental capacity. He thereby maintained that Jews and Greeks were two distinct and stable racial categories, with the Greeks representing the pinnacle of human development and progress. The Markan commentators seem to have duplicated this categorization when they presupposed that the phrase "Son of God" could have either a Greek metaphysical or a Jewish theocratic meaning. Whereas the Greek represented everything that Europeans desired (i.e., philosophy, metaphysics, science, and progress), the Semite represented

---

2. As Genette (1995, 189–99) argues, Renan claimed to have treated the Semitic languages as Bopp had treated the Indo-European languages. But unlike Bopp, Renan did not develop a chart based on the Semitic languages. Rather, his studies of the Semitic languages were based upon the chart that Bopp had developed for the Indo-European languages, creating "a sort of inverse of the latter" (Genette 1995, 194).

the opposite: what Europeans did not desire (i.e., stagnation, theocracy, and conservatism). As such, these categories were crucial to the second phase of colonialism as well as to the modernization of Europe (cf. Arvidsson 2006, 103).

Let us summarize the study so far. Interpreting the Markan designation of Jesus as the Son of God in the beginning of Mark's Gospel, the critically oriented commentators tend to base their interpretations on a binary division between a Greek (or Gentile or Hellenistic) and a Jewish (or Hebrew or Semitic) understanding of the title. Although not in complete agreement on whether the title as used in Mark is to be understood in a Jewish or Greek sense, the basic division is never questioned. The division seems to be based on essentialist and stable categories, which can be graphically displayed in the disposition displayed in table 3. The Greek understanding is seen as metaphysical or eternal and is connected to Pauline, Johannine, and Petrine thought. The Greek notion is tantamount to Christian doctrine and "could not arise on Jewish soil." Unlike Jews, Greeks could formulate metaphysical thoughts. The Semitic understanding, on the other hand, is seen as theocratic and official. The prominence of this binary distinction in the material analyzed indicates that the commentators reproduced the orientalist discourse with its racializing tendencies.

Table 3. The Greek/Jew Dichotomy in Orientalist Discourse

Greek	Jew
Metaphysical	Theocratic
Eternal	Official
Christian doctrine	Messianic kingship
Paul, Peter, John	Ordinary Jews

6
BETWEEN MAN AND BRUTE (5:1–20)

The Markan episode involving the Gerasene demoniac dramatically describes a meeting between Jesus and a man who is possessed by what turns out to be a legion of unclean spirits. Being a benchmark for anti-imperial readings of Mark (see ch. 15), its inclusion in this study is a given.

The following analysis of the nineteenth-century commentators focuses on three areas that are interesting from a postcolonial perspective. First, since several commentators argue that the exorcism took place in a non-Jewish area, "the heathen" becomes an important designation to analyze. Second, the matter of the demonic possession of an animal brought forth a discussion regarding the borderline between humans and animals that seems to connect to colonial discourse. Third, since the name "legion" involves a certain potential for anticolonial interpretation (see ch. 15), this possibility will be analyzed.

"The First Apostle of the Heathen"

In the popular *Expositor's Bible,* George Alexander Chadwick comments upon the episode. Although this commentary generally has a confessional tone, its position could well imply a critique against modernity, and, by implication, some aspects of colonialism as well. In order to make visible Chadwick's vivid style, I quote the initial paragraph of his commentary on the episode here in full:

> FRESH from asserting His mastery over winds and waves, the Lord was met by a more terrible enemy, the rage of human nature enslaved and impelled by the cruelty of hell. The place where He landed was a theatre not unfit for the tragedy which it revealed. A mixed race was there, indifferent to religion, rearing great herds of swine, upon which the law looked askance, but the profits of which they held so dear that they would choose to banish a Divine ambassador, and one who had released

> them from an incessant peril, rather than be deprived of these. Now it has already been shown that the wretches possessed by devils were not of necessity stained with special guilt. Even children fell into this misery. But yet we should expect to find it most rampant in places where God was dishonoured, in Gerasa and in the coasts of Tyre and Sidon. And it is so. All misery is the consequence of sin, although individual misery does not measure individual guilt. And the places where the shadow of sin has fallen heaviest are always the haunts of direst wretchedness. (Chadwick 1887, 142)

The extent to which this interpretation interplayed with colonial discourse is debatable. Dube (2000, 129) has highlighted the importance to colonial discourse of narratives that depict traveling to foreign lands. Chadwick's vivid depiction of Jesus' landing after a dramatic journey seems to tally with such depictions, evoking as it does the image of European travelers and missionaries arriving at godforsaken heathen shores. But it also needs to be recognized that Chadwick's description is based on Mark's depiction of a boat trip undertaken by Jesus. The question is how Chadwick interprets this boat trip.

Chadwick describes the area to which Jesus travels as a place populated by a "mixed race" that was greedy and indifferent to religion, and one on which "the shadow of sin has fallen heaviest," making it one of "the haunts of direst wretchedness." These images interplay rather closely with Protestant mission. That these descriptions not only designate ancient Gerasa but also "wretched" places in his contemporary world is signaled by his transition to the present tense. Chadwick here uses terms and phrases that are similar to those of Protestant evangelism and pietism, according to which the misery in the non-European world was seen as a product of sin that could be alleviated by evangelism and Christian conversion (Stuart 2002, 70–73). This similarity can be seen by a comparison to a text from *The Missionary Magazine and Chronicle*, an organ of the London Missionary Society, where "the Kaffir, the Hottentot, or the Bushman" in their "degradation" represent "the guilt and wretchedness in the world" against which the preaching of the gospel offers "the only antidote" (G. Smith 1863, 192–93). Although the relation between Protestant mission and European colonialism was complex (see ch. 4), the representation of non-Europeans as wretched and in need of Christian evangelism was surely an important motive for European colonialism.

6. BETWEEN MAN AND BRUTE (5:1–20)

Let us continue with Riddle's popular commentary. Although he has a more ordinary style, he offers a similar interpretation to Chadwick's. Unlike Chadwick, however, Riddle sees the local population as "heathen":

> The people were heathen, and as such were more affected by the loss of property and the fear of further damage than by the blessing wrought on the possessed man. Our Lord never came back—but the healed men[1] remained. The one spoken of by Mark and Luke wished to follow Jesus, but was bidden to publish the story of his cure among his friends. With what result we do not know, but doubtless he thus prepared the way for the gospel, which was afterwards preached everywhere. The possessed received Him more readily than the Gadarenes. Christ healed madmen where calculating selfishness drove Him away.[2]

Here it is important to note that Mark does not spell out whether the population was Jewish or non-Jewish. Riddle makes an assumption, probably based upon the existence of the swine.[3] He then points at this "heathen" identity as an explanation for their "calculating selfishness." Since the possessed man welcomes Jesus, Riddle seems to imply, the "heathen" population is even more wretched (to use a term that was common at the time) than him. When Riddle states that, afterward, the gospel was "preached everywhere," his interpretation points from the ancient context to his present time, in which preaching the gospel to the heathen was generally seen as an obligation among Protestant Christians (cf. Carey 1792). The basic division that supported this notion was the Christian/heathen opposition—an opposition that tended to be connected with other dichotomies. As mentioned in chapter 3, the Christian/heathen division was dominant during the first phase of European colonialism, and was accompanied by more sophisticated categories during the second phase.

That commentaries with a confessional tendency were affiliated with the discourse of Protestant mission is hardly surprising. To begin the analysis of the more critical ones, the commentary by Alexander B. Bruce in

---

1. Regarding the use of the plural ("men"), Riddle refers to Matthew's account, in which two demoniacs are cured (Matt 8:28–34). Mark and Luke describe only one.

2. Riddle 1879, 85. Due to different variants in the manuscripts, Riddle uses "Gadarenes," whereas Chadwick uses "Gerasenes" instead. This, however, does not affect their interpretation.

3. Plumptre (1897, 51), in a similar reading, designates the local population as "wild, half-heathen."

The Expositor's Greek Testament serves as a good start. Commenting on the last portion of the Markan episode, in which Jesus requests the healed man to go home and tell his people "what great things the Lord has done" (5:19), Bruce (1897, 373–74) states:

> The [cured] man desired to become a regular disciple. ... Jesus refuses, and, contrary to His usual practice, bids the healed one go and spread the news, as a kind of missionary to Decapolis, as the Twelve were to Galilee. The first apostle of the heathen (Holtz. (H. C.) after Volkmar). Jesus determined that those who would not have Himself should have His representative.

Bruce's designation of the cured man as a "missionary to Decapolis" and "the first apostle of the heathen" connects just as clearly to Christian mission as the less critical commentators above. What indicates the critical character of the commentary is the somewhat cryptic reference to two German works: *Hand-Commentar zum Neuen Testament* by Holtzmann (one of the commentaries included in the present study) and Volkmar. Holtzmann (1892, 153), however, only points out how the episode represents "the heathen swinishness" (*die Schweinerei des Heidenthums*), with reference to Volkmar for support. Since the interpretations of Bruce and Holtzmann are both rather brief (again, due to the genre in which they were writing), let us turn to Gustav Volkmar instead, and look into the scholarly discussion that was taking place around this episode.

Volkmar (1857) seems to have influenced several of the critical commentators in their readings of this particular episode.[4] As is evident by the term *Wissenschaft* in the title of his work, Volkmar was also a critical scholar. Compared to Bruce and Holtzmann, however, he gives a much more metaphorically rich interpretation of the episode:

> Even more threatening and terrible [than the great windstorm] is the kingdom of idols, this legion of evil spirits that possess the wretched people [*den armen Menschen*] over there in the heathen land [*drüben im Heidenland*]. Take it as an image—on the other side of the sea in the Gadara land. A whole legion of idols or spirits of idols had made the people miserable and driven them out of their senses [*Sinn*] and minds [*Verstand*]. ... Only the words of Christ are capable of overthrow-

---

4. Menzies (1901, 125) and Strauss (1879b, 186) make similar references to Volkmar.

6. BETWEEN MAN AND BRUTE (5:1–20)

ing all the unreason [*Unvernunft*] of the heathen world, possessed as it is by a legion of demons. Hereby the narrator [*Darsteller*] develops the most sensitive and beautiful poetry that until now has given rise to the greatest offense. ... For the Jew and the Judeo-Christian, the heathen land is something constantly awful. It is associated with the unclean, the swinish [*Säuisches*], and may not be entered. But as the poetical narrator shows in a beautiful way, when the legion of demons plunges, the idolatry and the swinishness or herd of swine of heathendom [*Sauerei oder Sauheerde des Heidenthums*] similarly plunges down into the abyss. The saved heathen, previously so shameless and senseless, is now sitting sensible and dressed "by the feet of Jesus," and the heathen land is hereby cleaned from the greatly offending uncleanness that was adhered to it. (Volkmar 1857, 229–30)

The difference between Volkmar's vivid account and the brief comments by Holtzmann and Bruce can be largely explained by the commentary genre. Volkmar presents his interpretation as a new way of understanding the Gospels' account of Jesus' exorcism in Gadara. Until now, Volkmar states, this episode "has given rise to the greatest offense." Searching for this offense—unexplained by Volkmar—I approached the scholar who is generally regarded as having been the most offensive of his time: Strauss. Judging from Strauss's (1860, 2:465–73) assessment of the Markan episode and its parallels, there seems to have been rather intense discussions stemming from the rationalists' questioning of the historicity of this story. Volkmar's solution, it seems, was to read the story in a poetic way. The author of Mark who interpreted the event in Gadara, the *Darsteller* as Volkmar calls him, was not so much a historian as a poet who used images that Volkmar found sensitive and beautiful.

More apparently than the previous interpretations, it seems, Volkmar's reading connects to the nineteenth-century discourse of Protestant mission. When he interprets "on the other side of the sea in the Gadara land" as an image of "over there in the heathen land," there is an allusion to his contemporary heathen land—the non-European territories of the nineteenth century. Furthermore, his playing on the words "swine" (*Sau*), "swinish" (*Säuisches*), and "swinishness" (*Sauerei*) with reference to the heathen duplicates the Christian/heathen divide and amplifies it even more than the less critical commentators. Nevertheless, being a critical scholar, Volkmar construes the division in a slightly different way. Instead of connecting the heathen with sin and guilt, as did the previous commentators, he associates the heathen with unreason (*Unvernunft*) and being out of one's senses (*Sinn*) and mind (*Verstand*). In this sense, Volkmar's interpretation belongs to the Enlightenment discourse. The scholarly interpretations of Mark 5:1–20, therefore, seem to be caught in the middle of overlapping Protestant missionary discourses that construed the Christian/heathen opposition in somewhat different ways.

The similarity between the scholarly interpretations and Protestant mission is rather evident. What Volkmar found beautiful in the story's poetics—and that was also noticed in the Markan commentaries—was how the cured demoniac, who in his possessed state symbolized the miserable, irrational, and swinish state of heathen people, ends up sitting sensible and dressed by the feet of Jesus.[5] Such a metaphor of a transition from fallen to saved, of course, would represent the civilizing aspects of Christian mission, which was a common trope in missionary discourses. Even if Germany was not a colonial nation at the time, the country had seen a recent increase in Protestant mission. As described by Gustav Warneck (1884, 89–99), the 1830s were characterized by a revitalization of Protestant mission and the forming of new missionary societies, such as *Gesellschaft zur Beförderung der evangelischen Missionen unter den Heiden* (formed in 1824 in Berlin), *Rheinische Missionen Gesellschaft* (formed in 1828), *Norddeutsche Missionsgesellschaft* (formed in 1836), and *Evangelisch-lutherische Missionen Gesellschaft* (formed in 1836 in Dresden). Volkmar's romantic imagery seems to fit well with this development.

Interestingly from my location, the affinity to Protestant mission can also be seen in a more graphic way by comparison with Swedish missionary magazines in which the civilizing aspect was a prominent motif as well. In the latter part of the nineteenth century, when photographs and lithographs were beginning to be used in the magazines, images became a powerful way of representing the identification of heathen nakedness with degradation and barbarism. Also, converted Africans were often depicted with Western-style clothes (see figs. 4 and 5). The commentators' interpretation of Mark 5:1–20, epitomized by Volkmar's work, have a noticeable counterpoint in such images of "converted heathens."[6]

Although there were some exceptions (Meyer 1880–1881, 1:266; Swete 1909, 99; J. Lange 1866, 47), it was common for orthodox, pietist, and critical commentators alike to take the demon-possessed man as an image of

---

5. The part where he sits at the feet of Jesus is rendered only in Luke's account.
6. "Counterpoint" stems from what Said (1993, 51) has called *contrapuntal reading*.

Figures 4 and 5. From *Svensk Missions-tidning* (1894/19, 265; 1901/26, 272), a magazine that was published under the supervision of the Church of Sweden Board of Mission. The captions read, respectively: "Three Zulu heathens" (above) and "Rev. Fristedt with his two evangelists Salomon (to the left) and Matthew (to the right)."

the wretched heathen who needed to be rescued by Christian mission. Although the relation between Protestant mission and colonialism was highly complex, it seems clear that these interpretations interplayed with the colonial discourse. It is important that we not speak lightly or condescendingly about these notions, since people devoted their lives and made large sacrifices for what they regarded as their divine obligation. On the other hand, it is equally important that we shine a critical light on their prejudiced and patronizing character. This is not to imply, however, that one should neglect that Protestant mission stood in an ambiguous relation to colonial discourse, something that should become more apparent as we explore another aspect of the interpretations.

Man, Brute, and Gender Trouble

When commenting on Mark 5:1–20, orthodox-oriented commentators tended to be skeptical of the interpretations by both Strauss and the rationalists. But if the story was, on the one hand, not a myth and, and on the other, not explainable in terms of rational causes, how was one to understand demon possession, and particularly the possession of an animal, which raised difficulties? When discussing these difficulties, the commentators become involved in discourses that are quite interesting from a postcolonial perspective.

The commentary of Henry Alford (1849, 60)—one of the English commentaries in this study—takes on the challenge posed by the rationalists. Acknowledging that the story about the Gerasene demoniac actualizes the question of demon possession in the Gospels, he plainly states, "the Gospel narratives are *distinctly pledged to the historic truth of these occurrences*" (60, italics original). One has to choose: either they did occur, or the Gospels are false. Consequently, he argues that these depictions are true and valid and are not to be dismissed as belonging to a bygone time. Explaining the phenomenon of demon possession, Alford (60) contends that it is not to be equated with bodily disease. The Gospels clearly distinguish between disease and possession, and it is therefore to be understood from the Gospels' depictions as a strange interpenetration "by one or more of those fallen spirits, who are constantly asserted in Scripture … to be the enemies and tempters of the souls of men." Such dreadful interpenetration, Alford (60–61) goes on to say, is more likely to occur "through various progressive degrees of guilt and sensual abandonment." In other words, certain people are more inclined to be possessed than others. Alford (61) here quotes from the biblical scholar Richard Chenevix Trench (1850), who holds that "lavish sin, and especially indulgence in sensual lusts, superinducing, as it would often, a weakness in the nervous system, which is the especial band between body and soul, may have laid open these unhappy ones to the fearful incursions of the powers of darkness."

The notion that demon possession was connected to sinfulness, sensual lusts, and a weakness in the nervous system is seen in some commentaries and seems to have been common during the mid-nineteenth century.[7] Riddle (1879, 84–85) expresses a similar understanding: "Mere sensuous life and demoniacal influence stand in some relation; hence this [story of the Gerasene demoniac] is a warning against sensualism." In order to analyze how these associations between demon possession, sinfulness, sensuality, voluptuousness, and weaknesses in the nervous system were construed in European colonial discourse, a detour into the discursive field of the nineteenth century is necessary.[8]

Weakness in the nervous system has a particular meaning in nineteenth-century science, especially biology. The Swiss comparative anatomist Georges Cuvier (1769–1832) was famous for his research on human skulls. By measuring the proportions between the midcranial area and the face, the Comaroffs (1991–1997, 1:100–101) explain, he sought to reveal the degree of dependence of an organism upon external sensations. Cuvier therefore claimed to have found a way to measure the development of reason and self-control. But as the Comaroffs (1:100–101) also point out, moral and spiritual capacity in Cuvier's work was most explicitly connected to the neurological dimensions. Seeing the nervous system as the locus of internal animation, Cuvier regarded it as determining the higher faculties of life such as intelligence and volition. The nervous system was then the location of a "soul or sentient principle" that Cuvier saw as underdeveloped among non-Europeans. In particular, the "negro" was seen as being governed by animal reflexes and reflexes of survival.

---

7. Similar to Alford and Trench, Olshausen (1847, 310–11) argues that demon possession is connected to a "predominating sensuality (more especially voluptuousness)" and a "debility of the bodily organisation, especially of the nervous system."

8. This detour is mainly informed by secondary sources, most important of which is the informative work *Of Revelation and Revolution* by Jean and John Comaroff (1991–1997).

By such claims, the new biology brought an older debate about the border between man and beast into the scientific discourses of modernity.[9] This was a time of anatomical plates, one of the most famous of which was Pierre (also called Petrus) Camper's (1722–1789) drawings of skulls, which illustrated the so-called facial angle. Camper's drawings (displayed in fig. 6), which became standard in nineteenth-century texts on racial difference, ordered the skulls in accordance with their alleged level of mental capacity: ape, orang-utang, negro, calmuck, Europeans, and "antique."

Significantly, the traits that the commentators described as increasing the risk of demon possession were also largely connected to the feminine.

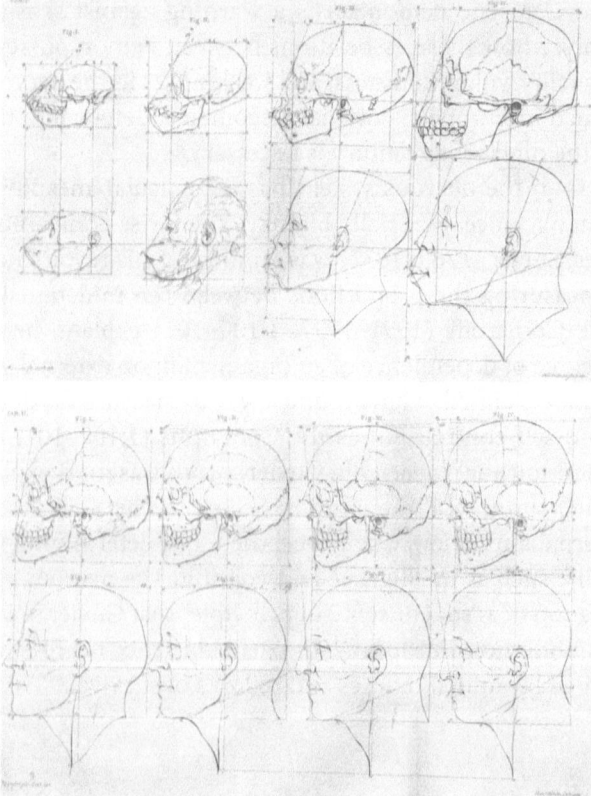

Figure 6. Pierre Camper (1791, 117–19): facial lines and angles.

---

9. Already during the first phase of European colonialism the status of non-European people was debated; see Fredrickson 2002, 36–37.

6. BETWEEN MAN AND BRUTE (5:1–20)

As the Comaroffs (1991–1997, 1:105–8) argue, nineteenth-century modernity entailed new distinctions in the construction of gender. The new biology offered rational explanations for a particular division of labor and hierarchical status between the sexes. In particular, weaknesses in the nervous system were used to explain female subordination. Since the uterus, biologists claimed, was directly connected to the central nervous system, women were liable to nervous disorders and responsive to control by males. Here Judith Butler and her analysis of the cultural embeddedness of contemporary biochemistry would be a welcome companion.[10] The following statement by an anonymous nineteenth-century physician tellingly indicates the way in which these "new scientific findings" were often harmonized with premodern ecclesial discourse: "It was as if the Almighty, in creating the female sex, had taken the uterus and built up a woman around it."[11] Moreover, as the Comaroffs (1:105–8) also point out, since the discourses of race and gender often intersected, non-Europeans were feminized. Women and non-Europeans alike were generally regarded as alien to reason and autonomy. In this way, the new biology produced an image of the ideal European man. Unlike women and non-Europeans, he was self-contained rather than dependent, driven by reason rather than sensory stimuli.

As one can see from this brief detour, there are significant similarities between how some of the commentators explain demon possession and the knowledge that was produced in nineteenth-century biology. As one can also see when Alford continues his interpretation of Mark 5:1–20, however, the similarity may imply friction. Alford (1849, 61) poses the question that he sees as most difficult: "How can we imagine the bestial nature capable of the reception of daemoniac influence?" Here he involves himself in an interesting comparison between "man" and "brute."

> If … the unchecked indulgence of sensual appetite afforded an inlet for the powers of evil to possess the human daemoniac, then we have their influence joined to that part of man's nature which he has in common with the brutes that perish, the animal and sensual mind. We may thus

---

10. Butler (1999, 135–41) discusses the work of a group of biogenetic researchers who in 1987 claimed to have found "the master gene" that filled the function of "the binary switch" that distinguishes between male and female. Their research, Butler argues, "reproduces that cultural sedimentation in the objects it purports to discover and neutrally describe."

11. The quote is from Comaroff and Comaroff 1991–1997, 1:106.

conceive that the same animal and sensual soul in the brute may be receptive of similar daemonical influence. But with this weighty difference: that whereas in man there is an individual, immortal spirit, to which alone belongs his personality and deliberative will and reason,—and there was ever in him, as we have seen, a struggle and a protest against this tyrant power; the oppressed soul, the real "I," calling out against the usurper;—this would not be the case with the brute, in whom this personality and reflective consciousness is wanting. (61)

As argued above, phrases such as "unchecked indulgence" and "sensual appetite" were part of the construction and feminization of non-European heathens and savages. Since these characteristics are seen as common to both human and animal, heathens and savages were seen as being more animal-like. Perhaps there is also a dual reference in the use of "brutes," which, apart from designating animals, can be directed pejoratively at people as well, as in Kurtz's well-known expression in *Heart of Darkness*: "Exterminate all the brutes!" (Conrad 1985, 87). But even if there are similarities between the desolate human and the brute, Alford also makes an important distinction. Unlike the brute, a human has an individual, immortal spirit and a deliberate will and reason, epitomized by "the real 'I.'"

Alford's explanation of the demon-possessed animals seems to imply a certain questioning of the degraded status of non-Europeans. On the one hand, his argument reaffirms a connection made in the new biology between demon possession and feminized heathens and savages—people who were represented by the "negro" in Camper's drawing; but, on the other hand, he makes the point rather strongly that despite the sensual appetites and the weak nervous system, this was a man with an immortal soul. Protestant mission was one of the discourses in which the determinism of the new biology was questioned.[12] According to the new science, some people were biologically inferior and had no chance of being delivered from a state of barbarism. Missionaries generally opposed this view and argued for the capacity to improve and the possibility of becoming civilized. A similar opposition seems to be present when Alford contends that a human, even if possessed, has something that an animal lacks: an

---

12. As the Comaroffs (1991–1997, 1:108) note, humanitarians as well as evangelicals resisted the reductionist understanding of non-Europeans and argued for the possibility of improvements.

immortal soul and a "real 'I'" that calls out against the usurper.[13] The opposition, it is important to notice, did not necessarily question imperial expansion per se, only the radical dehumanization that at times accompanied it.

The Oppressive Legion

Since the unclean spirits in Mark's account are called by the name Legion, one may ask whether any exegetes detect the anti-Roman signals that are thereby sent. Contrary to what one might expect, some do. In the Cambridge Greek Testament series, G. F. Maclear (1883, 88) begins his comment on the name Legion by offering a quote from an unacknowledged source: "He had seen the thick and serried ranks of a Roman legion, that fearful instrument of oppression, that sign of terror and fear to the conquered nations." These forces, Maclear further explains, "terrible in their strength, inexorable in their hostility, were the lords many." The source from which Maclear cites seems to be the work by Trench (1850, 140), which has much the same wording. Trench, in turn, refers to a commentary by Hermann Olshausen, first published in 1830. Also, Swete (1898, 91) offers a similar reading: "To a Palestinian of our Lord's time the name [Legion] would connote not only vast numbers ... and submission to a superior will... ; but the miseries of a military occupation by a foreign power."

Unlike some contemporary Markan scholars (cf. Gundry 1993, 260), these nineteenth-century commentators were evidently willing to acknowledge how the name Legion brings to mind the brutal and oppressive nature of Roman rule. But, then again, this is hardly to suggest that these commentators took Mark as an anti-imperial document. They refrain from discussing how this episode places Mark in relation to Roman rule. Also, as we will see below, when they interpret the episode about imperial tax (12:13–17), they find no opposition to Rome's order. If the dramatic expulsion of Legion evoked the fearful and oppressive nature of Roman rule, the commentators seem to presume that Mark understands this oppression as being only of a spiritual nature.

---

13. Here it is also possible to see a parallel to one of the political concerns of Protestant mission: the abolition of slavery. John Weasley, one of the Methodist missionary pioneers, claimed that slavery was contrary to nature: "the purchase of any human being could be made by Christ's blood alone" (quoted by Comaroff and Comaroff 1991–1997, 1:120).

To summarize, the interpretations of the Gerasene demoniac story (Mark 5:1–20) were found to interplay in three ways with the colonial discourse. First, the commentators—even if they construed the Christian/heathen dichotomy in slightly different ways—made vivid use of the common motif in Protestant mission of converting the heathen. Second, when discussing the phenomenon of demon possession, the commentators applied terms and knowledge from the new biology, claiming a connection between demon possession, a weak nervous system, and exaggerated sensualism—traits that were regarded in scientific discourse as being typical for women and non-Europeans. But even if the commentators became part of this production of knowledge, they also resisted the deterministic tendency that was often implied by its racial categorizations, upholding instead the possibility of cultural education and Christian conversion. Third, contrary to what one could expect, some commentators did notice that the name Legion evokes the oppressive nature of Roman rule. In a vague way, they indicated that Mark could be taken as a critique against empire. They did not, however, discuss this issue explicitly at this point, and we will see if they would discuss it elsewhere.

7
Submissive Heathen and Superior Greek (7:24–30)

The story about Jesus and the Syrophoenician woman has received quite some attention from postcolonial biblical scholars, most notably Kwok (1995, 71–83), Perkinson (1996), Dube (2000, 125–201), and Donaldson (2005). The attention received is primarily connected to the intersecting categorizations that are curiously staged in their meeting: gender, ethnicity, religion, and rural/urban. Other interesting features of the episode include traveling into a geographical borderland, Jesus' harsh attitude toward the woman, and the woman's way of turning the conversation.

Penetrating Gentile Territory

The episode in Mark begins by reporting that Jesus traveled to the region of Tyre (7:24). In relation to this text, Dube's (2000, 129) discussion of imperial motives in biblical texts again becomes helpful. Dube highlights how stories about traveling to foreign lands, often by using gender categories (e.g., equating women with land), were common in colonial discourse (94–95, 183). An important task here is thus to study how the Markan interpreters represented this journey.

As it turns out, we need not look far in order to find allusions to colonial or missionary travel expeditions. Approaching the commentaries, one soon runs into a debate concerning whether Jesus had crossed the borders of Galilee and entered a "foreign" or "heathen" territory or whether he remained in Galilee, in the regions that bordered Tyre. Let us begin with Riddle, who states the following in relation to the versions of Matthew and Mark:

> The interview with the heathen woman is striking and prophetic. The Jews reject the blessing; the Gentiles seek it with longing desire. The heathen world had been prepared for Him who was "a light to lighten the Gentiles."

... The Jewish world was closing against our Lord; the Gentile world was not yet open. He sought seclusion near the borderline, but "He could not be hid" (Mark vii. 24). The heathen mother found Him: she was a type of the longing, suffering Gentile world. (Riddle 1879, 138)

Riddle's taking of this text as prophetic implies that it somehow foretells a future development. By labeling the woman a "heathen mother" and regarding her as a "type," Riddle presents her as something that was quite familiar during the nineteenth century: "the longing, suffering Gentile world." Hence this designation oscillates between non-Jewish people in antiquity and non-Christian peoples in the nineteenth century who lacked what Europeans regarded as proper culture and religion. A similar double meaning is also seen in the other commentaries. J. Lange (1857, 219; 1865, 281), for instance, describes Jesus as traveling "into the boundary lands of heathenism" (*Gränzstriche der Heidenwelt*).

This double meaning is strengthened when we consider how "heathen" was understood etymologically at this time. According to *Encyclopædia Britannica* (1911, s.v.), *heathen* is usually ascribed to the Gothic *haiþi*, heath: "In Ulfilas' [4th century] Gothic version of the Bible, the earliest extant literary monument of the Germanic languages, the Syro-Phoenician woman (Mark vii. 26) is called *haiþno*, where the Vulgate has *gentilis*." No wonder that the interpretations of this episode in Mark oscillate between ancient and present referents. Being a character who had given rise to the term itself, the Syrophoenician woman was the heathen par excellence.

Some exegetes, however, criticized the traditional missionary interpretation. Meyer (1880–1881, 1:400), for example, criticizes the tradition of regarding the traveling as a missionary journey that anticipates the conversion of the heathen. As he dismisses a long list (seven to be precise) of previous Christian interpreters (from Chrysostom onward), the traditions surrounding this episode are quite clearly seen. He specifically criticizes Calvin, who argued that the purpose of Jesus' travels was "to give *praeludia quaedam* of the conversion of the Gentiles." Similarly, Gould (1896, 134) claims that "these are not missionary journeys, but are undertaken to enable Jesus to be alone with his disciples."

But although this challenges the traditional interpretation, Gould's language gives a rather different impression. Gould discusses whether Jesus did or did not "penetrate Gentile territory." The meaning of τὰ ὅρια, he contends, implies that Jesus actually "did penetrate the Gentile territory." If this was a retreat-like journey for spending time with his followers, one may wonder why Gould discusses it in terms of the highly active verb "penetrate," which connotes force and effort. Here, it seems, even if Gould has explicitly stated that Jesus did *not* travel as a missionary to the heathen, this is the very image that his language puts in play.

As Kwok (1995, 9) argued, Christian mission during the nineteenth century can be understood in terms of the function of the phallus in psychoanalytical discourse. "It is not mere coincidence," Kwok (9) says, "that missionary literatures describe Christian mission as 'aggressive work' and European expansion as 'intrusion' and 'penetration.'" This way of applying a psychoanalytic framework on European colonial discourse has been more extensively explored by Anne McClintock (1995).[1] Kwok's point is confirmed by Carey's influential work. Championing the obligation of Christians to convert the heathen, Carey (1792, 21–22) describes the first journey of Paul as "the first attack on the heathen world." Carey also states that Paul "penetrated as far as Derbe." Depicting "Gentile territory" as a space into which Jesus penetrates, therefore, Gould's interpretation interplays uncannily with a phallocentric tendency in European colonial discourse.

A further topic discussed in the commentaries revolves around the use of dogs and children as metaphors. Most commentators strive to reduce the inferiority that is implied by the word *dogs*. Alexander (1858, 198) represents this trend by pointing out the significance of the type of dog that is indicated: "The beauty of our Saviour's figure would be therefore marred by understanding what he says of savage animals, without relation or attachment to mankind." For Alexander, it is important to note that the dogs Jesus refers to are tame animals that belong to a human family by which they are loved. The woman's position is then less inferior as compared to her being likened to a "savage animal."[2] At the same time, however, there is no doubt that Alexander (199) also affirms that the woman is placed in an inferior position. Indeed, her attainment of help by

---

1. McClintock (1995, 1–4) introduces her study by pointing out the explicit sexualized character of a colonial map rendered in the beginning of the bestselling novel *King Solomon's Mines* by H. Rider Haggard (published in 1885). For the gendered nature of European colonial discourse, see Loomba 2005, 62–74, 128–45; and Hulme 1985.

2. Cf. Chadwick 1887, 198, who, in a similar manner, sees Jesus as domesticating the Gentile world.

Jesus is totally dependent on the acceptance of her inferiority: to give "a thankful consent to occupy that place [beneath the table] and to partake of that inferior provision."

The inferiority that Alexander ascribes to the woman is indicative of the way in which colonial discourse defined the relation between Europeans and non-Europeans.[3] Although, from a European perspective, Christian conversion involved being transferred from a savage to a cultured state, the converted "heathen" was still somehow inferior. Following Alexander's reading, Europeans were expected to love the converted "heathens" just as children love their puppies. As such, Alexander's interpretation uncannily corresponds to the design of standard collection boxes that were used in Swedish churches at the time. Adorned as they were with the submissive figure of a converted black African heathen (fig. 7), they helped establish an unequal relation in the intersection of religion and race.

Figure 7. A collection box used for "Heathen Mission of the Sunday School Children." The collection boxes were widespread in Swedish churches from the late nineteenth century up until the 1970s. Constructed with a joint that made the figure bow its dark brown body as coins were inserted, it keenly represents how the heathen were construed as racially submissive to the Europeans.

---

3. Cf. Kwok 1995, 78, who claims that "just like the Gentile woman [in Mark 7:24–30], colonized peoples were expected to be as subservient, obedient, and loyal as a 'devoted dog.'"

This relation of "benign" caretaking is reinforced by Riddle (1879, 138–39) when he comments on the fact that the woman asks Jesus for help: "A touch of nature in the mother's prayer! Maternal love remains even in heathenism; often leading to Christ." For Riddle the degenerated state of heathens seems to imply that their natural traits are disturbed. A heathen woman expressing maternal love is something unusual, signaling a step toward conversion from heathen superstition to salvation in Christ.

The Civilized Greek

This, however, is not the whole story. Since some commentators regard the woman as a model with which *Europeans* could identify, her submissiveness becomes significantly fraught with contradictions. In what appears to be a reversal of the colonial discourse, Chadwick (1887, 197) parallels the woman with Jacob the patriarch (Gen 32:22ff.) and describes her faith as "penetrating"; hence Jesus became "captive to a heathen's and a woman's importunate and faithful sagacity." Maclear (1883, 111) similarly sees her submissiveness as representing the humbleness of "our Church."[4] Since such interpretations allow a "heathen woman" to represent Irish or British Christianity, the Christian/heathen opposition is undermined, effectively transforming both colonizer and colonized into "heathens."

In some cases, however, this undermining of the Christian/heathen dichotomy was accompanied by the construction of another binary division. J. Lange (1858, 68; 1866, 67) exemplifies this when he emphasizes the woman's identity as "a Gentile, or Greek" (*eine Heidin* [*eine Griechin*]). As Lange seems to know, *Greek* has quite different connotations as compared to *Gentile* or *heathen*:

> Ἑλληνίς, according to the Jewish phraseology of the time, indicating a Gentile woman [*Heidin*] generally. This was not merely the result of the intercourse of the Jews with the Greeks especially; but it sprang from the fact that in the Greeks and in Greece [*Griechenthum*] they saw the most finished and predominant exhibition of this world's culture and glory [or Gentile worldview, *heidnische Weltanschauung*]. (Lange 1858, 68; 1866, 67)

Whereas the commentators discussed thus far have used the categories *Christian*, *Gentile*, and *heathen*, Lange introduces *Greek*. For Lange,

---

4. Similarly Riddle 1879, 139; and Alford 1849, 119–20.

moreover, *Greek* is not only an ethnic designation. As indicated by the term *Griechenthum*, it also signifies a particular culture and worldview that Lange regards as highly developed. Jesus' meeting with the woman, then, signifies a meeting with a culture that is apparently more civilized than his own. It is here interesting to note that the English translation of Lange's commentary (1866, 67) identifies the woman as "Gentile, or Greek," and in this way avoids combining the terms *Greek* and *heathen*. Since Lange connects Greece with the "world's culture and glory," the English translation refrains from using *heathen* when referring to the *Greek*.

As Lange brings in the civilized and philosophically sophisticated Greeks, he sets another binary division in play—the one between Greeks and Semites. In Lange's commentary, this division seems to exist together with the Christian/heathen division, thus highlighting the complexity of the Christian subjectivities these commentaries produced. Significantly, the Christian/heathen division is used in the homiletical and practical section of the English translation, where Lange (1858, 68; 1866, 68) describes Jesus as journeying "towards west, north, east, south"—which he regards as a "sign" (*Zeichen*). That this represents Christian expansionism along the lines of the Christian/heathen divide becomes clear when Jesus is described as working under the Father's government "in the dark [*finstern*] boundary of the heathen world [*Heidenlandes*]."[5]

These two binary divisions represent a tension within Protestant Christianity. Whereas the Greek/Semitic division is rendered in the exegetical section of Lange's commentary and belongs to modern orientalism with its philhellenism, the Christian/heathen division is presented in the homiletical section and is connected to the pietist tradition. Even if there was a competition between modernists and pietists, the two traditions coexisted in biblical studies. What made this coexistence possible, it seems, was the master term *Christian*, which was interchangeably manifested over against *Semitic* and *heathen*, both of which were important representations of the Other.

For Lange (1858, 68; 1866, 68), however, the Greek/Semitic division seems of greater importance. This one may see in the homiletical section, where he continues commenting on the episode by comparing *Heiden* with *Juden*: "The Gentile [*die heidnische*] longing everywhere feels from

---

5. My trans.; significantly, the English translation here renders *Heidenlandes* as "heathenism" (Lange 1866, 68).

7. SUBMISSIVE HEATHEN AND SUPERIOR GREEK (7:24–30) 115

afar and seeks after salvation, whilst the Jews reject it before their very eyes." Further, *die Heiden* are seen as "modest, tractable, docile, thankful table-companions of unthankful children." By depicting Jews as "unthankful children," Lange seems to be raising the position of the Gentile by lowering that of the Jew. There were thus two binary divisions involved simultaneously—Christian/heathen and Greek/Semitic—both of which were employed in the formation of an elevated European identity. For Lange, however, the latter seems predominant.

To summarize, the interpretations of this episode represent a rather complex and contradictory colonial heritage. On the one hand, the woman was seen as a prototype for the distant wretched heathens. In this interpretive tradition, Jesus' traveling to Tyre was seen as a missionary journey and was emblematic of Christian expansion. Upholding the woman's submissive acceptance of the position of a household dog, she became a type for the non-European world, the heathen par excellence. On the other hand, she was also seen as a Greek of a high-level culture. As the woman in this way became a representation with which Europeans could identify, the Christian/heathen dichotomy was undermined. In these cases, the woman's cleverness and faith were typically upheld. This undermining, however, could easily subvert into another dichotomic division. Europeans were at this time rather keen on identifying with the progressive Greeks over against the stagnated Semites.

8
The Embarrassing Parousia (8:31–9:1)

One of the features in Mark's Gospel that has been debated from a postcolonial perspective concerns eschatology and what is often referred to as the Parousia. Postcolonial biblical scholars have discussed the matter of how Mark's depictions of the future coming of a risen Christ in power and glory relate to imperial ideology. In chapter 17 I will return to Liew's contention (1999b, 1999a) that the Parousia in Mark duplicates the imperial ideology of "might is right." Of significance here, however, is the way in which Liew describes the approach that brought him to his conclusion. Referring to the way in which Foucault handles the problem of the Gulag in relation to the texts by Marx and Lenin, Liew (1999b, 8–9) regards European imperialism not as stemming from an unacceptable *distortion* of Mark's text, but as a *reality* from which it ought to be studied and criticized.

Although I do find this perspective important and necessary, I am not convinced that Liew has managed to show the ways in which Mark helped to fuel European imperialism. Pointing out what appears to be an imperial ideology in the text is not the same thing as showing how the text was actually interpreted and used in order to justify imperial expansion. In a limited sense, then, my analysis of the nineteenth-century Markan commentaries can serve as a test of the plausibility of Liew's reading.[1] If the Markan Parousia entails a "might-is-right" ideology that gave rise to Western imperialism, one would expect it to be visible in those Markan commentaries, which were written in the centers of the European empires.

As a first observation, the commentators show a high degree of disagreement when interpreting the Parousia in Mark. These disagreements,

---

1. Here I need to acknowledge the limited nature of this investigation. In order to actually test Liew's contention, one would need to dig much deeper into the intersections of Protestant mission, popular culture, and European colonialism and search for what meaning was given to the Parousia and what functions it had.

moreover, were not specific to the nineteenth century, but rather seem to have been discussed from the earliest times of Christianity (cf. 2 Pet 3). When the commentators interpret the explicit references to the Parousia in Mark (9:1; 13:26; 14:62), they make at least nine different suggestions concerning what the images of the returning Christ designate, some of which can be combined:

1. The transfiguration depicted in Mark 9:2–8 (Swete 1898, 186; Maclear 1883, 122)
2. The resurrection, the day of Pentecost, and the triumphant development of the church (Riddle 1879, 290; Swete 1898, 186; F. Cook 1878, 87, 280; Maclear 1883, 122)
3. The fall of Jerusalem (Chadwick 1887, 227; Riddle 1879, 290; many post-Reformation expositors according to Swete 1898, 186; F. Cook 1878, 87, 253; Maclear 1883, 122; Gould 1896, 251–52)
4. The imminent coming of Jesus as king and the realization of the kingdom (Meyer 1858, 328; 1880–1881, 1:430–31)
5. The future coming of Jesus to finally judge humankind (F. Cook 1878, 87, 280; Maclear 1883, 122)
6. The establishment of a spiritual rather than a worldly kingdom (Gould 1896, 159, 251; Swete 1898, 185; F. Cook 1878, 279)
7. The gathering of men into a true and lasting brotherhood (Swete 1898, 312; Riddle 1879, 198)
8. The gradual or progressive erection of Christ's kingdom in the hearts of people and in society at large (Alexander 1858, 230)
9. A warning or caution that the positions of Jesus and his judges would one day be reversed (Plumptre 1897, 212; Alexander 1858, 228; Swete 1898, 338; Menzies 1901, 173).

These interpretations of the Parousia might have interacted with European colonial discourse in several ways. The second suggestion, for example, about the triumphal development of the church, seems to stand in a symbiotic relation with what Protestant mission often called the gospel's victory march through the world.[2] Also, a combination of the fourth and the

---

2. *The Gospel's Victory March through the World* is a title of a work by Ussing

fifth suggestions reflects a commonly held belief that played an important role in Protestant expansion. As expressed by Barnabas Shaw, the founder of the Wesleyan missionary society in South Africa, the Gospels' declarations of an imminent end time were crucial for upholding the spirit since they kept the missionaries assured that "all nations shall serve him."[3]

An Ideology of Might Is Right?

In connection to the last point, the Parousia as interpreted in the commentaries served to motivate Christian expansion in another way. When commenting on the phrase "the Gospel must first be published among all nations" (Mark 13:10), F. Cook (1878, 178) states: "This statement is of extreme importance. A long interval before the end must be allowed for the publishing or preaching of the Gospel." Since the preaching of the gospel, Cook (139) explains, was only partially accomplished at the time of the early church, the phrase points significantly to "a later and fuller accomplishment hereafter, when the Gospel shall be actually preached to the whole world." The "extreme importance" that Cook ascribes to this statement is connected not only to the notion of a second coming and its implied judgment of all peoples but also to what was generally regarded as a unique moment in history when the gospel's message could potentially reach all the peoples of the world.

But even if Cook interpreted Mark's Parousia in a way that interplayed with Christian expansion, did it play the role of offering an ideology of "might is right," as Liew suggests? "Might is right" usually indicates that a superior power establishes the moral right: whoever wins the war gets to decide what is right and wrong. Although Cook's interpretation presupposes the existence of a superior power—even an unlimited divine power—this power is present in the form of a belief and an expectation. Although such a belief, if taken seriously, profoundly affects how people behave, it does not necessarily represent what is usually meant by "might is right." That is not to deny, of course, that such a belief played a key role in the justification of the Protestant mission. But even so, the commentators' lack of a singular meaning in Mark's Parousia and their extensive interpretive debates constitute reasons for skepticism in relation to Liew's claim.

(1902), a Danish theologian who describes what he regards as the success of the evangelical mission from the time of the early church to his present time.

3. See Stuart 2002, 67, who quotes from the *Memorials* of Barnabas Shaw.

When some commentators interpret Mark's Parousia in light of Matthew's, it takes on a far more violent and grandiose sense of divine retribution. But even then it is rather unclear from these commentators that they are part of constructing an imperial ideology. In relation to the parable about the final judgment of all nations (Matt 25:31–46), F. Cook (1878, 152) argues against interpreters who take "all nations" (Matt 25:32) as referring only to non-Christians or only to Christians. The presence or absence of Christian faith is not the specific focus, according to Cook (152); rather this parable about the final judgment deals with "moral duties discernible by the light of nature, and required of Christians and others alike." Further, the commentators disagree on crucial issues: Who are the ones to be condemned and on what grounds? In other words, even when interpreting a violent Parousia, like the one rendered in Matthew, the commentators are quite imprecise as to determining what is required in order to be saved. As such, these interpretations seem to offer poor support for the building of an empire.

However, there is another, rather paradoxical, way in which the interpretations interplayed with elevated European self-understandings. In between the lines in many of the commentaries there is a sense of struggle to explain the rather *problematical* images in Mark's Gospel. Bruce (1897, 294) makes this struggle plain when he states with a sigh of resignation: "What is said thereon [about the Parousia] is so perplexing as to tempt a modern expositor to wish it had not been there, or to have recourse to critical expedients to eliminate it from the text." In what one might regard as an expression of modern liberal discomfort, Bruce would most of all like to remove these images altogether. The Parousia is seen as a tiresome problem that makes modern scholars moan with unease. For enlightened Europeans, the fantastical image of Jesus descending in power from the clouds was, more than anything, embarrassing.

One way of handling this embarrassment was to associate these images with the Jewish rather than the Greek, thereby keeping them at a significant distance. Hence Menzies (1901, 239) sees the Parousia as "necessarily Jewish in colouring, and the scene in which they are looked for is the land of Palestine." Menzies regards Mark's Gospel as having been written for "the Western Church," and hence having been written "with the briefest statement of the return of the Messiah and his meeting with his saints." The less grandiose Parousia that is presented in Mark is here seen as connected to the West rather than the East. The powerful splendor of the Parousia is Jewish "both in its moral colour and in its incidents." But even so, and even if it stems from Palestine, Jesus did not use this language, according to Menzies (240). In relation to the East/West dichotomy, with which the downplaying of the Parousia is accompanied, Jesus ends up on the Western side.

The importance of these notions of East and West for European identities indicates a much more complicated use of the Parousia in colonial discourse than that of simply offering an ideology of might is right. The powerful and vindictive imagery of the Parousia, it seems, was regarded as being too primitive to be admitted as a part of the enlightened Western identity. In response to Liew, then, I would suggest that it was a *disavowal* of the Parousia, more than a straightforward *use* of it, that made European imperialism possible.

To summarize, the interpretations of the Parousia (8:31–9:1) were complex in relation to colonial discourse. On the one hand, the notion of eschatological judgment was a crucial motive for Protestant mission during the nineteenth century, especially given the unprecedented possibility of spreading the gospel to all people; on the other hand, the scholarly interpretations of these passages in Mark were highly diverse and contradictory. Most notably, however, were the recurring expressions of embarrassment over the notions of a grandiose second coming of Jesus. Critical scholars tended to distance themselves from these images, identifying them as Jewish rather than Greek. In this sense, and this I argued as a response to Liew's claim, elevated European identities were partly formed by disavowing the Parousia.

9
"Only Absolutely Spiritual" (11:1–11)

The next two Markan passages to be studied are Jesus' entry into Jerusalem (11:1–11) and the tribute question (12:13–17). Two factors make these texts crucial for the current investigation. First, royal as well as imperial power feature prominently in them. Second, when the commentators interpret these texts, they generally make use of a binary division between the spiritual and the worldly or between religion and politics. Although this binary is not without its contemporary advocates, scholars in the empire studies cluster (see ch. 3) sharply criticize its application to the ancient texts (R. Horsley 2001, ix–xii; Carter 2008, 20–22). Since this binary division was important for the reformulation of European colonial identities during the nineteenth century, they have great importance for this study. As a way to introduce the present chapter and the next, I will show how the terms were typically used in the commentaries.

The Spiritual and the Worldly

In the introduction to his commentary, when describing "the external conditions" of Mark's Gospel, Swete (1898, lxxiv–lxxxiii) divides his description into four aspects: geographic, political, religious, and miscellaneous. "Into the political conditions," he (lxxviii) states, "St Mark allows his readers only a passing glimpse." Mark shows little interest, Swete claims, in tetrarchs, procurators and "the complex political life" of Palestine. Swete (lxxix) offers no explanation for this alleged lack of political interest, stating, somewhat enigmatically, that it "is not due to ignorance," and thereby seems to assume that the reader will understand the reason. This lack of explanation indicates that Swete is leaning on what was then generally taken for granted regarding politics and the purpose of Mark's Gospel.

When it comes to "the state of religion" in Galilee and Judea, Swete (lxxix) says, "St Mark is less reserved." The way in which these external conditions are rendered is noteworthy, not least the terminology. The synagogues of Galilee and the temple of Jerusalem "control the ecclesiastical life of the two provinces." Similarly, the synagogue leader and chief priests are "ecclesiastical authorities." The scribes whom Mark depicts both in the north and in the south are "religious authorities." Moreover, the Pharisees and the Sadducees are "religious sects" that "divide religious opinion." Finally, Swete refers to the Saducean priests with whom Jesus comes in conflict as "the hierarchy."

The separation Swete makes between religion and politics when describing these external conditions significantly reflects the discourse of modernity and its division between the scientific, inquisitive West and the stagnant, theocratic East. Whereas issues that are connected with Roman rule (such as rulers appointed by Rome) are seen as "political," Jewish institutions (synagogues and temples) and issues connected to their influence are seen as "religious." The connection to nineteenth-century discourse becomes especially evident when Swete uses the term *ecclesiastical* to refer to the Jewish authorities. Similarly, in the designation "the hierarchy" there seems to be an echo of church structure, possibly with an anti-Catholic tone.

European colonial identities were to a high degree construed around a notion of Christianity as a spiritual religion. Unlike "superstitious" heathendom and "theocratic" Semitic religion, Christianity was seen as "spiritual," and thereby as being of a higher developmental level. In particular, Protestant Christianity's focus on the inner rather than outer was seen as religion in its highest sense. To be religious in the highest and most developed sense was seen as having a belief in a Supreme Being that was separated from and independent of worldly matters. The spiritual sense of Christianity was construed in opposition to what was seen as "Nature Religions" (animism, fetishism, heathendom, idolatry) as well as to national and nomistic religions (Judaism and Islam).[1] This is often seen in the commentators, exemplified by Gould (1896, 125), who sees Jesus' teaching in Mark 7:1–23 as striking "at the root not only of traditionalism, but of ceremonialism," the twin foes of spiritual religion.

---

1. See, e.g., *Nordisk familjebok*, s.v. "Hedendom"; *Chamber's Encyclopaedia*, s.v. "Idolatry"; and *Encyclopaedia Britannica*, 11th ed., s.v. "Religion."

Consequently, biblical scholars generally regarded Jesus as essentially a spiritual figure without any worldly or political aspirations. The weight of this hegemonic view was considerable. To suggest that Jesus had a political agenda was considered highly offensive, not unlike saying that the Gospels contain myths. As is well known, Strauss upheld the latter view. The former suggestion had been made in the preceding century by Hermann Samuel Reimarus (1778, 112–27; 1970, 78), who argued that the disciples of the historical Jesus understood his proclamation about a kingdom of heaven to indicate "a secular (*weltlichen*) and temporal (*zeitlich*) kingdom. It was not until the failure of this hope, when Jesus had died, that the disciples and evangelists began to build a "system of a spiritual suffering savior [*geistlichen leidenden Erlöser*] for the whole human race" (1773, 117). The provocative nature of Reimarus's thesis is shown not least by his choosing not to publish it. Eventually, his iconoclastic texts were published posthumously and anonymously by his colleague Gotthold Ephraim Lessing, appearing in the *Wolfenbüttel Fragments* (1774–1778). Although the Reimarus thesis could not be ignored by nineteenth-century biblical scholars, it was blatantly dismissed.[2]

Reimarus, however, had not questioned the basic division between the spiritual and the worldly. Rather, by depicting the historical Jesus as a political revolutionary, he transferred him to the opposite side of the divide, and it was therefore not a difficult task for biblical scholars to kindly but firmly shift Jesus back to where he "belonged." For a thorough deconstruction of the basic division, biblical scholarship would have to wait another two hundred years. In what follows, I will investigate how the spiritual/worldly divide was construed in the interpretations of two Markan passages, and how these constructions were affiliated with modern colonialism.

The Spiritual as Acquiescence

The Markan commentators repeatedly mention Reimarus's thesis in relation to the triumphal entry (Mark 11:1–11). Since the episode raised issues about the political aspirations of Jesus, Reimarus evidently became relevant. The space that is devoted to Reimarus, however, is limited. Meyer

---

2. According to Bammel 1984, 12–13, there were two main ways in which the thesis was refuted. Either Jesus was seen as altogether uninterested in worldly matters or he was seen as changing his attitude from having primarily accepted the popular messianic political orientation and later withdrawn in order to go another way.

(1880–1881, 2:61) simply states, "The triumphal entry of Jesus is not a final attempt to establish the Messianic kingdom in a political sense…, such a kingdom having been entirely foreign to His purpose and His function." Similarly, J. Lange (1857, 297; 1865, 373) dismisses Reimarus by referring to the disciples: "That the Lord never made a single attempt to set in motion a political lever, does not say enough: we find that His disciples never did so." The point here is not to evaluate these arguments, but rather to point out how the suggestion by Reimarus functioned to strengthen, rather than undermine, the spiritual/worldly divide.

The spiritual/worldly distinction also carried a certain anti-Jewish tendency. This is seen, for example, in relation to the peoples' call for the coming of David's kingdom (11:10), when Swete (1898, 236) discusses the extent to which "the Pharisaic conception of the Messianic kingdom admitted of spiritual ideas." In other words, the Jewish beliefs about the messianic kingdom are generally seen as worldly rather than spiritual. Similarly, Bruce (1897, 261) describes how Jesus entered Jerusalem in a way that was not "welcome to the proud worldly-minded Jerusalemites."

Gould renders an exceptionally clear case of this spiritual/worldly divide. Commenting on the passage, he (1896, 205–6) points at an apparent inconsistency in the narrative's presentation of Jesus. Previously, Jesus had repeatedly refrained from claiming power, and his way to Jerusalem had been described as a journey to his suffering and death. But as he rides into Jerusalem, Jesus accepts the very position that he had previously denied— his kingship. Such a proclamation was necessary in order to communicate the demand of Jesus to be accepted "as King, and not merely as Prophet." Having made his messianic claim, however, "he proceeds as before with his merely spiritual work." The key to these apparent contradictions is to be found in "the splendid self-consistency of Jesus' procedure, and in its absolute inconsistency with worldly ideas and policies." A certain anxiety might be detected in these repeated reassurances. Jesus, Gould insists, would use "only absolutely spiritual means."

The way in which these interpretations construed a spiritual/worldly division connects them noticeably to modernity with its increasing secularization, as well as to Protestant mission. Here the latter is of primary interest. Missionary magazines as well as historical overviews of Christian mission typically utilized this division.[3] By presenting the spiritual

---

3. For articles in missionary magazines see, for instance, Tottie 1884, 1885; Sör-

9. "ONLY ABSOLUTELY SPIRITUAL" (11:1–11)

in contrast to the worldly, writings on Protestant mission helped form a subjectivity that was both distinct from, and yet largely sympathetic to, colonialism. "Of course, English colonial politics is not driven by a will to serve God's kingdom," the German missionary historian Gustav Warneck (1881, 28) says, "yet it achieves—without knowing or wanting it—good conditions for the expansion of God's kingdom." In its struggle against the "spiritual power" (*geistige Macht*) of heathendom, Warneck (1876, 73) thus regards European colonialism as an important partner.

A similar viewpoint is found in Swedish missionary magazines: "Without doubt, the English are with all their mistakes of all nations on earth the one that has the power and means that are required to prepare the way for Christianity and ... protect its tender sprout among the heathens" (Tottie 1884, 118). In this magazine, published under the supervision of the Church of Sweden's Board of Mission, the colonial expansion was seen as preparing the way, that is, building railways and upholding law and order, thereby opening up the non-European lands for Christian mission. But while welcoming the colonial expansion, Protestant mission also distanced itself from it. Whereas the worldly imperial expansion was seen as involving politics, coercion, greed, and violence, the Protestant mission was considered to be based upon an essentially spiritual power (*Geistesmacht*) and free from coercion (cf. Warneck 1898, 1–7; 1901, 3–7).

Here I need to clarify that the principal distinction made between religion and politics in both the commentaries and the literature on Christian mission hardly represents the considerably complex social praxis of Christian mission and its complicated relations with colonial administrations. Even if the division between religion and politics was crucial for Protestant mission and its self-understanding, the division was quite difficult to uphold in the social settings where mission was pursued.[4] But even if the spiritual/worldly binary that the commentaries reproduced was hardly

---

berg 1887. For histories of Christian mission see Warneck 1881, 1884, 1901, 1903; Landgren 1871; Ekman 1893; and Ussing 1902.

4. Comaroff and Comaroff 1991, 8–9. Since the newly formed colonial states tended to lack a legislation that regulated the relation between church and state, there were often conflicts between mission stations and the colonial administration. In a letter to his brother in 1898, R. H. Walker, a leading Anglican missionary, wrote about such conflicts in the kingdom of Buganda: "Our work here is, on a small scale, so like the work and history of the Church in the 4th and 5th century. Many questions are just the same as were then settled. The relation of Church and State is continually cropping up." Cited from Hansen 2002, 157.

realized socially in the Protestant mission, it nevertheless made possible a self-understanding that affirmed and yet distanced itself from colonial expansion. Although this subjectivity, due to this distance, could involve certain resistance against the more cruel aspects of colonial rule, it typically refrained from questioning colonialism as such.

The Spiritual as Resistance

Interestingly enough, one commentary stands out in its construal of the spiritual/worldly division. George Chadwick (1887, 300–301) interprets the episode as follows:

> Thus He comes forth, the gentlest of the mighty, with no swords gleaming around to guard Him, or to smite the foreigner who tramples Israel, or the worse foes of her own household. Men who will follow such a King must lay aside their vain and earthly ambitions, and awake to the truth that spiritual powers are grander than any which violence ever grasped. But men who will not follow Him shall some day learn the same lesson, perhaps in the crash of their reeling commonwealth, perhaps not until the armies of heaven follow Him, as He goes forth, riding now upon a white horse, crowned with many diadems, smiting the nations with a sharp sword, and ruling them with an iron rod.

Like other commentators, Chadwick sees the entry story with its lack of swords as exhibiting a "spiritual power." But unlike other commentators, Chadwick poses more of an opposition between this spiritual power and "vain and earthly ambitions." That Chadwick sees earthly ambitions as designating imperial rule is evident in his reference to a "reeling commonwealth." With an unusual application of the Parousia, Chadwick warns what will happen to those who unheedingly prolong the imperial expansion. His commentary on Mark's entry story thereby construes the spiritual/worldly division in opposition to Pax Britannica.

In Chadwick's reading, the spiritual power of Jesus has political implications. In an illuminating parallel, he compares the spreading of the garments (Mark 11:8) to an anecdote about Sir Walter Raleigh and Queen Elizabeth, according to which Raleigh threw his beautiful new cloak before the Queen as she was standing in front of a puddle of mud (Marshall 1920, 342–45). As Jesus rides into Jerusalem, Chadwick (1887, 302) argues, he "openly and practically assumed rank as a monarch, allowed men to proclaim the advent of His kingdom, and proceeded to exercise its rights by

9. "ONLY ABSOLUTELY SPIRITUAL" (11:1–11)   129

calling for the surrender of property, and by cleansing the temple with a scourge." The challenge thereby posed to the rulers in Jerusalem, Chadwick (302) states, was harsh. Jesus had become an "Aspirant to practical authority, Who must be dealt with practically"; and hence "there could be no middle course between crushing Him, and bowing to Him."

As Chadwick upholds material matters (property) and practical authority in connection to Jesus, his commentary stands in a strained relation to the politically innocuous Jesus who characterizes the other commentaries. Whereas the spiritual/worldly division most often implied a silky relation to European colonial discourse, in Chadwick's case it involved friction. What made possible Chadwick's unique reading will be discussed in the next chapter.

To summarize, since the entry into Jerusalem (11:1–11) carries rather overt political connotations, the interpretations of these episodes interacted more directly with the issues of imperial power. It is not surprising that the commentaries here reproduced the spiritual/worldly division that was prominent in Enlightenment Europe as well as in Protestant mission. The spiritual/worldly division helped establish a subjectivity with a certain distance from the worldly colonial expansion. A limited resistance against particular aspects of the colonial discourse thereby became possible. At the same time, however, this distance also made possible a far-reaching cooperation with the European expansion. With the exception of Chadwick, the interpretations generally established an accommodating attitude to the colonial power as such.

10
AN IRISH CAT AMONG THE PIGEONS (12:13–17)

The episode about the tribute is one of the foundations of the dichotomous division between religion and politics that has had such fundamental importance for the development of Western societies. Being one of the most famous sayings by Jesus in the Gospels, the passage is often referred to in discourses about religion and politics during the nineteenth century as well as today.[1] As has been argued, this division played a crucial role in Protestant mission for establishing a critical, and yet cooperative, attitude toward the second-phase colonialism. Also, since issues about national independence, imperial rule and rebellion are discussed in the commentaries, more direct connections are opened to political issues. All in all, the episode is crucial for the present investigation.

The commentators generally take the question from the Pharisees and the Herodians as a trap. Either Jesus would answer in the negative and be arrested and put on trial in a Roman court, or he would answer positively and then lose popular support. The situation is therefore understood in a highly political sense. For example, J. Lange (1857, 317; 1865, 396) interprets the question, "Is it lawful to give tribute unto Cesar, or not?" (Matt 22:17; Mark 12:14), as being tantamount to asking, "Must we resist the dominion of the Romans, and rise up in rebellion?"

To little surprise, almost all commentators interpret Jesus' answer (Mark 12:17) as distinguishing between a worldly and a spiritual sphere, by which the claims of Caesar are harmonized with the claims of God. For instance, F. Cook (1878, 122) maintains that "our Lord distinguishes between temporal and spiritual sovereignty, and shews that the two are not opposed to each other." Similarly, Klostermann (1867, 236) distinguishes

---

1. Cf. Broadbent's (1998) study of how English biblical scholars interpreted this passage during the nineteenth and twentieth centuries.

between the external (*Aeußerliches*) demands of the Roman emperor and the internal self-devotion (*innerliche Selbsthingabe*) demanded by God. That these interpretations were connected to the modern division between church and state becomes evident in the commentary of Riddle (1879, 181), who makes a similar interpretation: "This answer settles in principle, though not in detail, the relations of Church and State." Having a "common origin in God," Riddle sees this relation as "friendly" and "without antagonism."

"Wherever Any King's Money Is Current, There That King Is Lord"

When interpreting Jesus' answer, several commentators give voice to an ideology of "might is right" by referring to a saying by Maimonides and other rabbis: "wherever any king's money is current, there that king is lord."[2] Jesus' showing of a coin in combination with the exhortation "render to Caesar..." is then taken as a paraphrase of this rabbinic saying. Hence Jesus is seen as telling his compatriots that since the Romans had taken control of their land and introduced Roman coinage, they ought to submit to the authority of Caesar. Thus Maclear (1883, 156) states that "the head of the Emperor on the coin, the legend round it, and its circulation in the country, were undeniable proofs of the right of the actually existing government to levy the tax." Similarly, Bernhard Weiss (1872, 392) takes the emperor's image on the coin to indicate the natural rightfulness (*die natürliche Rechtmäßigkeit*) of the tax duty. That this was seen as an ideology of might is right is evident in several commentaries and is generally unquestioned. Bruce serves as a good example:

> The coin showed that he [Caesar] was ruler *de facto,* but not necessarily *de jure,* unless on the doctrine that might is right. The really important point in Christ's answer is, not what is said but what is implied, *viz.,* that national independence is not an ultimate *good,* nor the patriotism that fights for it an ultimate *virtue.* This doctrine Jesus held in common with the prophets. He virtually asserted it by distinguishing between the things of Caesar and the things of God. ... By treating them as distinct Jesus said in effect: The kingdom of God is not of this world, it is possible

---

2. The saying is mentioned by Alford 1849, 158; Alexander 1858, 328; Meyer 1880–1881, 86; Riddle 1879, 181; Swete 1909, 276.

to be a true citizen of the kingdom and yet quietly submit to the civil rule of a foreign potentate. (Bruce 1897, 274–75, italics original)

In Bruce's reading, it is not of primary importance if Caesar had a right to rule over Palestine or if Jesus proposed a doctrine of might is right. The "really important point" is something else: a distinct separation between spiritual and worldly according to which worldly political issues such as national independence are of secondary importance for Christians. To quietly submit to a worldly emperor or "a foreign potentate" is compatible with being a true citizen of the kingdom of God. If society is ruled by a might-is-right doctrine, Bruce seems to argue, this is not offensive to Christians since they are citizens of a spiritual rather than a worldly kingdom. His reading therefore constructs the spiritual/worldly division in a way that fosters acceptance of the colonial discourse.

It is interesting to notice how the might-is-right ideology is connected to the distinction between spiritual and worldly. This can be seen in Menzies's (1901, 220–21) claim that Jesus was uninterested in politics: "[Jesus] is to be made to define his attitude towards the Roman government, a thing which he never thought of doing. Nor will he be drawn now into any political declaration; it would be wrong for him to be entangled in politics." Having defined Jesus as being uninterested in politics and indifferent to the question of how to relate to Roman rule, Menzies nevertheless continues by pointing out that Jesus clearly taught that taxes ought to be paid: "The fact that they use it [the money] shows them to be living in his [Caesar's] realm and under his protection, and common honesty declares that they ought to pay the price of these benefits. No doubt, then, they must pay the Imperial taxes, even though they are not mentioned in the Law." Living under Roman domination, Menzies argues, was beneficial, and therefore Jews ought to accept the taxes on the basis of "common honesty" regardless of what the Torah says. But, according to Menzies, whereas common honesty demanded the acceptance of imperial rule, Jesus was disentangled from such political issues. The alleged political indifference of Jesus then made possible the principle of might is right; Jesus is understood as accepting that whoever has conquered and gained control has the right to rule and collect taxes. Such construal of the spiritual/worldly binary surely helped to fuel the European expansion.

As discussed in the previous chapter, moreover, several commentators also have an anti-Jewish tone as they make the distinction between religion and politics. Meyer (1880–1881, 2:85, italics original), for instance, sees the question posed to Jesus as a "problem founded on theocratic one-sidedness, as though the Jews were still the independent people of God, according to their *divine* title to recognise no king but God Himself." Meyers here lets the Jews represent a position that blends spiritual and worldly in a flawed way. Jews who were striving for national independence were, in Meyer's reading, expressing a "theocratic one-sidedness." They somehow thought society could be ruled by God and were hence incapable of sorting out the spiritual from the worldly. Gould offers a similar reading:

> The difficulty with the Jews, and with all bodies claiming to represent God, is that they are zealous for him in a partisan way. ... These men were eager to assert God's claim against a foreign king. Jesus was anxious that they should recognize his real claims, those that involved no real conflict, but belonged in the wider sphere of common duties. (1896, 226)

To assert God's claim against a foreign king—to resist imperial domination—is seen as an expression of a partisan zeal that Jesus was anxious to correct. Significantly, Gould lets the Jews represent this sort of "flawed" religion that failed to acknowledge the sphere of common duties. The colonized populations of the nineteenth century, by implication, would also need to have their religious beliefs corrected so as to realize the real claims of God—claims that involved no conflict with European rule.

The Significance of Place

Whereas the interpretations discussed so far have fueled the colonial discourse, it is now time to look at one interesting exception. Having interpreted the triumphal entry as a critique of imperial expansion, Chadwick continues to read the tribute episode in an oppositional way. In keeping with the other commentators, Chadwick refers to the question posed to Jesus as a snare. But whereas the answer by Jesus (12:17) is generally taken as expressing a timeless truth about the relation between religious and political authority, Chadwick (1887, 326) refers to the statement in Matthew (10:16) about joining "the wisdom of the serpent to the innocence of the dove," and takes Jesus' saying as a strategic way of dealing with a dangerous situation in an oppressive society.

True, Chadwick (327) still agrees that the issue is not *only* a matter of handling a threatening situation: "Now the words of Jesus are words for

10. AN IRISH CAT AMONG THE PIGEONS (12:13–17)   135

all time; even when He deals with a question of the hour." Although this timeless message is to recognize a sphere "in which obedience to the law is a duty to God," Chadwick in the same breath clarifies that "it is absurd to pretend that Christ taught blind and servile obedience to all tyrants in all circumstances." Chadwick then develops his interpretation by comparing the first part of the exhortation (give to the emperor) with the second part (give to God). Just as the coin bears the image of Caesar, the whole creation and human existence bear the image of God. Chadwick here alludes to a biblical tradition (Gen 1:26–27; 9:6; 1 Cor 11:7; Jas 3:9) according to which God created humans in his own image, thereby relativizing the first exhortation in favor of the second:

> If most of all he demands the love, the heart of man, here also he can ask, "Whose image and superscription is this?" For in the image of God made He man. ... Common men, for whom the assassin lurks, who need instruction how to behave in church, and whom others scorn and curse, these bear upon them an awful likeness; and even when they refuse tribute to their king, He can ask them, Whose is this image? (329)

In a poetical manner Chadwick turns the dominant interpretation around by regarding the saying from the perspective of "common men for whom the assassin lurks." The question "Whose is this image" does not refer to a coin but to a human being that stands on trial for refusing tribute. Even if "their king" is rather vague as a referent (a tyrant of some kind?), it is clear that Chadwick regards Jesus as defending those who refuse to submit to the authority of a ruler, diverging thereby significantly from the other commentators. In Chadwick's reading, people living under oppressive regimes—perhaps under a foreign colonial power—could very well refuse tribute to the master. Since human beings, for Chadwick, are marked with the image of the Divine, and are not supposed to be living in slavery, refusing the tax is a way of rendering to God what belongs to God.

Like a cat among the pigeons, Chadwick's reading represents a lonely voice among the scholarly interpretations of this crucial passage. The other commentators see the demands of Caesar and the demands of God as two aspects of the same obligation; refusing tribute is seen as a crime against God as well as against Caesar. As Meyer (1880–1881, 2:87, italics original) argues, Jesus is saying that "you ought to do *both things*, you ought to be subject to God *and* to Caesar as well; the one duty is *inseparable* from the other!" Similarly, Lange (1857, 317; 1865, 396): "Jesus makes the payment of tribute a duty of virtual obligation [*Pflicht des faktischen Rechts*]." Swete (1898, 260), likewise, sees it as "two spheres of duty" that are "at once distinct and reconcilable"; and Alford (1849, 159) concludes that "these weighty words, so much misunderstood, bind together, instead of separating, the political and religious duties of the followers of Christ."

More clearly than at any other Markan passage, therefore, these readings supplied European colonial discourse with a gospel-based ideology of might is right. If Jesus in no way considered the political dominance of Rome to infringe upon the sovereignty of God, how could European world dominance possibly be a problem? The assumption that Jesus' interest was limited to the inner lives of human beings—and not to foreign rule over nations—provided little impetus for nineteenth-century European Christians to criticize colonialism. On the contrary, most scholarly interpretations of this famous saying served only to reinforce the elevated European self-image.

The exceptional interpretation by Chadwick, however, calls for further scrutiny. As on the entry story, discussed in the previous chapter, Chadwick here offers an exceptional reading. He is the only commentator in this investigation who reads the tribute passage as a call to tax resistance under certain conditions. One may then ask what made such an interpretation possible. Of course, it can be taken solely as an expression of his originality as an author. But it is also possible to connect his reading to a discursive context in which such a position would be intelligible. Chadwick's Irish location—unique as compared to the other commentators—here becomes interesting.

Born in 1840 in Youghal (southern Ireland), receiving his degree at Trinity College, Dublin, in 1862, and serving as the dean of Armagh's Cathedral from 1886 to 1896, Chadwick was most certainly rooted in the Irish culture (Leslie 1911, 28–29). Such a location might well imply being caught up in a complex relation to British rule. In the seventeenth and eighteenth centuries, resistance against English colonial rule pervaded Irish history. During the nineteenth century, however, when Ireland was forced into a union with Great Britain, the resistance took on somewhat new forms. True, the nationalist struggle was mainly a Catholic phenomenon, and Chadwick was Anglican. But anti-British sentiments were probably widespread in his context; and, as keenly exemplified by Stewart Charles Parnell (1846–1891), Protestants in Ireland could play

10. AN IRISH CAT AMONG THE PIGEONS (12:13–17)   137

important roles in the nationalist movement as well.³ Also, in connection with the disestablishment of the Church of Ireland by the British prime minister Gladstone in 1869, some Protestant clergy joined the movement for Irish home rule.⁴ Even though Chadwick's stance in relation to the particular situation in Ireland is unknown as far as I am aware, the combination of being Irish and belonging to a Protestant church that had been disconnected from the British Crown somehow points toward a position in the middle of the colonizers and the colonized.⁵ From such a location, empire appeared quite differently as compared to the location of the other scholars.

In sum, the episode about the tribute question carries even starker political connotations than the previous one. The interpretations were consequently dealing directly with questions about imperial rule and antiimperial struggle. As the episode was raising the question about rebellion, the commentators generally took the answer given by Jesus as a clear no. This answer, in turn, was given a theological motivation by the distinction between a worldly and a spiritual sphere, by which the claims of Caesar are harmonized with the claims of God. The harmonization involved an interesting paradox. On the one hand, Jesus was seen as being indifferent to politics—foreign rule was seen as a nonissue for him. On the other hand, Jesus was seen as defending the principle of might is right, which of course is a highly political principle. These interpretations interplayed closely with a colonial self-understanding. If Jesus thought the imperial dominance of Rome was perfectly acceptable to God, how could European world dominance possibly be a problem?

There was one clear exception to this dominant strand of interpretation. Chadwick regarded the enigmatic answer by Jesus as a way to handle

---

3. As president of the Irish Land League (founded in 1879), Parnell was a charismatic leader in the struggle for improvements for Irish tenant farmers—a struggle that included boycotts, disobedience, and even imprisonment (Hopkinson 2009; Nilsson 2010; Harrison 2010).

4. Although a minority, McDowell (1975, 99) tells about the Protestant clergyman Joseph Galbraith, who joined the home rule movement after feeling resentment against the disestablishment.

5. See Leslie 1911, 28–29. McDowell (1975, 72–73) mentions Chadwick as one of the bishops with "considerable intellectual distinction" and a "forcible preacher" who was elected during the forty years following the disestablishment of the Church of Ireland. It is important to notice that the disestablishment meant that Chadwick was not royally appointed, either as dean of Armagh or, later, as bishop of Derry and Raphoe.

a very threatening situation and as combining the wisdom of the serpent with the innocence of the dove. In a poetical manner, and by referring to the creation narrative, Chadwick took the episode as legitimating resistance against an oppressive regime. This exceptional reading becomes intelligible in relation to Chadwick's Irish location in the middle of colonizer and colonized.

11
THE CENTURION BETWEEN EAST AND WEST (15:39)

As Mark's Gospel approaches its end, Jesus dies on the cross and a Roman centurion who is standing in front of him says: ἀληθῶς οὗτος ὁ ἄνθρωπος υἱὸς θεοῦ ἦν (usually translated, "Truly, this man was the Son of God"). As will be discussed in part 3, Markan scholars often regard this saying as climactic. For the first time in Mark's narrative, a human character realizes Jesus' identity as God's Son. Since the character is a Roman officer, the saying is crucial for the current investigation.

Since the Roman soldier in Christian tradition is often considered to represent imperial Christianity, such that "Rome become Christian and Christianity become Rome," to use Moore's turn of phrase (2008, 107), it will be interesting to see if this interpretive tradition is found in the commentaries. Moore (104) also argues that the centurion's saying in combination with the disciples' shortcomings establishes a hierarchical opposition in Mark of "Gentile insight over Jewish blindness." Although Moore connects this ideological critique of Mark to the anti-Semitism of Nazi Germany, it could also be related to the nineteenth-century orientalist Greek/Jew opposition discussed above. These are questions that will accompany us as we approach the commentaries.

"A BELIEVING GENTILE SOLDIER"

Coming closer to the end of this investigation, I have learned to see some tendencies in the Markan commentators. In order to find an interpretation that contrasts "Jewish blindness" with "Gentile insight," I would begin by consulting J. Lange, who, as we saw above (ch. 7), depicted the Jews as "unthankful children." Lange (1857, 428; 1865, 528) renders an interpretation of Matt 27:54 that highlights the non-Jewish identity of the soldier: "Mark mentions, as the single witness of Christ's majesty in dying, this captain, who along with the captain in Capernaum (Matt viii.), and the captain Cornelius at Caesarea (Acts x.), forms a triumvirate of believing Gentile [*heidnischer*] soldiers, in the evangelic and apostolic histories."

Although Lange connects the centurion's belief to his "Gentile" identity, he does not go so far as to contrast this with the unbelief of the Jew. To the contrary, since the primary point for Lange is to claim that the centurion was uttering a Christian confession, he (1857, 428; 1865, 528) actually downplays the non-Jewish identity of the centurion. Even if the centurion was *Heiden*, Lange says, his words must *not* be taken "in a heathen meaning" (*im heidnischen Sinne*). Arguing against the reading by Meyer that I will soon discuss, Lange suggests that the centurion represents the broader phenomenon of "heathen becoming Christians."

> Heathen became Christians [*Heiden werden Christen*], and their conversion was announced by their Christian confession. Yea, the centurion may easily have been acquainted with Jewish opinions; and so the accusation, Jesus had made Himself Messiah and God's Son, was understood by the captain rather in a Christian sense, of a divine-human holy being, than in a heathen sense of a demi-god. The heathen coloring is exceedingly natural; but the germ [*Kern*] is evidently not a superstitious conceit [*abergläubischer Wahn*], but a confession of faith [*Glaubenszeugnitz*]. (1857, 428; 1865, 528)

Lange here contends that the centurion's saying ought to be taken not as heathen superstition but as a Christian confession of faith. Considering what Lange has previously written, the way he makes this argument is noteworthy. As we saw in chapter 5, Lange regarded the Jewish conception of Son of God as theocratic rather than metaphysical. The proposition that the centurion would understand, from acquaintance with Jewish opinion, that Jesus was the Son of God "in a Christian sense" (a divine-human holy being) is therefore farfetched in relation to his previous arguments, and indicates an eagerness to present the centurion as a "believing Gentile soldier." Lange's reading represents a dominant tradition of interpretation. Early in Christian tradition, the centurion was given the name Longinus and, according to Chrysostom, was believed to have become a saint and a martyr.[1] Although Lange does not uphold the particulars of this tradition, he maintains its basic validity.

---

1. In Homily 88, Chrysostom states that "some say that there is also a martyrdom of this centurion, who after these things grew to manhood in the faith" (1888, 522).

11. THE CENTURION BETWEEN EAST AND WEST (15:39)

Lange's depiction of the centurion's piety stands in conformity with several nineteenth-century commentators.[2] As expressed by Maclear (1883, 204–5, italics original), the saying is often taken in a triumphal way: "And what an end? All that he [the centurion] had dimly believed of heroes and demigods is transfigured. This man was more. He was *the Son of God*." According to Maclear, Mark depicts the death of Jesus as more heroic and triumphant than other deaths of great men. Being impressed in awe and wonder, the centurion became "a believing Gentile soldier."

Especially noteworthy is F. Cook (1878, 186), who argues that since the centurion was "more cultivated" than the other soldiers, he was "moved … by all that he had seen of our Lord's demeanour, especially by his last words." For Cook, then, the centurion represents a civilized imperial culture that is moved by Jesus and that understands the true nature of his divine identity. That such a figure was crucial for nineteenth-century Europeans is indicated by the manner in which Cook develops his argument. The confession by the centurion "was apparently drawn forth by the word 'Father,' twice repeated at the beginning and end of the crucifixion" (Cook, 186). Cook is here referring to Luke 23:34, 46, where Jesus calls God his Father—sayings that are not found in Matthew or Mark.[3] Whereas Cook (lxix) has previously warned against harmonizing the different Gospel accounts, this interpretation presumes a high degree of Gospel harmony. As such, his interpretation seems strained. In other words, Cook, like Lange, appears to have been quite willing to make a rather farfetched argument (by his own standards) in order to present the Roman centurion as a converted Christian.

As evident from other commentaries, however, this dominant tradition of interpreting the centurion's saying began to be questioned.[4] Already in the first edition of his commentary, Meyer (1832, 165; cf. 1880–1881, 2:279) suggested that the saying by the Roman centurion ought to be taken in a *heathen* sense, that "Son of God," for him, meant "ein Halbgott, ein Heroe" (a demigod, a hero). Meyer refrains, however,

---

2. Alexander (1858, 428–29), F. Cook (1878, 186), Riddle (1879, 237), Maclear (1883, 204–5), and Chadwick (1887, 434) all regard the centurion's saying as a (proto-) Christian confession.

3. Further, in Luke, the centurion says, "This man was innocent" (Luke 23:47).

4. Meyer (1880–1881, 2:279), Gould (1896, 295), and Bruce (1897, 333, 451) all take the saying in a "heathen" sense. Plumptre (1897, 178), Swete (1909, 388–89), and Menzies (1901, 282) take an intermediate position.

from discussing the interpretive implications of his argument. Similarly, Gould (1896, 295) briefly states that the centurion saw Jesus as "a hero after the heathen conception," but does not discuss what this might imply. Bruce, however, offers a little more material to work with. Discussing the common interpretation, according to which the centurion's "Christian" confession was seen as motivated by the heroic manner of Jesus' death, Bruce (1897, 451) states:

> This was a natural impression on the centurion's part, and patristic interpreters endorse it as true and important. ... But it may be questioned whether this view is in accord either with fact or with sound theology. What of the φέρουσιν in ver. 22? And is there not something docetic in self-rescue from the pangs of the cross, instead of leaving the tragic experience to run its natural course?

Based on historical as well as theological reasons, Bruce questions the traditional interpretation of the saying. If Mark (15:21–22) depicts Jesus as being too weak to be able to carry his cross and even to walk,[5] it seems historically questionable that Jesus' death could have been perceived as heroic and triumphant. Theologically, he seems to argue, since the traditional interpretation neglects the bodily weakness of Jesus and represses the tragic aspects, it can be criticized for docetism. Here Bruce makes room for a certain critique of the colonial discourse and its image of the moved and converted Roman centurion.

But Bruce was a lonely voice, and one can question whether Meyer's suggestion altered the understanding of the centurion in any significant way. As seen in the commentary by Plumptre, the centurion can still be elevated even if his words are not treated as a Christian confession per se:

> We must interpret them [the centurion's words] from the stand-point of the centurion's knowledge, not from that of Christian faith, and to him the words "Son of God" would convey the idea of one who was God-like in those elements of character which are most divine—righteousness, and holiness, and love. (Plumptre 1897, 178)

In Plumptre's view, that which was "most divine" to the Roman centurion were the qualities of righteousness, holiness, and love—all of which just

---

5. Bruce takes φέρουσιν in v. 22 as meaning "carry."

happen to be central terms in Christian tradition. Although the centurion had no knowledge of Christian faith, Plumptre's interpretation transforms him into a person who truly understood the Divine, thereby making him a Christian *avant la lettre*. By means of his pious words, then, the centurion still becomes an elevated image of imperial Christianity.

An Oriental in Disguise

As we approach the end of part 2, I will give Swete the last word on this particular Markan passage. Considering that his commentary has guided us into this exegetical landscape and in that sense made possible these postcolonial inquiries, it is not altogether inappropriate to point out how Swete's interpretation in one sense went against the grain of colonial discourse.

With reference to Joachim Marquardt's work on Roman antiquity, Swete (1898, 353) sees the centurion and the other soldiers as being "of provincial birth—not Jews, since the Jews were exempt from the conscription." Rather, they were "Palestinians and foreigners, serving under Roman orders." Swete thus depicts the Roman centurion as an oriental—a character who stands curiously in between Latin Rome and the Semitic East. What, then, did such a character mean with the phrase "Son of God"? Alleging that the centurion "borrowed" the phrase "Son of God" from the Jewish priests, Swete (366) thinks that he "could scarcely have understood [it] even in the Messianic sense." Even less, Swete here implies, does the phrase express a Christian confession. For the manner in which Jesus died, Swete (366) says, "impressed the Roman officer with the sense of a presence of more than human greatness. The Roman in him felt the righteousness of the Sufferer, the Oriental … recognized his divinity."

Although Swete's interpretation certainly reproduces a colonial dichotomy of a religious East and a rational West, it also, to a certain extent, undermines it by representing the two categories as blended in one and the same character. Avoiding the designation "Gentile" and suggesting instead a hybrid Roman-oriental identity, Swete's interpretation of the centurion's saying threatens one of the pillars of European colonialism: the racialized border between East and West. Of course, this threat should not be overstated. After all, the centurion's confession also uncritically anticipates imperial Christianity. But even so, in a departure from the mainstream and its quest for pure origins, Swete's imaginative use of historical criticism construes Christianity in a way that could potentially undermine the colonial discourse.

To summarize, a strong tradition in the commentaries takes the famous saying as a humble expression of Christian faith by a believing Gentile soldier and thereby as a triumphant representation of the universalism of imperial Christianity. That several of the commentators seemed anxious to defend this interpretive tradition, making rather farfetched arguments to achieve this end, indicates that their interpretations were interplaying with the colonial discourse in which empire and Christianity axiomatically fit together hand in glove. Some commentators, however, took a more critical stance in relation to the traditional interpretation. Bruce questioned what he regarded as a docetic tendency and Swete depicted the centurion as a provincial whose hybrid Roman-oriental identity could undermine one of the key dichotomies of European colonialism.

12
Conclusion: Mark and European Colonialism

The aim of part 2 has been to analyze scholarly interpretations of Mark's Gospel in relation to nineteenth-century European colonial discourse. Delimiting the material to sixteen biblical commentaries written mainly in Great Britain and Germany, I juxtaposed Markan interpretations with texts from Protestant mission and the academic field of orientalism, both of which in various ways tended to construe elevated European self-understandings during this period.

I have already acknowledged the limited nature of this study. The analysis undertaken here has an explorative character and needs to be supplemented by further studies. There is a rather obvious problem involved in letting sixteen commentaries from mainly England and Germany represent how biblical interpretations of Mark were related to European colonialism. Obviously, Mark was interpreted in a variety of ways, and European identity is a highly complex phenomenon. I have therefore avoided discussing European subjectivity in the singular, and have attempted to look for complexities and contradictions.

In spite of its limited character, and the plurality of self-understandings that existed in Europe at the time, however, this study upholds the existence of pan-European colonial discourses, with which orientalism and Protestant mission interplayed, and with which the commentators interacted. Biblical scholarship itself was also to some extent a pan-European enterprise. Part 2 has shown that the commentators interplayed with the colonial discourse in various ways, often by fueling it, sometimes by resisting some aspect of it, and, more seldom, by undermining it.

Taken together, the ways in which the commentators helped form European colonial identities are connected to three interrelated binary divisions: Greek/Semitic, Jewish/heathen, and spiritual/worldly. In order to illustrate these main findings of part 2, the three diagrams in figure 8 represent these three interrelated dichotomies.

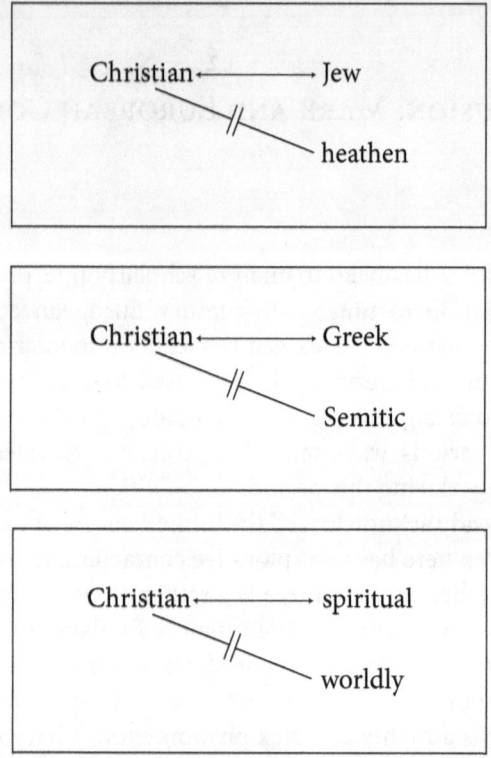

Figure 8. Three interrelated dichotomies (Jew/heathen, Greek/Semitic, spiritual/worldly), present in the Markan commentaries that helped construe Christian identity in nineteenth-century Europe. Whereas the two-way arrow indicates identification *with*, the broken line indicates identification *over against*.

The upper diagram exhibits how *Christian* was construed by identification with the *Jewish* over against the *heathen*. Here the commentators interacted closely with Protestant mission, where this dynamic was prominent. By interplaying with the orientalist field, moreover, the Markan commentators also construed *Christian* by identification with the *Greek* over against the *Semitic*, as represented in the middle diagram. The lower diagram, finally, displays how *Christian* was associated with the *spiritual* over against the *worldly*.

12. CONCLUSION: MARK AND EUROPEAN COLONIALISM 147

The tensions between these three dichotomies indicate the existence of considerable contradictions and anxieties in the colonial discourse and the subjectivities it formed. The strongest tension seems to be between the first two of these dichotomies. Making use of the essential and racialized notions of Greeks and Semites, the critically oriented scholars became part of the knowledge production of orientalist scholarship that imbued these categories with particular traits. Whereas the Greek was associated with progressiveness and metaphysical thinking, the Semitic was seen as stagnant and theocratic. Even though the Markan commentaries are rather brief (due to the genre), their constructions of these categories show a significant resemblance to works produced by famous orientalist scholars such as Renan. With the orientalist discourse, Europeans were offered a modern way of understanding themselves that partly challenged the older colonial discourse where ecclesial authorities were more or less unquestioned and where the Christian/heathen division was dominant. This modern development interpellated Europeans to a more "enlightened" colonial identity position that was formulated in partial opposition to an older ecclesial colonial identity. The Christian/heathen division, however, continued to play an important part, especially in the pietist strands of Protestant mission that tended to be critical of the increasing secularization of modernity.

The complex nature of the colonial heritage is perhaps seen most clearly in the interpretations of the Syrophoenician woman, who was seen on the one hand as representing the distant wretched heathen but on the other hand as representing the culturally elevated Greeks (and Europeans). The two dichotomies Christian/heathen and Greek/Semitic here interplayed in a contradictory way, making the woman an ambiguous figure. She belonged to the heathen "other" as well as to the Greek European "self" that had to share table with unthankful Semitic children.

The last of the three dichotomies, the one between spiritual and worldly, plays an important part in all commentaries and tended to involve both of the previously discussed dichotomies. Christianity was construed as a spiritual religion in opposition to the heathen as well as to the Semitic. Although the dichotomy was construed somewhat differently, it generally played a crucial role for the interpretation of the entry episode as well as for the episode about tax. With the exception of Chadwick's Irish-based oppositional interpretation, the spiritual/worldly division was mainly construed so as to downplay the political dimensions of the episodes. The kingship that was signaled by the entry story was interpreted as being of a spiritual kind and as involving no friction with imperial authorities. Similarly, the tribute question was generally taken as a harmonization between the claims of the emperor and the claims of God. The saying on tax by the Markan Jesus was generally seen as reflecting the doctrine of might is right and as endorsing imperial dominance—be it Roman or European. The prevalence of this interpretive tradition in the commentaries reflects the importance of the division between religion and politics for the development of secular modernity.

Since these three different ways of forming European colonial identities are somewhat conflicting, they are usually not acknowledged as being at work simultaneously. Said, for instance, argued that the orientalist discourse more or less superseded the Christian/heathen opposition. As this investigation has shown, however, such a description is inaccurate and could be seen as an expression of Hegelian secularism, which regards religion as an obsolete phase to be left behind in the name of liberal progress. It also gives a false impression of colonial discourse as free of tensions and anxieties. Since both Protestant mission and orientalism were important to European self-understandings, they are best understood in relation to each other.

In connection to the issues raised in the introduction about the truth claims of historical criticism, the scholarly interpretations studied here were to a great extent affected by their cultural and social locations in imperial Europe. Both critical and orthodox commentators affiliated themselves with social developments that were dominant at their time, sometimes by participating in them with a critical attitude, but more often by taking certain notions about Greeks, Jews, heathens, and so on for granted, sometimes even amplifying them. Designations such as disinterested and objective therefore hardly seem accurate. These designations, on the other hand, did play an important role for the self-understanding of critical scholars and were crucial for establishing biblical studies as an academic discipline, partly in opposition to Protestant orthodoxy. This is not to say, however, that this development is singularly emancipative and liberating. As this investigation has indicated, it could rather be understood as forming a new discourse that, like the older ecclesial discourse, was plagued with problems of Eurocentrism, colonialism, and misogyny. All scholars, even the most critical ones, were in different ways affected by the contemporary discourses and their truth effects. It therefore seems adequate to speak about a colonial heritage of biblical interpretation. With this heritage in mind, it is time to enter this study's main part: the investigation of Mark in its ancient imperial setting.

PART 3
MARK IN THE ROMAN EMPIRE

If there ever was a case of the construction of reality through text, such a case is provided by early Christianity.

—Averil Cameron (1991, 21)

13

MARK BEGINS TO CIRCULATE

To this point, I have refrained from engaging in the areas that are usually addressed in the trajectory of Mark and empire. Having studied how biblical scholars in nineteenth-century Europe interpreted Mark, however, I will now switch focus and embark on an exegetical journey myself. Whereas in part 2 I conducted a metacritical analysis of how the interpreters' contexts affected their interpretations of Mark, in part 3 I am focused on Mark's text itself at the time of its initial circulation, and how it related to Roman imperial discourse. In part 2 we saw how biblical scholarship, by generally standing in an uncritical and unreflective relation to European colonialism, often reproduced its hierarchical dichotomies and its harmonization of empire and gospel. Informed by these findings, in the present investigation of Mark I will explicitly engage in issues of empire and its effects on human subjectivity. Focusing on the same Markan episodes, then, in part 3 I apply various heuristic postcolonial concepts to Mark as a collective representation in order to study its interpellative force in relation to Roman imperial discourse. I begin part 3, however, with this chapter elucidating some preliminary features regarding Mark's Gospel: the discursive terrain in which it is primarily received, its date and provenance, its audience, and the significance of its written medium.

When describing the discursive terrain in which Mark's Gospel begins to circulate, one risks making stereotypical presumptions. As seen in part 2, nineteenth-century scholarship presumed the existence of a stable Greek and Jewish meaning of the phrase "Son of God." These problematic notions are being questioned in contemporary scholarship. In an influential work originally published in 1973, Martin Hengel (1981, 311–12) criticized what was then a standard division between Palestinian and Hellenistic Judaism, arguing instead that Judaism in Palestine was just as Hellenistic as the Judaism in the western Diaspora. All forms of Judaism were Hellenistic. Along the same lines, more recent scholarship questions and deconstructs the dichotomic divide between Judaism and Hellenism (Gerdmar 2001; Engberg-Pedersen 2001). But even so, as Gerdmar (2001, 18) points out, the Judaic/Hellenic divide is in some sense still axiomatic within biblical scholarship.[1] This could paradoxically be seen in Hengel (1986, 26–28), who, contrary to his previous position, contends that the earliest Christ followers' use of the title "Son of God" was largely independent of Hellenistic influence. The cult of the Roman emperors, according to Hengel, was a Hellenistic "official state religion ... at best a negative stimuli, not a model" (cf. A. Collins 2000, 86). Although Hengel's use of "Hellenistic" to designate the cult of Roman emperors differs significantly from that of nineteenth-century scholarship, it still fuels an essentialist dichotomy between a religious East and a secular West.[2]

Interestingly, Adela Yarbro Collins's (2000) treatment of the subject represents an increasing willingness among scholars to interpret the title "Son of God" in relation to Roman imperial culture.[3] Even if the current study is affiliated with this development, it is also important to acknowledge the problem of the very division discussed above. Although a range of different terms are used in contemporary scholarship—*Hellenistic*, *Greco-Roman*, *Gentile*, and even *pagan*—they often designate that which is not Jewish, and thereby risk reproducing a problematic dichotomic division.

Not only does such a division homogenize peoples in a problematic way, it also conceals the ancient imperial discourse that defined peoples as Roman subjects and that made Rome the center and the other lands

---

1. Gerdmar's (2001, 21–27) critical investigation of commentaries on 2 Peter and Jude confirms that the Judaism/Hellenism divide is still used in contemporary scholarship.

2. Hengel's (1986, 26–28) conclusion that the ruler cult's use of the phrase "Son of God" was "secular" and "official" implies that its use by the Christ followers in Palestine and Syria was religious. True, the East/West dichotomy is construed differently. Nineteenth-century scholars regarded Semitic religion as theocratic and therefore as flawed. Represented by Greek metaphysical beliefs, true religion for them was spiritual and could be separated from the political sphere. Hengel, on the other hand, here regards Semitic religion as a positive that stands in opposition to a religiously superficial West.

3. This willingness is also seen in works such as Bligh 1968; Kim 1998; and Hartman 2004, 30–31, 42–45. As seen in the previous chapter, this shift can be traced back to Deissmann.

and peoples the periphery. More particularly, it fails to acknowledge that Jews and Greeks shared the same fate of being subdued by the Romans. This lack in contemporary scholarship becomes evident from a postcolonial perspective.[4] Needless to say, how the categories Jews and Greeks are understood in relation to each other and in relation to Rome affects the reading of Mark's Gospel in its ancient setting.

In order to introduce this setting and map the discursive terrain in which Mark's Gospel begins to circulate, in the current chapter I first delineate Roman imperial discourse by briefly comparing how Greeks and Jews related to Roman rule and by pointing out the significance of the urban/rural divide. After a further discussion on the matters of date, authorship, provenance, and audience, I end the chapter by examining the significance of the medium by which the Gospel was circulated—written as compared to oral, and codex as compared to roll.

Roman Imperial Discourse

From the ancient authors (i.e., Livy, Dionysius of Halicarnassus, Plutarch, and Polybius) to the writers of today, there has been an immense production of literature about the Roman Empire.[5] As argued by D. J. Mattingly (1997, 7–9), contemporary scholarship on Rome is characterized by two tendencies: uncritical notions about the civilizing benefits of Roman rule, or a reversal of such preconceived notions. Based not least on the ancient historians themselves, the first perspective is predominant and implies a basically positive understanding of Roman rule as benevolent, peaceful, and orderly in its governance. Hence standard depictions of the transition from republic to empire typically present the battle of Actium in 28 B.C.E. and its victor Octavian/Augustus as having "given to the people of that world a century of undisturbed peace."[6] This predominating perspective also cherishes what it sees as the symbols of Roman prominence, such as the building of roads, sophisticated architecture, and the rule of law.

---

4. Samuel's (2007, 35–75) work on Mark pertinently addresses this problem.

5. In modern times, the most influential academic works on this subject are probably Gibbon 1776–1789 and Mommsen 1854–1856, for which he received the 1902 Nobel Prize in Literature.

6. M. Charlesworth 1936, 1.

The other, basically negative, tendency referred to by Mattingly conceives of Roman rule as having been oppressive, exploitative, and brutal. Although a minority perspective, Mattingly (1997, 10) points out nine works that focus on the "more unpleasant aspects of Roman domination and signs of resistance against Rome." A major work (not mentioned by Mattingly) that qualifies for this category is one by G. E. M. de Ste. Croix (1981). In his Marxist study of Rome's empire he explicitly takes a different perspective as compared to those who uncritically accept the benevolent intentions of the emperors. "By contrast," de Ste. Croix (374) states, "I am primarily concerned to show how imperial rule contributed to maintain a massive system of exploitation of the great majority by the upper classes." Even if scholars in this group would agree that Roman rule did imply a developed legal system, impressive cities, and better roads, they would also point out that Rome's impressive cities only benefited a small percentage of the population and that these projects were dependent on slavery as well as on a heavy taxing of the vast majority of peasant farmers.

Although Mattingly (1997, 9–10) is more critical of the first tendency, he criticizes both tendencies for assuming the existence of one widely shared social understanding of Roman rule in any given province. As an alternative, Mattingly calls for a multifaceted interpretation that is based (among other things) on a Foucaultian understanding of power, which overlaps with the postcolonial approach of this investigation. I need to point out, however, that since an encompassing nuanced analysis of Rome's empire far exceeds the limits of this project, the purpose of this description is only to enable an analysis of Mark's Gospel in this imperial setting. Since an empire such as Rome's was an immensely complex phenomenon, the space here allows merely a skeletal description; more detailed analyses of specific aspects of the imperial discourse will be conducted only when called for by the Markan narrative.

From a discourse-analytical perspective, then, one can describe the Roman Empire as a totality of textual/linguistic and extratextual/material dimensions. These dimensions, moreover, are all seen as signs, signifiers, or articulations that belong to a totality that creates meaning and permeates social reality, imbuing it with power. Although this is similar to a structuralist approach, I do not understand discourse as a fixed entity. Although signifiers might seem to be kept in a fixed place by closures, a discourse is also involved in constant rearticulations of signs and social practices that always imply a risk (or possibility) of destabilizing the fixed meaning. Further, as exemplified by Mark's (11:3) use of ὁ κύριος, there are also competing discourses in which signifiers receive a different meaning (see ch. 18).

Although discourse theory, unlike a traditional Marxist approach, poses no causative or determinative relation between a material base and a linguistic superstructure, discourse analysis can still benefit from Marxist-oriented studies such as those by Lenski (1966), Kautsky (1982), and de Ste. Croix (1981). The models developed by Lenski and Kautsky are established on the division of empires into different categories based upon the means of production.[7] Rome is then categorized as either an agrarian empire (Lenski 1966, 192–210) or a commercialized aristocratic empire (Kautsky 1982, 35–39). From this categorization it is possible to say something about the socioeconomic stratification of Roman imperial society. According to these scholars, the Roman Empire had a high degree of social stratification. While a small minority was affluent, most people were poor and lived under what contemporary Westerners would call dehumanizing conditions.

TRANSLATION OF MARXIST MODELS

Since the epistemological premises are different in discourse theory, however, some form of "translation" is necessary when these studies are used here (Jørgensen and Phillips 2002, 154–57). In discourse analysis it is not possible, for instance, to simply assume the existence of class consciousness from these theories of social stratification.[8] Rather, the purpose of discourse analysis is to find out what kind of social categorizations (class, gender, race, religion, etc.) were in use at a given time. The material aspects that, within a Marxist framework, are seen as being independent and determinant of the superstructure, are here seen as being intertwined with and inseparable from language and culture.

As these epistemological differences are acknowledged, in this investigation I can incorporate the results from Marxist-oriented studies. Roman imperial discourse can then be defined as including aspects that are mate-

---

7. These models are often referred to by biblical scholars who conduct empire critical studies; see Stegemann and Stegemann 1999, 7–14; Duling 2005; and Carter 2008, 52–55.

8. One should acknowledge that Lenski (1966, 74–79) is aware that his macromodel oversimplifies, and that the term *class* risks hiding the fact that "human populations are stratified in various ways."

rial as well as linguistic. The predominantly material dimensions—here seen as enmeshed in culture and textuality—include the means of production, the means of transportation, military technology, writing techniques, and so on. One can then state, in agreement with Lenski (1966, 192–210), that Rome was an agrarian empire. Although Kautsky (1982, 35–39) presses on the issue of commercialization, he generally agrees that agriculture was the fundamental means of production. As is generally agreed, the use of technology, such as the iron plow, animal power in agriculture, the wheel, and the sail, was important for the empire's magnitude.[9] The building of roads also warrants mention in this context.

Predominantly linguistic aspects, on the other hand, include oral speech and written texts that formed cultural and religious notions of the Romans as a superior people with a divine mandate to be rulers. These notions were already widespread during the period of the late republic. "Who," Cicero rhetorically asked, "once convinced that divinity does exist, can fail at the same time to be convinced that it is by its power that this great empire has been created, extended, and sustained?"[10] The naturalness of Roman rule was also established in the ethnographic literature during the imperial era. Here Rome was the self-evident center to which all other lands and peoples were compared, hence establishing a structure of center and periphery.[11] As exemplified by Tacitus's *Germania*, the far-

---

9. Crossan (1992, 43–46), the Stegemanns (1999, 9–10), Duling (2005, 53), and Carter (2008, 53) all refer to Lenski and Kautsky.

10. Cicero, *Har. resp.* 19. One could refer to many other texts from Greco-Roman antiquity as well. See, e.g., Virgil, *Aen.* 1.254–296, where Jupiter, "the Father of men and gods," grants the Romans "empire without end." See also the heading of the funerary inscription of the first Roman emperor: "Rerum gestarum divi Augusti orbem terrarum imperio populi Romani subiecit" (The achievements of the divine Augustus, by which he made the world subject to the rule of the Roman people; *Res Gestae Divi Augusti* 1.1). Other prominent examples include Livy, pref. 7; Aristides, *Roman Oratio* 104–105, 109; and Seneca, *Clem.* 1.1.2. See also Brunt 1978, who shows how divine will was an important ingredient in the self-understanding of the Romans.

11. Anticipating Montesquieu's theories of climate and human character, Pliny (*Nat.* 2.189–190) explains that whereas the Ethiopians are "burned by the heat" and the northern nations have "white frosty skins," the people that live "in the middle of the earth" have a healthy climate where "customs are gentle, senses clear, intellects fertile," and hence they are more fit than other people to have empires (*isdem imperia*). See also Pliny, *Nat.* 7.95–117; and Caesar, *Bell. gall.* 1.1; 4.1–5; 6.11–29.

ther away was a land from the center, the more barbaric and exotic were the depictions of its people.[12]

Roman imperial discourse also included aspects that have a combined linguistic and material character, such as military victories, public images, and symbols on monuments and coins, as well as buildings and architectures. Since the works of Simon Price (1984) and Paul Zanker (1988), these visual aspects have been generally acknowledged as crucial parts of Roman imperial discourse. Whereas literary representations were available only for the literate population, the images on coins and monuments had a much wider communicative effect. As highlighted by Davina Lopez (2008, 1–55) in her work on the apostle Paul, these visual images often used the category of gender to establish Roman superiority. Whereas Rome was often depicted as a self-controlled masculine body, the conquered nations (ἔθνη) were typically depicted as subordinate female bodies. A prominent example is the statue of Claudius subduing Britannia.[13] Such feminization, Lopez argues, established a range of interrelated hierarchical gendered dichotomies between ruler/ruled, masculine/feminine, self/other, active/passive, high/low, law/lawlessness, cosmos/chaos, and so on. A significant part of Roman imperial discourse, finally, included a wide range of social practices, such as the judicial system,[14] taxation,[15] enforced labor (ἀγγαρεία),[16] slavery,[17] patron-client relations,[18] the forming of colonies,[19]

---

12. For a treatment of ethnographic literature from a discourse-theoretical perspective, see Dench 2005, 37–92.

13. Other examples include the *Judea Capta* coin, the cuirassed statue of Augustus, and selected reliefs from the Sebasteion at Aphrodisias. What Lopez describes is a pattern of public visual representation, which means that there are also some exceptions—all female personifications are not derogatory in Roman imperial discourse. This is seen not least in the representations of Roma and Tellus (cf. Lopez 2008, 28).

14. For studies on Rome's judicial system, see Matthews 2010; MacMullen 2000, 10–13; de Ste. Croix 1981, 328–30; and Brunt 1978, 185–91.

15. I will discuss taxation in ch. 19.

16. I will discuss ἀγγαρεία in ch. 18.

17. Slavery in the Roman Empire has been investigated not least by Wiedemann 2005; Glancy 2002; Bradley 1994; and Alföldy 1985, 56–59.

18. For the significance of patron-client relations in Rome's empire, see Wallace-Hadrill 1989; Garnsey and Saller 1997; and Chow 1992, 38–82.

19. The Roman establishment of colonies, mostly for its veterans, has been studied by Broadhead 2007 and Salmon 1969.

the building and maintaining of cities,[20] festivals,[21] rituals,[22] triumphs,[23] and the activities of the Roman army.[24]

Taken together, Roman imperial discourse emerges as a powerful totality of discursive practices that includes religious, political, economic, and judicial aspects. In its striving to establish subordination without physical coercion, or what Gramsci called *hegemony*, the imperial discourse had an ability to synthesize itself with local traditions in various subtle ways, making Roman rule permeate peoples' lives to a high extent.

Internal Tensions

To this point, the description of imperial discourse leaves the impression of a fairly fixed hegemonic entity that simply ruled the peoples who lived around the Mediterranean Sea. Such an understanding, however, neglects the internal tensions of the imperial discourse as well as the responses and resistance to Roman rule. In order to address these tensions, I will further discuss Lopez's analysis.

Lopez helpfully highlights how issues of gender permeate Roman imperial discourse. At the same time, however, her approach seems to presume that imperial discourse was stable, fixed in meaning, and free from internal contradictions and tensions. In this sense, her study belongs to the second group of works criticized by Mattingly above, and can therefore be questioned. To this end, let us briefly look at Lopez's stimulating analysis of Tacitus's *Agricola*, where she discusses the speech by Calgacus, a military chieftain of the Britons,[25] who is quoted as saying:

---

20. See below, 164–66.
21. For the importance of festivals in the Roman Empire, see Price 1984, 53–77, 101–32; and Rives 2007, 105–17.
22. For the importance of rituals in the Roman Empire, see Price 1984, 234–48; and Frankfurter 2010.
23. Triumphant processions will be discussed in ch. 18.
24. The Roman army will be discussed in ch. 15.
25. The speech is delivered by Calgacus to the Britons just as they are about to enter the battlefield to fight against the Roman army. The purpose of the speech is to make the soldiers aware that they can avoid becoming the slaves of the Romans if they defeat them in this battle: "You have it in your power to perpetuate your sufferings forever or to avenge them today upon this field" (Tacitus, *Agr.* 32).

Rapists of the world [*raptores orbis*], now that earth fails their all-devastating hands, they probe even the sea; if their enemy has wealth, they have greed, if he is poor, they are ambitious; east nor west has satiated them; alone of all they covet with the same passion want as much as wealth. Robbery, butchery, rape [*rapere*] they falsely name *imperium*, they make deprivation, they call it peace.[26]

As Lopez points out, this is one of the most often quoted passages of Roman literature. The translation of *raptores* as "rapists" and *rapere* as "rape" is debatable, but is not of primary concern here.[27] Lopez reads the text as supporting her proposition that Roman conquest was perceived as sexual violence and slavery from the perspective of the subdued, which strengthens her apprehension of Roman imperial discourse as a unified and coherent quest for world domination. What she neglects, however, is the discursive location of the quotation above. Even if it is a military leader from the Britons who expresses this resentful critique of Roman domination, one should not forget that the quote derives from a work by Tacitus, who was, after all, a Roman aristocrat. As such, it hardly represents the perspective of the enslaved, as Lopez contends, but could rather be taken as pointing at an inherent tension and insecurity of the imperial discourse itself. By penning the long, reviling speech of Calgacus, Tacitus seems to express admiration for the foreigner's free spirit and desire for independence. Rather than representing the subdued, it seems to represent a subtle ambivalence toward the very discourse that placed him and his Roman aristocratic colleagues "on top." Therefore, without denying the force of imperial representations, I also allege an inherent instability and insecurity of the imperial discourse.

Responses to Roman Rule: Greeks and Jews

A second aspect that my description of Roman imperial discourse risks neglecting concerns the responses to Roman expansion. Even if the Roman Empire was extremely powerful, it could not silence all opposition. There

---

26. Tacitus, *Agr.* 30; Lopez's (2008, 109) translation; Lopez continues with a longer quote.

27. Lopez (2008, 109) defends this translation, successfully, in my view, by referring to the sexually charged images used in Roman visual representation of the conquered nations as female bodies.

always existed competing discourses that involved other kinds of articulations and ways of understanding the natural, the divine, the truth, and how people should relate to one another. Peoples (and groups within peoples) that were subdued by Rome took different positions, ranging from loyalty and acceptance via negotiations and diplomacy to anti-Roman resistance and violent rebellion. These groups and their ways of responding to and dealing with Roman authority varied in terms of both space and time, which highlights the slippery nature of the relation between dominant and subdued. In what follows I will briefly inquire into the particular dynamics of Greeks and Jews (respectively) under Roman rule. As I will argue, the Greek-Roman as well as the Jewish-Roman relation included opposition and antagonism as well as hybridity and mimicry.

The Roman expansion into the Greek east during the middle republic (the third and second centuries B.C.E.) was accompanied by a mutual antagonism. In Roman imperial discourse the Greeks were often depicted as effeminate, having been subdued by the masculine Romans (C. Edwards 1993, 92–97). This was exemplified during the first century B.C.E. by Sallust (*Bell. Cat.* 11.5), who describes how the warlike spirit of the Roman soldiers was easily softened by the charms and pleasures of Asia. The Greek life of pleasures was here depicted as soft (*mollis*) and was often contrasted with Roman military virtue. Cicero (*Quint. fratr.* 1.16) similarly warned against what he regarded as the deceitful (*fallaces*) and slippery (*leves*) attitude of Greeks and Asiatics.

In native Greek discourse, conversely, the Roman expansion provoked resistance. Even during the first century B.C.E., this is seen in the efforts of Mithridates VI. Along these lines, as is indicated by Livy (9.16.19–19.17), Greek writers contended that Rome would have been no match for Alexander the Great (Crawford 1978, 193). Exemplified by Chariton's novel *Chaereas and Callirhoe* from the first century B.C.E., the Greek heritage was celebrated and the Roman presence pushed to the margins.[28] Rome's power also ignited what is known as the Second Sophistic during the first century C.E., entailing a revival of Greek literature and a reimagination of what it meant to be Greek.[29] Hence there was a competition or struggle

---

28. As Samuel (2007, 35–51) argued, *Chaereas and Callirhoe* has many features that qualify it as a novelistic response from a subjected community, and hence as an ancient version of *The Empire Writes Back*.

29. Thurman 2007, 188–91. Similarly, Crawford (1978, 196–197) has pointed out the imperviousness of the Greek world to Roman customs.

between the native and the imperial discourses over the meaning of *Greek* and over the significance of Roman rule.

But even if there was antagonism, the Roman imperial and native Greek discourses were also involved in far-reaching mutual processes of ambivalence, mimicry, and hybridity (Thurman 2007, 188–92; Samuel 2007, 35–62). Parallel to the feminization of the Greeks in Roman discourse there is also what Catharine Edwards (1993, 95) calls "a cultural inferiority complex" connected not least to Greek philosophy and literature. For many educated Romans, familiarity with Greek literature, art, and customs was a source of prestige. In Greek discourse, in turn, there was also a tendency to valorize the masculinity of the Romans. Interestingly enough, this valorizing could entail an identification of what was *Roman* as *Greek*.

Writing his Roman history for Greek-speaking people, Dionysius of Halicarnassus set out to prove "that they [the Romans] were Greek" (*Ant. rom.* 1.5.1) and that their superior strength made their domination natural. The Romans were simply better at being Greeks than the Greeks themselves (cf. Lopez 2008, 58–59). As Thurman (2007, 189) argues, Greek identity was hybridized to the effect that Greek identity was somewhat disconnected from Greece as a geographic designation. This hybridization, however, did not imply a total collapse of differences between Greek and Roman (as the terms *Greco-Roman*, *Gentile*, and *pagan* indicate). As mentioned previously, such descriptions hide the complex power relations between the two.

As for the Jews, the situation is both similar to and different from the Greeks. Being conquered by the Romans two hundred years later, their time as a subdued nation is significantly shorter by comparison. Other differences include the geographic distance, the size of the populations, and the larger cultural and linguistic aspects. Also, whereas the Greeks had an imperial history of their own, the Jews had more experiences of being subjects to or having to deal with different empires from one time to another. This may have created differences between how Greek and Jewish discourses related to Roman power.

But even so, there are significant similarities. Thus the Jewish-Roman relation also entailed a mirrored antagonism. Most famously, as seen in the triumph of the Flavians after the Jewish War in 66–70 C.E., the Jews were depicted as a subdued and feminized nation in Roman imperial discourse. A derogatory attitude toward the Jews had been already expressed by Cicero (*Flac.* 67), who regarded the Jewish religion as a "barbaric superstition."[30] There are many examples in Roman discourse of Jews being ridiculed (e.g., Juvenal, *Sat.* 14.96–106). Reversely, expressed most clearly in the Jewish War, the Diaspora rebellion, and the Bar Kokhba revolt, there was an oppositional Jewish discourse. Applying the term גוי, Jews categorized the Romans as foreigners in a hostile sense.[31] The hostile attitude is evident in 4 Ezra 11:40–45, where Roman rule is described in terms of oppression and terror. Similarly, the *War Rule* from the Qumran community refers to Rome with the code term *Kittim* and depicts it as the army of Satan (1QM 1).[32] In a similar way, the Sibylline Oracles (5:162–173) denounces Rome as effeminate, unjust, unclean, murderous, impious, and doomed to end up in the nether regions of Hades. Later rabbinic sources (Gen. Rab. 65:1; Lev. Rab. 13:5) also give voice to the pollutant aspect of Roman rule and represent the Roman Empire as a pig or swine.

Side by side with the antagonistic attitudes, moreover, the Jewish-Roman relation also contained a complex of unsettled attitudes, including awe, loyalty, mimicry, and ambivalence. Even if the level of hybridization was probably lower as compared to the Greek-Roman relation, the complexity was considerable. Beginning with the Roman discourse on Jews, there was a grudging acceptance and respect for the Jewish religion for its ancient origin.[33] Hence Jewish worship earned admiration and attracted proselytes in Roman society.[34] Moreover, historians such as Tacitus often

---

30. Cicero here specifically defends the decision by Flaccus to prohibit Jews living in Asia to send money to the Jerusalem temple. But as Schäfer (1997, 181) notes, the designation *barbara superstitio* refers to the Jewish people in general, whom Cicero regards as standing in opposition to Roman values.

31. In Jewish history, the term גוי has changed meaning. Designating *nations* during the monarchy, it also acquired a more negative meaning (*heathen*) during the Roman era (M. Smith 1999, 192–93). As Stanley (1996, 105–6) contends, Jewish discourse did not relate to all foreign people in a similar way. The point here is to note the hostility with which Rome was sometimes treated.

32. J. Collins 1998, 168. See also Brooke 1991, who in his analysis of the Qumran pesharim argues that the Romans there are depicted as militarily mighty and economically threatening, but ultimately as no match for the God of Israel.

33. This comes to the fore in Tacitus's ethnographic account of the Jews (*Hist.* 5.2-13). Even if their religion is described as the opposite of and even "abhorred" (*incesta*) by the Romans (5.4), some of their rites are actually "sanctioned by their antiquity" (*antiquitate defenduntur*, 5.5). For treatments on the Jews in Roman discourse, see Stern 1974–1984; and Beard et al. 1998, 2:273–76, 320–29.

34. Schäfer 1997, 192–95. Also, as showed by Stern (1974–1984, 1:207–12), Varro

regarded this admiration as a threat. Roman attitudes toward Judaism therefore seem to include a large portion of ambivalence.

Jewish attitudes, in turn, were not as exceptional as is often upheld (cf. Goodman 1991). As with other peoples subdued by Rome, there was a spectrum of rather contradictory Jewish attitudes. As represented in Josephus's depiction of his sudden switching of sides (*J.W.* 3.340–408), the fluctuations between hostility and admiration could be rather intense. Having played a leading role in the anti-Roman rebellion, Josephus describes how he came face-to-face with the superior military power of Rome in Jotapata. In what is portrayed as a miracle, he presents himself as a messenger of the God of Israel who foretells of Vespasian's accession as emperor. As McLaren (2005) has argued, however, this sudden change is not to be taken as a complete acceptance of Roman rule. According to McLaren (48), a veiled criticism of Flavian omnipotence runs through the writings of Josephus. Springing from a position of imperial dependency, the writings of Josephus represent a subtle colonial ambivalence.[35]

Considering the importance of the communities of Diaspora Jews who were living in cities around the Mediterranean, the complexity of the Jewish-Roman relation becomes even more pertinent. Seen not least in the decision of Claudius to expel the Jews from Rome in the 40s, these communities were often dependent on Roman authorities for their protection, which affected the relation. An illustration of ambivalent Jewish attitudes toward Rome during the reign of Hadrian is found in a conversation among three Jewish rabbis:

> R. Judah, R. Jose, and R. Simeon were sitting. … R. Judah commenced [the discussion] by observing: "How fine are the works of this people! They have made streets, they have built bridges, they have erected baths." R. Jose was silent. R. Simeon b. Yoḥai answered and said: "All what they made they made for themselves; they built market-places, to set harlots in them; baths, to rejuvenate themselves; bridges, to levy tolls for them."[36]

---

identified the Jewish God with Jupiter. He therefore regarded Jewish worship as an example of pure worship that resembled the original cult of old Rome.

35. The ambivalence of Josephus has also been noted by P. Davies 1991, 173–74, who points out the cryptic way in which Josephus (*Ant.* 10.210) renders the accounts from Dan 2 about the destruction of the four world empires and the erection of God's empire.

36. B. Shabbat 33b; cf. b. 'Abodah Zarah 2b. Although the Babylonian Talmud was not completed until considerably later, N. de Lange (1978, 267–68) regards this

Reflecting different Jewish attitudes vis-à-vis Rome, the rabbis debate how to interpret four features of Roman imperial discourse (streets, marketplaces, baths, and bridges). As the three rabbis have one sentence each in this short story, a chiasmic structure is established that makes the silence of Rabbi Jose a central and curious feature. Placed in between the two oppositional understandings of attraction and repulsion, the silent Rabbi Jose serves as an apt representation of the ambivalence with which Jewish discourse related to the Roman Empire.

The City/Rural Division

Having outlined Roman imperial discourse and its complex relations to Jews and Greeks, I will now address a specific aspect that is of special importance to how this study perceives of Mark's audience: the relation between cities and countryside.

The importance of the cities for Roman domination has been a recurrent theme among scholars of the Roman Empire.[37] As stated by de Ste. Croix (1981, 10), "Greco-Roman civilization was essentially urban, a civilisation of cities." In the cities, Roman domination was visible in architecture, monuments, and inscriptions, and it was also the place of provincial administrations. Further, every Hellenistic city (πόλις) had its countryside (χώρα) from which it extracted taxes, rents, and dues, most of which were transferred to the central administration in Rome (Corbier 1991, 235). As many have pointed out, the specific definition of a city in Greco-Roman antiquity is a difficult matter.[38] Even so, it is still possible to distinguish a pattern in the Roman Empire of a city (πόλις) with an urban culture and a peasant countryside (χώρα). This pattern can be seen in the Markan episode about the Gerasene demoniac, which takes place in the χώρα of the Hellenistic city of Gerasa (5:1). After the event (5:14), the

---

conversation as accurately preserved from the time of Hadrian's reign and hence as bearing "the stamp of authenticity."

37. It is a key issue for Rostovtzeff 1957, 1:130–352; and de Ste. Croix 1981, 9–19. For a recent treatment, see Edmondson 2010.

38. This is seen when Pausanias 10.4.1, in the mid or late second century C.E., questioned whether Panopaeus in Phocis in central Greece could be called "a city" when it "possess[es] no government offices, no gymnasium, no theatre, no marketplace, no water descending to a fountain, but live in bare shelters just like mountain cabins, right on a ravine." A similar questioning could probably have been made in relation to Luke 1:26 and Matt 2:23, where Nazareth is called a "city."

swineherds run away to tell about what had happened in the city (πόλις) and in the countryside (χώρα). As Corbier (212) points out, this pattern was generally not imposed by the Romans but had developed during the classical period. But since Roman rule entailed an increase of taxation, it also tended to polarize the relation between city and countryside (234; de Ste. Croix 1981, 10–11). Although the relation between a city and its countryside varied in different parts of the empire, Corbier (1991, 212) still contends that "Rome helped to spread a 'town-and-territory' model of organization of space and of social life." Further, this pattern was also applied by the ancient authors as a metaphor for the empire as a whole: "What a city is to its boundaries and its territories, so this city is to the whole inhabited world, as if it had been designated its common town."[39] Referring to the city of Rome both as πόλις and as ἀρχή, Aristides (*Roman Oration* 58–71) regards the whole world as the city's χώρα (cf. Griffin 1991). This romantic imagery of the imperial discourse, however, was presumably contested by various local antagonistic discourses (cf. de Ste. Croix 1981, 11).

The division between πόλις and χώρα also often implied a difference in language and literacy. Whereas peasants typically spoke vernacular languages and were less familiar with the written word, urban dwellers could often speak Koine Greek and were more accustomed to urban literary culture. As Harris (1989, 333–37) pointed out, Roman power was practically as well as psychosocially connected to the written word (cf. Draper 2004b, 1). Practically, the emperor could communicate to the provinces via letters, instructing the legions and promulgating decrees. But literacy was also a prominent aspect of the aristocratic identity; the ability to read was important for the urban elite since it enabled an identification over against the uneducated rustics. As Harris (333) states, "access to the rhetorical education which was the mark of the elite was very restricted indeed." Similarly, Botha (1992, 205) has noted that literature was "an important facet of the life of an aristocrat." The significance of the written medium in Roman imperial discourse will be important to consider as we continue by locating the audience of Mark's written Gospel.

Further, as Rostovtzeff (1957, 1:192) states, what we know about the ancient Roman Empire is mainly its city life. This is particularly true of the literary sources, which indicate a general tendency among the urban

---

39. Aelius Aristides, *Roman Oration* 61. Cf. Dio Cassius 52.19.6.

population to identify themselves in opposition to the rural population.[40] According to Rostovtzeff (192), "for him [the man who lived in the city] the γεωργός or *paganus* was an inferior being, half civilized or uncivilized." Although we might expect to find a corresponding reversed and inverted identification among the rural people against the urban, no sources verify such an expectation.[41]

I would argue that the city/rural division is significant for our understanding of the development of the Christ followers as a collective. Initially based in rural Galilee, within a generation the Jesus movement had significantly transformed into an urban enterprise, most clearly represented in the Pauline letters. As stated by de Ste. Croix (1981, 433), this transition "cannot be understood by the historian … unless it is seen as the transfer of a whole system of ideas from the world of the *chōra* to that of the *polis*." The significant impact that this process of transformation had on the group's self-understanding has also been acknowledged in biblical studies, most notably by Wayne Meeks (1983, 10–11), who, in his important study of the first urban Christians, contends that the transition from a rural to an urban setting was of decisive significance for the development of the Christ followers as a group, since it implied the crossing of a "fundamental division in the society of the Roman Empire."

Locating Mark and Its Audience

From this broad and general mapping of Roman imperial discourse, let us now approach the more specific issue of Mark's provenance and audience. Two questions are then of immediate interest: (1) Is Mark's audience along the same lines as Greeks or Jews—as a group subdued by the Romans? (2) Are they part of or separate from Roman imperial discourse? As for the first question, Mark's audience, unlike the Jews and the Greeks, lacked a particular territory, and hence was not, in the same sense, a people or a nation (ἔθνος) subdued by Rome. On the other hand, they did identify the God of a subdued nation as their God, which placed them in a subordinate and suspect position in imperial discourse. Regarding the second question, I will here argue that Mark's audience was primarily located in urban

---

40. Pliny, *Nat.* 25.16; Plutarch, *Arist.* 7.5; Quintilian, *Inst.* 2.21.16; 5.

41. An exception here is, of course, the Gospel stories that do represent rural people. For an apprehension of the Gospels from this perspective, see de Ste. Croix 1981, 427–33; and Rohrbaugh 1993.

communities. As such, they were exposed to Roman imperial discourse on a daily basis. The extent to which they were actually interpellated by this discourse, however, is difficult to tell. Judging from Paul's letter to the Christ followers in Rome, there seems to have been both resistance (Rom 12:1–2) and accommodation (13:1–7). Further, their faith in Jesus of Nazareth as Christ, God's Son, and Lord, partly placed them in opposition to imperial discourse. Mark's audience, I therefore initially presume, is located on the fringes of Roman imperial discourse.

Date, Author, and Place

The task in this subsection is to describe more specifically how I envision Mark's provenance in this study. To begin with, I will briefly examine Mark's date, authorship, and place of writing.

Regarding the date, most scholars agree that the eschatological discourse in Mark 13 indicates a proximity to the war in Jerusalem in 66–74 C.E.[42] The main debate concerns whether Mark was written shortly before or shortly after the destruction of the temple in 70.[43] Since it seems unnecessary for my purposes to determine the exact date, I side with Marcus (2000, 37–39) and leave it as an unresolved issue. What is important for my understanding of Mark's Gospel, however, is the crisis that the war entailed for the Christ followers. In this sense, a dating around 70 is important. Further, since I am studying Mark as a representation of an identity position, my primary interest lies in the initial circulation of the text among the Christ-believing communities. Since the circulation would have taken several months, it seems reasonable to assume that Jerusalem had been already destroyed when Mark's Gospel was reaching its audi-

---

42. There are also minority voices such as Crossley 2004, who argues that Mark was written sometime between the mid-30s and the mid-40s. Since Mark presents Jesus as law abiding, it must have been written before these issues became controversial. As several reviewers pointed out, however, his argument has serious problems (Harrington 2005; Harrison 2005; Maloney 2005; Talbert 2006; Telford 2007). As is evident not least from Crossley's strained interpretation of the editorial comment in Mark 7:19, the use of legal issues as the only factor for determining the date is problematic.

43. For scholars who date Mark before 70 C.E., see Hengel 1985, 7–28; and A. Collins 2007, 11–14. Scholars who date Mark after 70 include Theissen 1992, 258–62; Incigneri 2003, 116–55; Head 2004; and Kloppenborg 2005.

ence.⁴⁴ In other words, this reading postulates that Jerusalem had fallen by the time of delivery.

Since the questions of provenance and authorship are interrelated, I will treat them together. There are two main suggestions concerning where Mark was written: either Rome, which is the traditional view, or a rural setting somewhere in the east (e.g., Galilee or Syria). Proponents of a Roman provenance often refer to external evidence, contending that someone named Mark had written the Gospel from the recollections of Peter's memories.⁴⁵ The earliest external source is the following much-discussed statement by Papias, bishop of Hierapolis: "The Presbyter used to say this, 'Mark became Peter's interpreter and wrote accurately all that he remembered.'"⁴⁶ Although Papias does not explicitly mention Rome, the greeting at the end of 1 Peter (5:12–13) connects both Peter and Mark to Rome. Even if there are other forms of external evidence, I will here focus on this statement by Papias.⁴⁷

Even if Papias's statement has been dismissed as unreliable due to its alleged apologetic tone (e.g., Telford 1995, 16–18) and/or its incompatibility with the findings of form criticism (e.g., Kümmel 1975, 95–96), there are reasons to follow scholars who argue for the statement's trustworthiness (Hengel 1985, 1–6, 47–53; 2000, 66–68, 78–89; Byrskog 2000, 272–97). As indicated in Papias's statement, the information rendered was given to him by the presbyter John, who died not long after 100 C.E.⁴⁸ As such, the connection between Peter and Mark that Papias provides goes back as early as the last decades of the first century. Rather than being invented on the basis of 1 Peter (as some suggest), therefore, the Papias note appears to be a synchronous and reciprocal confirmation of a tra-

---

44. For estimations of travel times in the Roman Empire, see Thompson 1998, 60–65. In addition to travel time, one also has to account for the time-consuming work of copying the manuscripts.

45. For proponents of a Roman provenance, see Hengel 1985, 28–30; Gundry 1993, 1026–45; van Iersel 1998, 31–41; Incigneri 2003, 59–115; and Head 2004.

46. Cited in Eusebius, *Hist. eccl.* 3.39.15.

47. The anti-Marcionite Gospel prologue to Mark (Regul 1969, 29) and Irenaeus (*Haer.* 3.1.1) indicate Rome as Mark's provenance. Clement states it explicitly (Eusebius, *Hist. eccl.* 6.14.5–7).

48. As Hengel (1985, 47, 150) and Byrskog (2000, 277–78) point out, this part of Papias's statement is often overlooked or dealt with in an unreasonably dismissive manner.

dition that connects Mark the Evangelist and Peter.[49] In response to the findings of form criticism, Hengel points out that Papias's note refers not to eyewitness testimony, but rather to what Mark *remembered* of Peter's stories. Further, Papias's professed apologetic tone has been questioned by Byrskog (2000, 272–73), who points out that even if Papias was not writing in a theological vacuum, his specific purpose for writing remains largely unknown.

Whereas external evidence seems to favor Rome, the internal evidence is more contested. Some scholars take it as indicating a rural eastern origin.[50] Even if the Latinisms speak in favor of a Roman provenance, the parables in Mark all come from the agrarian world, which, according to Theissen (1992, 238), indicates a rural setting. As Theissen (237–38) also points out, Mark's designation of the little Galilean lake as "sea" (θάλασσα) fits poorly in the cosmopolitan city of Rome, where "sea" would designate the Mediterranean. As will be seen below, however, this use of θάλασσα can also comply with a Roman provenance. Further, since the production of written texts would require considerable skills and financial resources (Gamble 1995, 42–108), it was a largely urban phenomenon, which makes the proposition of a rural origin less likely. Even if the content of Mark's narrative clearly has a rural flavor, it seems unlikely that the act of writing was carried out in a rural setting or that it was primarily directed to a rural audience. The written medium was largely utilized in urban settlements (Ong 1977, 86), and a written Gospel therefore indicates an urban rather than a rural setting (cf. Shiner 2003, 12).

Of course, we can never be sure about who wrote Mark's Gospel or where it was originally written. Even Byrskog (2000, 280) admits that agnosticism in relation to the Papias note is a possibility. But rather than leaving the question open, as do several Markan commentators (Guelich 1989, xxix–xxxi; Hooker 1991, 5–8; A. Collins 2007, 96–102), I am here following the dictum provided by Byrskog (2000, 280) that "an ancient

---

49. Mark the Evangelist is probably the same person as the John Mark referred to in Acts (12:12, 25; 13:5, 13; 15:37, 39) and the Mark referred to in Col 4:10; 2 Tim 4:11; Phlm 24. Although, as Byrskog (2000, 279–80) admits, these passages mostly connect Mark to his cousin Barnabas and Paul, they also indicate that a connection exists between Mark and Peter, and that Mark may have been assisting Peter in the same manner as he had assisted Paul and Barnabas.

50. For proponents of an eastern provenance, see Theissen 1992, 236–49; Myers 1988, 40–42; Waetjen 1989, 4–26; R. Horsley 2001, 30; and Marcus 1992, 25–37.

author is correct until proven otherwise." Mark's Gospel, I therefore presume, was probably written in Rome and was connected to Peter, who spent the last portion of his life there before being executed under Nero.[51]

Since identifying Rome as the location of Mark's provenance is at odds with what has become a standard position in empire-critical biblical scholarship, a clarification is needed.[52] R. Horsley (2001, 30) has vigorously argued that locating Mark's Gospel in Rome is an expression of how church tradition has reduced Mark's anti-Roman story to an "incidental stage-setting for the passion and crucifixion of Christ."[53] Horsley's critique is intelligible in relation to a discipline that has tended to be tone-deaf to political issues. The difference between a rural eastern and an urban Roman location is surely sociopolitically significant. In Horsley's reading, moreover, the rural location is connected to a clear-cut opposition to urban-based Roman imperialism.

But as indicated by the postcolonial perspective applied here, there are other ways to conduct empire-critical readings of Mark. Accordingly, the early traditions that connect Mark's Gospel with Peter and Rome need not be taken as a fondness for the imperial center. As indicated by the use of "Babylon" to designate Rome (1 Pet 5:13), the connection to Peter and the Roman provenance implies a subversive message (cf. Watson 1992). As an uneducated, Jewish, probably illiterate (Acts 4:13), Galilean fisherman, Peter represents a suspect and marginal position in Roman imperial discourse. As Mark's Gospel was circulating from Rome, with a connection to this leading apostle who had been a Jesus follower from the very beginning in rural Galilee, and who had been recently executed by Nero, its message was far from politically innocuous. Although the circulation of Mark from center to periphery imitates an imperial universality, the connection to Peter also establishes a sense of almost the same *but not quite* that undermines imperial authority.

---

51. John 21:18–19 (cf. 13:36) attests to the fact that Peter was executed, and confirmation that this execution took place in Rome under Nero can be found in 1 Clem. 5:4; Acts Pet. 37:8; Tertullian, *Scorp.* 15; Eusebius, *Hist. eccl.* 3.1.

52. Myers (1988, 40–42), Waetjen (1989, 4–26), and R. Horsley (2001, 30) all locate Mark in the rural east.

53. See also Myers 1988, 468, who criticizes Belo (1981) for being inconsistent when he places Mark in Rome. Cf. Incigneri 2003, 103–5.

For Whom?

Having argued that Mark's Gospel was written around the year 70 in Rome, I will now approach the issue of Mark's audience. Initiated by Richard Bauckham (1998b), and generally referred to as the Gospel community debate, a group of scholars have questioned the redaction-critical convention of reconstructing a community for each of the Gospels and suggests instead that the Gospels were written with a wider audience in mind.[54] Of particular interest relative to this study is Dwight Peterson's (2000) survey of the works by Kelber (1979), Myers (1988), and Kee (1983), all of which reconstruct a Markan community behind Mark's Gospel. Analyzing the interpretive strategy of these works, Peterson points out that in all cases the reconstructed Markan communities are used as a means of attaining interpretive control. Since such a community can only be reconstructed from the Gospel text itself, however, its use as an interpretive device fails to provide any firm ground, and the argument thus becomes "viciously circular" (Peterson 2000, 52–55, 107). Taking this criticism into account entails a shift in the understanding of Mark's origin. Even if Mark was written at a particular place, its primary audience was not limited to those who were living there. And more importantly, the meaning of Mark's text cannot be determined from the situation of a particular community. Since the audience is wide in scope, the meaning of the text similarly widens.[55] The Gospels are then seen as more open texts (Bauckham 1998a, 48) with gaps that different reading communities fill with somewhat different meaning.

The Gospel community debate intersects significantly with the purpose of part 3. If Mark was written with the purpose of being circulated more widely among communities of Christ followers in the Roman Empire, its status as a collective representation is strengthened. As we will see, such an apprehension of the Gospel audience entails a more diverse historical context and a more broadly conducted analysis. Since we may

---

54. Independent of Bauckham, Tolbert (1989, 303–4) and Hengel (2000, 106–15) have also argued that the Gospels were written for a wider readership. The debate has been summarized by Klink 2004, 2010a, 2010b. Bauckham (2010) has recently defended his thesis against Mitchell's (2005) critique regarding the patristic evidence.

55. Contra Incigneri 2003, 1–3, who describes the meaning by using the metaphor of biological conception. The author (father) and the community (mother) are the "genes" of the text that presumably generates the true meaning of Mark's text.

presume that the audience lived in different parts of the empire, moreover, the specific context in Rome becomes in one sense less important.

That is not to say, however, that Mark's Roman origin becomes unimportant. To the contrary, if Mark was written in Rome and if its author was affiliated with Peter, one can assume that this information was also communicated as the Gospel was being delivered in the communities. Here the distinction made by Foucault (1984) between an author's *function* and an *intention* becomes relevant. I would argue, then, that the connections between the author (Mark), Peter, and Rome—conveyed subversively with reference to Babylon (cf. 1 Pet 5:13)—had an important function as Mark's Gospel was being circulated. Granting that written communication from the imperial center in the form of imperial decrees and so on would be a common phenomenon in the cities where Mark's audience was located, the very distribution of Mark from the same center resembles an imperial structure of center and peripheries. But the simultaneous connection to a leading executed Galilean apostle makes the resemblance unstable and potentially subversive.

A City Audience

Establishing an understanding of Mark's audience also brings us to the issue of medium. The written medium, I would contend, primarily indicates an urban rather than a rural audience. The research development initiated by Werner Kelber (1997) here becomes significant, and his work will be further discussed below. In relation to the city/rural division, Kelber (17–18) points out that the domination of the oral medium among the Christ followers "corresponds with the sociological identity of the early Jesus movement." According to Kelber, this identity is connected to a rural location and implies "an ambivalence toward largely Hellenistic city culture." His discussion about Mark as a written Gospel, however, does not follow up on this interesting trope.[56]

By contrast, R. Horsley (2006, 2008) takes the city/rural antagonism more seriously, reckoning the written medium as a largely urban aristocratic phenomenon.[57] Hence, since Galilean peasants with their oral culture were detached from the scribal culture of the temple, they "would not

---

56. Kelber touches on this issue in his later essay (2004). His conclusions regarding Mark, however, are here rather meager (cf. Camp 2004, 207–8).

57. Contra Millard 2000, 154–84, who argues for comparatively high literacy

have any first-hand acquaintance with the written texts" (Horsley 2008, 60). Even though Horsley might be somewhat exaggerating the differences, he ought to be given credit for making explicit the city/rural relation and its implied differences in social status when discussing the significance of written and oral media. As discussed above, this relation often entailed social tensions that are important for understanding how Mark related to Roman imperial discourse. But even so, Horsley's conclusions regarding Mark's audience are questionable. Locating Mark in Palestinian villages (Galilee and Judea), Horsley (2008, 57–60) claims it to be written primarily for rural Jewish peasants (cf. Theissen 1992, 237–39; Rohrbaugh 1993; Waetjen 1989, 4–26). He thereby fails to discuss two pertinent questions: If Jewish rural peasants were the primary audience, and if this audience generally held negative sentiments toward the written medium, why would the written medium have been used?[58] And why would the text have been written in Koine Greek?

This is not to diminish the significance of the rural Galilean origin of the Jesus movement that is reflected in Mark's narrative (cf. Theissen 1978, 47–58). But the use of the written medium for the circulation of the Gospel indicates the beginning or continuation of a shift from rural to urban settings. As seen in Paul's letters, this shift had begun earlier. Hence the Stegemanns (1999, 265–66) maintain that "Christ-confessing communities came into being in various *cities* of the Roman Empire" (italics original). A precise geographic demarcation is difficult and not necessary for my purposes. We know from the letters of Paul that there were Christ-confessing communities in Antioch, Damascus, Ephesus, Philippi, Thessalonica, Corinth, and Rome. Of hermeneutical significance, however, is the suggestion that Mark, as a written Gospel, ought to be seen as primarily addressing communities most of which were located in the cities.

A certain dissonance between the medium and the narrative content here becomes visible. Unlike Kelber (1997, 129–30), then, who found a correlation between the written medium and the story's content, I find a conflicting message between the two. Whereas the written medium signals urbanity, the content of the story is centered on the countryside. Mark begins and ends in rural Galilee. The protagonist of the story draws his

---

rates in Palestine. According to Botha 1999, 236–45, however, this argument is based on the later claims of rabbis.

58. As Rohrbaugh (1993, 116) states, "fear of writing and those who could write was widespread among peasants who often resisted it as a tool of deception."

support in this rural area, and his closest followers are, like himself, of a rustic identity. The main characters of the story never enter a city until Jesus rides into Jerusalem, where he is crucified by the imperial authorities. The city/rural tension is especially pronounced when Peter is accused in the high priest's courtyard for being with "Jesus the Nazarene" and for being "one of them ... a Galilean" (14:66–72).[59] Further, representatives of the scribal city culture are presented in Mark as opposing Jesus (3:22; 7:1; 8:31; 10:33; 11:18, 27; 12:38–40; 14:1–2, 43, 53; 15:1–5, 31).[60]

Let us now return to Theissen's argument (discussed above) for an eastern provenance. Since Mark's use of θάλασσα can be explained by it being based on Peter's memories, I will argue for a different significance of the term. When Mark's story about God's Son from the Galilean countryside was proclaimed among Christ-believing city dwellers, they are curiously interpellated to a rustic position where "sea" (θάλασσα)—contrary to metropolitan common sense—signifies a little Galilean lake in northern Palestine. Indeed, Mark seems curiously fond of this word.[61] Despite the written medium, then, the scene of action in Mark's narrative entails a certain dissonance and resistance to the imperial city culture in which Mark's audience was living.

A Heterogeneous Audience

Since an urban location in contemporary biblical scholarship often implies a (mis)understanding of the Christ followers as educated, "upwardly mobile," and "middle class," a few words on the audience's social status are needed.[62] Many of Mark's allusions to imperial discourse are subtle and would have been interpreted differently according to the social status of the audience. The topic has occasioned a substantial amount of research, mainly with a focus on the Pauline communities.[63] I follow the position

---

59. As Matt 26:73 reads this episode, Peter is recognized because of his Galilean accent. In the context of a city, such an accent would surely be perceived as rustic.
60. But see Mark 12:28–34. Evidently, the opposition is not total.
61. For Mark's use of θάλασσα see 2:13; 3:7; 4:1, 39, 41; 5:1, 13, 21; and 6:47–49.
62. Whereas "educated" stems from Malherbe (1983, 29–59), the designations "upwardly mobile" and "middle class" are often based on Meeks (1983, 51–73). Although Meeks (53) points out that *class* is not a helpful term when discussing antiquity, he does use it and the term is present in scholarly debates.
63. Criticizing Deissmann's (1978, 62–72, 290–91) early-twentieth-century suggestion that the early Christ followers mainly belonged to the nonelite masses of the

of Friesen (2004), who criticizes what he sees as attempts to find a more "respectable" (i.e., middle-class) origin for contemporary Christians. According to Friesen, nearly everyone in the Pauline communities was poor—as was the vast majority in the Roman Empire (cf. Longenecker 2009). One can thus rather safely state that Mark's audience belonged to the urban nonelite rather than the aristocracy. On the other hand, they were not all destitute. Also, as is evident from Paul himself, being economically poor would not exclude being educated, literate, and schooled in Greek urban culture.

That Mark's audience was generally poor should not be taken as indicating that they were a homogeneous group. The contention regarding socioeconomic stratification seems relevant here as well: Mark's audience roughly reflects a cross section of urban society in terms of ethnicity.[64] Since urban life was greatly influenced by Greek culture, moreover, the vast majority of the audience could presumably speak and understand Greek. A significant portion was composed of Greek-speaking Jews, some of whom could also understand Aramaic and/or Hebrew.[65] Not unlike the Greek Syrophoenician in Mark 7:26, many had a straightforward hybrid identity (see ch. 16).

The Medium and the Message

As I conceptualize Mark's provenance and audience in this investigation, the issue of the written medium emerges. Since the force of Mark's Gospel as a collective representation is closely related to the medium with which it was distributed, a more careful examination of the medium, its message, and more specifically its bearing upon social location and social status

---

population, scholars during the 1980s—most notably Malherbe (1983, 29–59) and Meeks (1983, 51–73)—began to think that Deissmann had aimed too low, suggesting instead that the Pauline communities generally reflected a cross section of urban society. This "new consensus" has been challenged by Friesen 2004.

64. Although Mark's audience would have had a larger portion of Jews as compared to the general society, *Jew* is here not taken as indicating a particular ethnicity. The ethnically heterogeneous character of Mark's audience is indicated by the Pentecost account in Acts 2:5–13. See also Baker 2010.

65. The existence of Greek-speaking Jews is indicated by Acts 6:1; 9:29. The presumption that a portion of the audience knew Hebrew or Aramaic is here based upon the Aramaic phrases in Mark (5:41; 7:34) as well as the close (and yet tense) ties between the Christ followers and the Jewish synagogues.

in Roman imperial culture is called for. If the writing of Mark's Gospel indicates the beginning of a development in which the written medium becomes increasingly important, this would have significantly affected the Christ followers' self-understanding.

Originally published in 1983, the previously mentioned work by Kelber (1997) initiated a scholarly debate on the significance of oral and written media for Christian origins. Kelber's argument has received criticism as well as praise.[66] A disputed aspect is his (90–139, 184–226) proposition that the written Gospel signified a radical shift among the Christ followers.[67] Many have held that Kelber overstates the shift from oral to written media, thereby establishing a "great divide" between oral tradition and Mark's written text. According to Kelber's critics, oral and written media of transmission stood in close interaction during all stages of the Gospel tradition. An oral story may thus have been written down to facilitate its circulation; but when it reached its destination, it was once again orally conveyed, thus freeing itself from the written form; in this way a continuous process of textualization and reoralization took place (Byrskog 2000, 127–44; Hearon 2006, 9–10). Although this critique is basically sound, it seems nonetheless difficult to deny that the existence of a written Gospel, such as Mark, implied a shift of some kind, even if only initially.

The shift initiated by the written Gospel seems connected to the fixation of collective self-understanding. Thus in a number of essays about orality and scribality in early Christianity, the issues of fluidity and stability play a crucial role.[68] As Thatcher (2008a, 7) argues, oral speech is an event that takes place and draws its meaning from interactions in "the biosphere." In this sense, the oral medium has a more fluid character and implies that

---

66. For the most notable responses from biblical scholars, see Thatcher 2008a, 2.

67. Kelber (1997, 99) suggested that in the oral medium, represented most keenly by a prophetic *egō eimi* style of speech, Jesus was a highly present figure: as Jesus' words were pronounced, Jesus became present in the oral act of performance. The written Gospel, on the other hand, by transforming the word sounds to written signs, turned Jesus much more into a figure of the past. Drawing significantly on the linguistic turn of Continental philosophy, most pertinently represented by the recurring phrase, "the oral metaphysics of presence," which stems from Derrida, Kelber argued that the close connection between the signifier and the signified that is characteristic of oral speech is broken by deferment as soon as the word sounds are transformed into written letters.

68. See the edited volumes of Draper 2004a; Horsley, Draper, and Foley 2006; Thatcher 2008b; and Weissenrieder and Coote 2010.

stories are told somewhat differently depending on the situation. Here the concept of "hot memory," developed in later works by Kelber, is actualized.[69] Even if Mark as a written Gospel did not abruptly alter this oral culture and its use of hot memory, it was nevertheless connected to a crisis that the Christ followers went through in 70 C.E. that was caused by the war in Jerusalem as well as the cessation of memory carriers.

Mark as a written text seems to play a double role. Partly, it signifies continuity with orality—it is still an expression of hot memory that reshapes the tradition in light of the present. But the written medium also has the capacity "to harness and control the forces of orality" (Dewey 2008, 72–73). Rather than a simple transition from one medium to another, then, the written text is a blending of media contexts and of social worlds. As Hearon (2008, 109) points out, this also implies a shift from local to more centralized authority. When the text is circulated, the local storytellers receive competition from the written story that is circulating. The circulation of a written document enabled the gospel to more readily transcend local boundaries, which entailed the formation of a more stable identity. Mark as a written Gospel, then, signifies an important step toward a more fixed self-understanding. As we will discuss below, however, the fixation of self-understanding also stands in tension to the open character of Mark's story.

A pertinent question in relation to the issue of medium concerns how to conceptualize the act of delivery. Since the reading practices of first-century Christ followers are largely unknown to us, the question is difficult to answer. When Mark's Gospel was beginning to circulate, can we even be sure that the written medium was present during the delivery? Considering that reading entailed memorizing the text, it is conceivable that the delivery of the Gospel was made without the manuscript in hand. In that case, the written medium would only have a more indirect significance. It is thus crucial to question whether the written medium was present at the time of delivery.

---

69. Thatcher 2008b, 10–14. "Hot memory" is distinguished from the repetitive and preservative "cold memory." The notion of hot memory questions the understanding of Gerhardsson and Bultmann, who, despite their differences, tended to see a linear development from Jesus to the Gospels. Further, the distinction between hot and cold memory interestingly resembles Bhabha's (1990b, 294–97) notions of the pedagogical and the performative, which he sees as two important aspects of collective processes of remembering.

In one of the few studies on these matters, William Shiell (2004, 116–36) contends that recitations of texts among the early Christians reflected the wider reading practices of urban Mediterranean culture. Although Shiell can be criticized for presuming that trained lectors already existed in the Jesus movement during the first century (Verbrugge 2007), it seems reasonable to assume that their reading practices to some degree reflected those that were common in the urban Hellenistic culture in which they were located. Reading conventions here seem to include recitations both with and without a manuscript.[70]

But even if both possibilities are conceivable from the evidence of Greek and Roman reading conventions, one needs to ask whether it is likely that a newly written Gospel that was circulating would have been delivered without the book being present. Even if stories about Jesus had been and continued to be told orally, the arrival of these stories in a continuous written form would surely have been considered a noteworthy event in the community of Christ followers.[71] Presuming, then, that the newly arrived text was introduced and delivered for the first time at a meeting in a house church (Shiner 2003, 51), it seems highly probable that the book was present and visible at the gathering.[72] And if it was indeed present, it would in itself have communicated and signified. *What* it signified brings us to the question of whether the particular written medium was a codex or a roll (or scroll).

---

70. Quintilian (*Inst.* 11.3.142) states that a book indicates a "lack of confidence in your memory and it is a hindrance to a great many gestures"; he thus recommends that delivery should be made without a book. On the other hand, orators were often displayed in sculptures and reliefs holding a roll in the left hand while using the right hand for gestures. Shiell (2004, 40, 50, 113) discusses several such sculptures and reliefs.

71. True, the account by Papias (Eusebius, *Hist. eccl.* 3.39.4) indicates that there was skepticism toward the written word and a preference for oral tradition. Such skepticism, however, does not reduce the likelihood of the contention. To the contrary, the ambivalence indicates that the written medium was used and debated—and that it communicated a message in and of itself.

72. Contra Dewey 2004, 503–7. Although I agree with Dewey's primary point that the oral proclamations continued long after Mark's Gospel had been written, I am not persuaded by her suggestion that the written manuscript made "very little" difference to the use and transmission of Mark's Gospel. Indeed, as Dewey (502) also seems to mean, the notion of "Mark" as a "standard version" that was told and retold is conceivable only when Mark's Gospel becomes a written text. Most likely, this event had a significant impact on the Christ followers as a group.

The Codex and the Message

If Mark's audience was located in an urban context, it follows that they were familiar with different forms of the written medium.[73] In other words, they could tell the difference between a roll and a codex. As is well known, the standard book format in first-century C.E. Mediterranean culture was the roll. Not until the fourth century C.E. was the roll replaced by the codex.[74] Given the ubiquity of the roll as book format during the first and second centuries, one would expect the early Christian writings to have had the same form. "Remarkably," as Harry Gamble (1995, 49) notes, "they did not." Almost without exception, the earliest preserved Christian writings—the papyri—have the form of the codex.[75] It is therefore generally acknowledged that the Christ followers began using the codex at a very early stage and that their use of the codex soon became pervasive (Kenyon 1949). Debated questions are: How early? How to explain this odd usage of the codex as a literary form? Did the Christ followers pioneer its usage or did they merely adopt a usage that others had initiated? And more specifically: Was Mark's Gospel circulated in the form of a roll or a codex? Basing my argument somewhat on Gamble (1995) and more on Stanton (2004), I contend that Mark was circulated as a codex and that this medium in itself entailed an important object of identification for the Christ followers in Roman imperial city culture.

The codex as a literary form had predecessors—it did not arise from nothing. Interestingly for my purposes, the codex was probably a Roman innovation.[76] As denoted by the Latin term *codex* (literally "piece of wood"), it was a development from the wooden wax tablet that was used for utilitarian purposes such as notes, teaching aids, and drafts. The development of the parchment notebook (*membranae*) was an important

---

73. Being familiar with the written media is not the same as being able to read and write. But as Cavallo (1999, 65–71, 75) points out, life in a city included the presence of books and of being continuously exposed to oral proclamations of written texts.

74. Kenyon 1949. As Roberts and Skeat (1983, 5–10) and Stanton (2004, 178) point out, the development of the form (from roll to codex) needs to be distinguished from the development of the material (from papyrus to parchment).

75. Of the fifteen extant Christian manuscripts from the second century, thirteen are codices (Roberts and Skeat 1983, 40–41, 72–73; Gamble 1995, 49; Aland and Aland 1995, 102).

76. See Roberts and Skeat 1983, 22; Gamble 1995, 49–53, 65–66; and Stanton 2004, 173–81.

step. Being used for drafts of literary works at least from the Augustan age, the parchment notebook also figures in the New Testament.[77] In 2 Timothy the author instructs: "When you come, bring the cloak that I left with Carpus at Troas, also the books [τὰ βιβλία], and above all the parchment notebooks [τὰς μεμβράνας]" (2 Tim 4:13).

Although the parchment notebook initially had the same purpose as the wax tablet, it gradually developed into a literary medium.[78] The earliest evidence for a literary use of the codex is found in the Roman poet Martial (*Epigrams* 14.184–192; cf. 1.2), who refers to the works of well-known authors (Homer, Virgil, Cicero, Livy, and Ovid) *in membranis* or *in pugillaribus membranis*. Stanton (2004, 179) tellingly labels these as "pocket editions."[79] Since Martial's writings are so close in time to the initial circulation of Mark's Gospel, his use of the codex is particularly interesting. Even if it had not yet been accepted, it was probably somewhat known as a book format. As Stanton (2004, 179–80) points out, although the evidence for the codex as a book form is sparse, it is not completely lacking. Nevertheless, since the roll was still pervasive, using the codex for literature continued to be seen as an irregularity. Hence Gamble (1995, 65–66) regards the second-century codices as indicating an intermediate stage in the developing use of the codex. And it is to this intermediate phase, he argues, that the early Christian use of the codex belongs.

---

77. Horace (*Sat.* 2.3.1–2; *Ars* 386–90) provides two examples of parchment notebooks (*membranae*) being used for drafts of literary works. See also the following footnote.

78. The increasing literary use of the parchment notebook is indicated in the following sources: According to Suetonius (*Jul.* 1.56.6) Caesar's dispatches to the senate were written in the form of *memorialis libelli*, which probably means that he fastened a number of papyrus sheets together like a parchment notebook, but with a different material (Roberts and Skeat 1983, 18–19; Hengel 1985, 79). Horace (*Sat.* 2.3.1–2; *Ars* 386–390) renders two examples. From the mid-first century, Persius (*Sat.* 3.10–11) attests that *membranae* refers to a parchment notebook in codex form. Later in the same century, Quintilian (*Inst.* 3.31; cf. 10.3.32) makes a clear distinction between wax tablets and parchment pages; here the codex (*membranae*) appears to be more than a tablet and less than a book (Roberts and Skeat 1983, 21; Stanton 2004, 177).

79. Of course, "pocket edition" is not to be taken as signaling that reading during antiquity had the same private character as it has in Western societies today. But Martial suggests that the codex medium, since it was more easy to carry, "could keep you company wherever you may be." Hence he indicates that they could be used for private reading as well.

But when did the Christ followers *begin* to use the codex? A number of theories explain the shift from roll to codex by asserting some decisive event. Criticizing such "'big bang' theories," Stanton (2004, 167–69) contends that a gradual evolution of the codex medium is more likely than one single "trigger" factor.[80] Although Stanton here challenges Gamble, the hypothesis of a gradual evolution of the codex fits rather well with Gamble's argument that the Christian use of the codex belongs to an intermediate phase in the development of the codex as a literary form. The codices as used by the Jesus followers, Gamble (1995, 66) states, were neither notebooks nor fine literature; "they were practical books for everyday use: the handbooks, as it were, of the Christian community." And for such practical purposes, the codex might well have been adopted from the beginning and then gradually achieved more of a literary status, as Stanton suggests.

An evident consequence of Stanton's hypothesis is the questioning of the present "consensus" according to which rolls were used for the initial circulation of the Gospels.[81] If a gradual development from the use of the codex as a notebook to a more official medium is more probable than an *ex nihilo* explanation, as Stanton (2004, 181) holds, it follows that the Gospels were initially circulated as codices. The beginning of this gradual development is plausibly explained by the practical advantages of the codex.[82] Although the codex initially had a more private character, the border between private notes and official texts among first-century Christ followers could hardly have been clear-cut. It is therefore quite conceivable that the codex medium began to be transformed from notebook to official text during the latter half of the first century. Thus, with Stanton (2004, 190), I maintain the possibility that Mark was initially circulated in the codex form.

---

80. For a similar critique of "big bang" theories, see Epp 1997. Evidently, Epp and Stanton developed this critique, including the use of the particular phrase "big bang" theories, independently of each other.

81. Although Stanton (2004, 181, 189) refers to a consensus view, one can question the existence of such a consensus. Hengel (1985, 78–79), for one, thought that the Gospels were written on codices from the very beginning. The Alands (1995, 102) and J. K. Elliott (2000) express a similar standpoint.

82. Stanton (2004, 182–89) suggests that there were three different contexts of the Jesus movement in which the codex was initially used: (1) in the copying of excerpts and *testimonia* from Jewish Scriptures; (2) in drafts and copies of letters; and (3) in some of the Jesus traditions.

If we assume that the codex medium was used, it is interesting to examine what it communicated and signified for the Jesus followers. According to Raymond Starr (1987), literature in Roman imperial culture was primarily the domain of the aristocratic elite. The aristocracy mainly circulated literature in circles that were determined by friendship and social status. What did the codex signal in such a context? Evidence is sparse, but we can get some clues from Martial's way of presenting his "pocket edition." As seen in the beginning of the first book of the *Epigrams*, Martial connects himself with this curious form of book. In the introduction, Martial (no verse) refers to his work as "my little books" (*libellis meis*).[83] Similarly, in the very first epigram, Martial presents himself as world-famous for his "witty little books of epigrams" (*argutis epigrammaton libellis*). Further, and crucial for the argument here, he continues in the second epigram by making it clear that his *libelli* are in codex form (*membrana tabellis*). Whereas cylinders are needed for rolls, Martial exclaims, "one hand grasps me." Since he identifies himself with this particular book medium, it serves the function of representing him in absentia. The codex could be brought "wherever you may be," and hence Martial sees himself as being curiously present along with his codex.

The codex medium, it seems, helped to displace literature from its limited aristocratic domain, where it was connected to friendship and social status. Martial would have had no idea who might have "grasped him." As noted by William Fitzgerald (2007, 99), the codex here made possible a convenient way for "the man in the street" to have the poet as his companion. Similarly, as Guglielmo Cavallo (1999, 83–85) contended, the codex as a medium was connected to a widening of literary culture to the nonelite strata. Here is an interesting indication, therefore, that the use of the codex for literature points at a potential widening, even a displacement, of the literary culture that traditionally was the exclusive domain of the urban elite (cf. Roberts and Skeat 1983, 25).

The use of the codex medium as a literary device during the first century therefore seems to signal a new countercultural domain in the cities where literature was just starting to be used in a way that was indepen-

---

83. *Libellus* is diminutive form of *liber*. Martial's use of *libellus* has been debated. Fitzgerald (2007, 3) sees it as "one of Martial's most significant puns," since it can mean both "petition" and "little book." In the former sense it designates the occasion where an epigram is delivered on the day-to-day life of Roman elite culture.

dent of aristocratic circles.[84] Literary and sacred writings, the codex communicated, belonged not only to the elite, but also to the lower segments of the urban population. As Lovedale Alexander (1998, 82) points out, this message of the codex can explain both its attractiveness to the followers of Jesus and why it failed to catch on with equal speed among the dominant literary circles. In other words, the codex communicated newness and was probably connected to the Christ followers' countercultural self-understanding (Stanton 2004, 171–72). Further, since the codex was a Roman invention, the Christ followers' use of it as a literary medium indicates a borrowing or appropriation of a medium that in imperial culture was seen as suspicious. The use of the codex as a medium to distribute a Gospel, therefore, appears rather odd and can be seen as a catachresis in Spivak's sense.[85] Signaling a combination of newness and awkwardness, it pointed curiously toward an emerging urban cultural space on the fringes of imperial culture.

In summary, Mark's Gospel audience is here envisioned as being nonelite, economically poor, socially and ethnically heterogeneous, and primarily located on the margins of Roman imperial urban culture. Presuming with Stanton that the codex was the form in which Mark's Gospel was circulated (together, of course, with its oral delivery), the medium in combination with its content must have signaled a pertinent complexity of messages that considerably affected early Christian self-understanding in Roman imperial culture. Since a full discussion of these complex messages is possible only after an analysis of Mark's narrative, I will return to it below. But one can still state that the written medium in and of itself conveyed a message to Mark's audience. Indeed, as Stanton (2004, 172) suggests, there were even circumstances in which the mere presence of the codex conveyed a more important message than the written content itself. And as Epp (1997, 21) argues, in a time of relatively few personal possessions, a respected visitor's "props" would be strikingly visible to the congregation. The anomalous use of the codex in the Jesus movement signaled a newness that the Markan Jesus also gave voice to in the figura-

---

84. This goes somewhat against the argument by Starr (1987, 223), according to which Roman literature remained the preserve of the aristocracy. Starr, however, discusses bookshops and does not consider the codex as a book medium.

85. Although Spivak used *catachresis* for the use of linguistic words and concepts, its basic idea seems to be applicable to physical objects as well—especially if one adheres to the dictum, "the medium is the message."

tive saying of putting "new wine in new wine skins" (Mark 2:22). Being a Roman invention, this newness was the result of a catachrestic adaptation of a nascent Roman writing practice that opened an urban cultural space for the Jesus followers, the meaning of which was also affected by the specific content of Mark's Gospel. So as to ponder the nature of that meaning, we now turn to the study of Mark's narrative.

14
An Oppositional Beginning (1:1)

> They are all acting contrary to the decrees of the emperor, saying that there is another king named Jesus.
>
> —Acts 17:6–7

Approaching the content of Mark's Gospel with the aim of analyzing how it relates to Roman imperial discourse, we will not need much patience in terms of finding relevant material. The Gospel's very first verse (1:1) seems to be loaded with allusions to imperial discourse. The pregnant phrase runs: Ἀρχὴ τοῦ εὐαγγελίου Ἰησοῦ Χριστοῦ [υἱοῦ θεοῦ]. As I will argue, this phrase functions as a superscription to the entire work.[1] As such, its meaning is crucial to understanding Mark as a whole. As Evans (2000b), Samuel (2002), and Winn (2008, 92–99) contend, the phrase alludes to both Roman imperial and Jewish discourse. The very headline of Mark thus serves as a fitting point of departure for the present investigation.

A first question that needs to be addressed before getting involved in the exegetical discussions concerns the relation between modern exegesis and Mark's audience. The first sentence is obviously very short and would take only a few seconds to read. Since exegetes disagree about possible allusions and a polyvalence of meaning, how do their discussions relate to the actual circumstances of delivery? Would the audience have heard all the possible allusions that biblical scholars are pointing toward? One response to this question concerns whether one is referring to the first time the Gospel was heard. Presumably, more allusions and a more complex meaning would be grasped in subsequent proclamations of the Gospel. Another response concerns the character of the headline, which appears not to

---

[1]. For an introduction to the different kinds of narrative beginnings and their importance in ancient literature, see Smith 1990. See also Keck 1966; Boring 1990; and Matera 1988.

be an oral tradition but rather a literary construction by the author. As Marcus (2000, 143) states: "Mark has undoubtedly penned the first verse." Assuming that many other parts of Mark had been previously heard in different forms, the superscript would have struck the audience as a new composition, causing them to listen to it with special attention. Especially if Mark is here using the term *gospel* in a new way, it is quite likely to have been remembered. Further, we can also consider the presenter who was preparing to deliver the work. Quite likely, he or she was urged to carefully think through the manner in which the first sentence should be read. Where to put the emphasis? What does ἀρχὴ τοῦ εὐαγγελίου refer to? Most probably, the presenter concluded, as did Marcus (145), that "each word here is momentous." All in all, it seems reasonable to more deeply analyze this relatively short phrase.[2]

Who Is Number One? The Gospel's ΑΡΧΗ and the Codex

In most contemporary English Bibles, Mark begins with a title, such as "The Gospel according to St Mark." In such a title, "Gospel" refers to Mark's text. There are four Gospels, and Mark is one of them. This way of using "Gospel," however, was unheard of by Mark's audience. There were no texts referred to as "Gospels," and the text that began to circulate probably lacked such a title.[3] Therefore, the first verse in Mark's Gospel is here taken as a title, or incipit.[4]

Ἀρχὴ τοῦ εὐαγγελίου is a remarkably polyvalent phrase. Ἀρχὴ could mean "beginning" as well as "power" and "authority" (Liddell et al. 1996, s.v.). This is not so strange, perhaps, if we consider that being first, being number one, is connected to power. Words like *archbishop* and *archangel* make this clear. Hence a common term for the Roman Empire in Greek was ἀρχὴ Ῥωμαίων.[5] Not unlike how some patriots in the United States

---

2. A further reason for paying special attention to Gospel incipits (not only Mark's) is that they were popularly used on amulets and seen as representing the whole Gospel (Wasserman 2011, 45).

3. Hartman 2004, 13. For a different opinion, see A. Collins 2007, 2–3.

4. Although it is syntactically possible to read the first verse as the beginning of a sentence that continues with vv. 2 and 3, I here follow commentators who take 1:1 separately as a verbless title. See, e.g., A. Collins 2007, 130; Cranfield 1959, 34–35; Donahue and Harrington 2002, 59–60; Hooker 1991, 33; Taylor 1953, 152; contra Tolbert 1989, 239–48; Guelich 1989, 6–7; and Marcus 2000, 143.

5. For the use of ἀρχὴ Ῥωμαίων to designate Roman power, see Josephus, *Ant.*

regard their country as number one, the phrase ἀρχή Ῥωμαίων denoted the supremacy of Rome.

Since ἀρχή has this double meaning of "beginning" and "authority," there seems to be more to the incipit than a mere temporal designation (here begins); there is also a sense of authority or origin. Granted, further, that *gospel* was not used, as it is today, to denote a literary composition, it primarily carries the familiar meaning of the oral announcement (that had been ongoing since Easter) of the salvific significance of the Christ event.[6] With this meaning of *gospel* as something outside Mark's text, ἀρχή refers to Mark's work as a whole; Mark's composition then constitutes the beginning/authority of the gospel. Taking into account the open-endedness of Mark's story, this reading is not without merits. Ending in 16:8 with the women saying nothing to anyone, the lack of a narrative closure indicates a continuation outside the narrative; as Marcus (2000, 146) phrases it, "the *beginning* of the good news is over on Easter morning." After that the speaking about Jesus continued through the emerging church.

If Mark's text is the beginning/authority of the ongoing proclamations, the phrase ἀρχή τοῦ εὐαγγελίου somehow refers to Mark's document (i.e., to the written text) as protocanonized, as the origin of the continuous announcements of the Christ event. In that case, further, the issue of the document's medium becomes pertinent for how to conceptualize Mark's way of granting authority. As argued in the previous chapter, Mark was probably circulated in the form of a codex, a medium that signaled catachrestic newness and awkwardness in its imperial setting. The authority of Mark's text is thus curiously related to the codex.[7] And unlike the roll, the codex points toward an emerging cultural space displaced from the literary urban elite circles. Together with the document's medium, there-

---

15.361; 16.60; etc.; *J.W.* 4.657; 5.322; etc.

6. Boring 1990, 47–53. Also Stanton (2004, 52–59) holds that "gospel" in Mark 1:1 refers to oral proclamation, not the written text. Although Mark developed Paul's use of "gospel" and paved the way for the later use of "gospel" as referring to a written text, Stanton claims, Mark himself did not take that step. Of course, as A. Collins (2007, 130–31) argues, "gospel" could also refer ambiguously to the oral announcement as well as to Mark's narrative.

7. For a different suggestion of how to understand the relation between the medium and Mark 1:1, see Dronsch and Weissenrieder 2010, 222–28, who regard Mark's written Gospel as a medium that represents the absent body of Jesus and in that sense makes it present. They do not, however, discuss the specific kind of written medium.

fore, the gospel's ἀρχή, its authority, opens a subversive space in the imperial discourse.

The Gospel of Jesus Christ and the Gospel of the Flavians

The subversive message of the incipit becomes more articulated when we consider the term εὐαγγέλιον. Scholars have debated the origin of this term, whether it stems from a Jewish or Hellenistic context.[8] Unfortunately, it seems this debate is based upon a Judaism/Hellenism dichotomy and is thus caught up in a quest for pure origins. The interpretation suggested here rather strives to take into account how the audience perceived the term as alluding to Jewish tradition as well as to the Roman ruler cult.

Due to the explicit reference to Isaiah in verses 2–3, the use of εὐαγγέλιον echoes the Deutero-Isaian proclamations (Isa 40:9; 52:7; 60:6; 61:1) to preach the good news (εὐαγγελίζω) of the coming of God's rule. As Marcus (2000, 139–40) contended, since these allusions were connected to Jewish apocalypticism, Mark here strikes an apocalyptic tone with notions of the death of an old age and the birth of a new. Further, since these apocalyptic expectations were probably prominent among the rebels in Jerusalem, they could have carried rather strong anti-Roman sentiments at the time of Mark's circulation.[9] The question is, however, how the Markan audience would have heard those allusions. They would probably recognize that the movements initiated by John the Baptist and Jesus arose on the same soil as the rebellion and that they therefore in some ways were affiliated with the anti-Roman sentiments that eventually fueled the uprising. But they would hardly have taken the apocalyptic expectations in the same way as the insurgents. Considering that the Flavians, when Mark was delivered, had recently conquered Jerusalem and that the city would have been sacked by the time of Mark's delivery, the

---

8. Peter Stuhlmacher and Christian Strecker have taken opposite positions. Whereas Stuhlmacher (1991, 19–25) has argued that the term can be traced back via the historical Jesus to Deutero-Isaiah (Isa 52:7; 61:1), Strecker (1991, 71) has asserted "the Hellenistic ruler cult" as its primary basis. Whereas Strecker neglects how εὐαγγέλιον was used theologically and religiously in Hebrew Scriptures, Stuhlmacher seems to presuppose the existence of a Jewish understanding of the term that was unaffected by Hellenistic influence.

9. Josephus (*J.W.* 2.258–260; 2.433–434; 6.312–313; 7.29; *Ant.* 17.271–281) indicates that apocalyptic notions inspired the rebels. See also Marcus 2000, 140; and J. Collins 1998, 194–95.

14. AN OPPOSITIONAL BEGINNING (1:1)

anti-Roman apocalypticism probably appeared in a disillusioning light. In the face of this tragic defeat, Mark nevertheless upholds the very same tradition as victorious. Even if Rome won the war, Mark seems to say, their gospel is not the true gospel.

Here we enter the imperial semantic field with which the phrase 'ἀρχὴ τοῦ εὐαγγελίου interacts. Stemming from the early years of the Roman Empire, when internal strife had been ended by the battle of Actium and Octavian had been given the honorific name Σεβαστός (Augustus), εὐαγγέλιον began to be used in a new way that combined political and religious aspects.[10] This is especially visible in inscriptions about the introduction of the Julian calendar in the Greek cities. Responding to a letter from the proconsul of Asia (lines 1–30), the Greek assembly issued two decrees (lines 30–84), in which they in a praising manner decided to "reckon time from the birth [of Augustus]" (line 49).[11] The letter from the Roman proconsul as well as the assembly's flattering response were published in the form of inscriptions in numerous Greek cities, of which the most complete is the one from Priene from 9 B.C.E. (Danker 1982, 215–16). In an illuminating argument, Craig Evans (2000b, 68–69) has shown how Mark's incipit interacts with this inscription.

Since there had been no common calendar before this time (with each Greek city typically having its own), the establishment of a universal calendar was an important manifestation of Roman rule. Combining political and religious notions, the calendar inscription triumphantly celebrates the birthday of Augustus as "the beginning of all things" (τῶν πάντων ἀρχῆι, line 6), "the beginning of life" (ἀρχὴν τοῦ βίου, line 10), and the bringing of "a peaceful order" (κοσμήσοντα [δὲ εἰρήνην], line 37).

Especially close to the Markan superscription is the inscription's proclamation that "the birthday of the god [Augustus] was the beginning of the gospels that he brought to the world" (ἦρξεν δὲ τῶι κόσμωι τῶν δι᾽ αὐτὸν εὐαγγελί[ων ἡ γενέθλιος ἡμέ]ρα τοῦ θεοῦ, lines 40–41). As Koester (1990, 4) points out, the victories of Augustus gave the term εὐαγγέλιον a more elevated, dignified, and divine meaning than it previously had. Since Augustus's birthday was subsequently celebrated on a yearly basis, this elevated sense of εὐαγγέλιον was continuously reinforced in public festivals.

---

10. Friedrich 1964, 724–25. For the religious and political aspects of the transition from republic to empire under Augustus, see Beard et al. 1998, 1:167–210.

11. This and the subsequent indications of line numbers refer to document number 98 in Ehrenberg and Jones 1949, 74–76.

Further, at the time of Mark's writing, this dignified use of εὐαγγέλιον was actualized and rearticulated in connection with the ascension of Vespasian as emperor and the beginning of the Flavian dynasty. Resembling the glorification of Augustus, the Flavian rise was also described by Tacitus (*Hist.* 1.2) as having been preceded by a state of turmoil, conflagrations, and crisis (cf. Suetonius, *Vesp.* 1). Against this background, the "good news" of the Flavians was declared. Vespasian's crushing of the rebellion in Jerusalem was seen as the longed-for resolution of a crisis. Having secured the victory, Josephus (*J.W.* 4.618) recounts, rumors quickly spread the news that Vespasian had been proclaimed the new emperor in the East, upon hearing which "every city kept festival for the good news [εὐαγγελία], and offered sacrifices on his behalf."

In Josephus's indication of the East as the location of Vespasian's emperorship, yet another connection to Mark's incipit is established. In what seems to be compensation for Vespasian's obscure family background and lack of ancestral honors (Suetonius, *Vesp.* 1), the Jewish messianic expectations of a world leader from the East were projected onto Vespasian. Hence Tacitus (*Hist.* 5.13):

> There was a firm persuasion, that in the ancient records of their [the Jews'] priests was contained a prediction of how at this very time the East was to grow powerful, and rulers, coming from Judaea, were to acquire universal empire. These mysterious prophecies had pointed to Vespasian and Titus, but the common people, with the usual blindness of ambition, had interpreted these mighty destinies of themselves, and could not be brought even by disasters to believe the truth.

Similarly, Josephus (*J.W.* 6.312–313):

> What more than all else incited them [the Jews] to war was an ambiguous oracle, likewise found in their sacred scriptures, to the effect that at that time one from their country would become ruler of the world. This they understood to mean someone of their own race, and many of their wise men went astray in their interpretation of it. The oracle, however, in reality signified the sovereignty of Vespasian, who was proclaimed Emperor on Jewish soil.

The contention made above that the Jewish rebellion was fueled by apocalyptic messianic expectations is strengthened by these accounts. More interestingly, by proclaiming that Jewish apocalypticism actually foretold

14. AN OPPOSITIONAL BEGINNING (1:1)

the Flavian victory, Tacitus and Josephus also represent a Roman appropriation of Jewish messianic expectations. This is not to be confused with a Jewish interpretation that, in keeping with the Deuteronomistic tradition, regarded the Roman victory as a divine punishment against the Jewish people (N. de Lange 1978, 265). Unlike the Deuteronomistic interpretation, which provided a way for the subdued to uphold their God as being in control in times of defeat and hardships, the Roman appropriation of Jewish apocalypticism undermined the agency of the subdued. That Josephus, who was himself a Jew, reproduced the Roman appropriation of his own tradition indicates the profound extent to which an imperial discourse can speak through its subjects.

Rome's victory in Jerusalem and the subsequent ascension of Vespasian became a Flavian Actium that revitalized the religious and political notions of Roman power from the early days of the empire (Aitken 2005). As with Augustus, Vespasian's victory was invested with a divine aura, proclaimed as *good news*, and touted as the beginning of a new era of peace and stability—celebrated by the holding of various festivals. Unlike Augustus's triumph, however, the new beginning under Vespasian was also construed around Jewish messianic expectations that were seen as having been realized in Vespasian's victory, lending further legitimacy to his ascent to the emperor's throne.

The use of εὐαγγέλιον in Mark's incipit connects to these imperial notions of "good news," founded as they were on the fulfillment of Jewish messianic expectations and a new "beginning" established by a victorious founding event. In what appears to be a reappropriation of Jewish messianic expectations, Mark declares them to be fulfilled not by Vespasian and the Flavian dynasty, but in the life, death, and resurrection of Jesus. Although clearly distinguished from the anti-Roman uprising, Mark's incipit here represents a rather clear oppositional and subversive position that reclaims an indigenous tradition and its messianic expectations. While Rome was proclaiming the gospel of the Flavians, Mark proclaims the gospel of Jesus Christ.

From a postcolonial perspective, it is here important to note the extent to which Mark's use of these concepts initially seems to reproduce the imperial discourse. The notions of εὐαγγέλιον and a new ἀρχή, prominent in Mark as well as in Roman imperial discourse, were tied to a multidimensional superior and victorious strength. In the Flavian case, the military victory in Jerusalem was combined with oracles about Vespasian that invested him with a divine aura. Vespasian, it was told, restored the sight of a blind man and cured a man with a diseased hand (Suetonius, *Vesp.* 7; Tacitus, *Hist.* 4.81). In Mark's case, Jesus' power over evil spirits (Mark 1:21–28; 3:15, 20–27; 5:1–20; 6:7; 7:24–30; 9:14–29) was connected to his power to cure sicknesses (1:29–34, 40–45; 2:1–12; 3:1–6; 5:25–34; 6:5, 53–56; 7:31–37; 8:22–26; 10:46–52) and even to overcome death (5:21–24, 35–43; 16:1–8). Does Mark then merely present Jesus as a stronger and more powerful messianic version of Vespasian? Mark's beginning seems to signal such an opposition. It remains to be seen, however, whether Mark will also question the imperial dreams themselves.

In any case, as the key passage (1:14–15), which introduces the first main section of Mark (1:14–8:21), locates the beginning of Jesus' activities in Galilee and connects it to the arrest of John the Baptist, the oppositional tone of the incipit is reinforced. Mark here presents the very first saying of Jesus: "The time is fulfilled and the empire of God has come near; repent and believe in the gospel" (1:15).[12] Considering that Galilee at the time of the Jewish War had been "a hotbed of guerillas for over a century" (Smallwood 1976, 302), Mark's locating of the first saying of Jesus in this area in alignment with an imprisoned prophet surely would have sent oppositional signals.[13]

[Son of God] as a Sign of Colonial Ambivalence

Approaching the last phrase of the Markan superscript, we encounter a textual conundrum. In the latest edition of *Novum Testamentum Graece* (hereafter NA[27]), the textually uncertain [Son of God] has brackets and the sign "†" in the apparatus, signaling a "very difficult textual decision"

---

12. Regarding the translation of βασιλεία as "empire," one should note that although βασιλεία was connected to kingly rule, it was also used to designate the Roman Empire (Rev 17:18). True, for the Roman nobility it was important for ideological reasons not to use *rex* or βασιλεύς to designate the emperor. But for Greek-speaking people in general, βασιλεύς was used with reference to the Roman emperor (1 Pet 2:13–17; Josephus, *J.W.* 4.596; 5.563).

13. For a similar interpretation see Winn 2008, 178–79; Theissen 1992, 271; and Myers 1988, 124. A somewhat different reading is offered by Samuel 2002, who regards the incipit as fluid and slippery rather than directly oppositional. Although I agree that Mark's Gospel as a whole involves more subtle subversion than direct opposition, I do not see this being communicated in the incipit. Given the triumphant meaning these terms had in the imperial discourse, Mark needs more time in order to destabilize them.

(NA²⁷, 57*). Similarly, in *The Greek New Testament* (hereafter UBS⁴), the phrase is written within brackets and labeled {C} in the apparatus, indicating "that the Committee had difficulty in deciding which [textual] variant to place in the text" (UBS⁴, 3*). Since the textual evidence makes it possible to argue both ways, many scholars express uneasiness when deciding which text to read. Giving voice to this frustration, Alexander Globe (1982, 209) calls it "one of the thorniest New Testament textual cruxes." Similarly Adela Yarbro Collins (1995, 115): "it is notoriously difficult to decide which [variant] is the source of the other." Rather than contending that one of the variants was original, as most biblical scholars do, I will here locate the undecidability of the textual situation in the initial circulation of Mark's Gospel, relating it to the imperial discourse in which it emerged.

As noted by Peter Head (1991, 621–22), most contemporary commentators of Mark have, until quite recently, taken the phrase "Son of God" to be original. This trend reflects the development in the editions of the standard Greek texts. After the publication of Codex Sinaiticus in 1862, the phrase was generally omitted from the late-nineteenth-century editions of the standard Greek texts. Reconsidering the evidence, however, the assessment was revised in UBS³ (published 1966) and NA²⁶ (published 1979), where the phrase advanced from a possible variant in the apparatus to a bracketed part of the text itself. Commentators who take the phrase as original generally offer the following reasons for this assessment: (1) although a few important manuscripts omit the phrase, the external evidence is seen as favoring the longer version; (2) the omission of the phrase in some manuscripts is explained as an accidental oversight in copying, caused by the similarities of the endings (homoioteleuton) of the abbreviated *nomina sacra*; and (3) internal evidence—significant for the argument here—is generally regarded as the major factor for favoring the longer version. Mark's portrayal of Jesus as Son of God, climaxing in 15:39 with the saying by the Roman centurion, is seen as strongly indicating that the phrase was part of the original incipit. As Cranfield (1959, 38) states with reference to the internal evidence, it is "intrinsically probable" that the phrase would be found in the original beginning (cf. Head 1991, 622).

Judging from two recent commentaries on Mark, however, the issue is far from resolved: both A. Collins (2007, 130) and Marcus (2000, 141) see the shorter variant (without the phrase "Son of God") as original. Whether this reflects a turning of the trend can be debated; two rather recent commentaries render the longer version (Donahue and Harrington 2002;

Hartman 2004), as does Wasserman (2011). In any case, it is clear that the issue continues to be much debated, apparently stemming from the works of Ehrman (1991, 1993), Head (1991), and A. Collins (1995), which are referred to in the commentaries by A. Collins and Marcus.

Three arguments favor the shorter version as original:[14] (1) the external evidence is seen as giving diverse and early support for the shorter reading; (2) regarding the internal evidence, the depiction of Jesus as Son of God is rejected as evidence; although acknowledged as an important theme in Mark, the Markan depiction of Jesus as Son of God is not seen as necessarily implying that the phrase was part of the original incipit; and (3) the addition of the phrase is seen as being easier to explain than its omission (this, it should be noted, is the most important part of the argument). This last argument rests upon three additional features: (a) the dismissal of the possibility of an *intentional* omission; (b) the improbability that an *accidental* omission would have occurred in the very opening words of a work; and (c) the greater likelihood that the addition of the phrase is an example of "orthodox corruption" or, in a less provocative expression, of "tendentious reverential and doctrinal alterations" (Head 1991, 627).[15] Since part c of the argument presupposes that the scribes made intentional alterations in the text and since this is a debatable issue with significance for the argument here, I will give it some attention.

How are we to understand the copying of texts in early Christianity? Should we regard the copyists as mere copy machines who would never deliberately alter or embellish a piece of text? As pointed out by Tommy Wasserman, scholars disagree on this issue.[16] The influential nineteenth-century textual critics Westcott and Hort (1882, 282) dismissed any possibility of what they called "deliberate falsification." Generally viewed as the founders of modern textual criticism, their legacy has been followed by many subsequent scholars, who regard the willful changing of biblical texts to be a rare phenomenon, restricted to a few unfortunate examples. More recently, however, these views have been challenged. As stated by Kim Haines-Eitzen (2000, 9), "it has become increasingly clear that scribes were readers embodied in social, cultural, and religious contexts and that

---

14. These arguments stem from Ehrman 1991, 150–53; Head 1991, 626–28; and A. Collins 1995, 115–16.

15. Head (1991, 627) is here quoting C. S. C. Williams.

16. Wasserman 2007, 77–79. See also J. K. Elliott 1992, 18–19, who points at Mark 1:1 as an example of a textual uncertainty with theologically significant variants.

14. AN OPPOSITIONAL BEGINNING (1:1)

their contexts did shape their (re)production of texts." As she (111) is careful to point out, however, most of the variations in New Testament texts are due to accidental mistakes. Nevertheless, there is also evidence that scribes deliberately modified texts in the process of copying.

Focusing on the scribes of early Christianity, Haines-Eitzen (2000) explores how the copying of texts intersected with issues of authority, ideology, and power. Her main argument is that the scribes who copied early Christian literature were also involved in the study of these texts (16). Unlike scribes in larger societies, Christian scribes were not a hired professional group, separated from the users.[17] Thus their work was not only preservative but also performative. True, Haines-Eitzen delimits her study to the second and third centuries. But since the main shift in the reproduction of Christian texts seems to have occurred when the copying of texts became a more organized enterprise with the establishment of Christian scriptoria, and since this did not happen until after the third century (Haines-Eitzen 2000, 16), her main thesis regarding the scribes does seem relevant for the first century.[18]

A similar understanding of the early Christian scribes has been proffered by Bart Ehrman, who portrays the scribes as playing an important role in the contestation of beliefs and practices in the early years of Christianity. Being informed by reader-response criticism, Ehrman (1993, 29–31) sees all reading as a rewriting of text; when the scribes read their text, they rewrote it not only "in their minds" (as we all do) but also "physically" on the page. Consequently, the scribes are seen as "deeply rooted in the conditions and controversies of their day" (3). As the New Testament writings appear less stable than is often presumed and the quest for single and final autographs is probably misguided, the scribes' physical rewriting is rather to be seen as part of a continuous contestation of what it meant to be a Christ follower.[19]

---

17. Botha (2010, 347–52) has suggested that the scribes in the movement of Jesus followers were recruited from the networks of educated freedmen and slaves who, along with their ordinary work, were pursuing their own literary interests independently of their patrons and masters. Hence they were "behind-the-scenes" literates who placed their writing skills at the disposal of the Jesus followers in their spare time.

18. For a similar contention see Botha 2010, 351–52: the networks of second- and third-century scribes studied by Haines-Eitzen "were involved right from the beginning," and that "the shaping of early Christianity's literary character started there."

19. For a recent argument for the unstable character of ancient writings in gen-

Although Ehrman has opened an important development of textual criticism, his understanding of the scribes as a group can be criticized for being somewhat homogeneous. As Haines-Eitzen (2000, 112) points out, the motives for the deliberate modifications were not limited to orthodox harmonization, but might have been driven by other purposes as well. She particularly notes studies that have shown other kinds of motives, such as anti-Jewish sentiments and animosity toward women. Could there have been yet other motives for modifications? As she (106) makes clear, although texts were deliberately altered, text transmission in early Christianity cannot be characterized as uncontrolled and random. The deliberate changes were bounded and constrained by multifaceted discursive practices in early Christianity. The liberty that copyists sometimes took with their texts was shaped by the various discursive controversies that engaged the Christ followers.

The question is whether the textually uncertain Markan heading reflects a controversy that was prominent during the first century. As we saw above, scholars have viewed the adding of the title "Son of God" as an expression of orthodox harmonization. Another possibility that ought also to be considered is whether the addition or omission of the phrase might be a reflection of the controversy over how to relate to imperial authorities as Mark began to circulate.

The existence of such a controversy during the latter part of the first century is indicated by several places in the New Testament writings, especially by the narrative strategy of Luke–Acts.[20] In Acts 17:1–9 Luke describes the angry reactions against Paul and Silas when they had come to Thessalonica. Having spent three Sabbath days in the synagogue contending that Jesus was the Messiah, some of the Jews had become upset and accused them of "acting contrary to the decrees of the emperor, saying that there is another king named Jesus" (17:6–7). Since Luke presents these accusations of subversion and rebellion as false and motivated by envy (17:5), the Christ followers appear as innocent and politically innocuous. One can argue that this narrative strategy would not have been called for unless the question of subversion was an issue. Judging from

---

eral, see Botha 2010, 347. Botha contends that single, final autographs probably never existed.

20. The controversy is also reflected in the contradictory attitudes expressed toward Rome in Rom 13:1–7 and Rev 17–18, respectively.

14. AN OPPOSITIONAL BEGINNING (1:1)

the accusations in Acts, the issue concerned whether Jesus was "another king" (βασιλέα ἕτερον) who competed with Caesar.[21]

Assuming the existence of controversies over depicting Jesus as another king, there were motives for copyists to modify texts that were circulating among the Christ followers. I will argue that since "Son of God" was both a royal and an imperial title, there were motives for adding as well as removing the title in the Markan incipit. Considering the risks that being a follower of Jesus might have entailed, it is possible to imagine quite lively negotiations around what being faithful to Jesus meant, particularly in relation to imperial discourse. When the textual uncertainty of Mark 1:1 is located in this religio-political context, other motives for including as well as omitting "Son of God" become plausible.

A motive to add the title is indicated in accounts that depict early Christians as heroic and faithful witnesses and martyrs who did not hesitate to provoke the imperial culture (cf. Eusebius, *Eccl. hist.* 5.1.29-31). In this light, despite seeing cofollowers being prosecuted and executed for refusing to offer sacrifice to the emperor, a scribe would be quite eager to write "Son of God" as a title for Jesus. An addition of the title to Mark 1:1 can then be understood as an act of solidarity with executed cofollowers. Apart from orthodox harmonization, it can also be understood as an expression of opposition to the imperial order.

Further, the opposite is also possible: seeing and hearing about cofollowers being prosecuted and executed could be a motive for omitting, rather than adding, the title.[22] Considering the prospect of a highly agonizing death, it would not seem farfetched to assume the existence of fear and anxiety among Mark's audience. As is evident in Pliny (*Ep.* 10.96-97), several of those accused of being Christians, seemingly in fear of death,

---

21. Another illustration of this narrative strategy is how Luke's (23:1-25) portrayal of Jesus' trial before Pilate differs from Mark's (15:1-15).

22. The argument presupposes that identifying oneself as a follower of Christ might in some places have implied a threat of persecution at the time that Mark was beginning to circulate. In support of this presupposition, the following can be upheld: (1) Mark (4:17; 10:30; 13:19, 24) refers recurrently to διωγμός (persecution) and θλίψεως (tribulation, oppression). (2) According to Tacitus (*Ann.* 15.44), the Christ followers were blamed for the fire in Rome and executed in large numbers. (3) A later illustration of the situation is seen in the famous correspondence between Pliny (*Ep.* 10.96-97) and Trajan, in which Pliny asks for advice about how to deal with the Christians and their "evil superstition" when they are brought on trial. See also Incigneri 2003, 342; and Senior 1984, 105.

chose to deny their faith in Christ and offer sacrifice to the emperor instead. Even if Pliny's letter was written forty years after Mark, its indication that Christ followers gave up their faith when threatened would have been valid for Mark's time as well. Since the scribes were not a separate group, it is possible that fear of persecution and/or an unwillingness to provoke imperial authorities were motives for omitting the title "Son of God" from the Markan heading.

Since the suggestion of a deliberate omission of "Son of God" goes against the grain of scholarly opinion, I will point at three circumstances that, taken together, make the proposal more credible. First, since the oral medium was dominant when Mark was circulating, the text was not totally fixed. As Dewey (2008, 86) contends, Mark as a written Gospel continued to be transmitted orally, which meant that it was retold, rewritten, and adapted to different situations. In a situation where persecution was a palpable threat, the inclination to adapt the text by omitting the title would be considerable.[23] Second, since the very first sentence functioned as a headline for the whole Gospel, it was probably perceived as being of particular delicacy. The very first phrase pronounced at the occasion of delivering would be of exceptional significance to both friends and foes alike, for example, informers (*delatores*) from the local population (Remus 2002, 432). Third, since the headline already contained the terms ἀρχὴ τοῦ εὐαγγελίου, which challenged imperial discourse in ways that might have been perceived as threatening, the title "Son of God" would have likely created an even more dangerous situation.

To sum up, I am not arguing for the originality of either the longer or the shorter version. Rather, since I am arguing that the textual variants stem from the initial circulation of Mark's Gospel, the rendering of the title as [Son of God] most accurately represents the text in its initial circulation.[24] My primary point here is to locate the addition/omission of

---

23. This is supported by J. K. Elliott 1992, 26, who, in his discussion of textual problems in relation to theological and doctrinal issues, states that "in the earliest days of the church the very conditions under which the New Testament was copied would encourage alterations. Then, poor and isolated churches, often persecuted, were trying to preserve their foundation documents and adapt them to their everyday lives."

24. Cf. Swete (1909, 2) and Taylor (1961, 82), who have argued that Mark from its earliest days had two different beginnings, one with and one without the title "Son of God."

14. AN OPPOSITIONAL BEGINNING (1:1)

the title in a marginal movement negotiating its identity in an imperial religio-political context.

As this chapter concludes, it is interesting to note that the controversy that seems to be reflected in the textually uncertain headline has a parallel in Mark's narrative depiction of Jesus as Son of God. At the end of Mark's story, a Roman centurion stands before the cross and exclaims: "Surely, this man was God's son!" (15:39). I will return to this saying as well as to Mark's secrecy complex in chapter 20, but I can already state that the connection that scholars often make between the textually uncertain headline and Mark's way of presenting Jesus as Son of God is here affirmed. But rather than taking it as indicating the originality of the longer version, as is commonly done, I take it as representing the contestation and ambivalence of the designation "Son of God" in relation to the imperial discourse. As will be seen, Mark does not establish this relation in a clear-cut fashion. Anticipating how Mark's story will evolve, I take the headline's use of [Son of God] as a sign of what Bhabha has called colonial ambivalence.

15
IMPERIAL SATIRE (5:1–20)

> LEGION [Gk *legiōn*]. See ROMAN ARMY.
> *Anchor Bible Dictionary*, s.v. "Legion"

"What's in a name," Stephen Moore (2006, 24) asks as he begins a thought-provoking exploration of the Mark-and-empire trajectory. Springing from a sixteenth-century Shakespeare tragedy, the question poetically connects the past and the present. The significance of the question is also evident in relation to Mark's account of the Gerasene demoniac (5:1–20), where Jesus encounters an unclean spirit who presents himself with the baffling name "Legion" (5:9). Initially presented as an infestation by a single demon, the multiple character of the possession soon becomes evident as the name is pronounced together with the clause "for we are many." Besides numerousness, however, here I will argue that the name *Legion* also introduces an additional dimension: the incredible strength of the dreaded Roman army. Taken as a double reference, the name actualizes yet another way in which empire is inscribed in Mark's Gospel, and is truly fascinating from a postcolonial perspective.

Considering the vast number of scholars who have found this account to contain an unmistakable reference to the brutality of Rome's military presence in the East, the episode can qualify as a *locus classicus* for anti-imperial readings of Mark.[1] As an indication of the episode's benchmark

---

1. The following scholars have considered the story to contain a negative reference to the Roman military's occupation of the East: Olshausen 1833, 304; 1847, 321; Trench 1850, 140; Maclear 1883, 88; Swete 1902, 95; M. Baird 1920; Winter 1961, 180–81; Eitrem 1966, 72; Theissen 1978, 101–2; 1983, 255–56; 1992, 110–11; Gnilka 1978, 205; Derrett 1979; Hollenbach 1981; Kelber 1997, 53; Wink 1986, 43–50; Wengst 1987, 86; Myers 1988, 190–94; Malina and Rohrbaugh 1992, 208; Crossan 1992, 313–18; Wright 1996, 195; Waetjen 1989, 115–18; Carter 2000, 212–13; Dawson 2000, 160–62;

status, several have attempted to trace the anti-Roman reading backward in scholarly history. Among contemporary scholars, there are two different suggestions regarding the first instance of this interpretation. Sugirtharajah (2002, 92) and Moore (2006, 25) refer to Mary Baird, who contended in 1920 that the mentally deranged state of the demoniac could be understood in the light of the recruitment campaigns of the Roman army. Theissen (1992, 110) and Lau (2007, 351), however, point to the French scholar Théodore Reinach (1903), who offers a more substantial account than Baird. Reinach argues that the name Legion makes the episode a symbol of the Jewish people's hope for liberation from the Romans.

Curiously, however, as we saw in chapter 6, several nineteenth-century scholars take the name Legion as invoking the oppressive nature of Roman rule: Swete (1898, 91), Maclear (1883, 88), Trench (1850, 140), and Olshausen (1833, 304; 1847, 321). Since Olshausen's work was first published in 1830, the first reading of Mark 5:9 that recognizes its anti-Roman sentiment could therefore be redated to this year.

The typical nineteenth-century readings took the possessed man as representing the miserable status of the heathen. And the works that recognized the anti-Roman symbolism did not take it as a critique of imperial domination per se. Unlike the nineteenth-century interpretations, however, contemporary empire-critical readings characteristically take the saturated imagery of the possessed man as a poetical representation of the devastating effects of imperial domination, both past and present. Herman Waetjen (1989, 116), for instance, finds Mark's depiction of the demoniac to be a telling illustration of the mental derangement that often plagues colonized peoples. According to him, colonial rule fosters a systemic breakdown of the human personality. Similarly, Stephen Moore (2006, 27–29) takes the episode as an anti-imperial allegory, although of a more ambiguous kind. The representation of the possessed individual, Moore suggests, represents a longing for purity among God's people; to get rid of the unclean occupants from the (com)promised land.

Marcus 2000, 343–53; Dormandy 2000; R. Horsley 2001, 140–48; 2003a, 100–101; Sugirtharajah 2002, 91–94; Burdon 2004, 157–65; Head 2004, 253–56; Newheart 2004; Donaldson 2005, 102–4; Moore 2006, 24–44; Staley 2006; Samuel 2007, 127; Runesson 2007; Lau 2007; Rajkumar 2007; A. Collins 2007, 269–70; Joy 2008, 166–78; Garroway 2009. Please note that some of these scholars do not believe Mark as a whole opposes Roman rule.

Legion as Catachresis

The debate about whether λεγιών in Mark 5:9 alludes to the Roman military presence in the East is part of the wider controversy in biblical studies regarding the political aspects of New Testament writings. Scholarly opinion on this issue is gradually shifting toward an acceptance of the impossibility of separating the religious and political aspects of ancient society. This general shift is exemplified not least by Marcus (2000, 351), whose commentary in the Anchor Bible series interprets the story of the Gerasene demoniac as a satire on the Roman military presence in the East.[2]

A traditional interpretation is represented in the *Theological Dictionary of the New Testament*, where Preisker (1967) points out that λεγιών in the New Testament is given a rather unique meaning: "In the NT the word λεγιών is not used for the military world, as elsewhere. It is used to denote transcendent forces. It thus shows us where the Church militant has to fight its war, namely, where the struggle is between the kingdom of God and demonic powers." Preisker's argument seems to be that since λεγιών refers to nonhumans it cannot also carry its common referent to the Roman military. Although one would expect to find theological assertions in this dictionary, one must nonetheless wonder whether Preisker's understanding of the mission of the church is here directing his interpretation.

In the *Exegetical Dictionary of the New Testament* entry on λεγιών, the message is more complex. Franz Annen (1991) begins by pointing out what is generally known: λεγιών has been adopted from Latin and designates the largest Roman unit of troops. In Palestine, Annen continues, the most important legion was the Legio X Fretensis, which had the symbol of a boar on its standards. Discussing Mark 5:9, Annen states that even if the name is explicitly based on the great number of demons that dwell in the demoniac, the name *also* indicates "the violent, organized power of the world of the demons. Hatred and fear toward the Roman occupation power is evident." Here Annen seems to open the door for interpreting λεγιών as referring doubly to the numerous spirits and to the Roman army. Even if Legion primarily signifies a great numbers of demons, Annen seems to mean, there is an additional reference to "hatred and fear" of the Roman army. But if the door was beginning to open, it seems to close

---

2. To be precise, Marcus is here discussing the episode in its pre-Markan tradition. When it comes to Mark's position, he (2000, 352) is more vague.

again when Annen at the end of his entry forbids any attempts at such a reading: "λεγιών is used in the NT only for spiritual powers, and never for the military unit of the Roman army."

What is the logic behind Preisker's (and Annen's ambiguous) unwillingness to accept the double reference of λεγιών to the demons and the Roman army? According to Gundry (1993, 260), who takes a similar position, since the text explicitly associates λεγιών with numerousness ("for we are many"), it does not refer to the Roman army. But numerousness could have been expressed without any reference to Roman troops with terms such as χιλιάς, μυριάς, πλῆθος, ὑπερβαλλόντως, and ἀναρίθμητος. The explaining phrase "for we are many" is necessary in Mark's text to make the new use of λεγιών intelligible.

The suggestion that λεγιών would have passed unnoticed as a dead metaphor is simply unpersuasive. Everyday language is made up of metaphorical words and phrases that pass unnoticed as dead metaphors, for example, "the *branch* of an organization" or "kidney beans." But since Mark's curious use of λεγιών was in all likelihood previously unheard of, it could not have passed unnoticed in such a way.

A scholarly shift seems to be taking place toward realizing that the position taken by Preisker is misguided. As far back as 1974, when William Lane referred to Preisker's article, he stated rather hesitantly: "It is difficult to know what meaning to place upon the term" (Lane 1974, 184–85). Since Lane's commentary, the scholarly terrain has further shifted, shown not least by the social scientific methodology being established in the discipline. A response to Lane's hesitance is then to ask: What is so difficult with Mark's use of λεγιών? Or as Klaus Wengst (1987, 66, italics original) phrased it: "Can one conceive of any ancient hearer or reader who would *not* think of Roman troops in connection with the name 'Legion'—in contrast to modern commentators." According to Betz (1999, 507), further, the anti-Roman tendency in Mark 5:1–20 "should be obvious."

In contemporary English, of course, "legion" is a dead metaphor. The phrase "they are legion" simply refers to a very large or uncountable number of something. If anything, the expression signals acquaintance with biblical metaphors. Needless to say, Mark's audience would have heard it differently. In order to help modern readers hear what Mark's audience heard, Joshua Garroway (2009, 61) gives an analogy comparing how a similar story would be understood if it appeared in Iraq at the time of the U.S. occupation. When asked for his name, the demoniac would then answer (in Arabic): *"ismī 'Marines' li'annanā kathīrūn"* ("my name is 'Marines,' for we are many"). As Garroway points out, such a statement would doubtlessly have been heard as a reference to the U.S. military presence in Iraq. Although the analogy limps, like most analogies, it still illuminates the transparency of Mark's double entendre.³

It is important to note how λεγιών (or λεγεών as it was also spelled) was semantically tied to a Roman context. Loanwords generally vary in their degree of assimilation into a language, and λεγιών had a comparably low degree of integration in Koine Greek.⁴ As a military term it did not designate a military force in general, but specifically a *Roman* military unit.⁵ Its specific Roman connotation is seen clearly in Plutarch's biography of Romulus (*Rom.* 13):

> When the city [of Rome] was built, in the first place, Romulus divided all the multitude that were of age to bear arms into military companies, each company consisting of three thousand footmen and three thousand horsemen. Such a company was called a "legion" [λεγεών], because the warlike were selected [λογάδας] out of all.

In this foundational myth of Rome's empire, Plutarch describes the origin of the Roman legion, including the background of the term itself. Playing on one of the meanings of λέγω, "gather, pick up" (Liddell et al. 1996, s.v.), he explains that the warlike company was called

---

3. Garroway defends his analogy from the possible objection that Marines and Legion are different organizational units. There are two more important issues, however, not discussed by Garroway. (1) Since "legion" was a loanword in both Greek and Aramaic at the time of Mark, it is relevant to ask whether "marines" is being used as a loanword in present-day Iraq. Judging from consultation with friends with an Iraqi background, "marines" (written in Arabic) does seem to be in use as a loanword, which strengthens the analogy. (2) However, since it appears that demon possession is rare in Iraq, it is rather awkward to place a story about demon possession in present-day Iraq. Despite this problem, however, the analogy is helpful.

4. The various degrees with which a loanword is integrated into a language can be illustrated by the English language, where a loanword such as *Sitz im Leben* represents an inherently foreign case and words such as *umbrella*, *gas*, and *fail* are completely assimilated to the native word-stock. See Chalker and Weiner 1998, s.v. "Borrowing."

5. The earliest attestation is in Diodorus Siculus 26.5. The term is used frequently in papyri (i.e., Grenfell et al. 1898–2010 [P.Oxy.] 276, 9; 2760, 8–9; 3111, 5–6; Schubart et al. 1895–2005 [BGU] 272, 1; 802, XIV, 25; 1108, 3 etc.) and inscriptions (Dittenberger 1903–1905 [*OGIS*] 540, 15–18; 548, 9; 643, 7; 716, 4, etc.) to designate various Roman legions.

λεγεών because they were *selected* (λογάδας) among Rome's first multitude.[6] Further, in his biography on Otho, Plutarch (*Otho* 12) refers to the military forces of Otho and Vitellius as "two legions," δύο λεγεῶνες, and adds the explaining phrase "(as the Romans call the troops)" (οὕτω γὰρ τὰ τάγματα 'Ρομαῖοι καλοῦσιν).[7] An almost identical expression is used by Nicolaus of Damascus (*Vit. Caes.* 31). As indicated by these parenthetical remarks, the term λεγιών was specifically used for the Roman military. To denote military troops in general, a number of Greek terms could be used (τάγμα, σύνταγυα, σύνταξις, δύναμις, παρεμβολή, στρατιά), several of which Josephus and/or the Septuagint used and some of which were also used to designate Roman legions.[8] Even if the Roman army could be named with other Greek terms, then, the term λεγιών was only used for Roman troops. The foreign, unassimilated character of λεγιών as a loanword is therefore difficult to deny; even if Mark uses the term to signify a large number of unclean spirits, it nonetheless remains semantically tied to the Roman military.

The imagery of the Markan episode adds further weight to the double reference inherent in λεγιών. As pointed out by Duncan Derrett (1979), the text is imbued with military vocabulary. Once the name Legion has been revealed, several other military allusions are displayed: ἀποστείλῃ means *dispatch*, as of an officer sending a troop (5:10); ἀγέλη means *herd* but was also a local term for a band of trainees (5:11); ἐπέτρεψεν, *permitted*, could denote an issuing of a military command (5:13); and ὥρμησεν, *rushed*, a troop rushing into battle (5:13).

Apart from these general military allusions, some specific features allude to the particular situation at the time that Mark's Gospel was beginning to circulate. The tenth Roman legion, Legio X Fretensis, which was stationed in Decapolis at the time of Mark's composition, had a boar as their ensign, thus matching the herd of swine. Also, as argued by Lau

---

6. Later in the account, the size of a legion is doubled (Plutarch, *Rom.* 20). Plutarch's explanation tallies with the etymological background of the Latin term *legio* (Vaan 2008, 332–33; Beekes and Beek 2010, 841–42).

7. I concede that Plutarch uses a different style of Greek than Mark does. The example nonetheless indicates how closely connected the term "legion" was, not just to *any* military, but to the Roman military *in particular*.

8. Dionysius of Halicarnassus (*Ant. rom.* 6.42) referred to ten Roman legions with the phrase δέκα στρατιωτικὰ τάγματα. Similarly, Strabo (*Geogr.* 3.3.8) used the expression τριῶν ταγμάτων στρατιωτικὸν to designate three Roman legions.

(2007), although the number two thousand (5:13) is considerably less than a complete Roman legion, it amazingly corresponds to the size of the vexillation of Legio X Fretensis, which was initially dispatched to fight the first battle in the Jewish War (Josephus, *J.W.* 2.499–506).

Of course, λεγιών does not refer *only* or even *primarily* to Roman troops in Mark's text. When the demoniac answers λεγιὼν ὄνομά μοι, it is clearly a reference to the demons, and the fact that they are "many." Interestingly enough, however, there appear to be no texts before Mark that use λεγιών as a name for a large amount of demons, nor as an expression for "a countless number," as it is used in contemporary English.[9] Mark's use of the word, then, aptly illustrates a catachresis in Spivak's sense—a local, tactical maneuver that wrenches a term out of its place within an imperial discourse and uses it to open up a new arena of meaning, often in direct contrast to how it is conventionally understood.

All things considered, it is becoming increasingly difficult *not* to interpret the Latinism λεγιών in Mark 5:9 as alluding in a critical sense to the Roman domination in the East. But allowing this double reference, one can nonetheless interpret the episode in somewhat different ways. Before proceeding with my postcolonial reading, I will discuss a group of readings of the episode that have been instrumental for anti-imperial readings of Mark.

Functionalist Readings

An influential interpretation of the episode was offered by Paul Hollenbach (1981), whose impact can be seen in Crossan (1992, 313–18), Waetjen (1989, 115–18), and R. Horsley (2001, 141–48). Hollenbach approached the phenomenon of demon possession from a social scientific perspective. With the help of cultural anthropologists such as I. M. Lewis, Ari Kiev, and Erika Bouruignon, he argued for a correlation between mental illness and demon possession on the one hand and social tensions and oppression on the other. Thus Hollenbach (1981, 573) suggested that colonial domination ought to be seen as "the causal context of possession."

Particularly relevant to Hollenbach's study was Frantz Fanon's *Wretched of the Earth*. According to Hollenbach (1981, 573), both Fanon's Algeria

---

9. A possible Latin parallel is found in Horace, who refers to a "cohort of fever demons" (*Carm.* 1.3.30: *febrium ... cohors*).

and Jesus' Palestine were plagued by "oppressive colonialism." For Fanon, as discussed previously, colonialism generates a Manichaeism among the oppressed natives that is expressed in a "permanent dream ... to become the persecutor."[10] When this dream is not realized, Fanon claims, the psychic frustrations are canalized and transformed into different forms of ecstatic religion, such as trance dance and demonic possession. Demon possession, according to Hollenbach (576), can therefore function "as a 'fix' for people who saw no other way to cope with the horrendous social and political conditions in which they found their lot cast."

Mark's account of the Gerasene demoniac was for Hollenbach (581) an especially revealing and rare example of what social scientists had called an "oblique aggressive strategy" (Lewis), "a regression on the service of the self" (Bourguignon), and "at once both a disease and cure" (Fanon). The madness of the demoniac "permitted him to do in a socially accepted manner what he could not do as sane, namely, express his total hostility to the Romans; he did this by identifying the Roman legions with demons" (Hollenbach, 581).

With this interpretation Hollenbach explained the somewhat hostile attitude of the townspeople against Jesus after the exorcism—their asking him to leave their region (5:17). In his possessed state, the demoniac had expressed hostility toward the Romans in a socially acceptable way that stabilized the community and helped maintain a kind of peace, a colonial status quo. Since Jesus' exorcism disrupted this peace, Hollenbach argues, the locals became hostile.

Hollenbach's study broke new ground and initiated a new discussion on the political aspects of demon possession, shown not least by Crossan (1992, 313–18), who paradoxically included it in his work on the historical Jesus without claiming the story's historicity. Similarly, R. Horsley (2001, 147) rephrased Hollenbach's suggestions and interpreted the exorcism of Legion as a "demystification of (the belief in) demons and demon possession."

Although these readings are psychosocially insightful, we need to address some problems. First, it is not clear whether Hollenbach is discussing how an actual historical event might be understood or what Mark as a text might have meant to its initial audience. As I read Hollenbach, he seems to be doing the former, which invites criticism in terms of

---

10. Hollenbach 1981, 573, quoting Fanon.

historicity (cf. S. Davies 1995, 78–81). It is not that demon possession in general should be ruled out as a historical possibility, but rather that this particular episode contains some fantastical images that most academics would view as fictitious.

A more difficult problem, however, concerns Hollenbach's use of Fanon's writings. Fanon based his understanding of demon possession and ecstatic religion on his work as a psychiatrist in colonized Algeria. Being a modern scientist and influenced by Marxist thought, Fanon regarded religion in general and ecstatic religion in particular as an escape from reality. In his view (2004, 18–20), ecstatic rituals functioned as a kind of opium of the people, keeping the oppressed from seeing the real problem. The only solution was to transform aggressiveness into political struggle: "During the struggle for liberation there is a singular loss of interest in these rituals. With his back to the wall, the knife at his throat, or to be more exact the electrode on his genitals, the colonized subject is bound to stop telling stories." Without denying that ecstatic rituals at times could function as a delusion that stabilizes a colonial order, Fanon can also be criticized for upholding a problematic distinction between "telling stories" and struggling politically to end colonialism.

When used to interpret Mark's story, moreover, the inherently modern way of understanding possession becomes problematic. Fanon's understanding presupposes a secular sphere from which to criticize and reduce a religious phenomenon to a social function. Such a sphere would hardly have been available to Mark's audience. Hollenbach's study can therefore be criticized for pushing aside indigenous reports (Strecker 2002, 122; Donaldson 2005, 102–6) and reducing religious notions in a way that would have been foreign in a premodern context.[11] Further, Hollenbach's reading does not quite fit with Mark's narrative. According to his Fanonian reading, the exorcism ought to have made the Gerasene "stop telling stories," and begin to fight politically against the real cause of the problem—Rome's imperial order. For Mark, however, there are no such two opposite alternatives; Mark actually describes the cured Gerasene as being eager to tell

---

11. The reductionist stance is criticized by the anthropologist Lewis (2003, 105) as a "nostalgic picture of the pristinely innocent character of possession in its traditional, pre-colonial setting." As Lewis tried to show, demon possession and other kinds of ecstatic religion can also serve other functions, including that of being socially disruptive rather than stabilizing.

the story of Jesus (5:20). And storytelling is surely an important aspect of struggles for social change.

Imperial Hypermasculinity

In order to offer a postcolonial reading, I begin by placing the episode in its narrative context. After the incipit's counterimperial signals, Mark's story develops an oppositional plot that potentially interpellates the audience to an antagonistic position. Jesus' struggle with Satan (1:12–13), the arrest of John the Baptist (1:14), and the Galilean manifesto of God's empire being close at hand (1:14–15) clearly signal opposition. Jesus is depicted as attracting increasing support and as overcoming a growing hostility. Calling disciples (1:16–20) and teaching powerfully (1:21–22), Jesus is confronted with opposition from unclean spirits (1:23–24). As the demons are conquered (1:25–26; 3:11) and the illnesses are cured (1:30–34, 40–42; 2:1–12; 3:5), Jesus is portrayed as a victorious leader who attracts the support of an increasingly wider population (1:35–39, 45; 2:4; 3:7–10). At the same time, however, the opposition is extended to include several important social groups, such as the scribes (2:6), the Pharisees (2:16, 24; 3:6), and the Herodians (3:6). Although these groups would generally not have a common interest, Mark depicts them as forming a religio-political alliance against Jesus. Since Mark associates them with the unclean spirits, the story plots Jesus and his followers on a dangerously oppositional course in relation to an alliance of influential groups and unclean spirits in the local society.

The oppositional drama is significantly escalated as Jesus, in an echo of the Davidic monarchy, ascends on a mountain and appoints twelve followers (3:13–19). Here my reading merges with other political readings (R. Horsley 2001, 101–11; Myers 1988; Theissen 2002, 238) that highlight the plot's political dimension. This emblematic act presents Jesus and his Galilean disciples as forming a renewed Israel in opposition to the Judean administration and its collaboration with the Romans. As a further sign of the escalating conflict, the opposition to Jesus is intensified as his family and the scribes from Jerusalem come to indict him for being out of his senses and possessed by Beelzebul (3:21–22). These accusations, however, are countered as the Markan Jesus tells the forceful parable about plundering a strong man's house (3:23–27). With the militant imagery of binding and plundering, Jesus is symbolically associated with the revolutionary bandits who were the main initiators of the anti-Roman rebellion (cf.

15. IMPERIAL SATIRE (5:1–20)

Thurman 2003, 147). Resembling anti-imperial apocalypticism, the parable presumes Satan to be the spiritual ruler of the world.[12] As anticipated by the imperial terminology in the incipit, the intertwined demonic/social opposition to Jesus in Mark here appears to include Rome.

Whereas up to this point Mark's account has had a relatively high speed and intense action, the pace is slowed down in the relatively lengthy description of Jesus' teaching by the Sea of Galilee (4:1–34), where the seed parables about the empire of God are narrated. The poetic and enigmatic parables invite reflection and pause the oppositional plot. The more observant among the audience would surely hear the subtle allusion to Peter in the seed parable. With a wordplay on the name Πέτρος, which means "rock," the Markan Jesus describes how some seed is falling on "the rocky places" (τὸ πετρῶδες, 4:5, 16), thereby anticipating the subsequent failure of Peter (8:32–33; 14:66–72).

The last parable, the one about the mustard seed (4:30–32), is particularly interesting. God's kingdom is like a mustard seed, Jesus says, and explains that although it is "the smallest of all the seeds on earth," it eventually grows and "becomes larger than all garden herbs, and gets large branches so that the birds of the air can make nests in its shade." This imagery reminds one of how empires were often depicted in antiquity: a large tree in which birds build their nests. Ezekiel (17:23; 31:6), for instance, depicts an imperial dream for Israel with this image. Similarly, in Daniel (4:10–12, 20–21) such a tree represents the empire of Nebuchadnezzar. As seen in Suetonius (*Aug.* 94), Rome also made use of this image. A great palm tree in which doves build their nests symbolizes Rome's empire under the leadership of Augustus.

Although the Markan Jesus makes use of imperial imagery to describe the kingdom of God, there is also an unmistaken discrepancy. Rather than a large and mighty tree that usually represents an empire, Mark has Jesus use the image of a garden herb or shrub (λαχάνων) that in full size becomes between two and three meters tall. Matthew (13:32) tries to cover up the discrepancy by adding "and becomes a tree." But for Mark it remains a mustard shrub, which hardly represents an empire—almost the same *but not quite*, as Bhabha would have put it. As we will see, this subtle

---

12. 1 En. 6:1–8; 10:1–8; 1QM 1:14–15; 4Q286; Rev 12:9; 20:2. Apocalyptic literature will be discussed in ch. 17.

discrepancy will play an important role in the eventual undermining of the oppositional plot.

With the crucial line "Let us go over to the other side" (εἰς τὸ πέραν, 4:35), however, the narrative speed again increases; and the tranquil teaching scene passes into a dramatic boat trip in which the disciples fear for their lives, and Jesus, after being woken from an unexpected sleep, stills the storm (4:38–39). This remarkable trip brings Jesus to "the country of the Gerasenes" (5:1) and the beginning of the particular episode that is the focus of this chapter.

The designation "Gerasenes" is itself a conundrum. Located about 50 kilometers southeast of the lake, the surrounding χώρα of Gerasa could hardly have extended all the way to the lake. Perhaps Mark did not have what we might call an accurate understanding of geography. This seems to be what Matthew thought, since he replaced "Gerasenes" with "Gadarenes" (Matt 8:28). Some scribes have made similar attempts to "correct" Mark, and there is consequently textual uncertainty. Having strong external support as well as being the *lectio difficilior*, most scholars take "Gerasenes" to be the best reading.[13] Most likely, I would argue, the designation carries a poetic significance that is more important for Mark's narrative than accurate geography. According to a common suggestion, repeated by Moore (2006, 28), the name Gerasa stems from the Hebrew root גרש, which means "banish, drive out, cast out," and the like. This Hebrew wordplay strengthens the episode's poetical and allegorical character.

As the scene begins on the other side of the lake, it is important to recognize the narrative context. In an article on the imagery of this episode, Joshua Garroway (2009) points out a correlation between the seed parables and the expulsion of Legion in Gerasa. If the stilling of the storm (4:35–41) is taken as a scene connector, he persuasively argues, the events in Gerasa constitute a narrative illustration of the seed parable.[14] The above noted change of narrative speed adds further weight to Garroway's suggestion.

The disciples are now curiously absent—perhaps the audience assumes they are sleeping after the traumatic voyage. In any case, Jesus has evidently slept enough this night, and as soon as he gets out of the boat the

---

13. The difficulty is discussed in most commentaries; see, e.g., A. Collins 2007, 263–64.

14. The recurring marker "to the other side" (εἰς τὸ πέραν, 4:35; 5:1) strengthens the case for taking the boat trip as being a scene connector.

action continues when he is approached by a man "from the tombs with an unclean spirit" (5:2). Here the pace is somewhat reduced when Mark describes in several sentences (lengthy by Mark's standard) the man's condition: he is living among the tombs day and night, being uncontrollable and impossible to restrain even with chains and shackles, and crying out and beating himself with stones. Presumably performed with stark emotions by the orator, the powerful image of a deranged, asocial human being that the audience is here presented with seems highly symbolic, inviting an imaginative interpretation.

The subsequent interaction between Jesus and the possessed man adds further weight to the wild and desolate tone of the episode. It is not clear whether Jesus is speaking with the unclean spirit or the man; it seems to be a disharmonic combination of the two. The vagueness of the subject adds significantly to the description of the man's condition. "One can scent the spirit as well as hear the man," as Gundry (1993, 261) puts it. Further, as the catachrestical name λεγιών is pronounced (5:9), an association is established between the unclean spirits and the Roman military. Like the Roman military forces, the demons express a desire to stay in the area (5:10). The possessed man in his deranged state thus becomes a metonym for those subdued by Rome's army, which strengthens the already established oppositional plot. Indeed, the driving of Legion into the sea takes this plot to a climax.

Having previously likened the oppositional stance of Jesus to that of the anti-Roman bandits, Mark here intensifies this symbolism. As Garroway contends, Jesus' encounter with Legion illustrates the inevitable confrontation between the empire of God and the prevailing empire of Rome. Jesus is depicted as being victorious and overpowering Legion, which Garroway takes as imitating imperial ideology and hence as presenting Jesus as the ultimate Caesar. Let us explore this reading a little further. The Caesar for Mark's audience was Vespasian. Under his lead the Roman military had recently displayed its physical superiority in the East. Mark's catachrestic use of λεγιών with reference to demons that have a desire to stay in this particular area is therefore remarkable and calls for a juxtaposition of Jesus and Vespasian. The similarities displayed in table 4 seem especially pertinent.

TABLE 4. SIMILARITIES BETWEEN VESPASIAN AND JESUS

Vespasian	Jesus
Travels to a foreign land (Josephus, *J.W.* 3.8)	Travels to a foreign land (4:35–41)
Heals a blind man with spittle (Suetonius, *Vesp.* 7)	Heals a blind man with spittle (8:22–26)[15]
Heals a man with a withered hand (Dio Cassius 65.8.1)	Heals a man with a withered hand (3:3:1–5)
Is declared emperor in the East (Josephus, *J.W.* 4.618)	Is declared Son of God in the East (5:9)
Fulfills Jewish messianic expectations (*J.W.* 6.312–313)	Fulfills Jewish messianic expectations (8:29)
Establishes Rome's empire by crushing rebels with his legion	Manifests God's empire by driving out Legion (5:9–13)
Rescues the empire from internal instability	Rescues the man from self-immolation (5:3–4, 15)
Sends troops to Gerasa (Josephus, *J.W.* 4.488)	Sends the cured demoniac to Gerasa (5:17)

Most of these parallels I discussed in the previous chapter. Regarding the last parallel, it is interesting to note that, in Josephus as well as in Mark, the designation Gerasa fits poorly with the geography. Since the city was located some 80 kilometers from Jerusalem, it is difficult to understand why Vespasian would send troops there just when he was about to secure Jerusalem on all sides. Some scholars have therefore questioned the correctness of Josephus's account (Schürer 1979, 150; Smallwood 1976, 311). The geographic inaccuracy could add another poetic dimension to Mark. If Josephus was rendering stories, known to Mark's audience, about Vespasian's brutal and pitiless invasion of Gerasa, the driving out of Legion from the Gerasa area connects more directly to events that were perceived as contemporaneous for Mark's audience.[16] As far as Mark's audience was

---

15. This parallel has been explored more closely by Eve 2008.
16. Cf. Myers (1988, 191) and Wink (1986, 44–45), both of whom regard Vespasian's sacking of Gerasa, reported by Josephus, to be significant for the interpretation

concerned, I would argue, Vespasian had attacked Gerasa. Since Mark locates the encounter between Jesus and the legion of demons in the χώρα of the very same city, the anti-Roman symbolism is embedded in the painful poetics of Gerasa. The parallel between Jesus and Vespasian is thereby strengthened.

Considering the astonishing parallels, the resemblance between the Markan Jesus and Vespasian would surely have signaled competition and antagonism to Mark's audience. As Jesus drives out Legion, a challenge is posed to the audience as to who is the true ruler of the world. Jesus is here symbolically presented as taking the position of a true emperor, in effect turning the dichotomy between dominant and subdued on its head.

Moreover, the reversal is given a more sarcastic twist when the issue of gender is considered. According to Laura Donaldson (2005, 102–4), anticolonial readings tend to neglect how gender inflects Mark's story. She sees the possessed man's wrenching apart his chains and breaking up his shackles as a display of excessive, unruly maleness—or, in other words, as an expression of hypermasculinity. Taking the call by Donaldson in a somewhat different direction than she suggests, however, it seems relevant to reflect on the meaning of this image. The possessed man symbolically represents the suffering of those subdued by Rome. But there seems to be more to this rich, desolate imagery. If the self-immolating demoniac symbolizes uncontrolled strength and hypermasculinity, it also represents a critical satire on imperial masculinity itself. Whereas imperial discourse upheld the Roman military as an archimage of masculinity and regarded its victories as decisive for upholding peace and security, Mark depicts it as a perverted hypermasculinity. Since self-mastery was closely connected to masculinity in ancient Mediterranean culture (Moore and Anderson 1998), Legion in Mark's account is not masculine: it cannot control its strength and is therefore unmanly. And rather than sustaining peace and security, it is associated with mental derangement and self-immolation. If the episode in this way sarcastically critiques and mocks imperial notions of strength and masculinity, it also presents Jesus as the stronger one, the true man that with a simple verbal command controls and overpowers Legion (5:8). The degree of imperial reproduction in this episode is therefore considerable.

---

of Mark's account. They do not, however, consider the geographic problems in Mark or in Josephus.

Whereas my reading until this point more or less coalesces with Garroway's, here our ways part. According to Garroway, the imperial reproduction is undermined by the episode's second part. As Jesus instructs the cured demoniac (5:19–20), Garroway (2009, 68–71) argues, imperial ideology is subverted in that the cured demoniac becomes an image of the previously rendered allegory of the mustard seed. Although I agree about the connection to the seed allegory, I find unpersuasive Garroway's interpretation of it.

A crucial event for Garroway is the request by the locals that Jesus leave their region (5:17). This hostile attitude of the locals has generated different explanations among scholars.[17] Garroway here largely builds his case upon Marcus (2000, 353–54), who contends that there is a structural similarity between the hostile demons and the hostile locals. With this reading, the demonic opposition to Jesus does not disappear after the exorcism. Instead, as Marcus (353) states, "the reaction of the hostile townspeople to Jesus mirrors that of the demons in a remarkable way." From this alleged structural parallelism, Marcus (354) discusses the townspeople's negative reaction in terms of a "vicious counterattack" and interprets the episode as illustrating that the hostility "of demon-inspired people" has not hindered the proclamation of God's mighty work through Jesus.

In support of his argument, Marcus (353) points out four similarities between the demons and the townspeople: (1) they are both drawn to Jesus "almost against their will" (5:6, 14–15); (2) their initial reaction is one of fear (5:7, 15); (3) they entreat (παρακαλέω) Jesus (5:10, 17); and (4) the demons desire to stay in possession of the territory (5:10), "and so their human agents evict Jesus from it (5:17)." However, since some of these points are unconvincing, the parallel is rather dubious. Regarding point one, there are no signals in the episode indicating that the locals would be unwilling to come and see what had happened. In relation to point three, the verb παρακαλέω is used by the formerly possessed man not only in verse 10 and 17 but also in verse 18, which severely unsettles the parallel. Also, whereas in verse 10 the Legion entreat (παρακαλέω) Jesus not to send them (μὴ ἀποστείλῃ) out of the *country* (χώρα), in verse 17 the townspeople

---

17. A. Collins (2007, 272–73) regards their hostility as an expression of awe that often attends a divine manifestation. Hollenbach, R. Horsley, and Crossan, in turn, interpret it from the functional understanding of demon possession (see above). Sugirtharajah (2002, 93) and Runesson (2007), finally, see the negative reaction as typical of local elites who collaborate with colonizers.

entreat (παρακαλέω) Jesus himself to leave (ἀπελθεῖν) the *region* (ὅριον). The opposite directions (μὴ ἀποστείλῃ, "not send away" vs. ἀπελθεῖν, "go away") and the use of different words for "country" and "region" (χώρα and ὅριον) weaken the parallel. As to point four, it seems to consist of circular evidence. I simply cannot see where in the episode the townspeople are appointed as human agents of the demons. At most, we are left with a blurred similarity between the demons and the townspeople.

Since the existence of a parallel is doubtful, Garroway's explanation of the hostile attitude of the Gerasenes becomes equally unpersuasive. "Of course they are angry," Garroway (2009, 69) states, "they constitute the structural parallel to the legion on the previous scene." In what seems to be circular reasoning, he argues that the Gerasenes are hostile because they are a textual parallel to the demons. But if the parallel is dubious on textual grounds, which seems to be the case, their hostility remains enigmatic and needs to be understood in a different way. In Garroway's reading, the alleged structural parallelism becomes the basis for his argument that the second part of Mark's episode displays a subversion of the imperial concepts of kingdom and invasion. Whereas invasion in imperial discourse implies violence and brutality, Garroway (68–71) contends, invasion in Mark's narrative is achieved through preaching—or, metaphorically, through the planting of a mustard seed; hence the title of his article, "The Invasion of a Mustard Seed."

But is this a subversion of imperial discourse? The matter is quite complicated. Of course, expansion by military violence is different from expansion by preaching. But a postcolonial reading of the seed parable cannot neglect what lies in front of the text—how the text later becomes part of imperial discourses and in that sense carries the seed of imperial *expansion* rather than subversion. Since Garroway (67, 70) labels the Gerasenes *Gentiles*, associates them with demonic hostility against Jesus, and depicts them as "poised to be penetrated," a problematic reproduction of Christian imperial categorizations and imageries are set in play. Recalling the nineteenth-century readings that regarded the cured demoniac as "the first apostle of the heathen" (see ch. 6), one might ask how an interpretation that celebrates the proclamation of God's kingdom among demonized Gentiles is postcolonial.[18] As pointed out by David Joy (2008, 173), who is

---

18. Although it is somewhat unclear if Garroway claims to conduct a postcolonial interpretation, the essay is presented as a "riff on Moore's proposal" (Garroway 2009, 59).

located in an Indian multifaith context, interpretations that regard the episode as referring to "the unclean Gentile worship of idols" are often hostile to interreligious cooperation.

Being unconvinced by Garroway's reading of the episode's second part, I am left with the question of imperial reproduction. As we saw, Mark sarcastically turns the present order on its head. Those who are the world's number one, feared by all, are associated with unmanly and uncontrolled strength, even pure stupidity. Vespasian's messianic claim is falsified and replaced by the true Messiah, the true man, Jesus Christ. The oppositional plot that here reaches its climax in Mark's story involves a considerable portion of imperial duplication. This should not come as a surprise. The presence of an empire tends to imprint itself on bodies, thoughts, and how people understand themselves. It both sets limits for and makes possible certain ways of thinking and acting. What is more surprising, however, is that Mark also is offering something else. Although it will become more evident as the story continues, the oppositional climax itself already carries a seed that destabilizes the clear-cut anti-Roman position. As we saw from the parable section (4:1–34), Mark seems especially fond of such seeds.

Similar to Garroway, I find the seed parables to be crucial for understanding the Gerasene demoniac. These parables elaborate on the proclaimed manifesto of God's empire (1:14–15) and are dramatized in the intense events in Gerasa. Via the boat trip, the parables on the one side of the sea are linked to the events "on the other side" (4:35). As already mentioned, there are some subtle signals in these parables that undermine the oppositional plot. The seeds that fall on "the rocky places" (4:5, 16) anticipate a coming crisis concerning Peter, whose name means "rock." And the imagery of the mustard shrub in which the birds of the air can make nests (4:30–32) resembles, and yet differs from, the large trees that usually represent empires. By these features, the oppositional colliding of Rome's empire with God's empire becomes less clear-cut and the imperial reproduction of the oppositional climax is somewhat muted. Mark's Jesus, it seems, does more than replace Vespasian.

In this light, we are offered a new understanding of the local population's sending away of Jesus, as discussed above. Victories in the imperial culture were typically celebrated with triumphs. The conquering and manly acts of Jesus in Gerasa therefore generate expectations among the audience for triumph and salutation. Contrary to such expectations, however, the locals send Jesus away without showing any sense of gratitude. As will be seen, a similar pattern of unfulfilled expectations will be found in the entry story (11:1–11). What takes place after the victorious act on the mountain's steep bank, therefore, communicates a subtle yet significant reservation concerning the oppositional climax. Being only the beginning of what will soon become a narrative crisis, this reservation seems to represent the actual mustard seed.

16

Entering a Narrative Crisis (7:24–30)

> Can the subaltern speak?
> —Spivak (1988a, 294, 296)

"I cannot see the problem with this text," one of my students exclaimed, after having been assigned the task of conducting an ideological critique of Mark 7:24–30. Evidently, the student was familiar with Luther's (1983, 148–54) reading of the story. Taking the encounter between Jesus and the woman as a parable of a believer's relation to God, Luther took the Syrophoenician woman (or Canaanite in Matt 15:21–28)—with her insistent refusal to give up—as representing how a Christian ought to pray: even if God seems to be silent and dismissive, the believer ought not to give up. This is an important text, the student argued, since the experience of not having your prayers answered is common. Exegetically, the student might be right, at least according to Marcus (2000, 469), who states that Luther was on "the right exegetical track."

A more common interpretation takes the episode in a historical sense, whereby the woman represents the historical stage in early Christianity where non-Jews, to use Paul's imagery (Rom 11:17–24), were grafted into the olive tree. Even if this salvation-historical interpretation is also exegetically possible, it neglects the discourses of empire—ancient and modern—with which the text has interacted. Initially, indicated not least by the curious description of the woman as "a Greek, a Syrophoenician by birth" (Mark 7:26), this episode reflects a hybridity that was common in the ancient imperial setting.

In a postcolonial framework, the intersections of ethnicity, gender, and social status that appear in the episode are of particular significance. Initially it is interesting to note that although both Jesus and the woman are Roman subjects, their positions in relation to imperial discourse are far from similar. Unlike Jesus, who is presented as a Jewish Messiah with his base in rural Galilee, the woman's hybrid Greek-Syrophoenician identity locates her in the Hellenistic city of Tyre. The borderland on which their meeting takes place (7:24) might then serve as an image of the intersecting borders—man/woman, Jew/Greek, rural/city—that are actualized in their meeting. Judging from these divisions, it is difficult to tell who was dominant. Whereas the woman would probably represent the dominant from an urban Hellenistic standpoint, the opposite would be true from a Jewish Galilean perspective. Since the Markan Jesus is God's Son, one would perhaps expect him to somehow stand above such earthly borders. But in this episode he is curiously human and seems to be deeply enmeshed in the cultural complexity of the situation.

Given the complex categorizations that are set in play by this episode, a postcolonial perspective seems especially suitable. It comes as no surprise then that the episode has received ample attention from postcolonial biblical scholars.[1] Richard Horsley (2001, 212–15) has interpreted the woman as a representative of the non-Israelites who joined what he understands to be an anti-imperial movement for the fulfillment of Israel. Jim Perkinson (1996) has read it as a dislocation of the word of salvation, which opens up for a Christology of hybridity. Laura Donaldson (2005), in turn, has read the story from the viewpoint of the silent daughter, whom she sees as representing the indigenous subaltern.

Here I will analyze the meeting between Jesus and the woman. Beginning by discussing how we are to understand Jesus' harsh attitude, I continue by challenging the dominant tradition of labeling the woman a *Gentile*. I end the chapter by suggesting that the episode's way of introducing gender and ethnicity institutes a narrative crisis in relation to Mark's initial antagonistic plot.

A Prejudiced Jesus?

What immediately strikes a modern reader of this Markan episode is the dismissive, belittling, and even insulting attitude with which Jesus first treats the woman. The woman and her child are unmistakably equated with κυνάρια (little dogs), and since comparisons to dogs were generally regarded as insulting and dishonoring in Mediterranean culture (Michel 1965), the derogatory nature of the expression would not have escaped

---

1. See Kwok 1995, 71–83; Dube 2000, 125–95; and Rebera 2001.

Mark's audience. Typically, liberationist and feminist readings have tended to overlook this problem, focusing instead on the positive side. Since the woman succeeded in persuading Jesus, the story is taken as a message of inclusion. Hence Mary Ann Tolbert (1989, 185) states that "by faith, Greek can share the children's bread" (cf. Myers 1988, 205). Similarly, Herman Waetjen (1989, 134–36) argues that the episode communicates that table fellowship is not related to nationality, gender, or religious tradition; all those who respond in faith share the children's bread. In this way the woman is seen as a representation of the true disciple. Most influential, perhaps, is the interpretation by Elisabeth Schüssler Fiorenza (1983, 138), who upholds this woman as "the apostolic 'foremother' of all gentile Christians." A problem with these interpretations is the (often implicit) presumption that the woman became a Christian (or Christ follower) and the exclusion that this implies. Even if the child in this story was helped by the mother's acceptance of an inferior position, what about those mothers and fathers who find the position of a dog unacceptable? And what about those non-Jewish or non-Christian believers who are not interested in converting? Are they still to be regarded as dogs?

In a later work, however, Schüssler Fiorenza (1992, 162) acknowledges the problem. Referring to her previous interpretation, she clarifies that it "should not be used to deflect a critical theological discussion and ethical evaluation of the prejudice and discriminatory stance ascribed to Jesus." The first step in such a critical discussion would seem to be to ask whether Mark hints at any particular reasons for Jesus' harsh behavior. In this regard, two possibilities present themselves: either the insult is related to her having a non-Jewish religion/ethnicity, or it is related to her gender. In relation to the first hypothesis, being non-Jewish does not in itself seem to call forth a negative reaction from Jesus in Mark's Gospel. There are two episodes where Jesus cures (what appears to be) non-Jewish people: the Gerasene demoniac (5:1–20) and the healing of a deaf man (7:31–37).[2] And in both incidents Jesus shows no hesitancy to help these individuals simply because they are non-Jews. As for the second hypothesis, one can draw a similar conclusion. There are two female characters in Mark that are depicted as being helped by Jesus: Simon's mother-in-law (1:29–31) and the daughter of Jairus (5:21–24, 35–43). Although in this last instance

---

2. The non-Jewishness of the Gerasene demoniac is signaled by the geography. As for 7:31-37, non-Jews were often associated with deafness in Hebrew tradition (Marcus 2000, 472; cf. Isa 42:17–19; 43:8–9; Mic 7:16).

it is a male character who makes the request, this does not preclude the contention that in Mark's Gospel female gender is itself no reason for Jesus to respond negatively to a request.

Thus, rather than being related to one particular categorization, Jesus' apparently offensive attitude toward the Syrophoenician woman seems to be more connected to the combined effect of intersecting categorizations. In addition to gender and ethnicity, the meeting between Jesus and the woman also seems to be a meeting between rural Galilee and urban Tyre (cf. Theissen 1992, 61–80). As argued above (ch. 13), the urban/rural opposition was important in imperial discourse and often involved tension and hostility. That the woman represents the city is indicated first by the designation Ἑλληνίς, which in combination with the phrase Συροφοινίκισσα τῷ γένει implies that the woman was hellenized. The Phoenicians were a Semitic people, renowned for their dark red dye as well as their significant impact on the Mediterranean world during the first millennium B.C.E. (Peckham 1992). During the first century, however, the great days of Phoenicia were passed, and just like other peoples they were subdued by Rome (Pliny, *Nat.* 5.75–76). As Theissen (1992, 70) points out, most Phoenicians at the time of Mark's writing were not hellenized—that is, they could not speak Greek and were not accustomed to Greek culture. Those who were hellenized were usually the more affluent city dwellers.

A further indication to the woman's socially elevated urban identity is the term Mark uses for the bed on which the daughter was lying (7:30). Rather than κράβαττος, which designated the simpler mat or pallet on the floor (2:4–12; 6:55), the daughter was lying on a κλίνη, which implies a construction with legs.[3] That the woman had a "real bed" at home therefore points to a more affluent status. She would thus have been seen as occupying a dominant position relative to Jesus, who in Mark is located in the countryside.

In sum, Mark's depiction of the meeting between Jesus and the woman stages several intersecting categorizations and would therefore have sent complex signals to Mark's audience. Before continuing to interpret these signals, however, we need to deal with the rather pressing issue of the woman's identity.

---

3. As is evident from Mark 4:21, a lamp could be placed under a κλίνη.

Is She a "Gentile"?

A crucial question that is raised when this text is placed in a postcolonial frame concerns the designation or categorization of the woman. Although Mark describes her as Ἑλληνίς, which means "Greek," biblical scholars more often refer to her with the exegetically suspect designation "Gentile." Mark calls her ἡ δὲ γυνὴ ἦν Ἑλληνίς, Συροφοινίκισσα τῷ γένει, which literally means "the woman was Greek, a Syrophoenician by birth." The vast majority of commentators, however, translate Ἑλληνίς as "Gentile."[4] The reasons given for this interpretation are typically brief, indicating the existence of a scholarly consensus. This consensus, however, neglects to consider that if Mark had wanted to present her as non-Jewish in general, he could have done so by using the term ἐθνικός.[5] Also, the consensus appears to ignore the dictionary entries of Windisch (1964) and Bauer et al. (2000, s.v. "Ἑλληνίς").[6]

In what follows, therefore, I will exegetically challenge a dominant interpretive tradition by arguing that Ἑλληνίς in Mark means "Greek," and that although this for some of Mark's audience might have implied a general non-Jewish identity, most would have taken it as referring more specifically to the Greek culture that had spread from the time of Alexander the Great. The exegetical argument involves three steps: (1) the usage of Ἕλλην in 1 and 2 Maccabees; (2) the usage of Ἕλλην in the New Testament writings; and (3) the possibility of taking Ἑλληνίς, Συροφοινίκισσα τῷ γένει as indicating a hybrid identity.

1. Since Ἕλλην or Ἑλληνίς occurs only in Mark's Gospel, its meaning is often based on its use in other texts. Hence Lars Hartman (2004, 241) contends that Ἑλληνίς in Mark means *hedning* (the Swedish term for "Gentile," "pagan," or "heathen"), with reference to 2 Macc 4:36 and Sib. Or. 5:256. As is clear from these references, however, and from other Jewish writings,

---

4. See, e.g., Taylor 1953, 349; Hooker 1991, 183; A. Collins 2007, 366; Hartman 2004, 241; van Iersel 1998, 248. Exceptions are Guelich 1989, 382–85; and Marcus 2000, 461–62, who translate it as "Greek." Nevertheless, they interpret the designation as a "functional equivalent of 'Gentile.'"

5. Both singular and plural forms of Ἐθνικός are used in other NT texts to designate non-Jewish people in general: 3 John 1:7 (pl.), Matt 5:47 (pl.); 6:7 (pl.); 18:17 (sg.).

6. A. Collins (2007, 366) defends her translation of Ἑλληνίς as "Gentile" by a reference to Bauer et al. 2000. Collins, however, refers to only one of the two possible meanings that Bauer et al. give. Ἑλληνίς in Mark 7:26 can also mean "Greek in language and culture."

the use of Ἕλλην (the masculine form is more common) as a designation was connected to Greek domination and the threat that it entailed for Jews (cf. 1 Macc 1:1, 10; 8:18; 2 Macc 4:10; 11:2). To designate non-Jewish people and customs in general, the term ἔθνη was used. This is especially evident in 1 Maccabees (1:11, 13, 14, etc.). Hartman, however, refers to 2 Maccabees, where the usage of Ἕλλην is debated (Windisch 1964, 507–8). In 2 Maccabees the introduction of Greek culture and religion is depicted as defilement and as breaking the divine law (4:17). This is not to imply, however, that Ἕλλην and ἔθνη mean the same thing. Rather it indicates that Ἕλλην had become somewhat detached from the Greek nation and referred more to the dominant culture that an increasing number of people of diverse ethnicities were adopting. Even if Ἕλλην in 2 Maccabees exemplifies ἔθνη, the terms are not synonymous. Ἔθνη continued to be the wider term for non-Jewish people in 2 Maccabees (6:4; 8:5, 9, 16; 10:4, etc.; cf. Windisch 1964, 507–8). Hence Hartman's argument for taking Ἕλλην as being equivalent to ἔθνη is not persuasive.

2. Morna Hooker (1991, 183) justifies her translation by stating that Ἑλληνίς is "regularly used in the NT as the equivalent of Gentile." Assuming this to be a common view, she does not argue her case. Since this brings up the question of how Ἕλλην is used in New Testament writings, a somewhat more extended discussion is required.[7] Although the term mainly occurs in Paul's Letters and Acts, I will begin by looking at its use in John's Gospel. In John 12:20 the Ἕλληνες that were coming to worship at Jerusalem during Easter can hardly be characterized as Gentiles; rather they appear to have been Greek-speaking proselytes who were adhering to Jewish customs. Also, in John 7:35 Ἕλλην is used as a dual reference to Greeks (among whom the Diaspora Jews were living) and to Hellenistic Jews.[8] Here it is quite clear that "Greek" does not have the same meaning as "Gentile," but rather refers to Greek culture and language. This specific meaning is also evident in the use of the related term Ἑλληνιστί (John 19:20), which designates the Greek language. Hence in John Ἕλλην is not used as an equivalent of "Gentile."

Turning to Acts, we see some initial indications that Ἕλλην is related to Greek culture rather than non-Jewish people in general. The term Ἑλληνιστής is initially used to indicate Greek-speaking Jews (Acts 6:1;

---

7. The investigation that follows is indebted to Windisch 1964.

8. John 7:35 is then translated: "Does he intend to go to the scattered among the Greeks and teach the Hellenistic Jews?"

9:29), but in 11:20 is also used to describe how some Christ followers in Antioch began to preach the gospel to Greeks. Hereby Ἑλληνιστής receives the specific meaning "Greek" rather than "Gentile," which also spills over to the term Ἕλλην.⁹ After this important event, the author of Acts begins to use the pair Ἰουδαῖοι καὶ Ἕλληνες (Jews and Greeks) in combination. Is Ἕλληνες here equivalent to ἔθνη? Even if some places (i.e., 14:1-2; 18:4-6) may point in that direction, the terms are generally not synonyms. Unlike ἔθνη, Ἕλληνες in Acts is often closely affiliated with the Jews. For instance, the Greeks who were present in the synagogue at Iconium when Paul and Barnabas spoke (14:1; cf. 17:4) ought to be characterized as Godfearers rather than Gentiles. Conversely, as is evident in 4:25-27, ἔθνη has more of a negative meaning when used to designate Gentiles. Finally, since the author of Acts probably was non-Jewish (Col 4:11, 14), Ἕλλην to him would primarily signal Greek language and culture rather than the wider meaning of all non-Jewish people.

What about Paul then? In support of her presumption that Ἑλληνίς in the New Testament means "Gentile," Hooker refers to a Pauline declaration that she translates as follows: "to the Jews [sic] first, and also to the Gentile" (Rom 1:16). This translation is mistaken. Paul speaks of Ἕλληνες in Romans, 1 Corinthians, Galatians, and Colossians, most often in connection with Ἰουδαῖοι but twice in relation to βάρβαροι (Rom 1:14; Col 3:11). There are therefore two dichotomies that give meaning to his use of Ἕλληνες:

Ἰουδαῖοι καὶ Ἕλληνες
Ἕλληνες καὶ βάρβαροι

Already from these two oppositional pairs, it is evident that Ἕλληνες is not a synonym for ἔθνη. Whereas ἔθνη refers to all non-Jewish peoples, regardless of whether they are Greeks or barbarians, the term Ἕλληνες excludes the barbarians. And as is evident from Col 3:11, the Scythians were not included among the Ἕλληνες but were surely part of the ἔθνη.

Further, it is also quite clear that Ἕλληνες in Paul's writings, unlike ἔθνη, is used with the more specific meaning of Greek culture. One can argue that the desire for σοφία (1 Cor 1:22; Rom 1:14, 22) is described as being typical of Greek culture as opposed to non-Jewish people in general. Similarly, although Titus (Gal 2:3) was certainly a non-Jew, the

---

9. Similarly, Ἑλληνιστί (Acts 21:37) designates Greek language.

designation "Greek" also indicates his specific cultural and linguistic location. In some Pauline passages, however, the terms Ἕλληνες and ἔθνη become synonymous. Since in baptism the distinction between Jew and Greek is overcome (Gal 3:28), the pair "Jew and Greek" is used to represent a universalism. In these cases Ἕλληνες seems to represent ἔθνη in general. Also, Ἕλληνες and ἔθνη are used interchangeably in 1 Cor 1:22–24, the passage just mentioned. But since Ἕλληνες in 1:22 is connected to σοφία, which is a typical Greek marker, the term ἔθνη in 1:23 is used with the meaning "Greek," and not the other way around. In other words, ἔθνη is here used in a more narrow sense than usual.

As for Hooker's translation of Ἕλλην in Rom 1:16, it is evident that the use of Ἕλλην follows directly after Paul's assurance that he is obliged to both Ἕλληνες and βάρβαροι (1:14), a pair that is encompassed by the previous designation ἔθνη (1:13). This should make us careful not to take Ἕλληνες and ἔθνη as synonyms in Romans. True, in the section that is initiated by 1:16, Paul uses Ἕλλην and ἔθνος with a similar meaning. In 3:29–30, which sums up the argument from 1:16, it is stated that Ἰουδαῖοι and ἔθνη have the same God and that both περιτομή and ἀκρβυστία will be justified. But does this mean that Ἕλλην = ἀκροβυστία = ἔθνος, as Windisch (1964, 516) says? Analyzing how the terms are used, it is clear that whereas Ἕλλην is used only when paired with Ἰουδαῖος (1:16; 2:9, 10; 3:9) or with βάρβαρος (1:14), ἔθνος is used by itself (1:5; 2:14, 24). It therefore seems as if ἔθνος carries a wider significance and refers to all peoples regardless of whether they have accepted the Hellenistic culture—in other words, to Ἕλλην καὶ βάρβαρος. The word pair Ἕλλην and Ἰουδαῖος, on the other hand, seems to designate what Paul regarded as the civilized world.

It is interesting to note here that although both Ἕλλην and Ἰουδαῖος were subdued by Rome, they had rather different statuses in imperial discourse (see ch. 13). Whereas Ἕλλην was connected to an imperial civilization, Ἰουδαῖος was a more peripheral and even barbaric designation (Wanke 1990). Hence Paul's peculiar phrase Ἰουδαίῳ τε πρῶτον καὶ Ἕλληνι (to the Jew first but also to the Greek, 1:16, etc.) seems to oppose imperial discourse and its notion of where the world's center lies. Whereas the word pair Ἕλλην and βάρβαρος in Roman imperial discourse represented all those subdued by Rome,[10] Paul's use of the paired

---

10. Similarly, N. Elliott (2008, 50–51, italics original) argues that the phrase "Greeks and barbarians" has the meaning of "*the world's peoples as Rome's subjects.*"

terms Ἕλλην and Ἰουδαῖος presupposes a different center—the people of Israel and its one God.[11]

We can then conclude that although Ἕλληνες sometimes represents ἔθνη in Paul's writings, and although the terms are at some places used interchangeably, in general they are not synonyms (cf. Windisch 1964, 516). Whereas ἔθνη signifies non-Jewish people generally, Ἕλληνες designates the more particular culture, language, and customs that had spread predominantly in the Mediterranean cities from the time of Alexander. The Greek culture, further, inhabited the ambivalent space of being connected with the dominant civilized order and at the same time being subdued by Rome. The word pair Ἕλλην and Ἰουδαῖος, therefore, cannot be equated with the pair ἔθνος and Ἰουδαῖος. Even if Paul used both pairs in a way that challenged imperial discourse, they challenged it in different ways. Whereas the former pair primarily addressed the imperial city culture, the latter also included those nations and peoples that had refused to adopt the dominant culture.

3. The last part of the argument will be more constructive. According to a common understanding, represented by Vincent Taylor (1953, 349), the woman could not have a Greek and a Syrophoenician nationality at the same time. Although Ἑλληνίς means "Greek," says Taylor, since Mark further characterizes her as Συροφοινίκισσα τῷ γένει (Syrophoenician by birth), "it is probable that he means 'a pagan' or 'Gentile.'" In other words, if "Syrophoenician" refers to the woman's nationality, "Greek" must refer to something else, namely her religious identity. In what seems to be a vestige from the nineteenth-century quest for pure origins, Taylor does not consider the possibility of taking the designation "Greek" in combination with "Syrophoenician" as referring to a hellenized Syrophoenician identity—meaning that the woman, despite her being a native Syrophoenician, had adopted Greek cultural customs and was fluent in the Greek language. Although Mark's urban audience was certainly not familiar with the postcolonial concept of hybridity, many would recognize themselves in the mixed identity of this woman. For Taylor, however, writing in the 1950s, *hybrid* could still have carried the negative meaning of something "base and evil," and thus would not have appeared as a feasible alternative.[12] Windisch (1964, 509 n. 35), on the other hand, in what seems to be

---

11. Lopez (2008, 164–73) conducts a similar reading of Paul without, however, discussing the difference between the terms Ἕλλην and ἔθνη.

12. *Encyclopædia Britannica*, 14th ed., s.v. "hybridism."

an anticipation of the academic trajectory of cultural hybridity, explicitly suggests that Ἕλλην Συροφοίνιξ indicates "a hybrid."

To conclude this three-step exegetical argument, there are good reasons to take Ἑλληνίς (contra Taylor) as primarily signifying a Greek rather than a general non-Jewish identity. That Mark identifies the woman as a Greek Syrophoenician signals that she had adopted Greek customs and was in that sense "civilized." On the other hand, as previously argued, since the Greeks were also a subdued nation, the designation "Greek" was in itself ambivalent. To be a Greek, a Syrophoenician by birth, thus indicates that the Greek identity was added to a previously existing native identity. Or with Bhabha's understanding, as a Syrophoenician, the woman identified with the dominant Greek civilization in a complex ongoing process of attraction and repulsion.

Gender, Ethnicity, and Bread Crumbs

As we continue to ponder the complex ways in which this episode communicated to Mark's audience in their imperial setting, the woman's hybrid identity becomes a significant signal. Since Mark's audience in this study is located in urban Greek-speaking areas, a significant part of its members would have found in this woman a representation of their relation to Christ. Since the appellation Ἑλληνίς appears only in this passage of Mark's Gospel, her hybrid identity particularly stands out in the narrative. I begin, however, by mapping the narrative terrain in which this episode is located in Mark.

If the expulsion of Legion in 5:1–20 is a high point of the antagonistic plot, how does the episode about the Syrophoenician woman fit into this confrontational drama? Let us begin by exploring how the oppositional plot develops. The two interlacing healing stories that take place on the Galilean side of the lake (5:21–43) are followed by the episode in which Jesus appears to have offended the inhabitants of his hometown (6:1–6). At the same time, an increasing number of people approach Jesus and his disciples to ask for help (5:21, 24; 6:31, 53–56). The oppositional drama is reinforced as Jesus dispatches the Twelve a second time (6:7–13; cf. 3:13–19), repeating the claim of a renewed Israel. It is at this commissioning that the Twelve are specifically instructed to shake the dust from their feet in response to encountered hostility.

The oppositional character of this second sending out of the Twelve is further highlighted. Sandwiched between the commissioning (6:7–13)

16. ENTERING A NARRATIVE CRISIS (7:24-30)

and the return (6:30), Mark inserts the episode in which "King" Herod beheads John the Baptist (6:14-29).[13] From the beginning of Mark's Gospel, John the Baptist has been depicted as a forerunner of Jesus (1:4-11). His imprisonment was mentioned just as Jesus began to proclaim the gospel (1:14). In the subsequent narrative, John the Baptist is identified with the prophet Elijah (9:10-13; cf. 15:35-36), and Jesus uses the popularity of John to defend himself against the questioning of the temple authorities in Jerusalem (11:27-33). As the episode about John's execution is connected to Jesus' sending out of the Twelve, the antagonism between Jesus and his opponents is intensified and given an even more accentuated political dimension.

Here it is interesting to note that the death of John the Baptist was an incident of some renown that was even recorded by Josephus (*Ant.* 18.116-119), according to whom Herod executed John in order to prevent sedition. As is generally agreed, moreover, Josephus's recounting of the incident likely surpasses Mark's in terms of historical accuracy (cf. Taylor 1953, 310-11; Marcus 2000, 400). Assuming that Mark's audience was familiar with the execution of John the Baptist and knew that Herod had his reasons for killing him, Mark's description of Herod's unmanliness in not being able to control his women, and the erotically manipulative role played by Herodias in his reluctant accession to the beheading, borders on pure parody (cf. Myers 1988, 214-16).

But whereas the beheading of John the Baptist runs in sync with the oppositional plot, the episode about the Syrophoenician woman is different. Jesus here seems to contradict himself. In the passage that precedes this episode, he criticizes the Pharisees and scribes from Jerusalem for their interpretation of Jewish tradition that, Jesus argues, nullifies the word of God (7:1-13). In opposition to their understanding, Jesus instructs his disciples and the general public that all food is clean (7:14-23). Although this provocative teaching stands in continuity with the oppositional plot, it also expands and transcends it by pointing toward an opening of the table fellowship between Jews and non-Jews. Such an escalation, as we will see, also makes the plot vulnerable. When Jesus meets the Syrophoenician woman, his attitude is contrary to that which might have been expected from his teaching in the previous passage. In the debate around bread and

---

13. Mark here refers to the Galilean tetrarch Herod Antipas (see further Matt 14:1; Luke 9:7).

crumbs, children and dogs, the Markan Jesus appears to embrace the very same position that he just rejected in criticizing the Pharisees and scribes. The contradictory behavior of Jesus thus transmits a message of perplexity to Mark's audience, raising questions as to his offensive attitude. The previous teaching on the cleanness of all food seems to imply wider and more radical consequences than the Markan Jesus could handle, which brings the plot into a crisis.

Two other features indicate the emergence of a crisis at this stage of the narrative. First, having been previously depicted as standing in family-like alignment with Jesus (3:35), the disciples' hearts are now described as having hardened (6:52; 8:17-21). The second indication of an emerging crisis pertains to the narrative's foreshadowing of Jesus' death. The bread that Jesus and the woman discuss in 7:27-28 is, on a literary level, connected to the two enclosing episodes where bread is broken and miraculously distributed to feed multitudes of people (6:32-44; 8:1-10). These episodes, in turn, point ahead toward the Last Supper when Jesus breaks the bread as a symbol of his body (14:22).[14] The narrative therefore begins to enter into the mystery of Jesus' body and his identity as Christ and Son of God—a mystery that no human character in Mark's Gospel grasps.[15] This is one sense in which the beheading of John also plays into this narrative crisis. By foreshadowing the suffering and dying of Jesus, John's death contributes to the mystery surrounding Jesus and the question concerning who he actually is.

When the narrative crisis emerges, Mark's oppositional presentation of Jesus and its way of interpellating the audience becomes unstable. Three interrelated messages seem to be transmitted: first, the initial interpellation of Greeks; then, the disruption of the plot's male dominance; and finally, the more complex destabilization of the original plot, which establishes a new kind of subjectivity around Mark's Jesus as body/bread. As to the first, Jesus' negative response initially interpellates "Greek" to a submissive position. Although the episode plays on several boundary markers (see above), the label "Greek" has not been mentioned before, and is thus quite conspicuous here. Initially, the Greek is degraded by being associated with dogs and by the notion of a time lag (7:27). The challenge of this interpellation of "Greek," with which many in Mark's audience would identify, should

---

14. The parallel is strengthened by reference to the similar wording in 6:41; 8:6; and 14:22.

15. The only possible candidate is the Roman centurion in front of the cross (15:39), whose statement will be discussed in ch. 20.

16. ENTERING A NARRATIVE CRISIS (7:24-30)

not be underestimated. Jesus' hostile response plays on the hostility that Jews at times had displayed toward what they perceived as Greek domination. Since Mark was circulating close to or even at the end of the Jewish War, the enmity between Jews and Greeks would have been particularly acute at this time. As is evident from Josephus, the anti-Roman rebellion began with an incident that was related to the tensions between Jews and Greeks in Caesarea (*J.W.* 2.284-292). As the Jews were now being subdued and publicly disgraced and feminized by the Romans, it would have been especially critical for a Greek to accept the position of a dog underneath a Jewish table. Since the Greek is subjected under the already subjected, it might well have brought forth a crisis for the Greek part of Mark's audience. Harsh as it stands, this seems to be the episode's initial interpellation.

A second message is transmitted by the Syrophoenician's gender. Until this episode, Mark has refrained from portraying a female character who speaks directly to Jesus. True, after the healing of the woman with a flow of blood (5:24-34), the audience is informed that she told Jesus the truth in a frightened, trembling voice (5:33). But as a representation of Spivak's notion of an inaccessible blankness (see ch. 2), her speech is not reported. The Syrophoenician woman, on the other hand, doubtlessly speaks—something that performers of the Gospel would indicate by changing the tone of their voice. But even if this speaking woman and her silent daughter somehow represent the absent women in Mark, the audience will still have to wait before any female disciples become visible. The poor widow (12:42) and the woman who anoints Jesus (14:3-9) are presented as important characters, but can hardly be taken as disciples. Not until the very end are the female disciples made visible (15:40-16:8). Being introduced "from a distance," indicating their hidden position in the narrative, three such women have been mentioned by name (15:40). Since Mark states that these women had been following (ἀκολουθέω, same verb as in 8:34) and serving (διακονέω, same verb as in 10:45) Jesus during his time in Galilee, they are given the status of disciples. But why so late? Are these women who appear at the end of Mark's Gospel proof, as Thurman (2003, 160-61) contends, that Mark fails to question male privilege at a fundamental level? Are they to be seen as "consummate alternates," as Liew (1999a, 142) claims?[16] Or is it possible, with Spivak's help, to listen to

---

16. In Liew's reading, when the men failed their mission, the women are allowed to serve only as backups.

the subaltern voices and detect a narrative strategy in Mark that destabilizes gender categories and subverts the androcentric plot?

True, the plot's initial oppositional drama has been represented by the twelve male apostles and has left no room for female gender except in a marginal and subservient position (1:30). The anti-imperial plot has therefore basically been an androcentric project. With the narrative crisis that emerges in Mark's depiction of the Syrophoenician woman, however, the male-dominated plot is undermined. Presuming that Mark's Gospel is proclaimed repeatedly, the audience knows that, toward the end, Mark will retrospectively inform them about the female disciples who followed Jesus during his time in Galilee. The Syrophoenician and her silent, remotely involved daughter can then be taken as representing those subaltern women, doubly marginalized by Roman imperial and (apocalyptic) anti-imperial discourses—and silenced in the main parts of Mark's narrative. By presenting Jesus as being initially unwilling to help, but as changing his position after hearing the words of the female subaltern, Mark seems to be asking the audience to conceptualize the oppositional plot in a different way.

Here the unfinished and ironic character of Mark's Gospel needs to be given its full weight.[17] Having described how the female disciples see the empty tomb (16:1–7), the Gospel ends with the enigmatic description of them running away from the tomb saying "nothing to anyone, for they were afraid" (16:8).[18] As pointed out by Maria Olsson (2009), since the message of the resurrection is communicated to the audience as Mark's Gospel is delivered, the women's silence is an ironic "speaking silence." Further, the unfinished character of the Gospel also invites a constant rereading of the story. And each time that the story is reread, the irony of the silent women at the end of the Gospel increases, which, in turn, decreases the credibility of the narrative's nondepiction of the women as

---

17. For an exploration of the irony in Mark's Gospel, and the significance of Mark's ending in this regard, see Camery-Hoggatt 1992, 10–13, 176–77.

18. As argued by A. Collins (2007, 797–801), Marcus (2009, 1088–96), Gilfillan Upton (2006, 198), and Danove (1993), the proposition that Mark originally ends here has least difficulties. The shorter ending, the Freer Logion, and the longer ending were not part of the original Gospel narrative. As Danove (1993, 130–31) points out, external criteria establish that a conclusion with γάρ is at least acceptable according to the canons of literary practice. Also, investigations of narrative techniques confirm that the ending in 16:8 is consonant with the overall narration.

disciples, granting them in effect—not unlike Mark in the biblical canon—a curious status of "absent presence." The subversion of the androcentric plot in Mark's Gospel is therefore an ongoing process.

The episode's third message combines the two previous ones and adds further weight to the woman's disruptive role. Since the woman negotiates with and seems to influence Jesus, the subordinate position of the "Greek" appears to be rather unstable. Not only is it a position from which the woman can negotiate, it is also a position that seems to be curiously decentered. Jesus' initial offensive response to the woman appears to indicate a lack of control. In a catachrestical use of "dogs" that strips it of stigmatization, the woman appears to turn the tables by arguing that dogs are already eating (7:28), hence collapsing the time lag that Jesus initially had established.

That the Markan Jesus is not in control of events is further illustrated by the manner in which Mark has framed the encounter.[19] While traveling to Tyre, Jesus has attempted to escape notice (7:24), and the woman appears to have been informed about his arrival through rumors (7:25). Rumors about Jesus, prominent in Mark's account, were filled with expectations (1:28; 3:10; 5:20, 27; 6:56; 7:36) as well as fear (4:41; 5:15). As Jim Perkinson (1996, 70–71) persuasively argues, rumors are beyond control and lack all sense of a centered subjectivity. Perkinson here draws on Bhabha's (2004, 283–302) understanding of rumors as an expression of human subjectivity that is intersubjective, where *inter* is to be taken in its full sense of *between*. It is not possible, then, to clearly distinguish the messianic power of Jesus from its intersubjective articulations in the form of rumors. The healing of the woman's daughter begins before Jesus has even arrived on the scene and is affected by a "word," λόγος (7:29), pronounced by the woman. As Perkinson points out, the position from which the healing is affected is therefore a space *in between* Jesus and the woman.[20]

---

19. Contra Cranfield 1959, 249, who claims that the suggestion that the woman's reply did affect Jesus "seems to have little to commend it." Cranfield bases his position on Calvin, who thought the purpose of Jesus' coldness was to "wet her zeal and inflame her ardour" (248). Cranfield here represents a tradition of interpretations for which the image of Jesus being in control is important (see ch. 7). Mark's depiction, however, hardly signals control. Jesus tries to pull away but is caught off guard due to the rumors.

20. This becomes the basis for Perkinson's (1996, 79–82) elaboration on a decentered Christology.

In this unstable characterization of Jesus, the original plot of the story is further unsettled. The geographic movement to a border region on the fringes of Jewish territory as well as the woman's Syrophoenician γένος destabilize the notions of a renewed γένος of Israel (cf. Gal 1:14; Phil 3:5; 2 Cor 11:26; Acts 7:19). If Mark had begun to interpellate the audience as a renewed γένος (cf. 1 Pet 2:9), the narrative crisis destabilizes Mark as a founding document.[21] Whereas it previously revolved around a rather clear-cut opposition between Jesus and his disciples on the one hand and the intertwined political-spiritual opponents on the other, the sense of a homogeneous male collective centered on the unified subject of Jesus is subverted. As Perkinson (1996, 69) puts it, "the woman is clearly a disruptive figure, figured in the text itself as a disruption." Her disruption, moreover, seems to be of a benign kind. As the woman manages to turn a derogatory response to her favor, Perkinson (77–78) sees her (on a literary level) as qualifying for the role of Jesus' mentor, preparing him for his upcoming trials when her tactic will become useful (12:13–17, 18–27, 27–33).

In a further unsettling manner, the woman also destabilizes the insider/outsider boarder. Since Mark never mentions an actual conversion, she can be regarded as holding both an insider and an outsider status. On the one hand, her addressing Jesus as κύριε (7:28) can be taken as indicating that she becomes his follower. But it is also possible to take κύριε as a polite "Sir" that is connected to her concern for her daughter's need. By opening the story for both of these readings, the Syrophoenician woman receives an ambiguous insider/outsider status that blurs the borders around the identity position that Mark's narrative represents. Since the λόγος (7:29) that Jesus praises—and that seems to have affected the healing (cf. 4:14)—was spoken by the woman and thus originates in some sense from the outside, the external boarder of the "us" is made permeable.

At the same time, however, in the midst of this destabilizing narrative crisis, a new subjectivity also emerges. As ἄρτος enters the conversation between the two, Mark introduces a subjectivity around the bread as the body of Christ just as the narrative plot is being subverted. As mentioned, ἄρτος (7:27–28) alludes via the feeding miracles (6:30–44; 8:1–10) to the Last Supper (14:22–25). For Mark's audience, we may presume, distributing and eating the bread as a way of actualizing Christ's presence in their

---

21. One can debate when the notion of the Christ followers as a γένος began to develop. In any case, it had been established by the second century (Tertullian, *Nat.* 1.8; *Mart. Pol.* 3:2; 17:1; *Diogn.* 1).

midst would be a recurring ritual, crucial for the understanding of themselves as a group.

The notion of bread as the body of Jesus takes the destabilization of gender categories to yet another level. In the statement "this is my body" (14:22), τοῦτο refers doubly to ἄρτος and to Jesus as an extendable body. As noted by Graham Ward (2000, 102), "a certain metonymic substitution is enacted, re-situating Jesus' male physique within the neuter materiality of bread. The body now is both sexed and not sexed." The metonymic statement of Jesus about his ambivalently gendered body is then illustrated in Mark's subsequent depiction of how the body is treated. Having been handed over to the authorities (14:43–52), the body of Jesus is exposed to scourging (15:15), dressing and undressing (15:17, 20), beating (15:19), spitting (15:19), and humiliation (15:17–19), all adding up to making it too weak to carry the crossbeam (15:21).

Since masculinity in Mediterranean antiquity was "not a birthright" (Gleason 1995, 159) and "never entirely secure" (Moore and Anderson 1998, 250), Mark's crucifixion account seems to vacillate between depicting Jesus as truly manly and severely feminized. As the body is subsequently hung up on the cross, clothes removed (15:24), its gender status is highly negotiable: female or male? On the one hand, the account signals feminization. Again, as Ward (2000, 103–4) has it, "The body hangs … as that spent form left behind when the other has been gratified: as the body raped." Since protecting the boundaries of one's body constituted a key feature of ancient masculinity, the breached body of the Markan Jesus signals effeminacy (Gleason 2003). Also, Jesus' loud cry (15:37) before dying appears less than manly (Bowersock 1994, 74–76). On the other hand, considering the importance of self-mastery for the construction of masculinity, the silent endurance of suffering and cruelty would signal maleness (cf. Pilch 1995).

Given the Markan Jesus' identification of his body as bread and its implied destabilization of gender categories, the bread in the episode about the Syrophoenician woman obtains a remarkably rich meaning. Being introduced by Jesus in a negative statement (7:27), the bread becomes the item around which the conversation turns (7:28). Significantly, it is the bread's predisposition of falling to pieces, its inability to stick together as a unified whole, that makes possible the healing of the woman's daughter. Whereas Mark's plot initially framed Jesus as leading a male-dominated oppositional religious/political movement in rural Galilee, the narrative crisis reframes and transforms the plot and interpellates the audience to a decentered subjectivity and a blurring of the boundary markers. As bread, the body of Jesus opens a space for Mark's audience that is characterized by *différance* and transcendence of boundaries—ethnic boundaries, gender boundaries, socioeconomic boundaries, perhaps even religious boundaries.

In this sense, the episode connects intertextually to the pre-Pauline tradition of oneness in Christ (Gal 3:28; Col 3:11). But whereas the (pre-)Pauline formula proclaimed a homogeneous oneness, Mark's presentation of the unity in Christ is considerably more fractured and unstable. By rendering an encounter with disparaging remarks, by hiding the female disciples until the very end, and by narrating the disseminating nature of Jesus as bread, Mark offers a fractured oneness fraught with ambivalence and competing positions and categorizations. Judging from the Pauline letters, the competition between different parties among the Christ followers was at times hostile and could even include the use of "dog" (Phil 3:2). Mark's account thus seems to offer a critique against idealized notions of unity in Christ. As the object of identification for Mark's audience is being transferred into a body-as-bread with a decentered subject and blurred border, the collective subjectivity in Christ could hardly be seen as unified and free of tensions.

Although the decentered subjectivity that Mark's Gospel here begins to represent stands in a tension to the initial antagonistic plot, it nevertheless entails a subversive message. From a Roman point of view, Jesus as well as the woman represented the dominated—they are both Roman subjects. Cicero had already described the Greeks of Syria together with the Jews as "peoples born to slavery" (*Prov. cons.* 10: *nationibus natis servituti*). Similarly, Livy (36.17.5) regarded Syrians and Asiatic Greeks as "the most worthless of peoples among mankind and born for slavery." A story about subjected peoples—a Syrophoenician Greek and a Jew—who overcome enmity without a Roman intervention therefore suggests an incipient universalism beyond Roman control.

Nevertheless, the Syrophoenician brings forth a crisis. The plot's subversive character is then dislocated from a unified androcentric antagonism to the formulation of a decentered collective identification with a disseminating Jesus-as-bread that can deal with difference without an imperial master. This crisis affects a narrative turn that will have a continuous effect as Mark's story proceeds.

17
The Parousia as *Pharmakon* (8:31–9:1)

The *pharmakon* is neither the cure nor the poison, neither good, nor evil.
—Derrida (1997, lxxii)

An important trajectory in postcolonial biblical criticism involves what is often called "reading against the grain," an approach that calls upon the reader to adopt an attitude that differs from the text's implied reader.[1] This resistant-reading approach has been typically applied to biblical texts that are generally thought to promote liberation and justice. Searching for silenced voices, aporias, and tendencies to duplicate imperial discourse, such readings press at the points where emancipation uncannily subverts into oppression. In an emblematic illustration of this trajectory, Robert Allen Warrior (1991) reads the exodus narrative from a Native American perspective. Identifying with the indigenous people (the Canaanites) who ended up losing their promised land, Warrior provocatively points out how the exodus story justifies conquest and domination in the name of liberation and emancipation. Considering the foundational status of the exodus narrative for liberation theology, Warrior's reading marks a turning point in liberationist hermeneutics.

As previously mentioned (chs. 1 and 8), Liew (1999a) offers a similar critique of Mark's Parousia.[2] Considering the importance of eschatological hope to liberation theology, this critique is similarly provocative and

---

1. For a discussion of what it means to read against the grain, see A. Davies 2000, 12–19. The term *implied reader* is one of the concepts used in narrative criticism. See Malbon 2008.

2. For a similar discussion regarding the Parousia in Matthew's Gospel, see Carter 2005 and Neville 2007.

significant.[3] Although Liew does find anti-imperial elements in Mark, he nevertheless sees the Markan Parousia as undermining these elements. What makes Liew's claim particularly trenchant is how it connects to other New Testament writings. According to Heb 12:2, the cross has granted Jesus a position of unlimited divine authority. It is from this position, Paul wrote, that he will one day return to put all enemies under his feet (1 Cor 15:20–28). And as graphically depicted in Matthew (25:31–46), this is a return that will entail a rather violent form of judgment. Because these notions are generally regarded as being part of the Christian creed, Liew's critique of the authoritarian character of the Markan Parousia challenges that which Christians often take to be common belief. At the same time, however, these circumstances also make Liew's reading susceptible to criticism for harmonizing Mark with other New Testament texts and for not giving serious consideration to Mark's particular understanding of the Parousia.

While Liew's reading has been debated, it has not been generally accepted. Moore (2006) argues that the Markan Parousia is a milder and more muted affair than Liew claims. Comparing Mark with the book of Revelation, Moore (34) finds the Markan Parousia to be "in essence, a search-and-rescue mission, not a punitive strike." Similarly, Simon Samuel (2007, 79–81, 84–85) faults Liew for doing precisely what he claims not to be doing: idealizing Mark. According to Samuel, since Liew does not sufficiently exhibit the complex portraiture of Jesus in Mark, Liew's reading idealizes Mark as a colonial duplication. Further, Samuel argues, Liew misuses Bhabha's concept of mimicry, taking it to mean a straightforward reproduction or duplication, thereby disregarding that mimicry also includes mockery, menace, and subversion.

A more exegetical line of criticism has been delivered by David Neville (2008, 373–75), who questions the weight Liew implicitly lays on the verb ἀπολέσει in 12:9. Even if Liew refers to several Markan passages, his interpretation of the Parousia as a violent and tyrannical intervention, Neville claims, rests heavily on the parable of the Tenants (12:1–12), according to which the owner will "destroy the tenants" (12:9).[4] It could be questioned, Neville notes, if the coming of the owner of the vineyard

---

3. The importance of eschatological hope was especially emphasized by Moltmann 1967, who was influenced by the Jewish Marxist philosopher Ernst Bloch.

4. Liew (1999a, 103) refers specifically to 8:38–9:1; 12:9 36; 13:26; and 14:61–62.

(who is not the killed son) equates to the Son of Man coming in clouds with power (13:26; 14:62).

Even if these arguments against Liew's position are sound, they do not seem quite sufficient from a postcolonial perspective. For, as Moore (2006, 40–41) also points out, the imagery of a return "with great power and glory" (13:26) might be seen as a betrayal of "Mark's own latent desire for a top-heavy, authoritarian, universal Christian empire." One may then ask, if the Parousia in Mark is not to be seen as a punitive strike, how is it to be conceptualized?

Moore (2006, 40–44) has suggested a relocation of Mark's Parousia from the "official" apocalyptic speech in 13:1–37 to the two passages that enfold it, in which two female characters play a crucial role (12:41–44; 14:3–9). The two women in these passages, Moore holds, represent the real apocalypse in Mark. Drawing on what Derrida has described as the liminal concept of a gift beyond reciprocity, one could say that Mark's apocalypse points toward the breaking through of an impossible social world where models of economic exchange are deconstructed.

Despite the suggestive nature of this reading, it nevertheless renders Mark's depictions of an eschatological return (the "official" apocalypse) superfluous and expendable—at best. This, in turn, presupposes an understanding of the cross in Mark as "merely a bold entrepreneurial wager that yields an eschatological empire" (Moore 2006, 43). Considering the importance of the cross as a metaphor, it seems premature to give up on it and discard it as a hopelessly imperial metaphor. As I will argue here, therefore, although Moore's reading offers a justified critique against a Constantinian appropriation of the cross as a symbol, it overlooks what "cross" signified to Mark's audience and how the Parousia plays into the call to "take up the cross" (8:34) in Mark's narrative.

Unsettling the Oppositional Plot

To pick up the thread from the previous chapter, the meeting between Jesus and the Syrophoenician woman brought forth a crisis in Mark's narrative that entailed a subversion of the initial androcentric antagonistic plot. By metaphorically introducing the body that is to be given out and broken as bread, the story has begun to form a modified unimperial subjectivity, a universalism from below that resists Roman power without being overtly oppositional. This, in turn, was anticipated already in the seed parable, and the following antagonistic climax, where the empire of God was portrayed as almost but not quite an empire. Expanding on these notions and bringing the audience to accept them seems to be what the second dramatic section in Mark (8:22–10:52) revolves around.[5] In other words, the drama about the identity of Jesus continues to be, at the same time, a drama about the self-understanding of Mark's audience.

Since the second section depicts Jesus and the disciples as traveling between different regions, it is often designated "on the way" (ἐν τῇ ὁδῷ, 8:27; 9:33, 34; 10:17, 32, 46, 52). As will become evident, this is also the way that leads to Jerusalem (10:32) and the death of Jesus. Framed by two miracle stories in which blind men have their sight restored (8:22–26; 10:46–52), the section circulates around the disciples' attempt to "see" who Jesus is. Having already narrated a crisis, Mark has prepared the audience for the misunderstandings and quarrels that characterize this section. The most striking feature seems to be the disciples' inability to understand the unexpected messianic identity of Jesus. Although Jesus is transfigured on a mountain (9:2–9) and on three occasions foretells his suffering, death, and resurrection (8:31; 9:31; 10:33–34), the disciples are still unable to understand (9:10, 32). By this narrative strategy, the audience is interpellated into seeing what the disciples failed to see.

In what is often regarded as the story's turning point, the queries around Jesus' identity are initiated. On their way to Caesarea Philippi, Jesus asks the disciples to describe what people are saying about him (8:27). As already noted, Mark often indicates the variety of rumors about Jesus. Being not quite satisfied with what these rumors suggest, the Markan Jesus presses the disciples for their stance. Although here Peter seems to give what the narrator regards as a satisfactory answer (8:29), the inadequacy of his insight will soon become evident. Here the audience is reminded of the previously mentioned wordplay on the name Peter (Rock) and the "rocky places" of the seed parable.

In the scene that follows, several spatial markers indicate the dramatic turns. Having taught *openly* (παρρησίᾳ) about his coming suffering, death, and resurrection (8:31–32), Jesus is *taken aside* (προσλαβόμενος) by Peter, who is evidently upset and rebukes Jesus. However, refusing to accept this

---

5. I here follow the concentric structure suggested by van Iersel 1998, 68–86, according to which 8:27–10:45 forms a middle section that can be designated "the way." For similar suggestions see Cranfield 1959, 14; Hooker 1991, 27–29; Marcus 2000, 62–64; and Donahue and Harrington 2002, 46–50. For an overview of the debate, see A. Collins 2007, 85–93.

challenge on a one-to-one basis, Jesus *turns* (ἐπιστραφείς) away from Peter (8:33a). *Looking* (ἰδών) at the disciples, he rebukes Peter (evidently without looking at him): "Get behind me, Satan!" (8:33b). As indicated by the spatial markers, the argument involves significant physical movements and body postures that add weight to the accusations, something that a performer would surely try to illustrate during delivery.

The escalating development of teaching, rebuke, and counterrebuke culminates with the association of Peter with Satan. Peter, whose name ironically signals solid rock, and who has been depicted as having a primary position among the twelve male apostles (1:16; 3:16), serves as an important figure of identification for Mark's audience. In the original plot, Satan and his subordinate demons (cf. 3:22–23) had been unambiguously depicted, together with scribes, Herodians, Pharisees, Jerusalem leaders, and Roman imperial forces, as belonging to the opposing side against which Jesus and his disciples had been proclaiming, agitating, exorcising, and healing in order to champion the empire of God and a renewed Israel. Having been disrupted in the encounter with the Syrophoenician woman and the narrative crisis it entailed, the dramatic turn in 8:27–33 continues to subvert and modify the oppositional plot. Evil forces that had been previously connected with the opponents of Jesus and the Roman Empire are now depicted as permeating the anti-imperial leadership itself, as signified by the leading apostle. Empire, Mark signals, is just as much an internal as an external enemy. Further, whereas the satanic enemy has been previously associated with swinishness and uncleanness, it is here associated with Peter's "human thinking" (φρονεῖς τὰ τῶν ἀνθρώπων). The abject character of imperial discourse is thus significantly reduced.[6] This troubling lesson seems to need careful elaboration and is consequently repeated twice (9:30–37; 10:32–45), adding up to a powerful triad of empire-critical teachings.

At this point in the narrative, anti-imperial hermeneutics is typically troubled. I mention three examples. Belo (1981, 156, 238–40, 244–52) alleges the existence of a secondary textual layer in this narrative turning point—a "postpaschal discourse." Whereas the "prepaschal narrative" that has characterized the Gospel up to this point is messianic and teaches the practice of the hands (charity), the feet (hope) and the eyes (faith), the

---

6. *Abjection* is a term coined by Kristeva and refers to a psychosocial mechanism that establishes a subject's boundaries by repudiating certain phenomena as detestable and unclean (Macey 2000, s.v.).

postpaschal discourse begins with 8:31 and bears the stamp of theological predetermination and heavenly timelessness. Belo consequently defines his task as recovering the prepaschal layer that is hidden under the theological overlay.

Richard Horsley (2001, 231–53), for his part, suggests two other types of narrative layers that he terms "prophetic scripts" and "messianic scripts." The prophetic scripts that he sees as prominent in Mark's story revolve around a renewing of the people of Israel. By messianic scripts, on the other hand, Horsley means traditions of popular rebellious kingship that were common after the death of Herod in 4 B.C. and during the Jewish War of 66–70. The way in which Mark's story relates to these messianic traditions, Horsley claims, is "extremely unclear." According to Horsley (250–51), the closest Mark's story comes to presenting Jesus as being proclaimed Messiah by his followers is Peter's declaration here in 8:27–33. Although I agree that Mark's relation to popular messianic rebellion is ambivalent, Horsley's reading of 8:27–33 is strained. Horsley (92–93, 250–51) seems to take Jesus' rebuke in 8:33 as meaning essentially that Peter had been wrong to call him Christ in the first place (8:29). In order to make this reading intelligible, Horsley (250) alleges Mark 1:1 (the entire first sentence) to be a later addition made in the manuscript tradition.

Finally, Myers (1988, 242–45, 459–72) differs in some respects from the previous two. Criticizing Marxist-oriented readings for avoiding or suppressing Mark's representation of the cross as a political strategy, Myers explicitly rejects Belo's suggestion of a postpaschal discourse and suggests instead that the rebuke of Peter is to be taken as a sober reminder of the inevitable outcome of confrontational politics. But even if Myers succeeds in pointing to the cross as an emblem of nonviolent resistance, he neglects how Mark at this point unsettles his previously established antagonism. Jesus' rebuke of Peter, Myers (245) consequently argues, implies a "radical dualism" with "no middle ground." Ideally, perhaps, there would be no middle ground. But by associating Peter with "rocky places" as well as with Satan, Mark seems to display that the more ambiguous middle ground is a rather significant space for Mark's audience to consider.

As in the case of these anti-imperial readings, the postcolonial reading suggested here is struggling with long traditions of Christian theological interpretations that in this Markan passage have found a politically innocuous message of a spiritual savior whose sole agenda is to die for peoples' sins. From a postcolonial perspective it is simply inadequate to neglect that Mark's portrayal of the indictment, execution, and rising of

Jesus is a multifaceted drama that entails sociopolitical as well as spiritual dimensions. Unlike the anti-imperial readings, however, this postcolonial reading tries to highlight the way in which Mark's Gospel disrupts and dislocates its original oppositional plot. These tensions are crucial in order to conceptualize the potential of Mark as a collective representation in its ancient imperial settings.

ΣΤΑΥΡΟΣ as Catachresis

As the narrative crisis (7:24–30) and the association of Peter with Satan (8:33) have driven the androcentric oppositional plot into an impasse, Mark presents a short speech by Jesus (8:34–9:1) that serves as a way out of the aporia into a modified oppositional plot. Considering the harsh words recently uttered to Peter, the pitch here seems to be taken down and the tone is considerably more unobtrusive. As indicated by the repetition of the verb ἀκολουθέω, the speech begins with a chiasmic saying:

A   If anyone wants to follow [ἀκολουθεῖν] after me
B'   let him deny himself
B   and take up his cross
A'   and follow [ἀκολουθείτω] me

Surrounded by a repeated request to follow Jesus, the two parallel acts—denial of self and taking up one's cross—are clearly highlighted in the narrative. As pointed out by Joanna Dewey (2001, 23), this teaching has often been misread as a glorification of suffering and an encouragement to become a victim. But since victimhood seems to be the very problem that this saying sets out to cure, Mark's audience would probably have heard a different message.

In order to make this argument, a short digression on the cross in Roman imperial discourse is necessary. What did σταυρός signify to Mark's audience? According to Moore (2006, 43), the cross in Mark is mainly an "entrepreneurial wager" that acquires eschatological power. Expressed in the formula "no pain, no gain," Moore regards the cross as connected to imperial Christianity. And judging from the legendary imperial vision of Constantine ("in hoc signo vinces"), Moore's critique is incisive. When one considers that today the cross is the Christian symbol par excellence, the questions it raises are delicate—especially since our present time can be characterized as postsecular and post-Constantinian. As Mark's Gospel was circulating, however, σταυρός was not a symbol of Christianity, but rather signified the most repressive aspect of imperial discourse.[7] Focusing on the pre-Constantine setting, then, Mark's use of σταυρός needs to be reclaimed from the standards of imperial Christianity.

Although crucifixion was not a Roman invention, the Roman Empire made prominent use of this cruel form of punishment. Since it was considered too humiliating to be used for Roman citizens or for the elite stratum, it was generally limited to foreigners and people of low social status (O'Collins 1992). The elite's unwillingness to mention the cross in their writings is well known. In a famous defense of Rabirius, a Roman nobleman and senator who risked being condemned to death by crucifixion, Cicero wrote:

> How grievous a thing it is to be disgraced by a public court; how grievous to suffer a fine; how grievous to suffer banishment; and yet in the midst of any such disaster some trace of liberty is left to us. Even if we are threatened with death, we may die free men. But the executioner, the veiling of the head, and the very word "cross" [nomen ipsum crucis] should be far removed not only from the person of a Roman citizen but from his thoughts, his eyes and his ears. For it is not only the actual occurrence of these things or the endurance of them, but liability to them, the expectation, nay, the mere mention of them, that is unworthy of a Roman citizen and a free man. (*Rab. Perd.* 16)

It is significant that Cicero's repulsion for the cross is not only or even primarily connected to physical pain. The way he emphasizes linguistic aspects—the very word, thoughts, eyes, ears, expectations, and the mere mention—makes clear that the stabilizing effect of crucifixion was the particular meaning it was given in imperial discourse. In order to increase the deterring effect, crosses were often set up along the busiest roads (Hengel 1977, 87–88).

According to Laurence Welborn (2009, 306–7), the cross was a common topic among the lower strata and was only rarely discussed among the elite. Although the lower strata are not directly accessible, Welborn takes popular comedies to represent these wider segments of the

---

7. True, Paul crafted his arguments around the potentially offensive message of the cross (1 Cor 1:17–18; Gal 5:11; 6:12–14; Eph 2:16; Phil 3:18; Col 1:20; 2:14). Nonetheless, the cross was not a symbol for Christian faith and had not been appropriated by any emperor.

17. THE PAROUSIA AS *PHARMAKON* (8:31–9:1)

population. The frequent use of the cross in this literature, including gallows humor and vulgar taunts, indicates the large space occupied by the threat of the cross in the minds of the nonelite. Especially slaves lived in constant fear of a humiliating and painful death on the cross.[8] The elite's silence on this punishment and its frequent, brutal use in Roman imperial discourse prompt Welborn (309, italics original) to tellingly conclude that the cross was a *"material density ...* around which Roman power was constructed." For a significant segment of Mark's audience, then, the cross was a constant threat that implied a dependent and submissive subjectivity.

Considering the force of the material density of the cross in the imperial discourse, Mark's use of σταυρός as a metaphor is remarkable. The expression "take up one's cross" was probably used during the first century with reference to the condemned person's carrying of the crossbeam to the place of execution.[9] Metaphorical usage of σταυρός was rare. In the few extant instances it has a negative meaning (Bøe 2010, 74–77). Having already established Mark's inclination to utilize catachresis, his use of σταυρός is probably the most significant case. To use σταυρός as something to take up voluntarily would perhaps have been intelligible as a detached ironic joke in the context of a popular comedy. But since Mark at this point is free from irony, the saying appears remarkably awkward. By using σταυρός as a metaphor for following Jesus, its meaning in imperial discourse is subverted; the catachresis thus implies resistance against the stranglehold of the cross, making possible a new empowered subjectivity. Even if the risk of being crucified was still pervasive, the catachresis could potentially deconstruct its forceful material density, and affect a kind of liberation from the submissive subjectivity that the imperial discourse prescribed. Without being openly oppositional and rebellious, then, the catachrestic use of σταυρός was profoundly subversive.[10]

---

8. See Welborn 2005, 144–46. As is evident from Horace (*Sat.* 1.3.80–83), slaves could be crucified for arbitrary reasons.

9. The prevalence of the practice of carrying the cross to the place of execution is indicated in Plutarch, *Mor.* 554. See also Bøe 2010, 50–78, who argues that the Synoptic Gospels take this practice for granted.

10. Cf. Brandon 1967, 57; and Hengel 1989, 260, 270–71, who have suggested that "taking up one's cross" may have originally been a Zealot expression that was taken over by Jesus. Both base this suggestion on Schlatter 1925. Although there is no direct evidence of such usage of "the cross" among the Zealots, it could perhaps be inferred from the account of Josephus, which tells about Jewish rebels continuing resistance in the face of crucifixion (*J.W.* 5.446–459). If it was taken over as a phrase from the Zeal-

Although Paul in his letters had already begun using the cross in a catachrestical way, Mark's use differs by specifically referring to the literal situation of execution and by placing it in a call to follow after Jesus. If the cross for Paul was primarily a way of redefining the self into a more detached position vis-à-vis the dominating culture (Gal 6:14), for Mark it signified the social practice of "following." To use the cross in this catachrestical way, then, was not an invitation to suffering in general, nor did it encourage becoming a victim. Since the cross in imperial discourse upheld submission by victimization, the catachresis rather made possible the formation of groups for which the cross had lost its submissive power. Although it certainly remained a threatening aspect of imperial discourse, Mark's use of the term opened a new social space for the Markan audience to enter and incited them to establish or uphold their countercultural social practices.

The subversive message is strengthened by the universal address with which the teaching is initiated. Previously limiting himself to the disciples, Jesus is here described as summoning the "people" (ὄχλος, 8:34). The call about the cross then begins with the indefinite pronoun τις: "If *anyone* wishes…". Although in principle such a call would have included the elite as well, considering that this stratum generally avoided the topic of σταυρός, it is more likely that it was primarily directed to a nonelite audience (cf. 10:23).

Here it is important to clarify that the empowerment effected by the catachresis was not only a release from oppressive constraints in the imperial discourse, but also an acceptance of new bonds of allegiance and submissiveness. Mark presents the taking up of the cross as a metaphor for loyalty to Jesus, and thus it also implied being incorporated into the community of Christ followers, with its particular social practices and power problems.[11] The claims made here about liberation and empowerment are therefore to be understood in relation to the powerful effect of the cross as punishment in imperial discourse; they do not imply an idealization of Mark as a collective representation.

The catachrestic request to take up the cross, however, met considerable obstacles in both Roman imperial and Jewish discourses (Deut 21:23).

---

ots, however, its meaning in the mouth of the Markan Jesus is significantly modified compared to the openly rebellious meaning it would have had in a Zealot discourse.

11. As indicated by some of Paul's letters (Gal 3:28; 1 Cor 7:17–24; 11:2–16; 14:33–36), the issues of ethnicity, gender, and slavery were highly contested.

Rhetorically, then, Jesus' speech offers arguments—indicated by the recurring use of γάρ (8:35, 36, 37, 38)—that support his request and counter the objections. The paradoxical wisdom sayings (8:35–37) were apparently not sufficient. In order to address the issues of shame and humiliation that were connected to crucifixion, Mark introduces an apocalyptic notion of Parousia for the first time in the narrative by having Jesus foretell of his coming in power. The one who is ashamed of Jesus and his teachings, the Markan Jesus maintains, will end up being the subject of the Son of Man's shame in a future glorious coming (8:38). Even though Mark never uses the term παρουσία, it is implied in this and several other passages.[12] The point seems to be to neutralize the shame that would inhibit the catachrestical request in the first place—essentially countering one shame via another. This use of apocalyptic imagery thus seems to be connected to a counter-cultural social practice but might at the same time in itself reproduce the ideology that it strives to resist. This calls for further critical examination.

APOCALYPTIC WRITINGS AS RESPONSE TO IMPERIAL DOMINATION

Since the imagery of a Son of Man in 8:38 draws decisively on Jewish apocalyptic discourse (Dan 7 and 1 En. 46–48; cf. Wis 1–6 and 4 Ezra 13), a comparison to these writings is in order. Apocalyptic literature is generally described as having been developed from and influenced by various cultural and religious traditions, most notably Jewish prophetic and wisdom traditions, but also Persian, Egyptian, and Hellenistic traditions (Allison 1992; P. Hanson 1992). It is generally agreed that the bulk of Jewish apocalyptic literature was produced between 200 B.C.E. and 100 C.E. and that its background involved some sort of difficulty or crisis. Considering that these centuries for Jews were characterized by subjugation under foreign rulers, the development of the apocalyptic genre seems closely connected to an intensified exposure to imperial domination that began under the Seleucid Empire (P. Hanson 1992; Liew 1999a, 55–63).

---

12. Apart from 8:38, see particularly 13:24–27 and 14:61–62. These images resemble those in the Pauline writings of the Parousia (1 Cor 15:23; 1 Thess 2:19; 3:13; 4:15; 5:23; 2 Thess 2:1, 8), which Mark's audience presumably knew. The closest parallel is 1 Thess 3:13, in which Paul expresses his hope that God will strengthen the hearts of the Thessalonians, that they "may be blameless before our God and Father at the coming [ἐν τῇ παρουσίᾳ] of our Lord Jesus with all his saints."

The development and use of the Jewish apocalyptic literary genre, Liew (1999a, 57) claims, was a kind of "protest against colonialism" and therefore illustrates the agency of the subdued. Somewhat enigmatically, however, Liew overlooks the fact that these anti-imperial protests were also accompanied by imperial dreams of domination over other peoples and nations (e.g., Dan 2:44; 7:14, 27; 4Q246 II 1–8). His unwillingness to discuss the presence of such internalized imperial ideology in these texts he only passingly explains in terms of a reluctance to "blam[e] the victims" (Liew 1999a, 60). Since Liew shows no hesitation when it comes to discussing imperial duplication in Mark's Parousia, he seems to presuppose that Mark represents groups that were *not* factually victims. Such a presupposition needs to be challenged for drawing an arbitrary demarcation between who is and is not a victim, as well as for applying different standards to Jewish and Christian apocalyptic discourses.

This is not to say, of course, that Liew's highlighting of the political aspects of Jewish apocalypticism is unimportant. Somewhat similarly, for John Collins (1998, 283) apocalyptic literature is quite accurately understood from the perspective of liberation theology. But as Collins points out, although apocalyptic writings typically address issues of social and political oppression, they conspicuously lack a program for effective action. On the contrary, he argues, since human affairs are understood in these writings as being controlled by higher powers, their discourse tends to limit human initiative.[13] Collins refers to Daniel, whose message was to wait for the victory of Michael rather than to take up arms as the Maccabees had done. Similarly, in the aftermath of the destruction of Jerusalem in 70 C.E., 4 Ezra and 3 Baruch focus their attention on the mysteries of God. So if apocalyptic literature is revolutionary, Collins (283) states, this revolution is limited to the imagination. As Collins points out, this is not to be underestimated as a form of resistance in situations of social powerlessness. Apocalyptic writings can thus be understood as a kind of coded and elusive form of counterimperial speech that refrained from open resistance. On some occasions, however, violent fantasies and seething outrage seem to have fueled open defiance and violent revolts.[14]

---

13. Collins here seems to disagree with Liew's claim that apocalyptic writings represent a form of agency of the subdued.

14. See ch. 14 above. Even if there is scarce evidence regarding the social settings of apocalyptic writings, there is some support for this contention. As P. Hanson (1992, 280) argues, the "Animal Apocalypse" and the "Apocalypse of Weeks" in 1 En. 93 and

The Parousia as *Pharmakon*

Mark uses apocalyptic imagery with twists and modifications, the most significant of which is the blurring of the clear-cut apocalyptic boundary between the present and the coming age. The boundary between present and future is made permeable in the sayings of the Markan Jesus that refer to the empire of God as being at hand (1:15), likened to a growing seed (4:1–20, 30–34), received like a child (10:13–16), and connected to the love commandment (12:28–34). Hence Mark stands in an ambiguous relationship to the apocalyptic discourse, repeating some of its concepts and transforming their meaning.

A similar twist seems to be involved as Mark renders the apocalyptic saying in 8:38, our current focus. A pertinent question is to whom this Parousian threat is directed. It is not, as in Dan 7:13–27 (or, for that matter, in 1 Cor 15:24–25), a threat to annihilate the "evil imperial oppressors," whether in spiritual or human form. Rather, in Mark the threat is directed toward the disciples and connected to their reluctance to accept the catachrestic use of σταυρός. By implication, the threat is also directed toward Mark's audience. Mark's Parousia thus uses the Son of Man as a threatening metaphor that functions rhetorically in the very delivery of Mark's story to enable the audience to heed the catachrestic call to take up the cross with its implied countercultural practice.

Although this reading disagrees with Liew's interpretation of Mark's Parousia as a clear-cut reproduction of imperial ideology, Liew nevertheless offers a way in which the disagreement might be contained. Applying the Greek term *pharmakon*, which Derrida and Spivak have elaborated on, Liew (1999a, 150, 167–68) emphasizes the ambiguity of Gospel texts. Just as *pharmakon* can mean both "poison" and "medicine," Gospel texts are both safe and dangerous. As Liew makes clear, this vocabulary entails not a sorting out of Gospel texts into two dichotomous categories, labeling them either "medicine" or "poison," but rather a pressing of each text for its ambiguous potentials, showing "how 'medicine' and 'poison' are often one and the same thing" (167–68). Liew's (107) interpretation of Mark's Parousia as being, in the final analysis, "no different from the 'might-is-right' ideology" thus seems to fall short (by its own standards) in terms

---

91:12–17 fueled the Maccabean revolt. And, as previously argued, apocalyptic imaginations probably inspired the rebels in the Jewish War of 66–70.

of showing how it can also be heard as medicine. The reading offered here, therefore, does not negate so much as negotiate with Liew's reading. Taking Mark's Parousia as medicine, moreover, has the advantage of also implying a warning: it can become poisonous.

The Coming of Jesus and the Imperial Parousia

Having pointed out the rhetorical function of the Parousia in Mark, we are still left with the question of how to conceptualize the Parousia itself. Given the brevity of Mark's account in 8:38–9:1, such an analysis is difficult and we are bound to search for further clues in Mark that may assist the interpretation. Mark is rather sparse in this regard. The lengthiest description of the Parousia (13:24–27) briefly depicts the future coming of the Son of Man by means of heavenly signs. There is another brief portrayal in 14:62. Since explicit depictions of the Parousia are scanty, the search for further imagery that facilitates its conceptualization is warranted. As we have seen, Mark is fond of using narrative action to illustrate Jesus' enigmatic teachings (see ch. 15).

Such a search for a narrative illustration is not to be equated with the much-discussed issue of when to locate the Parousia in time—whether it is realized within Mark's narrative or if it is to be taken as referring to a future event outside the narrative. Christian interpreters over the centuries have been troubled by what appears to be a mistaken prediction by Jesus about the arrival of God's kingdom in power within a generation (9:1). A portion of that anxiety was seen in chapter 8. As Marcus (2009, 620) pointed out, there have been several suggestions to rescue Jesus from error by taking the Parousia as referring to various events, such as the transfiguration, the resurrection (and/or the ascension), the gift of the Holy Spirit, the miraculous growth of the church, and the destruction of Jerusalem. In the reading offered here, the declaration of the time of the coming by the Markan Jesus (9:1) is taken poetically (rather than literally) as referring to a future that is close at hand but not yet quite present.

But even if the search for a narrative illustration is not the same as trying to locate the Parousia in time, these discussions tend to overlap. The two suggestions of which I am aware that interpreters take as fulfilling the foretelling of Jesus' coming in power in Mark's narrative are the transfiguration (9:2–8) and the crucifixion scene (15:33–39).[15] In terms of a narrative

---

15. As shown by Taylor (1953, 385–86), a number of interpreters have argued that

17. THE PAROUSIA AS *PHARMAKON* (8:31–9:1)

illustration, however, these scenes lack an important ingredient. Even if they include apocalyptic elements, they are wanting of an actual arrival of Jesus.

For a narrative illustration, therefore, it seems as if the entry story (11:1–11) constitutes the best option. This is clearly a scene where Jesus arrives, and it has a noticeable messianic flavor. More to the point for this reading, its character resembles how a parousia was understood in imperial culture. As Brent Kinman (1999, 280–84) has argued, the parousia terminology in imperial discourse was closely associated with the phenomenon of celebratory welcomes and the arrival of a powerful ruler or deity.

Since these allusions bring us to the entry story (11:1–11), I mention them here as a transition to the next chapter. Literally meaning *presence* or *arrival*, παρουσία was used in imperial discourse as a technical term to designate a divine epiphany, the official visit of an emperor, or some other high-ranking official, to a city.[16] As Oepke (1967, 859) attests, there is no sharp distinction between religious and political usage. When Mark alludes to these imperial images for the coming of Jesus, a pertinent task is to analyze how the Gospel places the audience in relation to imperial discourse. As we approach the next chapter, then, Mark's way of illustrating the Parousia will be an issue to keep in mind.

---

the foretelling of Jesus' coming in power at least partly is fulfilled in the transfiguration. For an interpretation of the crucifixion scene as a realization of the Parousia, see Myers 1988, 389–92.

16. Radl 1993; and Oepke 1967. See also Deissmann 1978, 368–73; and G. Horsley 1981, 46.

18
WITH BHABHA AT THE JERUSALEM CITY GATES (11:1–22)

> This suit is black [pause] not.
> —Borat[1]

In Mark's story about Jesus' entry into Jerusalem (11:1–11), a number of royal and messianic signals appear for the first time in the narrative: instead of walking, Jesus has here mounted an animal; there are garments placed on the colt as well as on the road; and the crowd spreads leafy branches and salutes the arriving Jesus by acclamations of "he who comes in the name of the Lord" with reference to the kingdom of David.[2]

How might such an entry story relate to Roman imperial discourse? Whereas some scholars read it in oppositional terms,[3] others take it as a politically innocuous representation.[4] Most commonly, however, the issue is avoided. Being informed by the analysis of the nineteenth-century commentaries in part 2, I suspect that the answer (or the lack thereof) is related to a specific location and its dominating regime of knowledge. A prominent example of an innocuous reading is Gould (1896, 205–6), who argued that the key to a correct understanding of this episode can be found in the binary division between the spiritual and the worldly—

---

1. The quote is from the movie *Borat: Cultural Learnings of America for Make Benefit Glorious Nation of Kazakhstan (2006)*.
2. A previous version of ch. 18 is Leander 2010.
3. As already mentioned in ch. 9, Reimarus (1970, 92) constitutes an early example. Although focusing on Matthew's account, his reading also affected the interpretation of Mark. For contemporary oppositional readings, see Brandon 1967, 349–50; Belo 1981, 178–79; Myers 1988, 290–97; and R. Horsley 2001, 109–10.
4. Catchpole 1984, 322–23; and Roskam 2004, 159–61. However, interpretations that refrain from explicitly discussing the issue often presuppose an innocuous interpretation. This contention can be drawn from their interpretation of Mark 12:13–17. See, e.g., Taylor 1953, 477–80; Cranfield 1959, 369–72; and Gundry 1993, 692–700.

the very same division that fueled the European missionary movements. This is not to say, however, that oppositional readings are independent of discursive affiliations. When R. Horsley (2001, 109–10) describes Jesus' entry into Jerusalem in terms of "liberation from oppressive foreign rule," the reading is quite clearly connected to anticolonial liberation struggles. Needless to say, the same goes for a postcolonial reading such as the one suggested here. Unlike most other readings, however, the approach applied strives to be more transparent and involves an explicit reflection over the interconnections between location and interpretation. As will be seen, the reading of this particular episode will explicitly engage with Bhabha's concept of mimicry as a way of conceptualizing the manner in which it relates to imperial discourse.

Triumphal Entries and Mark's Anticlimax

In what follows, the terms *triumphal entry, celebratory welcomes*, and *Parousia* will be used interchangeably. Since this study locates Mark's audience in the wider imperial cultural context, I begin by analyzing how this phenomenon was depicted in imperial discourse.[5] Judging from numerous sources, triumphal entries and processions were relatively common in antiquity. Indeed, there are several accounts of Greek,[6] Roman[7] and Jewish[8]

---

5. My analysis is indebted to Catchpole 1984; Duff 1992; and Kinman 1999.

6. Alexander the Great's entry into Jerusalem, as told by Josephus (*Ant.* 11.332–336), is a famous example. See also Polybius (16.25.1–9), who describes how King Attalus of Pergamum received a triumphant welcome upon entering Athens. Similarly, Athenaeus (*Deipn.* 6.253c) describes how Demetrius was triumphantly received in Athens, and saluted as "the only true god." Moreover, after Mithridates's victory over the Romans in the first century B.C.E., he was welcomed and hailed as "God and Saviour" in the cities of Asia Minor (Diodorus Siculus 37.26).

7. Roman emperors generally received grandiose welcomes when they traveled. For instance, Suetonius (*Nero* 25.1–3) offers telling descriptions of Nero's entrances to different cities, including Rome. See also Plutarch (*Ant.* 24.3–4) regarding the welcoming of Antony into Ephesus. Further, Josephus (*Ant.* 16.12–15) discusses Marcus Agrippa's entry into Jerusalem. There is also the somewhat different, but related, Roman triumph in which the ruler, rather than having a procession in a foreign (sometimes vanquished) city, had it in his own city instead—i.e., in Rome (Josephus, *J.W.* 7.132–157). See also Versnel 1970.

8. There are many examples from the Hasmonean period—the victory over and entry into Gaza by Simon Maccabeus (1 Macc 13:43–48; 14:7), Jonathan Maccabeus's glorious reception when entering Askalon (1 Macc 10:86; 11:60), and the honor-

triumphal processions. Being both political and religious manifestations, they elevated rulers and granted them authority and power.[9] Presumably, the phenomenon was well known and spoken about extensively. As argued by A. Collins (2007, 514–16), the widespread attestations of such stories give reason to regard them as a specific literary genre to which Mark 11:1–11 belongs.

When analyzing various accounts of celebratory welcomes, a basic common structure becomes evident.[10]

(1) The prominent person is greeted near the city gates and hailed by the citizenry, often as a divine revelation.
(2) He (they are all male) is then formally escorted into the city, accompanied by hymns and/or acclamations.
(3) The procession typically ends in the city's temple, where some kind of ritual takes place—either a benevolent sacrifice or a hostile expulsion of some kind.

The entry story in Mark's Gospel has a similar pattern. Jesus is greeted by "many" (11:8) outside the city. With garments and leafy branches he is escorted into the city, accompanied by shouts that acclaim him as a longed-for king (11:9). The messianic and royal undertones with their divine and political connotations reinforce the suggestion that the episode alludes to the wider imperial phenomenon of celebratory welcomes. An important difference, however, is how the procession ends. The procession continues, as expected, through the city and into the temple. While there, however, the customary ritual does not take place. Jesus quickly looks around

---

able reception of Apollonius into Jerusalem (2 Macc 4:21–22). Also, Josephus (*J.W.* 2.433–434) describes how Menahem (a Jewish insurgent during the war against the Romans), armed with Herod's weapons, entered Jerusalem "like a veritable king," after which he became a leader of the rebellion.

9. This is shown most clearly by the decree that granted celebratory welcomes to Augustus in the cities he visited; see Dio Cassius 51.20.2–4.

10. Catchpole (1984), Duff (1992), and Kinman (1999) describe the pattern somewhat differently. Most notably, Catchpole (1984, 321–23) differs by suggesting that a procession is always preceded by a military victory. Since several of the sources do not support this claim, it probably should be seen as reflecting Catchpole's attempt to reject Reimarus's (1970, 92) thesis that the public parade "could aim at nothing other than a secular kingdom."

and then retires, for, as Mark says, "it was already late" (11:11). Thus, as depicted by Mark, the procession's ending is anticlimactic.

Several scholars have recognized the anticlimactic character of the entry story and explained it in two different ways. The first line of interpretation is represented by Kinman (1999), whose argument is based on the account in Luke. The arrival of prominent guests at a city implied certain expectations as to provision of a customary welcome, the neglect of which was viewed as an insult, sometimes leading to severe consequences; hence, that Luke 19:28–44 makes no mention of Jesus having received such a welcome is interpreted as indirectly signaling an insult. A. Collins (2007, 516–21) approaches Mark's account along similar lines—that Jerusalem's leaders appear not to have given Jesus a proper welcome when he arrived at the city indirectly signals an affront. This notwithstanding, Mark's account differs from Luke's in several crucial ways. Since Mark makes no prior mention of earlier visits to Jerusalem, Mark's audience would likely not have expected the city's leaders to know of Jesus' prominence and would thus not have regarded the absence of an official welcoming as an insult. Moreover, Mark depicts Jesus in less royal terms than does Luke, which further lowers expectations of a grand official welcoming at the temple and reduces the impression that an insult had been committed by its omission.

A second suggestion comes from Duff (1992), who also emphasizes the importance of the concluding ritual in triumphal entries. Somewhat differently from Kinman and Catchpole, however, Duff regards the concluding ritual as an act of appropriation in which the ruler symbolically takes possession of the city. By postponing the concluding ritual and describing it as a condemnation rather than an appropriation, Mark "gives his 'triumphal entry' an ironic twist" (70). Although Duff might be seen to exaggerate the case for a particular ritual of appropriation—the concluding ritual appears to have been more diverse in character—his argument is still quite suggestive. Particularly telling is his conclusion that Mark "teases his readers with what seem to be triumphal allusions but never satisfies their expectations" (70).

Jesus' Entry as Mimicry

Although it thus seems clear that the depiction of Jesus' entry into Jerusalem both resembles and differs from narrations of imperial triumphs, it is far from obvious how one should interpret this. Where does the episode place the Markan Jesus in relation to imperial discourse and how does it thereby interpellate the audience? As Mark has Jesus and the Twelve stroll out of the city at twilight (11:11), having been deprived of the concluding ritual, a gap is established in relation to imperial discourse. A way of conceptualizing the effects of this enigmatic narration is offered by Bhabha's concept of mimicry. Taking the entry story as mimicry implies that its relation to imperial discourse fluctuates ambivalently between on the one hand appearing original and authoritative and on the other hand as being articulated with a significant difference. What Mark depicts could then be termed as being almost the same *but not quite* an imperial triumph.

An illustration of the parodic and rupturing aspects of mimicry from contemporary popular culture is the mockumentary movie *Borat: Cultural Learnings of America for Make Benefit Glorious Nation of Kazakhstan*, in which a Kazakh journalist tries to imitate a dominating American culture. Trying to tell jokes as instructed by a U.S. teacher, Borat imitates yet subverts the teaching, thereby becoming almost the same *but not quite* an American.[11] The delayed climax in the Markan account has a curious similarity to Borat's attempts to imitate American joke telling: in both instances there is a problem of timing. To tell a successful joke, Borat is supposed to say the word "not" at exactly the right moment, and as he fails by being either too late or too soon, the attempt to educate (or civilize) him appears as a parody that undermines the authority of the dominant culture. In a similar vein, when Jesus enters Jerusalem, the delay of the final climax makes the entry come across as a parody on imperial triumphs.

If one takes it as mimicry, the anticlimax is not primarily expressing hostility in the way that Collins suggests, but is rather destabilizing imperial notions of power. Further, the colt itself can be seen as signaling irony and ambivalence.[12] As an animal "on which no one has ever sat" (11:2), it serves as a telling image of the third in-between space that is opened up by the story's imitative displacement of imperial parousia.[13] Before expanding further on the effects of this mimicry, however, I would like to point

---

11. The menacing effect is perhaps seen most clearly when Borat, visiting a rodeo, irst excites the crowd with chauvinist, pro–U.S. remarks, then sings a fictional Kazakhstan national anthem to the tune of "The Star-Spangled Banner," which receives a strong negative reaction.

12. Even if Jewish tradition granted that a king could ride on a colt or a donkey (Gen 49:8–12; Zech 9:9), there seems to be no such precedents in Roman discourse.

13. The open character of the term πῶλον (it could mean horse, donkey, or camel) supports the newness with which Bhabha associates the third space.

260 DISCOURSES OF EMPIRE

out two more components of the entry story that feed into this particular interpretation. Also, as mentioned in the previous chapter's analysis of Mark's Parousia, I will discuss the implications of reading the entry story as an illustration of the future coming of Jesus in power.

Forced Labor (11:3)

In 11:3 there is an enigmatic phrase that tends to trouble commentators. As Jesus instructs his disciples to obtain the colt that is to be used in his entry, he effectively tells them to take it without permission from a local village (11:2). He further instructs that if questioned, they are to respond by saying, ὁ κύριος αὐτοῦ χρείαν ἔχει (11:3). Following these instructions, the disciples proceed to fetch the colt, and when challenged as expected (11:5), they dutifully utter these words (11:6). Immediately, as if by magic, all objections are dropped. What was it that made the bystanders voluntarily relinquish the colt? And who does ὁ κύριος refer to? It appears that there are various possible ways of filling this space with meaning.

The title ὁ κύριος (with a definite article) has occurred only once before in Mark (5:19). There it ambiguously refers to Jesus or God. Similarly, in 11:3 it is quite unclear to whom it refers. Taylor (1953, 454–55) gives three alternatives: *the Lord* can refer either to Jesus, to God, or to the owner of the animal. Somewhat reluctantly, Taylor decides upon the third option, as does Hartman (2005, 421). A. Collins (2007, 518), on the other hand, chooses the first option—Jesus. Here I will follow Collins, but with a certain twist that amounts to a fourth option. As some commentators mention, the scene in which an animal is acquired for transportation resembles the Roman practice of requiring the local population to procure beasts of burden, generally known as ἀγγαρεία (forced labor). To my knowledge, discussions regarding how this particular allusion places Mark in relation to Roman imperial discourse are quite meager.[14]

---

14. Four more recent commentators mention the allusion: Gundry 1993, 627–28; Perkins 1995, 658; Hartman 2005, 414, 422; and A. Collins 2007, 518. Perkins comes closest to a discussion when she states that Jesus is different from the Roman occupying power since he promises to give the animal back to its owner. In his otherwise brilliant analysis, Derrett (1971, 243–48) seems to overlook the imperial allusion when he argues that the acquisition was consistent with Jewish customs according to which a rabbi had the right to impress animals for transportation. In that case, as Derrett says, the phrase should have been rendered "our master [*mārān*] needs it." In another

18. WITH BHABHA AT THE JERUSALEM CITY GATES (11:1–22) 261

Ἀγγαρεία is a Persian loanword that stems from the Persian Empire (ca. 500–300 B.C.E.), which developed a postal service by enforcing local transportation. As shown by Derrett (1971) and Wink (1992a, 202–4), its use during the time of the Gospels is well known. That the Romans practiced ἀγγαρεία is made clear in the Passion Narrative, where Roman soldiers *compel* (ἀγγαρεύουσιν) Simon of Cyrene to carry Jesus' cross (Mark 15:21; Matt 27:32). It is also shown in the Sermon on the Mount, where Jesus teaches about going two miles if anyone *forces* (ἀγγαρεύουσει) you to go one mile (Matt 5:41).

As argued by E. A. Judge (1981, 39), forced labor was generally a source of bitterness and friction in the Roman provinces. Roman soldiers carried heavy loads, and in order to keep pace they compelled local populations and their beasts of burden into service. There are even stories of whole villages fleeing so as to avoid being pressed into carrying such loads (MacMullen 1963, 88). When the Greek philosopher Epictetus (contemporary with Mark) writes about freedom, he makes use of ἀγγαρεία in a telling image: "But if there be a press [ἀγγαρεία], and a soldier should lay hold of it [your ass], let it go, do not resist, nor murmur; if you do, you will receive blows, and nevertheless you will also lose the ass" (*Diatr.* 4.1.79).

As indicated by the many laws and imperial edicts that were aimed at regulating the practice of ἀγγαρεία, it was both hated and disputed by the local populations. One such edict, inscribed in both Greek and Latin, is preserved from a pillar in Galatia, dated by Judge (1981, 40–42) to 18 or 19 C.E. Here the local population is compelled to supply carts, mules, and donkeys as means of transportation for their imperial masters in exchange for specified payments, and in certain cases for free. The edict also regulates who has the right to use these services, particularly mentioning the Roman knights involved in "the needs of the Augustus" (τοῦ Σεβαστοῦ χρήαις).[15] From these regulations it seems possible to derive a phrase that

---

interesting article, Stauffer (1956, 85–86) contends that the phrase was an official requisition formula that prepared for the "königlichen Adventus" of Jesus. Categorizing the Markan Jesus as a nonpolitical king, however, Stauffer makes a pro-imperial interpretation based on the previously discussed division between spiritual and worldly (ch. 9). In sum, there seems to be a lack of discussion about the disruption that is signaled when a popular Galilean leader entitled "Son of God" makes use of an imperial requisition formula.

15. Comparing the edict to the phrase in Mark, one finds the word χρήαις in the edict is similar to χρείαν in Mark. They are different forms of the noun χρεία, which means "need." Χρήαις in the edict is in the dative plural and has an older spelling.

may have been typically used in the requisition of an animal: "Augustus has need of it" (cf. Derrett 1971, 246). Or even more likely, since Augustus was generally referred to as "Lord," the phrase can be rendered, "The Lord has need of it"—the very enigmatic phrase that Jesus instructs his disciples to use.

The phrase in 11:3 would therefore have echoed familiarly with a well-known yet detested standard phrase for Roman ἀγγαρεία. But what is the subtext? If one judges from the imperial edict, a person such as the Markan Jesus would have lacked all legal rights to make use of ἀγγαρεία, and even less so his disciples.[16] On the contrary, Jesus and his disciples belonged to the wider category of people who, as Roman subjects, could be compelled to supply the Romans with means of transportation. Due to the story's low verisimilitude, the depiction appears miraculous and humorous. By twisting the roles and presenting Jesus and the disciples as successfully practicing ἀγγαρεία, Mark's requisition story imitates and mocks the Roman use. This ironic imitation also accentuates a competition over the title ὁ κύριος, which in an imperial requisition doubtlessly would have referred to the emperor. In Mark, as we saw, the referent is rather vague. What I would suggest, then, as a fourth option (referring to the three mentioned above) is to take the phrase "The Lord has need of it" as a mimicry of the imperial practice of ἀγγαρεία and the word ὁ κύριος as a reference to Jesus' being almost the same *but not quite* the emperor.[17]

In imperial discourse, the meaning of ὁ κύριος was construed around phallocentric notions—masculinity, strength, power, and domination. When Mark uses this term to designate a rural Galilean Son of God who makes use of the official impressment phrase, ὁ κύριος is destabilized from a natural or self-evident meaning and becomes what Ernesto Laclau (1990, 28) has called a floating signifier. In the context of the entry story's mimicry, the imitation of Roman ἀγγαρεία becomes parodic. Not only is the referent of ὁ κύριος displaced, but Mark also disturbs in a more profound sense the meaning of "Lord"—the power, attitude, and social practice that is associated with the title (cf. 10:42–44).

---

16. Contra Derrett (1971), who argues that Jesus' instructions contain important legal implications from a Jewish perspective. He does not, however, discuss the imperial allusions of the phrase.

17. This reading of κύριος complies with the meaning the title seems to have in Mark 5:19. As argued in ch. 15, 5:1–20 presents Jesus as similar to and yet different from Vespasian.

THE PEDAGOGICAL AND THE PERFORMATIVE (11:9–10)

There is yet another way in which the text coaxes its way into the third space in between imperial discourse and its antagonistic response. As R. Horsley (2001, 109–10) has persuasively argued, the Hosanna cries in 11:9–10 are recitations of the Hallel psalms that were sung during the Passover in remembrance of the exodus.[18] The Hosanna cries therefore invoke the exodus tradition and the Jewish longing for liberation from foreign rule. Since the exodus tradition was important for motivating the anti-Roman uprising, it was probably known by Mark's audience.[19] The anti-Roman message is further supported by the reference to "the kingdom of David," which evokes memories of the short yet significant period wherein Judea was a great power in the Near East (Meyers 1992, 360–61).

In line with the development of Mark's plot, however, it is not surprising to find that when the memory of the exodus appears in the entry story, it is disturbed and modified by the story's mimicry of triumphant processions. In Mark's account (11:9–10), the Hebrew cries are used quite differently than they are in the Jewish Passover remembrance of the exodus. According to Marvin Pope (1992, 291), Mark's way of narrating the Hosanna cries is a "misapprehension of a well-known Hebrew term," which he seems to regard as rather unfortunate and regrettable.[20] But this "misapprehension" can also be understood in terms of Bhabha's distinction between the pedagogical and the performative (see ch. 2). The odd use of Hosanna then appears as a performative enunciation of a national memory that both adds to and supplants its meaning. When the anti-Roman prayer of the exodus tradition (Hosanna, save us [from the Romans]) is used to praise

---

18. Although these psalms were used both at the Feast of Tabernacles and Passover (Taylor 1953, 456), the literary context in Mark makes the Feast of Tabernacles less likely since that feast marked the conclusion of the harvest. Passover, with its political connotations, fits much better with the genre of the entry story.

19. The accounts by Josephus indicate that the exodus tradition was important for fueling anti-Roman sentiments (*J.W.* 2.258–263; *Ant.* 18.85–87; 20.97–98, 168–171). Cf. Hooker 1991, 259, who claims that the Hosanna cries among Jews were perceived as an "appeal to God to save his people from foreign domination." In Mark, however, she believes they are rather to be taken as cries of homage. But would this exclude the possibility that traces of anti-Roman sentiment might still be heard?

20. Since *Hosanna* in Hebrew means "save now," Pope argues, the cry in Mark 11:10 should not be translated "Hosanna in the highest," but rather "Save/help, please, O Highest." These are liturgical texts that cry to the anointed king for deliverance.

Jesus as he enters Jerusalem, Mark redefines and dislocates its meaning from a ritual that recalled a past founding event—the pedagogical in Bhabha's terms. Being relocated to a mimicry of celebratory welcomes, the Hosanna cries are used performatively as homage and acclamation. The original anti-imperial meaning can still be heard but is also made unstable as it is transferred into a more elusive mimicry of imperial triumphant processions. In relation to Rome, this places the Markan Jesus in a less confrontational but more ambivalent and subtly subversive position than that which the exodus tradition would have allowed.

The Entry as an Illustration of the Parousia

Here let us return to the question of Mark's Parousia, discussed at the end of the previous chapter. The coming of the Son of Man in a mighty cloud, as taught by the Markan Jesus, presents a paradox. Located in the eschatological future, it is also an event that is anticipated in the present.[21] The expectation of a future coming, Mark's story conveys, affects the understanding of the present. The way in which the future coming is conceptualized is therefore important, hence the quest for a narrative illustration.

Taking the entry story as a narrative illustration of the Parousia has several merits. It fits well with Mark's blurring of the apocalyptic curtain (see ch. 17). It also fits with the entry story's eschatological undertones. The Hosanna cries (11:10), in their rearticulating of a past founding event, acclaim the coming βασιλεία, commending what appears to be an already achieved victory. In that sense of eschatological anticipation, the entry story celebrates a victory that, in Mark's narrative, is yet to come. Nonetheless, it occurs performatively in the very celebration, pointing toward the ambiguous notion of God's nonimperial empire as present and as not yet present. Considering how Mark's entry story, by its parodic mimicry/

---

21. Contra Myers (1988, 248, 389–92), who takes the crucifixion of Jesus as the realization of the Parousia foretold in 8:38–9:1; 13:26; and 14:62. The crucifixion scene, however, is lacking in power and glory, not to mention clouds. Besides being exegetically unpersuasive, Myers's overrealized interpretation of Mark's eschatology can be criticized politically as well as spiritually for promoting a dangerous utopianism. In fairness, however, Myers also seems ambivalent. The Gospel's "most salient lesson," he states (394), is that those who follow Jesus are often unsure of who he is, "but struggle to trust him nevertheless." So everything is not yet completely revealed, and Myers's eschatology does not appear so realized after all.

mockery of celebratory welcomes, subtly subverts imperial notions of strength and triumph, the Markan Parousia helps establish a third space in between imperial and anti-imperial discourses that feeds into Mark's dislocated plot.

The Janus Face of the Temple Incident (11:12–22)

Although delayed, Jesus' visit to the temple does indeed occur on the following day. Since the dramatic events that transpire on that visit (11:12–22) are significantly related to Mark's stance vis-à-vis imperial discourse, it is necessary to briefly discuss the interpretation of the drama as it continues. Since Myers takes this as a key passage for his reading of Mark, I will discuss his interpretation and offer my own alternative reading.

Sandwiched between a twofold story in which Jesus curses a fig tree for bearing no fruit (11:12–14, 20–22), the temple incident is often taken as communicating a not so subtle condemnation of the temple.[22] This is the basis for Myers's (1988, 297–306) reading of the episode as an exorcism of the temple. With reference to the passage about the poor widow (12:41–44) and the following foretelling of the temple's destruction (13:1–2), Myers (303) regards the temple institution as exploiting the poor. Taking the temple incident as alluding to the parable about the strong man (3:23–27) and his "goods" (σκεῦος, 3:27), Myers (303) argues that the divided house in 3:25 veritably corresponds to the temple and its "goods" (σκεῦος, 11:16). Here emerges Myers's (304) main thesis: "*This* is the apocalyptic struggle to bind the strong man and plunder his house." Further, in relation to the following instructions on prayer, Myers (305) continues along the same route: the "mountain" that is to be thrown into the sea (11:23) in Mark's narrative context "can only refer to the temple." Myers's reading thus sustains an intense antagonism between Jesus and the disciples on the one hand, and the temple institution and its satanic imperial order on the other. What appears striking from a postcolonial perspective, however, is how Myers's reading of the temple incident as an apocalyptic struggle has an uncanny intertext in the Roman destruction

---

22. See Telford 1980 and many scholars following him. Annette Weissenrieder (2010) has suggested that the fig tree refers not to the Jerusalem temple but to Rome. Although she is right to point out that visual representations of fig trees were commonly used as symbols of Roman power, she does not consider the obvious intertext for Mark's audience: the destruction of the Jerusalem temple.

of the Jerusalem temple. As the war had probably just ended when Mark's narrative was beginning to circulate, this event would surely have been present in the minds of Mark's audience when the dramatic temple scene was conveyed. The agent that finally binds the strong man and plunders the house (the temple), then, turns out to be none other than the Roman army. As Mark seems to be giving divine mandate to the Roman war against the Jews, the temple institution is radically altered as a symbol.[23] Whereas Myers took it as representing Rome's imperial order, it also seems to represent unfruitful Jewishness justifiably punished by Rome's army.[24] Since the apocalyptic struggle thus becomes associated with the Roman destruction of Jerusalem, it seems important to point out the sinister side of the temple incident. Elevating Rome's army as God's appointed instrument for punishing the Jews is surely not what Myers intended. By ignoring this interpretive potential, however, his dualistic reading dangerously idealizes the drama.

To be clear, I am not here arguing that the temple incident as depicted by Mark unequivocally grants Rome a divine status or unambiguously expresses a desire to gain Rome's favor. After all, Jesus' activities in the temple constitute a rather provocative disruption of a powerful institution, and as such can hardly be thought of as deeds that would unequivocally attract the favor of Rome. As Carol Meyers (1992, 364–65) points out, the restoration and enlargement of the Jerusalem temple under Herod the Great had established friendly relations with Rome. Being a grandiose center for Mediterranean standards, the Jerusalem temple represents a Roman-friendly metropolis. Also, taking into account the rural identity of Jesus and the Twelve, the rural/urban division gives further weight to the disruptive and antagonistic character of the incident. When Mark depicts Jesus as driving out the sellers and buyers in the temple, referring to the temple elite as "bandits" (λῃστῶν), it signals an attack against

---

23. As David Seeley (1993, 275) has noticed, Mark enables the Romans to "absolve themselves of responsibility by claiming that the destruction [of the Jerusalem temple] had been divinely ordained" (cf. Mark 12:9; 13:2).

24. As Moore (2006, 35) contends, Mark here grants Rome the role of God's scourge along Deuteronomistic lines (see, e.g., Deut 28:25–68). As previously mentioned, the Deuteronomistic tradition can be seen as one in which the subdued is granted a certain sense of agency. In Mark's case, however, the divine wrath is directed against *the Other* (as represented by the temple) rather than the self, which constitutes a crucial difference.

an urban institution that was closely intertwined with Roman imperial order. The condemnation of the temple is therefore a condemnation of its Roman dependency.

But this condemnation also has a reverse or Janus side. When the Roman destruction of Jerusalem is taken into account, an alternate image presents itself. The "bandits," in this alternate interpretation, do not refer to the temple elite but to the Jewish anti-Roman insurgents.[25] The aggressive temple acts by the Markan Jesus are then associated with Rome's military victory over these "bandits." Hence the anti-imperial message of the temple act is haunted by the Janus-faced grant of status to Rome as a divine avenger.

When the Roman destruction of the temple is juxtaposed with the anti-imperial reading, the meaning of the temple drama begins to fluctuate. Here a link is established with the entry story and its anticlimactic ending. As a delayed ending of the entry story, the temple incident expands the mimicry/mockery slippage into a more intense ambivalence. Whereas the entry story signals a playful slipping between imitation and parody, the delayed temple drama signifies a wider gap between two conflicting messages. Fluctuating between an attack against and an exaltation of Roman imperial order, the temple incident represents a profound colonial ambivalence.

Even though more could be said about Mark's depiction of the temple incident, it seems sufficient for my purposes here to see the drama as an expression of the deep ambivalence in relation to Roman power that seems to permeate Mark's Gospel. On the one hand, Jesus is depicted as disrupting business-as-usual in the temple of a Roman-friendly city, and thereby subverting imperial social order. On the other hand, by enfolding Jesus' disruption in a cursing of a fig tree, Mark also grants divine legitimacy to the Roman destruction of the temple and the suppression of the Jewish insurgents. Vacillating between aggression and admiration, fear and desire, the temple act generates a colonial ambivalence that undermines a clear-cut position in relation to imperial discourse, and instead pulls the audience into an interstitial third space of negotiation.

---

25. Just as Josephus (*J.W.* 1.304) refers to Jewish insurrectionists as "bandits" (λῃστής) who were hiding in "caves" (σπηλαίοις), the Markan Jesus' use of the term "den of bandits" (σπήλαιον λῃστῶν) might refer to Jewish anti-Roman insurgents.

19
The Emperor Breaks the Surface (12:13–17)

> Is it lawful to pay the penalty to Caesar?
> —Mark 12:14

It is difficult for a postcolonial reading of Mark's Gospel to avoid the passage in which Jesus pronounces the famous words, "Render to Caesar the things that are Caesar's, and to God the things that are God's" (12:17). As Taylor (1953, 478) puts it, the saying "has deeply influenced all subsequent discussions of the complex relationships of Church and State." Given the saying's ambiguity, however, it would be fairer to say that its influence stems more from the various traditions of *interpreting* it. As we saw in chapter 10, the nineteenth-century interpretations of the passage typically applied the division between a spiritual and a worldly sphere, which resulted in a harmonization of the claims of Caesar and the claims of God. As a first step in the analysis of this passage, therefore, I will conduct a small survey in which contemporary commentaries are compared to the nineteenth-century ones studied in part 2. I will then focus on the question of how Mark's audience was addressed by this passage. To what position in relation to Rome's imperial order were they interpellated? Unlike the other Markan passages that are scrutinized in this study, this one has the relation to Rome written all over its forehead (so to speak), addressing rather directly the essential question of this study. But even so, the nature of the episode is curiously ambiguous, leaving a lot of room for hermeneutical variation. Taking into account the episode's place in Mark's narrative, as well as the specific meaning of taxation in Roman imperial and Jewish discourses, I will suggest that this episode, despite its ambiguity, established an unmistakable sense of friction in relation to imperial discourse.

Comparing Interpretations

The statement on Roman taxes by the Markan Jesus clearly attracts amazement—"they marveled" (12:17). But what message did Mark's audience receive regarding the issue? Despite the amazement, the statement does not precisely specify what belongs to Caesar and what belongs to God. Given the ambiguous character of the statement, the interpretive possibilities are considerable. As Marcus (2009, 825) has noted, "the answers to this question [what belongs to God and to Caesar] have been legion, and have often depended on the political leaning of the commentator." This clear-sighted recognition echoes the outstanding comment by Myers (1988, 313): "Exegetes who otherwise think the Gospel of Mark has little to do with political discourse feel free at this point to insert their own." Apart from the interpreter's particular political leaning, however, there is also the issue of basic presuppositions—typically unacknowledged—that are taken for granted. As we saw in chapters 9 and 10, an example of such a presupposition is the division between religion and politics.

And yet, even if the ambiguous character of the statement as well as the inevitability of inserting preconceived notions are recognized, biblical scholars will continue to interpret the saying. Indeed, the statement seems to be asking of its readers to do just that. Hence Myers went ahead and inserted a political interpretation of his own, as did Marcus. The same, of course, applies to this study. In addition to offering my own reading, however, I also attempt to make visible how scholarly interpretations have been affected by epistemic presuppositions that have changed from one historical period to another. What follows then is a brief survey of previous interpretations that, for the sake of comparison, will only include commentaries.

In contemporary Markan scholarship the interpretations of the saying vary widely from one end of the spectrum to the other. On the one side are those who regard the saying as a forthright call for tax resistance, and on the opposite side are those who consider it a clear-cut call for payment. There are also those who consider the saying to provide no definite answer in either direction, and even others who fall along the spectrum in subtly diverse ways. While I admit that the attempt to categorize these various positions is fraught with difficulties, it nonetheless appears necessary for comparison's sake. I have thus taken a selection of sixteen contemporary commentaries as well as the nineteenth-century ones that I here previously studied, and placed them into four interpretational categories, intended to

19. THE EMPEROR BREAKS THE SURFACE (12:13–17)

facilitate a comparative analysis. The results of this classification can be seen in the following formation and table 5.

(1) The first category interprets the saying as an unambiguous call to pay the tax. The claims of God and the claims of Caesar are here seen as harmoniously integrated. There is no conflict between the two. Four[1] contemporary and thirteen[2] nineteenth-century commentators belong to this category.

(2) In the second category the saying is taken as an instruction to pay the tax, but also as a warning to be cautious. The claims of God and the claims of Caesar are not always reconcilable. There are situations, and here some refer to Acts 5:29, when loyalty to God implies resistance to the ruling authorities. Eight[3] contemporary and two[4] nineteenth-century commentators belong to this category.

(3) The third category reads the saying as a call to resist the tax. When one compares the claims of God and the claims of Caesar, the latter falls short. Since Caesar has no legitimate

---

1. Taylor (1953, 478–80), Hooker (1991, 278–81), Gundry (1993, 692–700), and France (2002, 464–69) all argue that there is no opposition between the claims of Caesar and God. Hooker (1991, 281) finds the answer to be unequivocal. The authority of Caesar and the obligations that this entails cannot be escaped. As Taylor (1953, 480) states, the claims of the state are within the divine order. Similarly, Gundry (1993, 694, 699), finds that the answer emphasizes the obligation "to pay tax and follow Jesus."

2. F. Cook 1878, 122; Gould 1896, 224–27; J. Lange 1865, 396; Meyer 1881, 85; Alford 1849, 159; Swete 1898, 260; Riddle 1879, 181; Maclear 1883, 154–56; Menzies 1901, 220–21; Weiss 1872, 392; Klostermann 1867, 236; Holtzmann 1892, 243–244; and Bruce 1897, 273–75.

3. Although arguing in different ways, Cranfield (1959, 369–72), Gnilka (1979, 150–54), Lane (1974, 421–25), Perkins (1995, 673–74), Witherington (2001, 323–26), Donahue and Harrington (2002, 345–48), Hartman (2005, 446–49), and Marcus (2009, 815–26) belong in this category. Even if the saying is taken as a call to pay the tax, these commentators also see an implicit critique against the divine claims of the emperor. According to Marcus (2009, 825), it still distinguishes the position of Jesus from that of a Zealot, and thus he sees it as exegetically sounder to take Jesus as advocating payment rather than a "tax revolt." Witherington (2001, 326) takes a similar position. Hartman (2005, 448–49), in turn, makes clear that the answer presents two empires that stand in an oppositional relation to each other. Although taxes can be paid, there were other demands that could not be accepted.

4. Plumptre 1897, 137; and Alexander 1858, 328.

claim, all things belong to God, the true Lord. One[5] contemporary and one[6] nineteenth-century commentary belong to this category.

(4) In the last category, the saying is taken as being ambiguous, and thus as offering no real answer to the question about taxes. Three contemporary commentators (no nineteenth-century ones) belong to this category.[7]

Table 5. A comparison of how commentators interpret Mark 12:17

Interpretations	Contemporary	Nineteenth-Century
1. Pay the tax (forthright).	25%	81%
2. Pay the tax (cautiously).	50%	12%
3. Resist the tax.	6%	6%
4. The saying gives no answer.	19%	0%

At the outset, the limited character of this survey needs to be acknowledged. There were more commentaries written on Mark's Gospel during the nineteenth century than the sixteen studied here. Similarly, the scope of contemporary scholarship on Mark is significantly wider than the commentaries included in the survey. Despite the limited nature of the survey, however, the results indicate the occurrence of two significant developments in contemporary scholarship.

---

5. Although not clear-cut, Liew (2007, 109–10) reads Jesus' answer as a challenge to Roman authority. For readings that clearly take it as a call *not* to pay the tax, see R. Horsley (2001, 43; 1993, 306–17) and (to a lesser extent) Myers (1988, 310–14) and Belo (1981, 186–88). Since their works are not commentaries, they are not part of this particular comparison.

6. Even if ambiguous, Chadwick (1887, 325–30) takes the saying as legitimating a refusal to pay the tribute. For a more comprehensive discussion, see ch. 10.

7. Van Iersel (1998, 370–72), Evans (2000a, 240–48), and A. Collins (2007, 550–57) take this position. According to van Iersel (1998, 372), Jesus' saying "definitely does not answer the question." A. Collins (2007, 552) similarly sees the saying as being "too general ... to provide a practical guide for conduct." According to Evans (2000a, 247), the statement is such that regardless of whether one is for or against the payment of taxes one can agree with it.

First, whereas more than three-quarters of the nineteenth-century scholars fall into the first category, contemporary interpretations are considerably more heterogeneous. Even if the binary division between spiritual and worldly is still quite common, contemporary scholars are not quite as eager as their predecessors to presume a harmonious relation between the claims of God and Caesar. Second, as is indicated by the increase from 0 to 19 percent in the fourth category, the evasive nature of the answer has been far more recognized in contemporary scholarship. In addition, commentators in other categories have often stressed the answer's ambiguous character.

The Emperor Surfaces

The interpretation of the episode suggested here is based on how Mark's narrative has thus far related to the Roman imperial discourse. Mark's incipit set the tone by alluding in an oppositional way to imperial notions of gospel, of new beginnings, and of divine sonship. Mark's plotting of Jesus and the Twelve as a Jewish rural movement continued along this oppositional path. However, beginning outside Gerasa with the request that Jesus depart (5:17) and outside Tyre with the Greek Syrophoenician woman (7:24–30), the antagonistic plot began to vacillate. Peaking with the turbulent exchange between Jesus and Peter (8:27–33), the dualistic antagonism was dislocated by an aporetic impasse. As the story continued, Mark's plot became subversive in a new sense, represented by the catachrestic use of σταυρός (8:34–9:1), the mimicry of triumphant processions (11:1–11), and the colonial ambivalence expressed in the temple incident (11:12–22).

In the previous narrative, imperial discourse has been only alluded to in more or less subtle ways. It is not until the narrative's last section on Jesus' chastisement of the temple authorities that three explicit representations of imperial discourse are brought to the surface: the emperor, the coin, and the issue of taxation. The surfacing occurs in three steps. First, when the issue of authority is broached (11:27–33), Jesus repudiates the temple officials by referring to the popular memory of John the Baptist, who had been executed by Herod (6:14–29). The political character of the drama, already introduced in the entry story, is now further articulated. The second step occurs as Jesus continues by telling the parable of the Tenants (12:1–12), which indicates that what happened to John the Baptist will also happen to Jesus: he will be seized and killed (12:8). Mark here makes clear that the temple officials took this parable as an accusation (12:12). By implication, however, it is also an accusation against their patrons, the Roman authorities who are to effect the execution (15:1–39). The third step, finally, is the actual surfacing of the emperor himself, in the form of an image on a coin.

In the two previous steps, Mark has depicted the success of the Galilean's political rhetoric and use of parable to handle the temple authorities. In what appears as an attempt to recover their honor, the temple authorities send some of the Pharisees and Herodians to catch Jesus in a "verbal trap" (12:13). Since Jesus had become too popular to merely apprehend (12:12), they set out to manufacture a situation that would make arrest more feasible. This constitutes the beginning of the episode in question.

To set their scheme in motion, the Pharisees and Herodians first employ the device of flattery, praising Jesus as being honest, unaffected by the opinions of others, unwilling to compromise his views, and a true teacher of the way of God (12:14). Having thus prepared the way, their plans are brought to fruition in the form of the following question: "Is it lawful to pay taxes to the emperor, or not?" (12:14). With this question, it appears as if Jesus has been caught between a rock and a hard place. The matter of taxation was presumed to be so delicate as to effectively ensnare Jesus no matter how he answered. Similar to the earlier episode about the Syrophoenician woman (7:24–30), the drama here highlights the capacity to maneuver cleverly in a potentially dangerous situation. He begins by requesting a coin (12:15), the granting of which makes the opponents lose the initiative (12:16a).[8] As Jesus proceeds, questioning them about the image and inscription on its face (12:16b), the tables are effectively turned and the scene is set for the climactic, "Give to the emperor the things that are the emperor's, and to God the things that are God's," which certainly impresses his inquisitors (12:17). But what is it about this statement that so impresses?

Even if the preparatory question about the image and inscription on the coin (12:16) makes the statement on taxes (12:17) appear reasoned,

---

8. Mark does not tell what emperor was depicted or what was written on the denarius. Commentators (e.g., Hartman 2005, 437; Marcus 2009, 824) often suggest that the denarius had a laurel-crowned head of Tiberius surrounded by the text "TI[BERIUS] CAESAR DIVI AVG[VSTI] F[ILIUS] AVGVSTVS." By not spelling this out, Mark seems to lift the issue of Roman imperial discourse to a more general plane. It could be any emperor.

and even well founded, the logic is concealed. That the coin showed Caesar's head and inscription does not make clear whether it is lawful to pay the tax. What seems to attract amazement, then, is the combination of Jesus' clever counterquestions and the statement's profound ambiguity. Indeed, it is the very evasiveness of the aphorism that releases him from the hazardous scheme and attracts admiration. Interestingly enough, the perplexing nature of Jesus' response seems to represent what Roman aristocrats found so repugnant among those who had been subdued by Rome.[9] The evasiveness was thus probably heard as a subtle form of resistance to Roman rule. Also, the way in which the entrapment was construed in the first place has implications for the message Mark sends in relation to the issue of imperial taxation. In order to further pursue these issues, two subjects are of particular importance: the significance of taxation in Roman imperial discourse, and Mark's use of the term κῆνσος in 12:14.

Opening a Metonymic Gap: ΚΗΝΣΟΣ and the Issue of Taxation

I will argue here that Mark's use of κῆνσος, arises from its use in Jewish anti-Roman discourse, was a catachresis that opened what postcolonial critics often call a *metonymic gap* (to be described below). In order to make this argument, I will discuss the issue of taxation and the specific function of the *census* in Roman imperial discourse.

Taxation or tribute in general was closely connected to empires in antiquity.[10] The logic was quite simple. After a people had been subdued by military power, tribute was imposed on them, both as a sign of their subjugation and as a means of financing the maintenance of the empire. This is evident from the description of Alexander the Great's empire in 1 Macc 1:4: "He gathered a very strong army and ruled over countries, nations, and princes, and they became tributary to him [αὐτῷ εἰς φόρον]."

---

9. As mentioned previously (ch. 13), Cicero (*Quint. fratr.* 1.16) regarded such evasiveness as characteristic for dominated Greeks and Asiatics. These attitudes, Cicero argues in his letter, are a result of subjugation, which involves being schooled in excessive complaisance (*nimiam adsentationem*).

10. According to Fleming and Badian 1993, 779, there was a general distinction between tribute and taxation in the ancient Near East. Whereas tribute consisted of the payment made by a subdued state to the dominant power, taxation consisted of revenues collected within a given country. As we will see, a similar distinction existed in the Roman Empire.

Similarly, the emergence of Rome as a superpower was marked by their having subdued and thoroughly crushed kingdoms from all ends of the earth, to the effect that the conquered "paid them tribute" (διδόασιν αὐτοῖς φόρον) each year (1 Macc 8:4). In addition, in his account of Pompey's victory over Jerusalem in 63 B.C.E., Josephus (*J.W.* 1.154) concludes by noting that both the country and Jerusalem were "laid under tribute" (ἐπιτάσσει φόρον); and Cicero (*Flac.* 28.69) also regarded the laying of Jerusalem under tribute as a sign of subjugation or even slavery: the Jewish nation had then been "conquered, laid under tribute and made a slave" (quod est victa, quod elocata, quod serva).

The collection of revenue, therefore, was one of Rome's most important imperial endeavors. Varying over time and place, the array of taxes in kind and cash was bewildering. From the time of Augustus, Roman imperial discourse knew of two main forms of taxation: direct and indirect (Spencer 2000; Balz 1991). The direct tax, *tributum* (φόρος), existed in two forms: a tax on land (tributum soli) and a poll tax or "head tax" (*tributum capitis*). Then there were also different forms of indirect tax, *vectigal* (τέλος), such as a sales tax and taxes on transported goods. Taxes were often collected by a system of "tax farming," whereby the government employed private corporations of tax collectors (*publicani*), whose desire for profits implied regular abuses.[11] As a further indication of the imperial nature of Roman taxation, from the time of the Third Macedonian War, Roman citizens were exempted from direct taxation (Ando 2010, 185); and the fact that provincials were thus made to carry a larger financial burden became a source of resentment. In Roman discourse, however, the provincial tax was seen as a reasonable payment for "perpetual peace and tranquility," and complaints were regarded as groundless (Cicero, *Quint. fratr.* 1.1.34).

Apart from being connected to the ongoing payment of taxes, and the varying degrees of resentment that this involved, Mark's term κῆνσος also curiously brings to mind the specific phenomenon of the Roman *census*. The term κῆνσος that Mark 12:14 uses is rather peculiar, to put it mildly.[12] The use of κῆνσος to designate the tax itself is unheard of in texts outside

---

11. Luke's (19:2–8) description of Zacchaeus illustrates this phenomenon. See also Spencer 2000.

12. According to R. Horsley (1983, 70–71), "the Latin loan word is not very common in non-literary sources." In terms of literary sources, there appears to be no text that uses the term before the third century.

19. THE EMPEROR BREAKS THE SURFACE (12:13-17)

the New Testament.[13] When Mark recounts that the Herodians and Pharisees asked Jesus, ἔξεστιν δοῦναι κῆνσον Καίσαρι ἢ οὔ; this would literally have been like asking, "Is it or is it not lawful to pay the tax registration to Caesar?" On the other hand, unlike "tax registration," κῆνσος would have called to mind the Roman *census* and the particular meaning that it had in imperial and Jewish discourse.

Being a Latin loanword, one would expect κῆνσος to designate the making of inventories of populations and properties to be taxed. But the verb δίδωμι in combination with the question of a denarius (Mark 12:14-15) indicates that the conversation concerns the actual paying of tax itself (cf. Josephus, *J.W.* 2.402, discussed above). Commentaries and dictionaries tend to glide over the problem of the Latin loanword.[14] Symptomatically, Greek-English lexicons give a rather confused impression.[15] The present consensus among scholars that κῆνσος and φόρος were synonyms would seem to be the case of an unverified assumption being upheld by the process of frequent repetition. The exception that verifies the rule is Derrett's (1970, 329) significant assertion that "in spite of frequent statements by commentators to the contrary it is unknown even whether *census* was a poll tax at all."[16] To Derrett (313-38), however, this assertion has no implications respecting his interpretation of the episode. In what seems to be an attempt to normalize Mark's awkward

---

13. In the few cases outside the NT where κῆνσος occurs, it is used with the meaning "tax registration" or as a title for the official responsible for the registration.

14. Marcus (2009, 817) simply states that the Greek term "came to mean the tax itself." Similarly, Balz (1991) makes the unsupported claim that φόρος and κῆνσος are synonyms.

15. The supplement to Liddell et al. (1996) modifies the entry on κῆνσος from the 1968 and 1996 editions. According to the latest supplement, κῆνσος means, like the Latin *census*, "assessment (for tax purposes)." Inscriptions are mentioned that verify this meaning. This, the supplement also claims, is how the term is used in Matt 17:25 and 22:19 (and presumably in Mark 12:14 as well). Bauer et al. (2000), in turn, also point out how κῆνσος was given the same meaning as the Latin *census*. Despite these occurrences, however, Bauer et al. (unlike the supplement to Liddell et al.) state that κῆνσος is used in Matthew and Mark to mean tax or poll tax. Bauer et al. therefore take the same position as Liddell and Scott (1972, the so-called middle Liddell that is founded on the 7th edition from 1883), who state that whereas κῆνσος generally means *registration of taxation*, in the NT it means "*the tax* itself."

16. As Goldschmid (1897, 208-10) argues, *census* (or its Greek and Hebrew equivalents) never designated a special tax and it never appeared in the lists of taxes against which the Jewish people complained.

use, Matthew (22:19) has Jesus employing the term in the expression τὸ νόμισμα τοῦ κήνσου (literally "the census coin"). But as indicated by Luke's (20:22) rendering of the passage, φόρος would have represented the correct terminology.[17]

My point here, however, is not to blame Mark (or Matthew) for using awkward language, but rather to acknowledge with appreciation that the faulty use of κῆνσος is a case of catachresis that helps to open a *metonymic gap* in the episode. Ashcroft, Griffiths, and Tippin (2000, 137–38) describe a metonymic gap as

> that cultural gap formed when appropriations of a colonial language insert unglossed words … from a first language, … that may be unknown to the reader. Such words become synechdochic of the writer's culture … [and] "stands for" the colonized culture in a metonymic way, and its very resistance to interpretation constructs a "gap" between the writer's culture and the colonial culture. The local writer is thus able to represent his or her world to the colonizer (and others) in the metropolitan language, and at the same time to signal and emphasize a difference from it. In effect, the writer is saying "I am using your language so that you will understand my world, but you will also know by the differences in the way I use it that you cannot share my experience."

As will become clear below, the way in which Mark uses κῆνσος is indeed an example of an unglossed word that signals "you cannot share my experience." It therefore aptly exemplifies a metonymic gap. But whereas Ashcroft, Griffiths, and Tippin discuss a particular writer who clearly belongs to a colonized culture, in Mark's case the writer is more vague. Also, since Mark largely renders material that already existed in oral form, that material does not receive the same sense of "the writer is saying." Nevertheless, if the tradition from Papias is taken as valid (see ch. 13), there existed a connection between the author and the apostle Peter. Not unlike the manner in which the term θάλασσα (sea) was used to designate the little Galilean lake in northern Palestine (Mark 2:13, etc.), Mark's use of κῆνσος represents a setting that is foreign to Mark's audience and hence communicates distance. Let us look more closely at this distance.

Of great significance is the fact that *census* also became a loanword in Hebrew and Aramaic. When the Roman *census* had been conducted

---

17. Also, some manuscripts substitute κῆνσος for ἐπικέφαλαιον, which indicates that the term κῆνσος was perceived as inaccurate.

under Quirinius in 6 C.E. the Aramaic and Hebrew קנס (*qns*) began to be used as a synonym for "fine," "penalty," or "punishment."[18] But even if the term was used with this meaning in a variety of different contexts, both as a verb and as a noun, its association with the loathed imperial taxation was still present. Hence in a midrash on Gen 3:14 (Gen. Rab. 20:1), R. Levi apocalyptically foretells that God, as he throws the nations to burn in Gehenna, will ask them, "Why did you fine [קונסים, based on the root קנס] my children?"[19]

This Hebrew and Aramaic usage of קנס as penalty is comprehensible in relation to the significance of the *census* in imperial discourse and the resentment with which it was associated among Jewish groups. Unlike the continuous taxation, the *census* was a more isolated event. As Ando (2000, 352) points out, the Roman *census* was an "extraordinary novelty." Already during the monarchy, the *census* was introduced by the Romans as a way to keep track of the taxable population and its property. At the end of the republic its occurrence seems to have declined, perhaps due to rapid territorial expansion (Ando 2010, 186). During the reign of Augustus, however, the *census* appears to have been conducted several times throughout the empire, although not in all provinces at the same time (contra Luke 2:1).

Apart from its having been driven by economic motives, a *census* involved religious as well as political aspects (Ando 2000, 350–62). The religious aspect is evident from the ritual of purification (*lustratio*) that constituted the concluding part of the *census*.[20] Moreover, since the information that was gathered far exceeded what was necessary for the levying

---

18. Klausner 1925, 161–62; and Goldschmid 1897, 208–10. This usage is also verified in Hebrew and Aramaic dictionaries: Sokoloff 2002, 497–98; Klein 1987, 585; and Jastrow 1992, 1393–94. See also Hengel 1989, 136, who points at the connection between the Jewish resentments against foreign domination and the manner in which the term *census* became a loanword meaning "fine" in both Hebrew and Aramaic.

19. Jastrow's (1992, 1393) translation. According to Stemberger and Bockmuehl (1996, 89), R. Levi was a third-generation Amoraic rabbi who lived in Palestine during the latter part of the third century.

20. As seen in the summary of Livy's book 29, the concluding part of a *census* was the ritual known as *lustratio*. After the *census* was conducted by Marcus Livius and Gaius Claudius, "the rite of purification [*lustrum*] was completed by the censors [*censoribus*]." Invoking the deity Mars, the main ingredient was a circular procession of purification and averting of evil. It especially denoted a new beginning signified by the *census* (Linderski 2003).

of taxes, the *census* was more than a financial endeavor; it communicated Rome's ultimate ownership of the land and property. A *census* therefore involved a more penetrating enterprise than the perpetual collecting of money and/or goods. Especially in its initial phase, according to Ando (354), the *census* encroached upon social life in a way that was both greater and more enduring than simple physical interference.

The impact and significance of the *census* was therefore more than merely establishing a basis for calculating taxes. Each household's copy of its most recent *census* return gave physical form and bureaucratic permanence to an otherwise abstract relationship to the emperor. Considering the impact of such interaction with imperial bureaucracy, Ando (2000, 362) tellingly argues that the Roman *census* "interpellated provincials as individual subjects." The *census* can in its entirety therefore be seen as a discursive practice by which households were defined and interpellated as Roman subjects.

Judging from the writings of Josephus and his depiction of the first Roman *census* that was conducted among the Jews in 6 C.E., the catachrestic use of קנס began as a response against the Roman *census*. Having described how Augustus replaced the ethnarch Archelaus with a Roman proconsul and added Judea to the province of Syria, Josephus (*Ant.* 17.354–18.2) explains what happened when Quirinius, the newly appointed legate of Syria, was sent to conduct a *census* of the Jewish population:

> Although the Jews were at first shocked to hear of the tax registration [ἀπογραφαῖς], they gradually calmed down, yielding to the arguments of the high priest Joazar, the son of Boethius, to go no further in opposition. Those who were convinced by him declared [ἀπετίμων], without hesitation, the value of their property. But a certain Judas, a Gaulanite from a city named Gamala, having recruited Saddok, a Pharisee, pressed hard for resistance. They said that the tax registration [ἀποτίμησιν] implied downright slavery, no less, and appealed to the nation to claim its independence. (*Ant.* 18.3–4, my trans.[21])

Josephus describes how from initial shock Jewish attitudes toward the Roman *census* fluctuated between acceptance and resistance. If the *census*

---

21. The translation is indebted to R. Horsley (1993, 81), who has criticized the tendency in translations and interpretations to depict Judas the Galilean and the Fourth Philosophy as being violently rebellious (77–89). Rather, Horsley argues, they should be seen as advocating nonviolent tax resistance.

interpellated provincials as Roman subjects, as Ando argues, the advocates of resistance refused to accept the interpellation, regarding it as being tantamount to slavery.[22] The catachrestic use of the term קנס seems to stem from this setting of resistance. Even though Josephus does not depict Judas the Galilean (as he is more often called; cf. Acts 5:37) as having organized a violent rebellion (*J.W.* 2.118, 433; 7.253; *Ant.* 20.102), the repeated mention of his initiative indicates that it was remembered and continued to motivate anti-Roman resistance at least until the Jewish rebellion in 66–74 C.E.

From Negation to Negotiation

We are now in a better position to discuss the scheme to entrap Jesus as well as the ambiguous saying in Mark 12:17. Mark's curious use of κῆνσος echoes the Hebrew and Aramaic catachrestical application of the term with the meaning "penalty." For a significant section of Mark's audience, however, this expression represents something culturally foreign, a metonymic gap, or what Bhabha (2004, 313) has called an incommensurable element or a "stubborn chunk" of cultural difference.

Of course, one can discuss if there were members among Mark's audience who understood this phrase from the Hebrew or Aramaic perspective. It is possible that conversations took place among Mark's audience in which an Aramaic- or Hebrew-speaking person would explain how קנס was used in Jewish discourse. In that case, the question posed by the Pharisees and Herodians obtains a more pronounced anti-Roman flavor, increasing the expectation that Jesus will answer in the negative when asked: "is it or is it not lawful to pay the *penalty* to Caesar?" (12:14b). Construed around an anti-Roman discourse in which taxation is seen as slavery, this expectation makes it appear as if the bind is particularly difficult for Jesus to escape. At the same time, however, considering that

---

22. As seen above, Roman discourse also regarded taxation as slavery in certain circumstances. This fact calls into question the emphasis that is often placed on Jewish theocratic beliefs as being the primary motivator of anti-imperial resistance (Brandon 1967, 32; R. Horsley 1993, 83–84, 316). Without denying the religious component (cf. Josephus, *J.W.* 2.118, 233), it seems reasonable to view opposition to the *census* as involving more than the mere question of monotheism or theocracy. As is evident from the difficulties of conducting the *census* in Gaul (Derow 2003a), resistance against the Roman *census* was not necessarily connected to religious monotheism.

the plot to ensnare Jesus was executed on the sole initiative of the temple authorities who collaborated closely with the Romans, this anti-Roman attitude rings peculiarly hollow, appearing even more hypocritical than the initial flattering of Jesus (12:14a). This hypocrisy, moreover, is not without its due share of Markan irony. The hypocritical flattery has an ironic subtext of communicating the truth. Mark's audience would certainly agree that Jesus is honest, unaffected by the opinions of others, unwilling to compromise his views, and a true teacher of the way of God. Similarly, even if those who organized the plot did not believe so, Mark seems to imply, the Roman *census* truly was a punishment.

Having thus discussed the conspiracy to entrap Jesus, a subsequent question concerns the answer that extricates Jesus from the plot (12:17). Regardless of whether Mark's use of κῆνσος was heard as a metonymic gap or from the inside perspective, the scheme to entrap Jesus is construed around an anti-Roman discourse. The answer seems to send three interrelated messages. The first message is connected to the sense of distance and foreignness that is signaled by the question. For Mark's urban audience, taxation was perceived somewhat differently as compared to the rural Jewish context of the Markan Jesus and his followers.[23] It is then significant that Mark asks the audience to consider the issue of tax not only from their own urban locations, but also from a Jewish rural perspective, where taxation was considerably more contested.

But whereas the attempt to entrap Jesus was designed in a highly polarized setting, his enigmatic answer seems to resist that polarization. If the Jewish anti-Roman discourse construed a subject by negation, Jesus' ambiguous answer does not seem to comply smoothly with this antagonistic discourse.[24] Rather, it appears to leave an opening to ponder and negotiate over what factually belongs to Caesar now that God's empire is emerging. To use Bhabha's terms, the enigmatic answer interpellates Mark's audience into a subject formed around *negotiation* rather than *negation*.

---

23. On the one hand, taxes were surely a source of friction in the cities as well (Tacitus, *Ann.* 13.50–51; Philo, *Spec.* 2.92–95; 3.159–163). On the other hand, resistance to taxation was generally not as strong in the cities as compared to the countryside. As Perkins (1984, 195) notes, unlike rural peasants, city dwellers did not have to confront the problem of having to pay taxes even when crops had failed.

24. If the message had been a clear-cut "don't pay," the issue of tax would have likely appeared in the interrogation by Pilate (Mark 15:1–15).

19. THE EMPEROR BREAKS THE SURFACE (12:13–17)

A second message is related to Paul's teachings on tribute and tax in Rom 13:1–7. Although Paul's exhortation was probably intended to address the turbulent tax protests that were occurring at the time in Rome, his proposition that "there is no authority except from God" (Rom 13:1) could have been interpreted to mean that the authority of the emperor had been bestowed and sanctioned by the Divine.[25] Following this line of reasoning, then, some among Mark's audience certainly could have concluded that Christ followers should pay their taxes in accordance with the emperor's divine mandate. In Mark's depiction of this drama, however, there is no mention of such a mandate. Even if Mark refrains from precisely indicating that which belongs to Caesar and that which belongs to God, the very division between God's and Caesar's claims makes clear that the requirement to pay taxes is not justified by divine mandate. Rather, the reason for eventually paying is to be found in the verb ἀποδίδωμι or "render what is due" (Liddell et al. 1996, s.v.), implying that what is "due" depends upon the situation. If some had understood Paul as having delivered a timeless endorsement of the emperor's divine authorization, Mark reframes the matter of taxation as dependent on the situation. To anyone who had expected Caesar's claims to be divinely justified, Mark must have come as a great disappointment. As is evident from the anti-Roman context of Mark's drama with the conspicuous use of κῆνσος, its juxtaposing of God and Caesar is accompanied by friction.

The explicit and outspoken manner with which the issue of tax is presented constitutes a third message. As mentioned, the emperor himself surfaces in the narrative as an image on a denarius. Even if Jesus' answer is ambiguous, Mark here brings the issue of Rome to the surface and asks the audience to consciously involve itself in considering the contested issue of Rome's power. How does the emergence of God's empire affect the audience's relation to Caesar's empire? In light of Bhabha's description of mimicry as being both a subconscious effect of colonial discourse and a conscious subversive strategy (see ch. 2), the surfacing of the emperor in Mark's story can be seen as a means of bringing the issue of Rome to the conscious level. The audience is invited to openly examine the issue of imperial domination that otherwise tended to be dealt with in an unre-

---

25. Rom 13:1–7 probably addresses the particular situation of tax protests in Rome under Nero. For an insightful discussion and interpretation of Rom 13:1–7, see N. Elliott 2008, 150–56. See also Telbe 2001, 141–209, who warns against taking Paul as a naïve supporter of Roman rule.

flecting manner. Here it is interesting to note that, despite its evasiveness, the answer by which Jesus extricates himself from entrapment is represented as a bold position—"they marveled" (12:17b). It thus seems that the episode on taxation establishes a certain distance in relation to imperial demands, by which Mark's audience is granted a sense of negotiating agency. Although this agency, due to its exposed position in the fringes of imperial culture, takes the form of a split subject who speaks under the powerful influence of imperial discourse, it is nonetheless granted a certain independence.

20
THE SECRECY COMPLEX AS A THIRD SPACE (15:39)

> A contingent, borderline experience opens up *in-between* colonizer and colonized. This is a space of cultural and interpretive undecidability produced in the "present" of the colonial moment.
> —Homi Bhabha (2004, 295–96)

As the end of Mark's Gospel approaches, a fascinating character appears on the scene—a Roman centurion. As we saw in chapter 11, nineteenth-century interpreters made prominent use of him in their constructions of Christian imperial identities.[1] From a postcolonial perspective, such a character invites careful scrutiny: how does he, and his curious saying, affect Mark's stance vis-à-vis Rome? For the present investigation, such an analysis involves a reconnection with the incipit, previously discussed in chapter 14. As argued there, the textually uncertain title "Son of God" represents the ongoing negotiations of Mark's audience with imperial discourse, and can thus be regarded as a sign of colonial ambivalence. This ambivalence, I briefly suggested, is also present in Mark's way of presenting Jesus as Son of God throughout the Gospel narrative, seen most pertinently in the famous saying by the Roman centurion in front of the cross. In what follows, we will further explore this suggestion.

SON OF GOD IN MARK'S NARRATIVE

Although narrative criticism, with its understanding of the text as a closed unit, is insufficient for the purposes of this study, it can still serve as a point of departure for probing into the messianic secret in Mark.[2] Apart from

---

1. Bruce (1897, 451) and Swete (1898, 353) are possible exceptions.
2. For introductions to narrative criticism, see Malbon 2008; Resseguie 2005; Powell 1990; and Moore 1989.

the textually uncertain incipit, Jesus is presented as God's Son in Mark's introductory scene, where he is baptized by John (1:9–11). Here the divine voice that calls Jesus "my beloved son" reveals knowledge to the implied reader that the other characters in the narrative lack, thereby forming a major theme in Mark: seeing Jesus as God's Son and realizing what that means. Initially, only the unclean spirits express knowledge of Jesus' identity as Son of God (3:11; 5:7; cf. 1:24, 34). At the narrative's midpoint, the divine voice is heard again on the mountain of transfiguration (9:2–9), and even though Peter, James, and John are present, they are unable to understand who Jesus is (9:10, 32). In the final section of Mark, Jesus is identified as the Son of God on four separate occasions (12:6–7, 35–37; 14:61–62; 15:39), but it is only at the end of Mark's narrative that a human character appears able to recognize Jesus' true identity as the Son of God.

Being long awaited by the implied reader and uttered close to the end of the narrative, just as the main protagonist has died, the saying by the Roman centurion surely qualifies as a narrative climax; but is it as clear-cut as is usually assumed? Scholars often argue for the inclusion of "Son of God" in the incipit with reference to 15:39 as a triumphant conclusion, alleging that the identity of the suffering and crucified Jesus as God's beloved Son is here finally realized and expressed by a human character.[3] All ambiguity in Mark's Gospel is then settled, stabilized, and fixed. But is this a plausible reading? Does the saying really represent a realization of Jesus' true identity, not to mention a confession? And does it dissolve the secrecy complex?

There are two problems with this reading. First, as Moore (1994, 65–81) contends, narrative criticism, with its penchant for a closed, unified story, often turns a blind eye to contradictions and aporias[4] in the narrative.[5]

---

3. Here it suffices to mention three: Cranfield 1959, 460; Lane 1974, 41, 576; Donahue and Harrington 2002, 60, 449.

4. *Aporia*, a Greek word meaning "unpassable path" or "impasse," has been used by Derrida to describe the undecidability of meaning (Wolfreys 2004, 19–25). According to Derrida (1993, 12–13), an aporia tends to paralyze the reader.

5. This critique also seems to be somewhat valid for Robert Fowler (1991), who applies reader-response criticism to Mark's Gospel. By distinguishing between story and discourse, he (208) interprets the centurion's saying as ambiguous at the story level, whereas it clearly expresses the "narrator's understanding of Jesus" at the discourse level. This reflects Fowler's (23) overall assessment that "the coherence [of Mark's Gospel] lies at the discourse level." Fowler, however, does not discuss the incoherence with which Mark's Gospel relates to Roman imperial discourse on both levels—a rela-

Being influenced by the current in literary theory known as New Criticism, narrative critics typically emphasize the autonomous unity of the text—the integrity of the whole—and are driven by a "holistic passion."[6] With such premises in hand, the saying of the centurion is often taken in a triumphant way—he "see[s] the rule of God in Jesus" (Rhoads et al. 1999, 114–15). The contradictory signals in the narrative (to be explored below) that make the saying appear enigmatic are then glossed over in the quest for a unified narrative.

A second problem concerns the implied reader, understood in narrative criticism as an aspect of the narrative itself. Although at times a helpful device, this theoretical, construed "reader" becomes curiously detached from any discursive contexts and is oddly impervious to either political or religious interests, with the exception of those held by the implied author. Thus from the detached perspective of the narrative's closed world, the implied reader understands the centurion's saying as "self-evident." This allegedly self-evident meaning, however, begins to crumble as soon as the text is located in time and space and is understood in relation to other (con)texts. That the character expressing the revealing formula represents the imperial order in the province of Judea should in itself make us careful not to neglect the imperial discourse that is thereby brought into the text.

As several scholars (Johnson 1987; Shiner 2000; Van Oyen 2003) have arugued, the centurion's saying does not even come close to dissolving the secrecy complex. Shiner (2000, 15), for instance, takes the saying as an "ironic and uncomprehending vindication" that leaves the Markan veil of secrecy intact. According to Shiner, however, for Mark's audience the message was clear. As with the mocking acclamations of Jesus as king of the Jews (15:18), the audience did not doubt that the centurion's saying, regardless of his intention, expressed the truth about Jesus. In this sense, therefore, Shiner still seems to interpret Mark as a stable representation.

Of particular importance relative to this study, however, is how the character's profession draws the imperial discourse into the hermeneutical enterprise and how that affects the narrative's complex interpellation of Mark's audience. Κεντυρίων is another Latin loanword in Mark's Gospel, denoting a Roman army officer who is in charge of a *centurio*—or one

---

tion that seems difficult to neglect since the character expressing the "confession" is a Roman soldier. In other words, even if Jesus is clearly represented as God's Son on the discourse level, the meaning of that title in relation to Rome is far from evident.

6. See Resseguie 2005, 21–25; Culpepper 1983, 3; and Malbon 2008, 41.

hundred soldiers. Thus the centurion clearly invokes the Roman order, which had at the very top of its hierarchy a divinized emperor to whom all subjects were to offer sacrifice as a sign of allegiance and devotion. As Kim (1998) argues, the saying clearly echoes the imperial cult and, more specifically, the title of its most revered figure: *divi filius* Augustus.

Possibly, then, the saying was received as being a straight-out conversion in the sense that the centurion realizes that Jesus rather than Augustus is the true Son of God. But as Johnson (1987, 15–16) points out, it is difficult to find anything in Mark that prepares the audience to expect that a Roman officer can understand the mystery of Jesus' identity, and even less that he can express faith in Jesus as the Son of God. Unlike Luke (7:1–10) and Matthew (8:5–13), Mark says nothing about Roman soldiers being merciful or respectful to Jesus. On the contrary, Roman troops have been associated with evil spirits (5:1–20), and they are the main representatives of those disapprovingly designated by Mark (10:42) as "rulers of the peoples that lord it over them." Moreover, to prove such a remarkable turnaround reliable, one would expect to see a marked change of perspective—perhaps a mood of repentance—on the part of the centurion. But since the centurion is depicted as nonchalantly continuing in his ordinary manner when approached by Pilate about the status of Jesus (15:44–45), the audience must have been left wondering about the depth of his understanding and the credibility of his words. Although recognizing the words as true, the audience would also wonder if the centurion knew what he was saying. This combination of recognizing the saying as true and yet improbable causes the stable meaning of the narrative climax to unravel and dissolve, thus drawing the audience into an aporia of doubt and hesitation respecting their relation to Rome.

A Third Space of Identification

A first hermeneutical possibility as we are entering this aporia is connected to the abundance of irony, parody, and mockery over the fate of Jesus. After the verdict of Pilate (15:1–15), Jesus is removed from the city by Roman soldiers, who mockingly rig him out with an outfit that (hardly anyone would miss) alludes to imperial insignia—a purple robe, a crown, and a scepter (15:16–20). Almost *but not quite* like Vespasian, who was proclaimed emperor on Jewish soil, Jesus is hailed as king of the Jews—presumably under the command of the renowned centurion. Having been crucified at Golgotha, Jesus continues to be mocked by passersby, chief

20. THE SECRECY COMPLEX AS A THIRD SPACE (15:39)

priests, scribes, and fellow convicts alike (15:29–32). In this regard, several scholars (Johnson 1987, 16–17; Fowler 1991, 204–8; Moore 2006, 32–33; Thurman 2007, 221) have suggested that the centurion's apparently realized statement continues along these lines and is thus expressed in a sarcastic tone. On the literary level, this reading is supported by Jesus' ardent plea to let the cup pass (14:36) and the crying out on the cross (15:37). As Bowersock (1994, 74–76) has argued, such direct and uncontrolled expressions of grief were at variance with how masculinity was construed in Greek and Roman discourses. Rather than expressing admiration, the centurion's saying would then be understood as an ironic insult.

But even if the sarcastic interpretation is possible, it presupposes that the person delivering the story was doing so with gestures and intonations that communicated irony and sarcasm. While the sarcasm in Mark's previous scenes is depicted in an explicit and overt fashion (15:20, 29, 31, 32), the centurion's remark has no such indicators, thus reducing the likelihood of a sarcastic interpretation. In addition, some supernatural occurrences are connected with Jesus' death that further undermine this line of interpretation. As Mark narrates how darkness fell upon the land for three long hours (15:33) and how the temple curtain was torn from top to bottom (15:38), the centurion's saying acquires an awesome character.

In considering the awesome nature of the portents, especially the eclipse of the sun, an interesting parallel to Mark's account can be found in Roman ruler mythology. As one can see in the account by Dio Cassius (56.46), the Roman practice of apotheosis of rulers was founded on the account of Romulus's death and divine ascension (cf. Beard et al. 1998, 1:148–49, 208–10). The divinization of Caesar was closely connected to the story about Romulus and became the basis for Augustus and the succeeding emperors receiving of divine status and the title *divi filius* (θεοῦ υἱός). Similar to Mark's account, the stories about the death of Romulus typically include a supernatural darkness (Dionysius of Halicarnassus, *Ant. rom.* 2.56). The following description of the Romulus myth comes from Plutarch (*Rom.* 27.6–7):

> Suddenly strange and unaccountable disorders with incredible changes filled the air; the light of the sun failed, and night came down upon them, not with peace and quiet, but with awful peals of thunder and furious blasts driving rain from every quarter, during which the multitude dispersed and fled, but the nobles gathered closely together; and when the storm had ceased, and the sun shone out, and the multitude, now

gathered again in the same place as before, anxiously sought for their king, the nobles would not suffer them to inquire into his disappearance nor busy themselves about it, but exhorted them all to honor and revere Romulus, since he had been caught up into heaven and was to be a benevolent god for them instead of a good king.

The portents, particularly the failing light of the sun, connect Mark's account to that of Plutarch. But even if it seems probable that the portents accompanying the death of Jesus would have been heard as an echo of the death of Romulus, the meaning that was thereby communicated can still be debated. For example, A. Collins (2007, 768) suggests that the Roman centurion was heard as recognizing Jesus rather than the emperor as the true ruler of the world; but this explanation does not consider how Mark's account resembles, and yet *differs* in significant ways, from the imperial script.[7] I mention only three observations. First, in Plutarch's account, the death/ascension of Romulus is mediated via the paternal care of the nobles (οἱ δυνατοί) for the anxious multitude (ὁ ὄχλος), thereby establishing credibility by rendering what imperial discourse defined as a natural hierarchy between the elite and the rest of the population. In Mark's depiction, on the other hand, the chief priests (corresponding somewhat to the nobles) incite the people (ὁ ὄχλος) *against* Jesus; and as the disciples are dispersed, Mark provides no paternal nobles to care for them and assure them about the miracle that is about to occur. Second, in what seems to be an attempt to establish the least imperially trustworthy account possible, Mark identifies three women of peasant origin as witnesses to the death (15:40–41) as well as to the resurrection (16:1–8). Plutarch mentions no female character. And third, whereas the actual death of Romulus is curiously absent from Plutarch's account, Mark graphically depicts what could be taken as a feminizing as well as a heroic death of Jesus (see ch. 16).

---

7. This suggestion by A. Collins seems at odds with her comments on the Gerasene demoniac (5:1–20), where she finds "no theme of opposition to Rome" (2007, 269), a contention that she supports by referring to the very centurion in 15:39 "expressing faith in Jesus." Yet again, still discussing the Gerasene demoniac, Collins (269–70) suggests that "it would be a culturally logical step for the audience to link the kingdom of Satan with Rome." What seems like contradictions in Collins's commentary, however, could support the argument made here regarding Mark's ambivalent and subtly subversive way of relating to Roman power.

20. THE SECRECY COMPLEX AS A THIRD SPACE (15:39)

Just as Mark's account gains authority by its resemblance to Roman ruler mythology, it also undermines that power by its way of differing from it. The combination of resemblance and nonresemblance draws Mark's account into the ambiguous space in between the dominant and the dominated, bringing us back to Bhabha (2004, 171–72) and his understanding of mimicry as being "less than one and double," and as effecting a separation from origins and essences upheld in imperial and nationalist discourses alike. In what appears to be an ancient illustration of Bhabha's (170) colonizer/colonized "the natives expel the copula" characterization, Mark lacks a mediating group of nobles to take paternal care of the frightened disciples. Indeed, considering the aristocratic avoidance of the cross as a topic of conversation, this lack in Mark is not without its logic. As the dying Jesus is presented as being almost *but not quite* a new Romulus, then, the rupturing effects on the originality and authority of imperial discourse are profound.

Returning to the aporia into which the audience was brought, we are now able to formulate where the saying of the centurion seems to have located Mark's audience in relation to imperial discourse. As the saying is presented as true and yet improbable, the awesome account both powerfully resembles and profoundly subverts imperial ruler mythology, thus opening a third space of identification for the audience that is empowering and yet not ruled by imperial logic. The "almost *but not quite*" grants the audience a certain distance that is strengthened by Mark's presentation of the centurion as being unaware of the meaning of his own words. Regardless of what the centurion meant, the audience knows. Rome is thereby given a secondary importance. Even if it is not a position that directly opposes Roman power, then, it still destabilizes it by depriving it of its priority of interpretation and its right to dictate standards.

B(h)ab(h)elian Performance

In order to conclude the argument in this chapter, I will bring the textually uncertain incipit (1:1) into the discussion. I begin, however, by pointing out a parallel in the essay "Des Tours de Babel" by Jacques Derrida (2002), in which he interprets the Genesis story about the tower of Babel as a myth not only about the inevitable need of translation, but also about the divine rupturing of rational imperial transparency—a myth about the impossibility of completion, of finishing, and of totalizing. Since Babel, Derrida (104–11) claims, every reading is a rewriting, every reading is a translation. Babel, the word itself being impossible to translate, is then a myth that unsettles the notion of the original by pointing out its lack, and its constant desire to be translated. For Derrida, this is Babelian performance, and hence the Babelian demand: translate me. This demand resonates particularly well with the postcolonial perspective applied here, and most pertinently with Bhabha (not only considering his name). Hence Mark's portrait of Jesus as [Son of God], with its undecidability both in terms of the original manuscript and the narrative, can be seen as representing the B(h)ab(h)elian demand: translate me, interpret me.

In relation to the textual uncertainty of the incipit (1:1), biblical scholars usually see two options: either include or exclude the phrase "Son of God." Both of these options, however, would signal that the textual problem is negligible, which it clearly is not. I have instead suggested that the phrase be rendered with brackets and that these be regarded not as unhappy markers of a lost original text, but as significant aspects of the text itself, contributing to the interpretation of the narrative. Taking the textual uncertainty as stemming from negotiations and variations during the initial circulation of Mark, the brackets signify the contested and charged nature of Jesus as Son of God in the oral and heterogeneous culture of the Christ followers; they express how the Gospel of Mark from its very beginning established a space (with Bhabha's term, a third space) where the identification emerged in between imperial rule and anti-imperial opposition. Since it is "notoriously difficult to decide which [variant] is the source of the other" (A. Collins 1995, 115), the addition/omission of the phrase probably goes back to a very early stage, and the brackets surrounding "Son of God" can then be seen as referring to a primordial act of B(h)ab(h)elian performance, or even better, of colonial ambivalence.

As argued in this chapter, the very same colonial ambivalence is present in the Markan narrative, particularly in its depiction of Jesus as Son of God. Since the first sentence functions as a headline for the narrative as a whole, the brackets can also be seen as adequately signifying the aporetic climax in Mark 15:39. There is no human being in Mark's Gospel that fully comprehends what it means that Jesus is God's Son. The disciples try but fail. The Jewish authorities denounce the claim with outrage. The Roman centurion utters the right words, but their meaning slips away, much like the naked man who ran into the woods when Jesus was arrested (14:51–52). Mark does not offer a fixed position vis-à-vis Rome, but points instead toward a continuous process of destabilizing identifications. As a representation of a collective identity, Mark's Gospel brings forth negotiations around what it means to be an anticipator of God's unimperial empire—a universalism from below—in the midst of the empire of Rome. In this way, given its circular and unfinished disposition, Mark forms a self-understanding that, potentially at least, causes empire to crumble.

21

How Mark Destabilizes Empire

> Generally speaking (and putting it rather too mildly), Mark does not enjoin its audience to respect human authorities.
> —Stephen Moore (2006, 36)

Equipped with the thoughts of Bhabha and Spivak, and fueled by an interest to move beyond a colonial heritage in Markan interpretation, in part 3 I have analyzed the various ways in which Mark's Gospel negotiated a space in Roman imperial discourse. Taking Mark to be a significant representation of a collective identity, I have detected the complex ways in which its narrative positioned first-century Christ followers in relation to Rome's order. In this chapter I will summarize the findings of part 3.

Presenting the imperial context in which Mark's Gospel began to circulate, I delineated Roman imperial discourse as a powerful totality of linguistic and material practices that made Roman domination natural, but that also involved internal tensions and contradictions. Challenging the Judaism/Hellenism divide that tends to affect biblical scholarship, the positions of Greeks and Jews were located in the imperial discourse whereby similarities as well as differences were found. The differences, of course, are related to their disparate histories. Whereas Greeks had a history of being dominant, Jews had a history of being exposed to various imperial powers. Their ways of relating to Rome were therefore different in important respects. Even so, both Jews and Greeks were subjected to Roman rule and related to Rome with antagonism as well as with mimicry, ambivalence, and hybridity. The traditional distinction between Jew and *Gentile*, then, tends to hide the fact that Greeks and Jews shared the fate of being subdued by imperial Rome.

After discussing the significance of the city/rural relation in Roman imperial discourse, I dealt with the issues concerning Mark's date, provenance, authorship, and audience. Since Mark's Gospel was based on stories that had been transmitted orally from the time of the first Jesus followers (who mainly dwelled in rural environs), the written medium indicates an urban rather than a rural provenance. This contention was supported by external evidence that, while contestable, appears to point toward Rome as the place of writing and "Mark" as an author with connections to the apostle Peter. I have here approached Mark's Gospel, written in Rome by an author with close connections to a recently executed illiterate Galilean apostle and circulating from center to periphery, as an event that reproduces as well as subverts Roman imperial discourse. Based upon a scholarly consensus, moreover, the writing of the Gospel was located close to the end of the Jewish War in 70 c.e. Furthermore, Mark's Gospel was taken as addressing a wide audience rather than a particular community in Rome. Representing a cross section of the nonelite population, the audience was understood as ethnically and socially heterogeneous and as economically poor. Since the written medium was more of an urban than a rural phenomenon, the audience was primarily located in Mediterranean cities.

Searching for the interpellative effect of Mark's Gospel, I analyzed the written medium and its complex messages. Alleging the presence of the written medium at the place of Mark's delivery, I argued that it, on the one hand, signifies the beginning of a shift toward a more controlled mediation of the Jesus traditions. On the other hand, however, this stabilization stands in tension with the open-ended character of Mark's story as well as with the specific form of written medium that was probably used for the circulation of Mark's Gospel—the codex. Whereas the standard book format in Roman imperial city culture was the roll, Mark was probably delivered in the form of a codex. Being itself an important object of identification for the Jesus followers, the irregular character of the codex as a literary medium significantly signals a displacement from aristocratic circles. Further, since the codex was a Roman invention—developed from the wooden wax tablet—it was a form of cultural borrowing that placed the Christ followers on the fringes of imperial culture. Signaling anomalous and catachrestic newness, it helped form a new cultural space in the urban environment of the Jesus followers.

In chapters 14 to 20, I analyzed the content of Mark's story. Beginning with the incipit, the dense phrase that immediately strikes the reader runs: Ἀρχὴ τοῦ εὐαγγελίου Ἰησοῦ Χριστοῦ [υἱοῦ θεοῦ] (1:1). Loaded with imperial allusions, the incipit interplays with the imperial discourse in three interrelated ways. First, since ἀρχή has the wider meaning of "beginning" and "authority," a remarkable message was communicated in combination with the codex as a literary medium. If we take ἀρχή as referring to Mark as a protocanonized written document and τοῦ εὐαγγελίου as referring to the Christ followers' ongoing proclamations of the saving event in Christ, the initial phrase ἀρχὴ τοῦ εὐαγγελίου designates "the beginning" as well as "the authority" that legitimates continuous gospel proclamations. At the delivery of Mark's Gospel, then, as the speaker pronounces the initial phrase, the beginning/authority obtains a countercultural connotation by becoming subtly connected to the codex in the hand of the speaker. The way in which Mark as a written Gospel legitimizes and stabilizes the ongoing gospel proclamation is thus paradoxically connected to the cultural space opened by the codex form.

Second, the incipit as a whole interplays significantly with the inauguration of the Roman imperial era. As expressed on calendar inscriptions, the new beginning under Augustus was proclaimed in terms of a religiopolitical gospel. More particularly, since the rise of the Flavian dynasty coincided with the initial circulation of Mark, the incipit was probably perceived more directly in relation to these events, especially its accompanying messianic claims for Vespasian. After several years of internal strife and crisis, the Flavian victory in Jerusalem became a prominent trope in imperial discourse and helped legitimize the ascension of Vespasian as a new emperor. In reminiscence of Augustus's victory in Actium, which inaugurated the imperial era, the Flavian victory was celebrated as divinely ordained "good news" (εὐαγγελία). As Rome was proclaiming the gospel of a new imperial beginning under Vespasian to be the fulfillment of Jewish messianic expectations, Mark's headline proclaimed the countergospel of an alternate beginning under God and his anointed Son—the true fulfiller of the Jewish messianic expectations.

Third, the textual uncertainty of the title "Son of God" was located in the presumed debates among Christ followers over how to relate to Roman power. Considering the way in which υἱός θεοῦ as a title for Jesus challenged imperial discourse, one can conceive of motives for adding as well as omitting the title in Mark's very first sentence. Rather than arguing for one or the other of these variants as being the original, then, I took [Son of God] as a sign of colonial ambivalence, and I located the textual uncertainty in a minority movement that negotiated its identity in an imperial context.

As Mark introduces the Gospel narrative, several signals indicate that the headline's initial oppositional message will become escalated: Jesus' collaboration with John the Baptist (1:9), who is reported as being imprisoned (1:14); Jesus' struggle with Satan (1:12–13); and the rural setting in which the plot is located. The first part of Mark's Gospel (1:14–8:21) thus narrates an oppositional plot wherein Jesus and the Twelve, in anticipation of the coming empire of God, collide with the local Jewish collaborative authorities and the unclean spirits.

In a dramatic climax of this collision, Jesus encounters a possessed man whose unclean spirit presents itself as "Legion" (5:9). Since the Latin loanword λεγιών was solely used to designate Roman troops at the time of Mark's writing, the name represents a catachresis (in Spivak's sense) that refers doubly to the unclean spirits and Rome's military, thereby giving the episode a rich metaphorical character. By depicting the presence of Roman troops in the East symbolically as possession by unclean spirits, the author uses the deranged state of the possessed man to mock Rome's most precious icon: the imperial army. In the dramatic scene, filled with military vocabulary, Jesus dispatches Legion into a herd of swine that rushes into the sea and drowns. Playing on the notion of masculine strength that imperial discourse connected to the Roman army, and particularly to the Legio X Fretensis that stood under Vespasian's command, the author's catachrestic use of "Legion" illuminates the strength of Jesus by subtly mocking the potency of Rome's prize legions. As Jesus is juxtaposed with Vespasian, Rome is symbolically defeated in the image of a herd of drowning swine, and Jesus is depicted as having total manly control and hence as being the true ruler of the world.

Since Mark here turns the present order on its head, I pointed out the extent to which the episode reproduces the imperial discourse. But even in this very climax of Mark's oppositional plot, there are signals that prefigure its displacement and remodeling. These signals were found when the dramatic scene in Gerasa was taken as an illustration of the seed parables (4:1–34) where Peter's failure is anticipated (4:5, 16), and where God's βασιλεία, by being presented as a mustard shrub rather than a large tree (4:30–32), is depicted as almost *but not quite* an empire. Corresponding to such disturbing signals, the second part of the Gerasa episode includes a similarly disruptive motion. As Jesus has conquered Legion and his victory has become evident in the drowning of the two thousand pigs, certain expectations of a celebratory triumph are evoked. By not fulfilling these imperial expectations—Jesus is not even granted a thank you by the hostile local population—Mark's story here subtly distances itself from the imperial discourse. A seed is thus sown that will eventually disrupt the initial oppositional plot.

Moving forward to the episode about the Syrophoenician woman (7:24–30), I devoted an exegetical analysis to Mark's description of her as Ἑλληνίς, Συροφοινίκισσα τῷ γένει, which literally means "Greek, a Syrophoenician by birth." Challenging the consensus among biblical scholars that translates Ἑλληνίς as "Gentile," I argued that Ἕλληνες in New Testament writings is not identical with ἔθνη and that "Greek Syrophoenician" indicates a hybrid hellenized identity with which a majority of Mark's audience could easily identify. Since the tradition of interpreting this woman as a *Gentile* was important during the nineteenth century, and since it continues to influence contemporary scholarship, I will return to it in part 4.

Up to this point, Mark's narrative has revolved around a more or less clear-cut oppositional plot with an escalating conflict between Jesus, the twelve apostles, and an expanding crowd on the one hand, and their intertwined spiritual and religio-political opponents on the other. If the encounter with the Gerasene demoniac was a symbolic peak in this plot, the meeting with the Syrophoenician represents its breakdown. In a turnaround from the previous radical teaching about an inclusive table fellowship (7:1–23), the negative answer to the woman's request places the Markan Jesus in the very same position as the Pharisees and scribes whom he had just criticized. This brings the plot into a crisis that revolves around three interrelated issues: ethnicity, gender, and the identity of Jesus as bread.

First, with the harsh imagery of children and dogs, the episode initially places *Greek* underneath *Jew*. The critical nature of this interpellation of "Greek" is evident when we consider that the Jews at the time of Mark's circulation were being publicly disgraced and feminized in the aftermath of Rome's humiliating victory in Jerusalem. Being subjected under the already subjected could certainly entail a crisis for those of Mark's audience who identified themselves as Greek.

Second, in terms of gender, since the Syrophoenician is the first woman who actually speaks to Jesus in Mark's Gospel (and in a notably bold manner at that), the episode marks a destabilization of the plot's androcentric character. Up to this point in the narrative, all the main protagonists have been males, whereas women have been left to occupy only marginal and subservient roles. If we presume that Mark's Gospel had been previously heard, the belated presentation of the female disciples who followed Jesus during his time in Galilee (15:40–16:8) is anticipated by the sharp wit of the Syrophoenician woman. Since the unfinished and ironic character of Mark's Gospel invites continuous rereadings, and since each rereading ends with a retrospective account about the silenced female disciples, the disruption of the androcentric plot is an ongoing process.

The third aspect of the narrative crisis in 7:24–30 involves more of a constructive onset. While the oppositional plot is in the process of being disrupted, the meeting between Jesus and the woman—a Jew and a Greek—also begins to form a new subjectivity. Representing two peoples subjected to Roman control, seen in imperial discourse as peoples born to slavery, their overcoming of enmity represents a universalism from below, beyond Rome's control. This emerging subjectivity, in turn, is formed around bread (the conversation turns around the bread crumbs) as the body of Christ. Via the surrounding feeding miracles (6:30–44; 8:1–10), the bread referred to by Jesus and the woman (7:27–28) alludes to the Last Supper (14:22–25), when Jesus identifies his body with bread that is extendable and transcends its male gender. Significantly, it is the bread's brittle character that enables the saying words to be pronounced—a brittleness that corresponds to the feminization of Jesus' body at his execution. The decentered nature of this new subjectivity of *différance* is further illustrated by the geographic borderland that functions as a metaphor for the interstitial space between Jesus and the woman from which the word (λόγος, 7:29) of healing is pronounced. Also, taking into account the story's subversive underlying message about a miraculous overcoming of enmity between a Greek and a Jew without Roman intervention, the narrative crisis begins to interpellate the audience into a modified oppositional subjectivity that transcends boundaries of gender, ethnicity, and possibly religion.

Having been initiated by the narrative crisis in 7:24–30, the middle section of Mark's Gospel (8:22–10:52) continues to destabilize the oppositional plot and offers a remodeled version instead. The destabilization is effected by a narrative strategy that plays on the imagery of blindness and seeing, presenting the disciples as being "on the way" with Jesus, but as failing to see who he is. The peak is represented by the dispute between Jesus and Peter over Jesus' messianic identity, when Peter is associated with Satan (8:27–33). Portraying the evil imperial forces as infusing the leading apostle, the original plot with its androcentric anti-imperial opposition here enters an impasse. As empire turns out to be an internal as much as an external threat, the audience is moved into an aporia from which they are soon offered a way out via the catachrestical saying about the cross (8:34). Located on the way, in a setting of geographical transition, the remodeled plot challenges imperial discourse in a more indirect and yet profound way.

Challenging previous postcolonial interpretations of the cross as an entrepreneurial wager that gains eschatological power, I offered an alternative interpretation. Since the cross, in this pre-Constantinian imperial setting, represented a constant threat to a significant segment of Mark's audience, implying an utterly dependent and submissive subjectivity, the instruction to voluntarily take up the cross as a sign of loyalty to Jesus potentially defused the repression with which it was associated in imperial discourse; Mark's catachrestic use of the cross as a metaphor contributed significantly to the opening of a social space that threatened and undermined the authority of imperial rule. I therefore suggested a post-Constantinian reclaiming of the cross as a metaphor. Without idealizing Mark as a collective representation, the narrative at this point offers resources that make possible a certain empowerment.

The first Parousia reckoning in Mark (8:38–9:1), I then argued, serves the important rhetorical function of preserving the unstable catachrestic use of the cross in Mark's account. Criticizing the one-sidedness of readings that take the Parousia as a clear-cut reproduction of imperial ideology, I suggested that Mark's Parousia ought to be taken as *pharmakon*, which could mean "poison" as well as "medicine." Although apocalyptic sayings tends to reproduce and legitimize imperial power—then serving as *poison*—Mark here uses an apocalyptic saying as a rhetorical *medicine* that serves to strengthen the modified plot and enable the countercultural social praxis that was represented by the imperative to take up the cross.

Further, since Mark is relatively reserved in the depictions of the coming of Jesus in power, and since the entry story (11:1–11) depicts what during Mark's time was generally referred to as a parousia (the official visit of a high-ranking official), I suggested that the entry story be taken as a narrative illustration of the coming of Jesus in power. Given the parodic way in which the entry story both imitates and subverts the notions of imperial triumphs, Mark's Parousia then obtains a playful connotation that, in a difficult situation, invites the audience to anticipate a victory yet to come.

The entry story also brings Mark's Gospel into its third section, which takes place in Jerusalem (11:1–16:8). With its royal and messianic signals in combination with parody, the entry story intensifies the modified oppositional plot and is crucial for Mark's way of representing an identity position vis-à-vis Roman imperial discourse. In a clear case of mimicry (in Bhabha's sense) the entry story resembles and yet differs from celebratory welcomes in imperial discourse. Just like an emperor, Jesus instructs his followers to acquire a colt by ἀγγαρεία (11:3), seats himself upon it, and then enters the city, hailed and welcomed by the people. But since, as a rural Galilean, Jesus lacked any legal right to ἀγγαρεία, and since the procession anticlimactically ends without a concluding ritual (11:11), the entry story vacillates between mimicry and mockery of imperial triumphs. Also, the entry story rearticulates Jewish national discourse in a way that resonates with Bhabha's conception of the pedagogical and the performative. Since the anti-Roman Hosanna cries are rendered as acclamations of Jesus, the pedagogical repetitions of the exodus as a past founding event are transformed into performative enunciations that both add to and substitute the meaning. This rearticulation of the oppositional exodus tradition adds further weight to the subversion and modification of the original plot of Mark's Gospel.

If the entry story vacillated in a rather subtle way between mimicry and mockery of imperial triumphs, the continuation of the episode significantly widens the gap between conflicting messages. Sandwiched in between a twofold scene about a withered fig tree (11:12–14, 20–22), the delayed ending of the entry story is depicted in the rather aggressive temple incident (11:15–19). Fluctuating between an anti-imperial attack against a major metropolitan Roman-friendly institution and a divine justification of Rome's war and destruction of that very institution, its relation to imperial discourse is ambivalent in the extreme.

A more subtle ambivalence is displayed as Mark depicts the legendary discussion about paying taxes to Caesar (12:13–17). Whereas the issue of Rome's empire until this point has been treated in an indirect manner, here it surfaces and becomes an explicit issue in the form of a direct question that is posed to entrap Jesus and facilitate his arrest. Considering the importance of taxation in imperial discourse, the question basically addresses the legitimacy of Roman rule. Due to the awkward use of κῆνσος (12:14)—which probably stems from the Jewish appropriation of the Latin *census*, with the meaning "penalty"—the question posed to Jesus opens a metonymic gap that subtly subverts the legitimacy of Roman taxation. The ambiguous, and yet clever, answer by the Markan Jesus (12:17) transmitted three interrelated messages.

First, whereas the urban location of Mark's audience implied a less hostile attitude toward Roman taxation, the episode asks the audience to consider the question of taxes from a local Jewish perspective in which Roman taxation was seen in more oppositional terms. At the same time, whereas the polarized perspective construed a subjectivity around *negation*, the ambiguous answer interpellates to a position of *negotiation*. Second, assuming that Paul's exhortation in Rom 13:1–7 was known to Mark's audience and interpreted by some as delivering a timeless message about the divine mandate of imperial rule, Mark here sends a correcting message. Rather than granting unconditional priority to the emperor, Mark relativizes his claims and opens the possibility of resisting imperial demands. God and Caesar are thus not easily reconciled, and sorting out what belongs to whom depends on the situation. Third, as the episode brings up the issue of Roman power in an explicit way, Mark's subtle ambivalence becomes openly displayed. Mark's audience is then asked to make a conscious effort to deal with Rome's claims in a more tactical way. Rather than relating to Rome in an unreflecting manner, Mark's drama on tax grants them a certain agency, stimulating them to ponder and distinguish between those aspects of Rome's order they could accept and those they could not.

Approaching the end of Mark's Gospel, the audience is presented with the Roman centurion and his now famous saying about the crucified Jesus being God's Son (15:39). When Mark is read as a closed narrative unit, the saying appears to be a climax that expresses a realization of Jesus' true identity, longed for by the implied reader. As the narrative is located in its imperial setting, however, the saying's questionable credibility causes the stable meaning to dissipate. Even if the saying for Mark's audience appears true, the centurion also seems unaware of the meaning of his own words, which leaves unresolved the question of how the saying places Mark's audience in relation to Rome's order.

Due to the portents in connection with the death of Jesus, moreover, the saying receives an awe-filled meaning. With the centurion's Roman identity, these portents establish a rather close resemblance to the apotheosis of Romulus, presumably well known to the audience. By differing in significant ways, Mark's account represents a mimicry of Roman ruler mythology. The lack of an intermediary group of nobles as well as the reverence for a Son of God who is feminized and heroic at the same time subvert the aristocratic scripts of Roman power and distort its construal of masculinity. The saying by the Roman centurion, then, does not resolve the Markan secrecy complex as much as it brings Mark's audience into a third space of identification that establishes a critical distance to imperial discourse and that is not ruled by imperial or anti-imperial logic.

With the subsequent ironic ending, in which women are leaving the empty tomb in fear and silence, Mark's Gospel refrains from offering a narrative closure, and invites instead continuous rereadings of the story.

The position to which it thus interpellates—even though it draws extensively on Roman imperial discourse—is not possible to determine as pro- or anti-Roman. True, the way in which Mark's Gospel engages with imperial discourse reflects pro- as well as anti-Roman attitudes. It ranges from antagonistic reversal to divine justification of Rome's destruction of the Jerusalem temple. Most of its dealings with imperial discourse, however, take place in the more ambivalent terrain represented by mimicry/mockery, catachresis, metonymic gap, and the opening of a third space. The position's evasive character, I here argue, was more threatening to imperial discourse than was downright opposition. As represented by the mustard seed, the real threat to imperial discourse did not lie as much in the oppositional contrasting of Jesus and the emperor as it did in the playful, yet profound, destabilizing of imperial notions of strength and triumph that were enacted in anticipation of God's unimperial empire.

Part 4
Uninheriting a Colonial Heritage

22
Different Marks in Different Empires

When the missionaries first came to Africa, they had the Bible and we had the land. They said, "Let us pray." We closed our eyes. When we opened them, we had the Bible and they had the land.
—Desmond Tutu[1]

The future is very much animated by the past-present.
—Ananda Abeysekara (2008, 2)

I am calling for more studies that triangulate close attention to contexts of modern scholarship, including how this encounter echoes, refracts, suppresses, and distils possibilities from earlier moments and from the interpreter's own location.
—Denise Buell (2010, 180)

With the primary aim of studying the stance of Mark's Gospel vis-à-vis Rome, in this study I have attempted a multifaceted treatment of the Mark-and-empire trajectory. Applying contemporary postcolonial theory as an interpretive grid, I have studied Mark in two different empires, Rome's and Europe's, thereby probing the divergent kinds of ties between Mark and discourses of empire. Here in part 4 I will discuss these different entanglements and locate the findings of the study in the contemporary discussions on religion and politics and the adjacent trajectory of the postsecular.

At a recent conference in Bethlehem, Palestine, Richard Horsley posed the following intriguing question: "What do you make of this anti-imperial Jesus movement which in fact became the chaplain of empire?" (quoted in Ferguson 2012, 86). In a response to this question, Christopher Ferguson, the World Council of Churches representative to the United Nations in

---
1. Quoted in Gish 2004, 101.

New York, contends that "we must locate ourselves in that movement" in a way that takes into account how Protestant tradition, by its division between private and public, much too often is "letting empire off the hook" (Ferguson 2012, 86, 91). As I have argued in this study, the author of Mark asked his audience to do just that: he asked his (mainly urban) audience to identify with a disturbing Jewish renewal movement that originated in the periphery of the civilized world. The kind of identification Mark asks for is not of the clear-cut opposition and confrontation that often characterized popular anti-Roman movements. It could rather be described as an identification that repositions from negation to negotiation.

I have reached this understanding of Mark by a postcolonial approach and its concomitant parallel analysis of Mark in ancient and modern empires. Alleging that a study of a Gospel's way of relating to Rome's empire tends to be affected by and intertwined with contemporary discourses of empire, I began this study by describing the contemporary heuristic and theoretical perspective through which the material was approached. By introducing postcolonial theory as a form of discourse theory in part 1, I laid the theoretical groundwork for the subsequent examination of Mark's Gospel in nineteenth-century Europe (part 2) and in ancient Rome (part 3).

In part 1, as the mutual challenges of postcolonial criticism and biblical studies were discussed (ch. 3), I found reciprocal critiques between the fields. First, I challenged the secularist tendency in postcolonial criticism by the more recent questioning of the ideological underpinnings of the secularization theory as well as by the adjacent reflections over the new visibility of religion in a postsecular condition. Second, in the opposite direction, I made a postcolonial critique against the relatively low degree of critical self-consciousness in the historical-critical paradigm of biblical studies. Historical-critical approaches are good at seeing biblical texts as products of social contexts, but are not as good at seeing biblical scholarship as a product of social contexts. Here I raised the question of (dis)continuity with the origin of modern biblical scholarship. The postcolonial approach, I argued, stands in fractured and critical continuity with modern biblical scholarship.

As an expression of this fragmented continuity, there are similarities as well as differences between the nineteenth-century interpretations analyzed in part 2 and the postcolonial reading offered in part 3. As for similarities, in both cases historical claims are made about Mark's Gospel and its stance vis-à-vis ancient Rome. Also, they are both in different ways connected to contingent historical contexts, thereby reflecting how the past gets caught up in the present. Unlike nineteenth-century scholarship, however, the postcolonial approach makes visible its social context by situating its claims in a particular theory, time, and geopolitical location. This particular feature of the postcolonial approach involves a certain distancing from the conducted analysis in order to make visible what one could call a colonial heritage in biblical scholarship.

As an important step in this distancing, I will here connect this study to the contemporary discussions on the colonial heritage of modernity and the postsecular trajectory with its questioning of the dichotomous division between politics and religion. This trajectory is particularly interesting in a location—Sweden—that is often described as one of the most secularized countries in the world (Pettersson 2009, 80). Since the three postcolonial critics (Said, Spivak, and Bhabha) who hitherto have informed this study have refrained from discussing secularism as part of a colonial heritage, I will here introduce some other postcolonial scholars who could assist our conceptualization of the past-present correlation.

The Postsecular Condition

Three important works that elaborate on the intersections between the postcolonial and the postsecular are Talal Asad (2003), Dipesh Chakrabarty (2000), and Ananda Abeysekara (2008). Rather than seeing the secular as a natural and emancipative development in modern societies, Asad has analyzed how the secular and its redemptive project are constructed in contrast to the religious, thereby excluding other forms of community. The notion of the secular as a social space free from religion, universally valid for all peoples, he seems to hold, represents a neocolonial heritage.

Along similar lines, Chakrabarty (2000, 4) has argued for the impossibility of thinking of concepts like political modernity or liberal democracy without drawing extensively on the intellectual and theological traditions of Europe. These allegedly universal terms are inherently European and need to be "provincialized." But, he (4) also argues, whether one likes it or not, this heritage is now global, and a program for a simple rejection of modernity would be "politically suicidal" (45). These concepts are therefore not only unavoidable; they are indispensable for criticizing socially unjust practices. At the same time, Chakrabarty is troubled by the use of these concepts. Not only are they used as though they were universally valid, regardless of the context. They also risk justifying the violence that accompanies the imperial or triumphalist moments of modernity. Finding no clear-cut answer to this dilemma, Chakrabarty still votes for inhabiting modernity in a way that relates to the past in a new manner, seeing the past as caught up in, and yet "disjointed" from, the present (108).

Picking up on the trajectory initiated by these two works, Abeysekara (2008, 154), a religious studies scholar from Sri Lanka, appreciates Chakrabarty for pointing towards a path of thinking that "take[s] the past seriously without necessarily being bound to or dictated by all its concerns." Exploring this path, Abeysekara contends that liberal democracy involves a promise that can never be quite fulfilled. Drawing extensively on Derrida, Abeysekara claims that democracy always entails a promise, and that a promise by definition is deferred. This deferred nature of democracy is interesting for this study since it connects with Mark's way of establishing an anticipation of something that is to come in the future. Further, in relation to such an ambiguous concept as liberal democracy (what Spivak would have called *pharmakon*), Abeysekara (2–3) suggests a negotiating attitude that he curiously calls *un-inheriting*: "By un-inheriting I mean a pathway of reflecting upon the postcolonial conceptions of heritage, history, and identity that is not reducible to a ready-made binary of remembering/forgetting, embracing/abandoning." Uninheriting modernity, Abeysekara claims, may bring forth futures that are not dictated by the past. Thus uninheriting seems to resonate with Spivak's catachresis. Abeysekara, however, avoids Spivak's secularist tendency.

Somewhat similar to uninheriting, Abeysekara (3) also speaks of "mourning secular futures." I take it as implying on the one hand a sympathetic stance to the (impossible) promise of secularism that a distinction between the private and the public, between the religious and the political, could make pluralism and diversity possible. But it also implies facing the wars conducted in its name, as well as its problematic exclusions. For better and for worse, religion is becoming increasingly visible in the public sphere, not least in European societies. The mourning of secular futures therefore involves giving up on secularism as a self-evident politics, and beginning to think about the important ways in which the intervention of religious discourses within the public sphere may, as Abeysekara (169) states, "help us pose the question of democracy vis-à-vis minority differences in a new way."

While I thus regard the concepts mourning and uninheriting as useful and as compatible to the postcolonial approach applied here, I am somewhat surprised by Abeysekara's low degree of interaction with Spivak and

Bhabha.[2] Spivak's way of seeing postcolonial modernity as a space that one cannot avoid inhabiting, and yet must criticize, seems crucial for a project such as Abeysekara's. As already mentioned, Spivak's understanding of catachresis seems to dovetail with Abeysekara's uninheriting. At the same time, catachresis questions Abeysekara's (4) pessimism over "improving" democracy "in the name of itself." Unlike Abeysekara, Spivak and Bhabha invest significant hope in the revisionary force of postcolonial criticism and offer concepts that could potentially transform societies and social practices. Abeysekara's work would have gained from engaging with these interventions in the colonial heritage. They might have muted his fascination of Derridean aporias (248, 255, 277), which seems to generate a rather pessimistic stance. Indeed, Abeysekara (277–78) ends with an aporia that leaves the reader in an impasse of inactivity and paralysis. As one reviewer points out, it remains unclear even at the end of Abeysekara's book whether religion has any place in his thinking (Pecora 2010).

Therefore, in relation to a religious tradition represented by Mark's Gospel, with a potential of contributing politically and theologically in contemporary postsecular societies, the terms *uninheriting* and *mourning* in relation to a colonial heritage are here pooled with other concepts, such as *catachresis* and *reclaiming*. With these concepts, we are better equipped to address the past-present dynamics that in this study I am bringing up for scrutiny.

Uninheriting Mark's Colonial Heritage

Focusing on seven passages in Mark (1:1; 5:1–20; 7:24–30; 8:31–9:1; 11:1–22; 12:13–17; 15:39), in part 2 of this study I examined the relation of sixteen German and English Markan commentaries to nineteenth-century European colonial discourse. Part 2 concluded (ch. 12) with a representation of three interrelated dichotomous divisions that were crucial for a European colonial subjectivity and that constitute a colonial heritage in Markan interpretation.

First, the traditional Christian/heathen division continued to play an important role in the commentaries and helped fuel a Christian imperial universalism. The Gerasene demoniac (5:1–20) was seen as "the first

---

2. While Abeysekara engages somewhat with Spivak, he does not discuss her use of catachresis. Bhabha, in turn, is mentioned in only one place.

apostle of the heathen," the Syrophoenician woman (7:24–30) as representing "the longing, suffering Gentile world," and the Roman centurion (15:39) as "a believing Gentile soldier."

Second, side by side with this traditional division, and seen most clearly in the interpretations of the Markan incipit (1:1), scholars with a more modern and (for its time) critical approach also made ample use of the Greek/Semitic division that was common in orientalist scholarship. The commentators identified *Christian* with *Greek* over and against *Semitic*. Whereas the Greeks were seen as progressive and as capable of metaphysical thought, the Semites were seen as stagnant and theocratic.

The tensions and anxieties that these interrelated processes of identification entailed indicate a certain instability in the European self-understanding. But there was also a third division, the one between spiritual and worldly. Since the Jew as well as the heathen were associated with the worldly, this instability was somewhat reduced. Seen not least in the interpretations of the triumphal entry story (11:1–11) and in the tribute question (12:13–17), this binary division—crucial for nineteenth-century Protestant Christianity—functioned as a lubricant that removed the friction between Mark's Gospel and imperial domination, be it Roman or European. Although this distinction involved a certain complexity, it nevertheless helped Protestant mission to benefit from the colonial expansion and still dissociate itself from it.

With an ambition of moving beyond, or uninheriting, this colonial heritage, in part 3 I applied a postcolonial optic for studying Mark's Gospel in its ancient setting. Focusing on the same Markan passages as in part 2, in the investigation in part 3 I read Mark as a collective representation and analyzed how its potentials for interpellating the audience were related to Roman imperial discourse. Whereas a modified Saidian approach served as the basis for part 2, the investigation in part 3 largely rested on the works of Bhabha and Spivak and their heuristic concepts—mimicry, colonial ambivalence, hybridity, third space, catachresis, and *pharmakon*, all addressing the slippery nature of the relation between the dominant and the dominated. Mark's Gospel begins antagonistically, I then argued, by presenting a countergospel according to which Jesus is more powerful and manly than even the Roman emperor. As the interconnected issues of ethnicity and gender bring the story into a crisis, however, the oppositional plot begins to turn on itself. By the wit of a hybrid female, the plot's unified and androcentric character becomes subverted and remodeled around the brittleness of Jesus as bread in a way that relates to imperial discourse in more complex ways. While at times opposing and at other times justifying Roman rule, most of its dealings take place in a more ambivalent terrain. The story's playful and evasive character was more threatening to imperial discourse than would have been its downright opposition. In part 3 I thus offered ways of conceptualizing Mark as a form of subversion and resistance that does not imply a direct and oppositional anti-Roman stance.

In its ancient imperial setting, then, Mark's Gospel addresses a mainly urban audience and tells a story about a rural Galilean Christ, the true Son of God. Represented not least by how terms such as θάλασσα (Mark 2:13, etc.) or κῆνσος (12:14) open a metonymic gap, Mark asks its audience to identify with a space located at the rural outskirts of the civilized world, inhabited by a people that imperial discourse regarded as suspect and semibarbaric. In this way, Mark carries a potential of forming a countercultural self-understanding that entails friction against the dominant culture.

When this subversive potential, inherent in Mark's Gospel, is placed side by side with the nineteenth-century commentaries on Mark, some interesting features come into sight. Evidently, there are different Marks in different empires. Written as they were in the centers of European empires, the commentaries tended to reproduce hierarchical binaries—Greek/Jew, Christian/heathen, and spiritual/worldly—in their readings of Mark's story, thereby helping to construe European subjects in a dominant position.

With respect to the first binary, the postcolonial reading suggested instead that Jews and Greeks were to be seen as sharing the fate of being subdued by Rome. This was especially seen in the inflamed meeting between Jesus and the Greek Syrophoenician woman—the only place in Mark (7:24–30) where "Greek" is used—that became a significant turning point for Mark's potential of forming a self-understanding that is subversive in another sense than being directly oppositional.

The second binary, the Christian/heathen division, constitutes a topic in its own right and will be dealt with below. The last binary, the spiritual/worldly division, played a crucial role in the commentaries. That this division was difficult to uphold in terms of a social practice in the colonies does not diminish its importance for the subjectivity of Protestants in nineteenth-century Europe. The postcolonial reading suggests a twofold way to uninherit this, still influential, interpretive tradition. First, it is criticized in terms of being historically unsound in that it presupposes a division between two spheres that were inseparable in Mark's premodern setting. In addition to this exegetical critique, there is also the postsecular condition and the new visibility of religion that quarrel with the spiritual/

worldly division from a contemporary point of view. To formulate a contemporary theopolitically engaged Christian subjectivity thus demands a thinking that in some ways transcends this modern dichotomy.

Here one needs to acknowledge that the nineteenth-century readings of Mark from locations in imperial centers hardly represent a new phenomenon. Beginning already during the fourth century, under Emperor Constantine, the Gospels have been continuously read from the perspective of the dominant. Such hegemonic transferring of Mark from margin to center needs to be uninherited in order that Mark may be appreciated and reclaimed as initially inhabiting a position in the margin. This post-Constantinian reclaiming of Mark as a text from the periphery is perhaps illustrated most clearly in the episode about the Gerasene demoniac (Mark 5:1–20), whose desolate state nineteenth-century commentators generally took as symbolizing the wretched state of "the heathen." In relation to the colonial heritage of biblical interpretation, I have here maintained that the demon-possessed man represents a need to be saved *from*, rather than *by*, empire.

Heathens, Pagans, and Gentiles:
On Christian Appropriation of an Anti-imperial Dichotomy

As Mark has been scrutinized from a postcolonial perspective, a recurrent subject has been the deconstruction of the Jew/Gentile divide that was prominent in the nineteenth-century quest for pure origins, as well as a subsequent reimagination of Greeks and Jews as having shared the fate of being subdued by Rome. Despite a general academic realization that these terms are extremely slippery as designations—seen not least in Hengel's questioning of the Judaism/Hellenism divide that was previously discussed (ch. 13)—contemporary usage of the designations *Jew*, *Greek*, *Gentile*, and *pagan* (*heathen* is generally avoided) are still haunted by notions of stable, fixed, and essential entities.

Of course, one could argue that since these designations are commonly used in the ancient sources, biblical scholarship cannot simply stop using them. Is our best option as scholars then to make visible the problems but nevertheless use these designations in our writings? *Jew* and *Greek* surely have to be used. But when it comes to *Gentile* and its cognate terms, a postcolonial uninheriting is a more satisfactory approach. As was seen in the common translation of Ἑλληνίς as "Gentile" (Mark 7:26), discussed in chapter 16, there is an interpretive tradition that defends the usage of "Gentile" even when it is exegetically possible, indeed preferable, to use the term "Greek" instead.

This brings us to a discussion of how to refer to non-Jewish people when interpreting biblical writings. Since we are dealing with several target languages, the discussion is somewhat complicated. The English term *Gentile* does not carry exactly the same connotations as the Swedish *hedning* or the German *Heide*. Since in English there has been a shift from using *pagan* and *heathen*, the Swedish and German terms seem to carry a more noticeable colonial heritage. But is the term *Gentile* really free from such connotations? Here opinions vary. Amy-Jill Levine (1993) seems to find no problem with the term, seeing it rather as synonymous with *Christian*. Another dictionary entry (Browning 2009, 128–29) is more cautious, however, warning that the term *Gentile* is "only meaningful in relation to Israel and the Jews for the rest of mankind." A more outspoken and sharp-eyed critique has been delivered by Neil Elliott (2008, 46), according to whom the use of "the Gentiles" rather than "the nations" constitutes a confusion of social analysis with ideology.

In various contemporary Christian contexts, it is not uncommon to find the term *Gentile* being used enthusiastically as an indication of a Christian universalism that exceeds ethnic boundaries. The term *Gentile* fuses all non-Jewish ethnicities into one category, thereby signaling the complete irrelevancy of ethnic difference. Indeed, the Roman centurion in front of the cross (Mark 15:39) is typically seen primarily as representing Gentiles rather than Rome's empire. There is nothing wrong with empire, it is then hinted, as long as it is Christian. This is not to neglect that such a nonethnic Christian universalism can be and has been useful in combatting slavery and racism. But this universalism presupposes an imperial master and risks suppressing ethnic difference (cf. Buell and Johnson Hodge 2004, 236–37). If the universalist enthusiasm lacks a self-critical reflection of Western colonialism, it risks reproducing the colonial legacy; the use of Gentiles becomes yet another brick in the tower of Babel.

Part 2 of this investigation has made visible the colonial heritage of the term *Gentile* and its cognates. Seeing the Greek Syrophoenician woman as a *heathen* mother, a nineteenth-century commentator was surprised that she could show maternal love for her daughter. Her submissive behavior, further, represented how Europeans expected the "heathens" to behave as they were being civilized. Echoes of this colonial heritage can be heard in contemporary commentaries. When Cranfield (1959, 246), for instance, discusses Jesus' traveling in Mark 7:24, he states: "How far Jesus penetrated into this pagan area is not indicated." The same phrasing is used by Harrington (1993, 612). Similarly, Hartman (2004, 255, 257) points out that the event takes place in *"hednaland"* (literally "land of the heathen") and sees Jesus as "making a thrust into a pagan area" where demons were presumably prevailing.

Hence, when biblical commentators refer to the woman as a *Gentile* or *pagan*, this is typically a designation that carries a religious essence that easily becomes transferred to non-Christian (or non-Jewish) peoples in general. One can make a similar point regarding the translation of ἔθνη in the New Testament in general. In the light of the present volume, therefore, I suggest that "nations" is generally preferable to "Gentiles" as a translation of ἔθνη. And, as I have argued, Ἕλλην ought to be translated "Greek."

As Stanley (1996, 105) contends, those who, from a Jewish perspective, could be lumped together as *Gentiles* would have defined themselves as Greeks, Romans, Phrygians, Galatians, Cappadocians, and members of other ethnic populations. Since *Gentile* was not used as a self-designation in Mediterranean culture, then the argument that Ἑλληνίς in Mark 7:26 means "Gentile" presupposes the perspective of a Jew under domination. When biblical scholars write about Mark's Gospel, however, their audience is typically Christian. Christian interpretations seem to have appropriated a Jewish anti-imperial rhetoric and placed it in a dominating imperial center, where it has become a powerful tool in the hands of the masters. Whereas the hostile use of Ἕλλην, ἔθνη, and גוי in Jewish discourse could have served as a protection against imperial domination, in Christian discourse the terms *pagan*, *heathen*, and *Gentile* have more often been used by the dominant to exclude and degrade the Other (Forward 2005).

In what might exemplify what Derrida (1998, 29–30) has called globalatinization, the Christian appropriation of the anti-imperial terminology seems to stem from the Vulgate translation, which reads, "mulier gentilis Syrophoenissa genere" (a Gentile woman, a Syrophoenician by birth). As previously seen (ch. 7), the term *heathen* can be traced back to a fourth-century Gothic translation of the Vulgate, in which the woman is designated *haiþno*, from the Latin *gentilis*. The Gothic origin is supported by the *Oxford English Dictionary* (s.v.), which also states that the word began to be used in Germanic languages to mean "non-Christian, pagan," after the introduction of Christianity. Is this not the time for biblical commentators to discontinue designating the Syrophoenician woman as a "Gentile" and her land as "pagan"? Is this not the time to uninherit rather than reproduce and normalize the colonial heritage?

From Darkness to Light?

When the idea of a parallel focus on ancient and nineteenth-century empires has been discussed at seminars, I have been warned not to establish a new kind of dualist structure of darkness and light. The nineteenth-century readings, the warning goes, risk becoming a dark foil to my postcolonial reading. Although I regard this as a serious challenge, it remains to be seen whether the warning has been heeded. As I have stated, the postcolonial perspective involves moving beyond and uninheriting the colonial heritage of academic research, including biblical interpretation. Given the affiliation of nineteenth-century academic discourses with European colonialism, they are inevitably associated with a certain "darkness." At the same time, however, I have been careful to locate this study in the complex development of modern biblical scholarship, which, after all, was established during the nineteenth century and has developed into a scholarly field where various critical perspectives on biblical interpretation, including postcolonial criticism, are cultivated.

The entanglement of the nineteenth-century commentators with the Protestant mission is similarly ambiguous. If the commentators largely placed Mark in the center of European imperialism, it seems as if the above humorous anecdote of Archbishop Tutu represents a development in which Mark's Gospel was actually retransferred from its awkward place in the center back to the imperial periphery. Ironically, one could then argue, European colonialism and the Protestant mission were only returning the gospel to port. This argument is somewhat similar to Gallagher's (1994b, 22) contention that the Christian missionary enterprise, despite its "chauvinistic cultural limits," also brought the tools (i.e., education) with which the colonial yoke could be shaken off. As Donaldson (1996a, 3–4) has pointed out, however, this counterhegemonic use of missionary education is to be seen as a way in which the colonized were able in some very surprising ways to appropriate imperializing strategies (i.e., language suppression) in a manner that enabled resistance to colonization. In other words, regardless of the intention of the Protestant mission, it did at times imply that when Mark's Gospel became a text with which groups in the periphery of the European empires began to identify, its subversive potentials began to resurface. As indicated by the ironic tone in Tutu's quote at the beginning of this chapter, and by the struggle he was part of, such resurfacing blurs the light/darkness dualism that this study risks producing.

This is not to deny, however, that postcolonial criticism—with its critical tools and ways of understanding social change, difference, and culture—has in some sense "enlightened" my understanding of the ecclesial and activist contexts with which I identify. And again, other perspectives and interpretations might also show the shortcomings and dark spots of this interpretive perspective, forcing me—God forbid—to critically reflect upon what might be an inevitable academic or activist self-centeredness inadvertently embedded in this study's probing of Mark and empire.

Provincializing Historical Criticism

As indicated in the introduction and discussed more fully in part 1, postcolonial criticism questions certain epistemological presumptions in the historical-critical paradigm. The extent to which the scholar's interest, location, and zeitgeist affect the interpretation of the biblical text has been seen throughout this study. It became especially noticeable when the interpretations of the tribute episode (12:13–17) were compared in table 5 (ch. 19). Only one of the nineteenth-century commentators in the investigation interpreted the tribute episode as a questioning of the ruling authorities. As this scholar was the only one located in Ireland, it is difficult to avoid the contention that the scholar's location influences how Mark's story is understood. In imperial centers, such as England and (eventually) Germany, issues of imperial domination appeared different as compared to the colonized Ireland. Although unacknowledged in the commentaries, these differences implied that Mark's text was approached with different presumptions and interests, resulting in different interpretations.

The trajectory of location as well as center and periphery, however, also risks simplifying and/or reducing the complex nature of biblical interpretation to a question of geopolitical location. As exemplified by this study, although the Swedish and Gothenburg/Hammarkullen location is intertwined with this postcolonial reading, there is no automatic connection between living in Sweden and reading the Bible in a particular way. Indeed, given the increasingly heterogeneous character of biblical studies in Sweden, the notion of a particularly Swedish perspective seems farfetched.[3] Also, postcolonial readings are conducted from a variety of

---

3. The situation has changed significantly compared to the 1950s, when almost all Swedish biblical scholars signed the so-called exegetical declaration on the issue of female ministers (referred to in ch. 1). The divergent positions among contemporary

geographic locations, Western as well as non-Western. Even if my specific location in a diasporic suburb is intertwined with the application of a postcolonial perspective, the correlation is not causative, but should rather be understood as a matter of identification. Since postcolonial criticism has been developed in a vacillation between center and periphery and is characterized by hybrid identifications across cultural borders, the actual geographic place of the interpreter is perhaps not as significant as the willingness to identify with experiences of marginalization and alienation. Spivak (Spivak and Harasym 1990, 121) adopts a similar position in her argument against the notion of a transparent subject:

> What we are asking for is that … the holders of hegemonic discourse should de-hegemonize their position and themselves learn how to occupy the subject position of the other rather than simply say, "O.K., sorry, we are just very good white people, therefore we do not speak for the blacks." That's the kind of breast-beating that is left behind at the threshold and then business goes on as usual.

In other words, whereas there is no subject position that automatically generates an empire-critical approach, postcolonial criticism furnishes and enables its practitioners to identify with the experiences of marginalization in self as well as in others when researching biblical texts. Given the Eurocentric heritage of biblical scholarship, this interpellative force of postcolonial criticism corresponds to what Abeysekara calls un-inheriting Eurocentricity and what Chakrabarty calls provincializing Europe (see above). As I have tried to demonstrate, however, such provincializing is not tantamount to a neglect of the disciplinary history, nor does it denounce issues of historical plausibility. To the contrary, and as Spivak (1990, 228) aptly phrases it, it involves entering an academic space that "one cannot not want to inhabit and yet must criticize."

One may then ask to what extent the claims made here about Mark's countercultural or even subversive character are simply a reflection of the postcolonial perspective. Does this contention, contingent and informed by a particular perspective as it is, say anything about Mark in its ancient setting? As stated in the introduction, the way in which Mark's primary audience heard and understood the Gospel's story is impossible to know.

Swedish exegetes on the issue of same-sex relations give witness to a considerably more complex situation in the present.

Regardless of perspective, or any supposed lack thereof, the actual primary reception of the story remains unknown. Even so, my findings in this study do involve claims of historical plausibility. In this study I have presumed, moreover, that the audience was diverse and that the story was thus heard in somewhat different ways. True, there were also social practices (e.g., teaching, repetitive rituals) that regulated the reception and helped form a collective self-understanding that deviated from the cultural norms. But still the presence of various competing discourses (Roman, Greek, Jewish, and other local discourses) would have established different kinds of overdetermined subjects, implying diversity in how Mark was heard. In other words, any historically plausible contention about Mark's Gospel needs to acknowledge the plurality of ways in which it was initially received.

Since the choice of a postcolonial perspective has involved a substantial amount of historical investigation of Mark as a collective representation, I do indeed make historical claims about Mark in its ancient setting. But the postcolonial perspective also generates a historical plausibility that interacts more transparently with the present. Being critical of unacknowledged entanglements between academia and discourses of empire, I framed the questions in triangular ways (cf. the epigraph from Denise Buell above) that imply a critique of knowledge that is often taken for granted. Further, as the heuristic concepts supplied by postcolonial criticism have helped to inform the understanding of Mark in its ancient setting, they also connect this understanding to contemporary discourses on empire, Christian subjectivity, and social change.

Reclaiming Mark

Although there are surely subversive elements in the other Gospels (cf. Segovia and Sugirtharajah 2007), Mark's story, with its ambiguities and gaps, offers an amazingly rich and exciting source for construing a post-Constantinian Christian self-understanding. This contention is indirectly supported by Schildgen's (1999) study of the reception of Mark from the second century until today, in which she discusses Mark's "absent-presence" in the biblical canon. When Mark receives attention, the inattention that it commonly receives is reversed, indicating "changing historical and cultural forces" (Schildgen, 33). During Christianity's long and troublesome intertwinement with empires through the centuries, Mark has been rather absent compared to the other Gospels. Represented foremost by increasing academic influence over biblical studies, the new interest in Mark by nineteenth-century scholars was indeed connected to "changing historical and cultural forces." It is not until the contemporary empire-critical readings, engaged with in this study, however, that Mark can uninherit its colonial heritage and become reclaimed as a voice from the margin.

From a Swedish location, one might ask how this reclaiming complies with a Lutheran context. Although Reformation theologies are divergent, Lutheran churches have often been quite uncritical of state power, shown not least by the tradition of national churches in the Nordic countries. At the same time, Lutheran tradition has also emphasized the vernacular, and Lutheran churches are often keen to adapt to various contexts. In the present, a postsecular society poses new, challenging questions about the relationships among church, theology, and politics. Could churches rooted in the Reformation be part of the increasing visibility of religion in the public sphere? With my postcolonial approach, I strive to contribute to a theology that identifies with the margins and intervenes critically and yet playfully in this emerging theopolitical sphere.

Although in this study I have engaged extensively with and been inspired by anti-imperial hermeneutics, I also offer a diverging suggestion on how Mark relates to empire. Correlated to the way in which postcolonial criticism relates to anticolonial discourses, Mark has been pressed for the subtle ways in which it both reproduces and undermines imperial discourse. Its most subversive traits can be discerned in its slipping between mimicry and mockery, as well as in its open and unfinished character, inviting as it does continuous rereadings that subvert the initial androcentric plot with its absent-present women, disintegrating bread crumbs, and frail disciples. If empire imposes universalism on the basis of military and economic superiority, Mark represents a reworked universalism from below that identifies with the margin and disturbs imperial hegemony in anticipation of God's unimperial empire. To be a follower of Christ is, with Mark, not a fixed and transparent affair, but one that continues to be negotiated in the present, affirming the unfinished character of the self as it searches for unexpected signs of the Divine.

Bibliography

The abbreviations used in this study are listed in *The SBL Handbook of Style* (Alexander et al. 1999, 68–237).

ANCIENT SOURCES

Aristides, Aelius. 1898. *Aelii Aristidis smyrnaei qvae supersunt omnia*. Orations XVII–LIII. Edited by Bruno Keil. Berlin: Weidmann.
Aristides, Aelius. 1976–1980. *P. Aelii Aristidis Opera quae exstant omnia*. Orations I–XVI. Edited by Friedrich Walther Lenz and Charles Behr. 4 vols. Leiden: Brill.
Aristides, Aelius. 1981–1986. *The Complete Works*. Translated by Charles Behr. 2 vols. Leiden: Brill.
The Apocryphal New Testament: A Collection of Apocryphal Christian Literature in an English Translation. 1993. Translated by J. K. Elliott. Oxford: Oxford University Press.
The Ante-Nicene Fathers. 1884–1887. Edited by A. Cleveland Coxe. 10 vols. Edinburgh: T&T Clark. Repr., Grand Rapids: Eerdmans, 1989–1990.
The Apostolic Fathers. 1912–1913. Translated by Kirsopp Lake. 2 vols. LCL. London: Heinemann.
Athenaeus. 1928–1951. *The Deipnosophists*. Translated by Charles Burton Gulick. 7 vols. LCL. London: Heinemann.
Augustus. 2009. *Res Gestae Divi Augusti*. Translated by Alison E. Cooley. Cambridge: Cambridge University Press.
Bibeln. 2000. Bibelkommissionens översättning. Örebro: Libris.
Biblia Hebraica Stuttgartensia. 1990. Edited by K. Elliger and W. Rudoph. 4th ed. Stuttgart: Deutsche Bibelgesellschaft.
The Babylonian Talmud. 1935–1948. Translated under the editorship of I. Epstein. 8 vols. London: Soncino.
Caesar. *The Gallic War*. 1958. Translated by H. J. Edgards. LCL. Cambridge: Harvard University Press.

Cassius, Dio. 1914–1927. *Roman History*. Translated by Earnest Cary. 9 vols. LCL. London: Heinemann.

Chrysostom, John. 1888. *Homilies on the Gospel of Saint Matthew*. Nicene and Post-Nicene Fathers 10. New York: Christian Literature.

Cicero, Marcus Tullius. 1923. *The Speeches: Pro archia poeta, Post reditum in senatu, Post reditum ad quirites, De domo sua, De haruspicum responsis, Pro plancio*. Translated by N. H. Watts. LCL. London: Heinemann.

———. 1927. *The Speeches: Pro Lege manilia, Pro Caecina, Pro Cluentio, Pro Rabirio, Pro Rabirio Perduellionis*. Translated by H. Grose Hodge. LCL. London: Heinemann.

———. 1953. *The Speeches: In Catilinam I–IV, Pro Murena, Pro Sulla, Pro Flacco*. Translated by Louis E. Lord. LCL. London: Heinemann.

———. 2002. *Letters to Quintus and Brutus; Letter Fragments; Letter to Octavian; Invectives; Handbook of Electioneering*. Translated by D. R. Shackleton Bailey. LCL. Cambridge: Harvard University Press.

The Dead Sea Scrolls in English. 1995. Translated by Geza Vermes. 4th ed. Sheffield: Sheffield Academic Press.

Diodorus Siculus. 1933–1967. *The Library of History*. Translated by C. H. Oldfather et al. 12 vols. LCL. London: Heinemann.

Dionysius of Halicarnassus. 1937–1950. *The Roman Antiquities*. Translated by Earnest Cary on the basis of the version of Edward Spelman. 7 vols. LCL. London: Heinemann.

Epictetus. 1925–1928. *The Discourses as Reported by Arrian, the Manual, and Fragments*. Translated by W. A. Oldfather. 2 vols. LCL. London: Heinemann.

Eusebius. 1926–1932. *The Ecclesiastical History*. Translated by Kirsopp Lake. 2 vols. LCL. London: Heinemann.

The Greek New Testament. 2002. 4th ed. Stuttgart: United Bible Societies.

The Holy Bible: New Revised Standard Version. 1989. London: HarperCollins.

Horace. 1926. *Satires, Epistles and Ars Poetica*. Translated by H. Rushton Fairclough. LCL. London: Heinemann.

———. 2004. *Odes and Epodes*. Translated by Niall Rudd. LCL. Cambridge: Harvard University Press.

Josephus. 1926–1965. Translated by H. St. J. Thackeray et al. 10 vols. LCL. London: Heinemann.

Juvenal and Persius. 2004. Translated by Susanna Morton Braund. LCL. Cambridge: Harvard University Press.

Livy. 1919–1959. Translated by B. O. Foster et al. 14 vols. LCL. London: Heinemann.
Martial. 1993. *Epigrams*. Translated by D. R. Shackleton Bailey. 3 vols. LCL. Cambridge: Harvard University Press.
Midrash Rabbah. 1983. Translated under the editorship of H. Freedman and Maurice Simon. 10 vols. London: Soncino.
Nicene and Post-Nicene Fathers. 1886–1888. Edited by Philip Schaff. First series, 14 vols. Repr., Christian Classics Ethereal Library. Online: http://www.ccel.org/fathers.html.
Nicolaus of Damascus' Life of Augustus. 1923. Translated by Clayton Morris Hall. Smith College Classical Studies. Northhampton, Mass.: Collegiate Press.
Novum Testamentum Graece. 2006. Edited by Eberhard Nestle et al. 27th ed. Stuttgart: Deutsche Bibelgesellschaft.
Pausanias. 1918–1935. *Description of Greece*. Translated by W. H. S. Jones and H. A. Ormerod. 5 vols. LCL. London: Heinemann.
Philo. 1918–1935. Translated by F. H. Colson and G. H. Whitaker. 10 vols. LCL. London: Heinemann.
Pliny the Elder. 1938–1962. *Natural History*. Translated by H. Rackham, W. H. S. Jones, and D. E. Eichholz. 10 vols. LCL. London: Heinemann.
Pliny the Younger. 1969. *Letters and Panegyricus*. Translated by Betty Radice. 2 vols. LCL. London: Heinemann.
Plutarch's Lives. 1914–1926. Translated by Bernadotte Perrin. 11 vols. LCL. London: Heinemann.
Plutarch's Moralia. 1927–1969. Translated by Frank Cole Babbitt et al. 15 vols. LCL. London: Heinemann.
Polybius. 1922–1927. *The Histories*. Translated by W. R. Paton. 6 vols. LCL. London: Heinemann.
Quintilian. 2001. *The Orator's Education*. Translated by Donald A. Russel. 4 vols. LCL. Cambridge: Harvard University Press.
Sallust. 1921. Translated by J. C. Rolfe. LCL. London: Heinemann.
Seneca. 1928–1935. *Moral Essays*. Translated by John W. Basore. 3 vols. LCL. London: Heinemann.
Septuaginta. 1935. Edited by Alfred Rahlfs. Stuttgart: Württembergische Bibelanstalt.
Suetonius. 1913–1914. Translated by J. C. Rolfe. 2 vols. LCL. London: Heinemann.
Tacitus. 1925–1937. *The Histories and The Annals*. Translated by Clifford. H. Moore and John Jackson. 4 vols. LCL. London: Heinemann.

———. 1946. *Dialogus, Agricola, Germania*. Translated by William Peterson and Maurice Hutton. LCL. London: Heinemann.
Tertullian. 1968. *Le premier livre Ad nationes de Tertullien: Introduction, texte, traduction et commentaire*. Translated to French by André Schneider. Neuchâtel: Institut Suisse de Rome.
Virgil. 1999. *Ecloges, Georgics, Aeneid I–IV*. Translated by H. Rushton Fairclough. LCL. Cambridge: Harvard University Press.

Modern Sources

Abeysekara, Ananda. 2008. *The Politics of Postsecular Religion: Mourning Secular Futures*. Insurrections: Critical Studies in Religion, Politics, and Culture. New York: Columbia University Press.
Adam, A. K. M. 2000. *Handbook of Postmodern Biblical Interpretation*. St. Louis: Chalice.
Ahmad, Aijaz. 1994. *In Theory: Classes, Nations, Literatures*. London: Verso.
Aichele, George, et al., eds. 1995. *The Postmodern Bible*. New Haven: Yale University Press.
Aitken, Ellen Bradshaw. 2005. Reading Hebrews in Flavian Rome. *Union Seminary Quarterly Review* 59:82–85.
Aland, Kurt, and Barbara Aland. 1995. *The Text of the New Testament: An Introduction to the Critical Editions and to the Theory and Practice of Modern Textual Criticism*. Translated by Erroll F. Rhodes. 2nd ed. Repr., Grand Rapids: Eerdmans.
Alder, Ken. 2002. *The Measure of All Things: The Seven-year Odyssey That Transformed the World*. London: Little, Brown.
Alexander, Joseph Addison. 1858. *The Gospel According to St. Mark*. New York: Scribner's.
Alexander, Loveday. 1998. Ancient Book Production and the Circulation of the Gospels. Pages 71–111 in *The Gospels for All Christians: Rethinking the Gospel Audience*. Edited by Richard Bauckham. Edinburgh: T&T Clark.
Alexander, Patrick H., et al., eds. 1999. *The SBL Handbook of Style: For Ancient Near Eastern, Biblical, and Early Christian Studies*. Peabody, Mass.: Hendrickson. Online: http://www.sbl-site.org/downloadAsset.aspx?asset=SBLHS09 .pdf.
Alföldy, Géza. 1985. *The Social History of Rome*. Totowa: Barnes & Noble.

Alford, Henry. 1849. *Matthew–Mark.* Vol. 1, part 1 of *The Greek Testament: With a Critically Revised Text.* 4 vols. in 6. London: Francis and John Rivington, 1849–1857.

Allison, Dale C., Jr. 1992. Apocalyptic. Pages 17–20 in *Dictionary of Jesus and the Gospels.* Edited by Joel B. Green and Scot McKnight. Downers Grove, Ill.: InterVarsity Press.

Althusser, Louis. 2001. Ideology and the Ideological State Apparatuses: Notes Towards an Investigation. Pages 85–131 in *Lenin and Philosophy and Other Essays.* Edited by Louis Althusser. New York: Monthly Review Press.

Ando, Clifford. 2000. *Imperial Ideology and Provincial Loyalty in the Roman Empire.* Classics and Contemporary Thought. Berkeley: University of California Press.

———. 2010. The Administration of the Provinces. Pages 177–92 in *A Companion to the Roman Empire.* Edited by David Stone Potter. Malden, Mass.: Blackwell.

Annen, Franz. 1991. λεγιών. Pages 345–46 in vol. 2 of *Exegetical Dictionary of the New Testament.* Edited by Horst Balz and Gerhard Schneider. 3 vols. Grand Rapids: Eerdmans, 1990–1993.

Appiah, Kwame Anthony. 1991. Is the Post- in Postmodernism the Post- in Postcolonial? *Critical Inquiry* 17:336–57.

Arvidsson, Stefan. 2006. *Aryan Idols: Indo-European Mythology as Ideology and Science.* Translated by Sonia Wichmann. Chicago: University of Chicago Press.

Asad, Talal. 2003. *Formations of the Secular: Christianity, Islam, Modernity.* Cultural Memory in the Present. Stanford: Stanford University Press.

Ashcroft, Bill. 1996. On the Hyphen in "Post-Colonial." *New Literatures Review* 32:23–31.

Ashcroft, Bill, Gareth Griffiths, and Helen Tiffin. 1989. *The Empire Writes Back: Theory and Practice in Post-colonial Literatures.* London: Routledge.

———. 2000. *Post-colonial Studies: The Key Concepts.* Routledge Key Guides. London: Routledge.

Baird, Mary M. 1920. The Gadarene Demoniac. *Expository Times* 31:189.

Baird, William. 1992. *From Deism to Tübingen.* Vol. 1 of *History of New Testament Research.* 2 vols. Minneapolis: Fortress.

———. 2003. *From Jonathan Edwards to Rudolf Bultmann.* Vol. 2 of *History of New Testament Research.* 2 vols. Minneapolis: Fortress.

Baker, Cynthia M. 2010. "From Every Nation under Heaven": Jewish Ethnicities in the Greco-Roman World. Pages 79–99 in *Prejudice and Christian Beginnings: Investigating Race, Gender, and Ethnicity in Early Christian Studies*. Edited by Laura Nasrallah and Elisabeth Schüssler Fiorenza. Minneapolis: Fortress.

Balz, Horst. 1991. κῆνσος. Page 287 in vol. 2 of *Exegetical Dictionary of the New Testament*. Edited by Horst Balz and Gerhard Schneider. 3 vols. Grand Rapids: Eerdmans, 1990–1993.

Balz, Horst, and Gerhard Schneider, eds. 1990–1993. *Exegetical Dictionary of the New Testament*. 3 vols. Grand Rapids: Eerdmans.

Bammel, Ernst. 1984. The Revolution Theory from Reimarus to Brandon. Pages 11–68 in *Jesus and the Politics of His Day*. Edited by Ernst Bammel and C. F. D. Moule. Cambridge: Cambridge University Press.

Barr, James. 1961. *The Semantics of Biblical Language*. London: Oxford University Press.

Barrett, Michèle. 1991. *The Politics of Truth: From Marx to Foucault*. Cambridge: Polity.

Barsky, Robert F. 1993. Discourse Analysis Theory. In *Encyclopedia of Contemporary Literary Theory: Approaches, Scholars, Terms*. Edited by Irena R. Makaryk. Toronto: University of Toronto Press.

Barton, John. 1990. Eisegesis. Pages 187–88 in *A Dictionary of Biblical Interpretation*. Edited by R. J. Coggins and J. L. Houlden. London: SCM.

Bauckham, Richard. 1998a. For Whom Were the Gospels Written? Pages 9–48 in *The Gospels for All Christians: Rethinking the Gospel Audience*. Edited by Richard Bauckham. Edinburgh: T&T Clark.

———, ed. 1998b. *The Gospels for All Christians: Rethinking the Gospel Audience*. Edinburgh: T&T Clark.

———. 2010. Is There Patristic Counter-evidence? A Response to Margaret Mitchell. Pages 68–110 in *The Audience of the Gospels: The Origin and Function of the Gospels in Early Christianity*. Edited by Edward W. Klink. London: T&T Clark.

Bauer, Walter, F. W. Danker, W. F. Arndt, and F. W. Gingrich. 2000. *Greek-English Lexicon of the New Testament and Other Early Christian Literature*. 3rd ed. Chicago: University of Chicago Press.

Beard, Mary, John North, and Simon Price. 1998. *Religions of Rome*. 2 vols. Cambridge: Cambridge University Press.

Beckingham, C. F. 1979. Edward W. Said: Orientalism. *Bulletin of the School of Oriental and African Studies* 42:562–64.

Beekes, Robert, and Lucian van Beek. 2010. *Etymological Dictionary of Greek*. 2 vols. Leiden Indo-European Etymological Dictionary Series 10. Leiden: Brill.

Belo, Fernando. 1981. *A Materialist Reading of the Gospel of Mark*. Translated by Matthew J. O'Connell. Maryknoll, N.Y.: Orbis.

Berger, Peter L. 1999. The Desecularization of the World: A Global Overview. Pages 1–18 in *The Desecularization of the World: Resurgent Religion and World Politics*. Edited by Peter L. Berger. Grand Rapids: Eerdmans.

Bernal, Martin. 1991. *Black Athena: The Afroasiatic Roots of Classical Civilization*. 2 vols. New Brunswick, N.J.: Rutgers University Press.

Betz, Hans Dieter. 1999. Legion. Pages 507–8 in *Dictionary of Deities and Demons in the Bible*. Edited by Karel van der Toorn, Bob Becking, and Pieter W. van der Horst. 2nd ed. Leiden: Brill.

Bhabha, Homi K. 1990a. The Third Space: Interview with Homi Bhabha. Pages 207–21 in *Identity: Community, Culture, Difference*. Edited by Jonathan Rutherford. London: Lawrence & Wishart.

———. 1990b. DissemiNation: Time, Narrative, and the Margins of the Modern Nation. Pages 291–322 in *Nation and Narration*. Edited by Homi Bhabha. London: Routledge

———. 1992. Postcolonial Criticism. Pages 437–65 in *Redrawing the Boundaries: The Transformation of English and American Literary Studies*. Edited by Stephen Greenblatt and Giles Gunn. New York: Modern Language Association of America.

———. 2004. *The Location of Culture*. New York: Routledge.

Bird, Phyllis A., et al., eds. 1997. *Reading the Bible as Women: Perspectives from Africa, Asia, and Latin America*. Semeia 78. Atlanta: Scholars Press.

Bligh, Philip H. 1968. A Note on Huios Theou in Mark 15:39. *Expository Times* 80:51–53.

Bøe, Sverre. 2010. *Cross-bearing in Luke*. Wissenschaftliche Untersuchungen zum Neuen Testament 2/278. Tübingen: Mohr Siebeck.

Boer, Roland. 2001. *Last Stop before Antarctica: The Bible and Postcolonialism in Australia*. Bible and Postcolonialism. Sheffield: Sheffield Academic Press.

Boeve, Lieven. 2008. Religion after Detraditionalization: Christian Faith in a Postsecular Europe. Pages 187–209 in *The New Visibility of Religion: Studies in Religion and Cultural Hermeneutics*. Edited by Michael Hoelzl and Graham Ward. London: Continuum.

Bondurant, Joan V. 1988. *Conquest of Violence: The Gandhian Philosophy of Conflict*. Princeton: Princeton University Press.

Borg, Annika. 2004. *Kön och bibeltolkning: En undersökning av hur Nya testamentets brevtexter om kvinnors underordning tolkats i bibelvetenskapliga kommentarer under 1900-talet*. Uppsala: Uppsala universitet.

Borg, Marcus J. 1998. *Conflict, Holiness, and Politics in the Teachings of Jesus*. Harrisburg, Pa.: Trinity Press International.

Boring, M. Eugene. 1990. Mark 1:1–15 and the Beginning of the Gospel. *Semeia* 52:43–81.

Botha, P. J. J. 1992. Greco-Roman Literacy as Setting for New Testament Writings. *Neotestamentica* 26:195–215.

———. 1999. Schools in the World of Jesus: Analysing the Evidence. *Neotestamentica* 33:225–60.

———. 2010. "Publishing" a Gospel: Notes on Historical Constraints to Gospel Criticism. Pages 335–52 in *The Interface of Orality and Writing: Speaking, Seeing, Writing in the Shaping of New Genres*. Edited by Annette Weissenrieder and Robert B. Coote. Wissenschaftliche Untersuchungen zum Neuen Testament 260. Tübingen: Mohr Siebeck.

Bowersock, G. W. 1994. *Fiction as History: Nero to Julian*. Berkeley: University of California Press.

Bowie, Malcolm. 1995. Lacan, Jacques. Page 429 in *The New Oxford Companion to Literature in French*. Edited by Peter France. Oxford: Clarendon.

Bradley, Keith R. 1994. *Slavery and Society at Rome*. Key Themes in Ancient History. Cambridge: Cambridge University Press.

Brandon, Samuel George Frederick. 1967. *Jesus and the Zealots: A Study of the Political Factor in Primitive Christianity*. New York: Scribner's.

Broadbent, Ralph. 1998. Ideology, Culture, and British New Testament Studies: The Challenge of Cultural Studies. *Semeia* 82:33–61.

Broadbent, Ralph, Ivy George, David Jobling, and Luise Schottroff. 1999. The Postcolonial Bible: Four Reviews. *Journal for the Study of the New Testament* 74:113–21.

Broadhead, Will. 2007. Colonization, Land Distribution, and Veteran Settlement. Pages 148–63 in *A Companion to the Roman Army*. Edited by Paul Erdkamp. Malden, Mass.: Blackwell.

Bromiley, G. W., ed. 1979–1988. *International Standard Bible Encyclopedia*. 4 vols. Grand Rapids: Eerdmans.

Brooke, George J. 1991. The Kittim in the Qumran Pesharim. Pages 135–59 in *Images of Empire*. Edited by Loveday Alexander. Journal for the Study of the Old Testament Supplement Series 122. Sheffield: Sheffield Academic Press.

Browning, W. R. F., ed. 2009. *A Dictionary of the Bible*. 2nd ed. Oxford: Oxford University Press. Online: http://www.oxfordreference.com.ezproxy.ub.gu.se/view/10.1093/acref/9780199543984.001.0001/acref-9780199543984-e-742.

Bruce, Alexander Balmain. 1897. The Synoptic Gospels. Pages 1–651 in *The Expositor's Greek Testament*. Edited by W. Robertson Nicoll. New York: Doran.

Brunt, P. A. 1978. Laus Imperii. Pages 159–91 in *Imperialism in the Ancient World*. Edited by Peter Garnsey and Charles Richard Whittaker. Cambridge: Cambridge University Press.

Buell, Denise Kimber. 2005. *Why This New Race: Ethnic Reasoning in Early Christianity*. Gender, Theory, and Religion. New York: Columbia University Press.

———. 2010. God's Own People: Specters of Race, Ethnicity, and Gender in Early Christian Studies. Pages 159–90 in *Prejudice and Christian Beginnings: Investigating Race, Gender, and Ethnicity in Early Christian Studies*. Edited by Laura Nasrallah and Elisabeth Schüssler Fiorenza. Minneapolis: Fortress.

Buell, Denise Kimber, and Caroline Johnson Hodge. 2004. The Politics of Interpretation: The Rhetoric of Race and Ethnicity in Paul. *Journal of Biblical Literature* 123:235–51.

Burdon, Christopher. 2004. "To the Other Side": Construction of Evil and Fear of Liberation in Mark 5.1–20. *Journal for the Study of the New Testament* 27:149–67.

Butler, Judith. 1999. *Gender Trouble: Feminism and the Subversion of Identity*. Tenth anniversary edition. New York: Routledge.

Byrskog, Samuel. 2000. *Story as History—History as Story: The Gospel Tradition in the Context of Ancient Oral History*. Wissenschaftliche Untersuchungen zum Neuen Testament 123. Tübingen: Mohr Siebeck.

Calhoun, Craig, ed. 2002. *Dictionary of the Social Sciences*. Oxford: Oxford University Press. Online: http://www.oxfordreference.com.ezproxy.ub.gu.se/views/ENTRY.html?subview=Main&entry=t104.e298

Cameron, Averil. 1991. *Christianity and the Rhetoric of Empire: The Development of Christian Discourse*. Berkeley: University of California Press.

Camery-Hoggatt, Jerry. 1992. *Irony in Mark's Gospel: Text and Subtext*. Society for New Testament Studies Monograph Series 72. Cambridge: Cambridge University Press.

Camp, Claudia V. 2004. Oralities, Literacies, and Colonialisms in Antiquity and Contemporary Scholarship. Pages 193–217 in *Orality, Literacy, and Colonialism in Antiquity*. Edited by Jonathan A. Draper. Leiden: Brill.

Camper, Pierre. 1791. *Dissertation physique; sur les différences réelles que présentent les traits du visage chez les hommes de différents pays et de différents âges; sur le beau qui caractèrise les statues antiques et les pierres gravées. Suivie de la proposition d'une nouvelle méthode pour déssiner toutes sortes de têtes humaines avec la plus grande sûreté*. Utrecht: Wild & Altheer.

Carey, William. 1792. *An Enquiry into the Obligations of Christians to Use Means for the Conversion of the Heathens*. London: Hodder & Stoughton.

Carpenter, Joseph Estlin. 1911. Religion. Pages 61–76 in *Encyclopedia Britannica*. 11th ed. Chicago: Encyclopædia Britannica.

Carter, Warren. 2000. *Matthew and the Margins: A Sociopolitical and Religious Reading*. Bible and Liberation. Maryknoll, N.Y.: Orbis.

———. 2001. *Matthew and Empire: Initial Explorations*. Harrisburg, Pa.: Trinity Press International.

———. 2005. Constructions of Violence and Identities in Matthew's Gospel. Pages 81–108 in *Violence in the New Testament*. Edited by Leigh Gibson and Shelly Matthews. New York: T&T Clark.

———. 2007. The Gospel of Matthew. Pages 69–104 in *A Postcolonial Commentary on the New Testament Writings*. Edited by Fernando F. Segovia and R. S. Sugirtharajah. London: T&T Clark.

———. 2008. *John and Empire: Initial Explorations*. New York: T&T Clark.

———. 2010. Review of Adam Winn, *The Purpose of Mark's Gospel: An Early Christian Response to Roman Imperial Propaganda*. *Review of Biblical Literature*, http://www.bookreviews.org.

Cassidy, Richard J. 1978. *Jesus, Politics, and Society: A Study of Luke's Gospel*. Maryknoll, N.Y.: Orbis.

Catchpole, David R. 1984. The "Triumphal" Entry. Pages 319–34 in *Jesus and the Politics of His Day*. Edited by Ernst Bammel and C. F. D. Moule. Cambridge: Cambridge University Press.

Cavallo, Guglielmo. 1999. Between *Volumen* and Codex: Reading in the Roman World. Pages 64–89 in *A History of Reading in the West*. Edited by Guglielmo Cavallo and Roger Chartier. Cambridge: Polity.

Chadwick, George Alexander. 1887. *The Gospel According to St Mark*. Expositor's Bible. New York: Hodder & Stoughton.

Chakrabarty, Dipesh. 2000. *Provincializing Europe: Postcolonial Thought and Historical Difference*. Princeton Studies in Culture/Power/History. Princeton: Princeton University Press.
Chalker, Sylvia, and E. S. C. Weiner, eds. 1998. *The Oxford Dictionary of English Grammar*. Oxford: Oxford University Press.
Chamber's Encyclopaedia. 1875–1876. American rev. ed. 10 vols. Philadelphia: Lippincott.
Charlesworth, James H., ed. 1983–1985. *The Old Testament Pseudepigrapha*. 2 vols. New York: Doubleday.
Charlesworth, M. P. 1936. The Flavian Dynasty. Pages 1–45 *The Imperial Peace: a.d. 70–192*. Vol. 11 of *Cambridge Ancient History*. Edited by S. A. Cook, F. E. Adcock, and M. P. Charlesworth. Cambridge: Cambridge University Press.
Chow, John K. 1992. *Patronage and Power: A Study of Social Networks in Corinth*. Journal for the Study of the New Testament Supplement Series 75. Sheffield: JSOT Press.
Christensen, Torben, and William Robert Hutchison. 1982. Introduction. Pages 5–9 in *Missionary Ideologies in the Imperialist Era, 1880–1920: Papers from the Durham Consultation, 1981*. Edited by Torben Christensen and William Robert Hutchison. Århus: Aros.
Claesson, Bo, ed. 2003. *Samer och ursprungsbefolkningars rättigheter: Rapport från Värdegrunden*. Göteborg: Centrum för värdegrundsstudier.
Clark, Elizabeth A. 2004. *History, Theory, Text: Historians and the Linguistic Turn*. Cambridge: Harvard University Press.
Clévenot, Michel. 1985. *Materialist Approaches to the Bible*. Maryknoll, N.Y.: Orbis.
Coggins, R. J., and J. L. Houlden, eds. 1990. *A Dictionary of Biblical Interpretation*. London: SCM.
Collins, Adela Yarbro. 1995. Establishing the Text: Mark 1:1. Pages 111–27 in *Texts and Contexts: Biblical Texts in Their Textual and Situational Contexts: Essays in Honor of Lars Hartman*. Edited by Tord Fornberg and David Hellholm. Oslo: Scandinavian University Press.
———. 2000. Mark and His Readers: The Son of God among Greeks and Romans. *Harvard Theological Review* 93:85–100.
———. 2007. *Mark: A Commentary*. Hermeneia. Minneapolis: Fortress.
Collins, John J. 1998. *The Apocalyptic Imagination: An Introduction to Jewish Apocalyptic Literature*. Biblical Resource Series. Grand Rapids: Eerdmans.

———. 2005. *The Bible after Babel: Historical Criticism in a Postmodern Age*. Grand Rapids: Eerdmans.

Comaroff, Jean, and John Comaroff. 1991–1997. *Of Revelation and Revolution*. 2 vols. Chicago: University of Chicago Press.

Conrad, Joseph. 1985. *Heart of Darkness*. Repr., Penguin Classics. London: Penguin.

Cook, Albert B. 1990. Review of Herman C. Waetjen, *A Reordering of Power: A Socio-political Reading of Mark's Gospel*. *Christian Century* 107:376–77.

Cook, F. C. 1878. St. Mark's Gospel: Commentary and Critical Notes. Pages 199–308 in *The Holy Bible, According to the Authorized Version (A. D. 1611): With an Explanatory and Critical Commentary and a Revision of the Translation by Bishops and Other Clergy of the Anglican Church*. Edited by F. C. Cook. London: Clowes.

Cook, Richard B. 2003. Review of Troels Engberg-Pedersen, ed., *Paul beyond the Judaism/Hellenism Divide*. *Biblical Theology Bulletin* 33:169–71.

Cooley, Alison E. 2009. *Res Gestae Divi Augusti: Text, Translation, and Commentary*. Cambridge: Cambridge University Press.

Corbier, Mireille. 1991. City, Territory and Taxation. Pages 211–39 in *City and Country in the Ancient World*. Edited by John Rich and Andrew Wallace-Hadrill. London: Routledge.

Cranfield, C. E. B. 1959. *The Gospel According to Saint Mark: An Introduction and Commentary*. London: Cambridge University Press.

Crawford, M. H. 1978. Greek Intellectuals and the Roman Aristocracy in the First Century B.C. Pages 193–207 in *Imperialism in the Ancient World*. Edited by Peter Garnsey and Charles Richard Whittaker. Cambridge: Cambridge University Press.

Crossan, John Dominic. 1992. *The Historical Jesus: The Life of a Mediterranean Jewish Peasant*. New York: HarperOne.

———. 2007. *God and Empire: Jesus against Rome, Then and Now*. San Francisco: HarperSanFrancisco.

Crossan, John Dominic, and Jonathan L. Reed. 2004. *In Search of Paul: How Jesus's Apostle Opposed Rome's Empire with God's Kingdom: A New Vision of Paul's Words and World*. San Francisco: HarperSanFrancisco.

Crossley, James G. 2004. *The Date of Mark's Gospel: Insight from the Law in Earliest Christianity*. Journal for the Study of the New Testament Supplement Series 266. London: T&T Clark.

Cullmann, Oscar. 1970. *Jesus and the Revolutionaries*. Translated by Gareth Putnam. New York: Harper & Row.
Culpepper, R. Alan. 1983. *Anatomy of the Fourth Gospel: A Study in Literary Design*. Philadelphia: Fortress.
Dalman, Gustaf. 1909. *The Words of Jesus Considered in the Light of Postbiblical Jewish Writings and the Aramaic Language*. Translated by D. M. Kay. Edinburgh: T&T Clark.
Danker, Frederick W. 1982. *Benefactor: Epigraphic Study of a Graeco-Roman and New Testament Semantic Field*. St. Louis: Clayton.
Danove, Paul L. 1993. *The End of Mark's Story: A Methodological Study*. Biblical Interpretation Series 3. Leiden: Brill.
Davies, Andrew. 2000. *Double Standards in Isaiah: Re-evaluating Prophetic Ethics and Divine Justice*. Leiden: Brill.
Davies, Philip R. 1991. Daniel in the Lion's Den. Pages 160–78 in *Images of Empire*. Edited by Loveday Alexander. Journal for the Study of the Old Testament Supplement Series 122. Sheffield: Sheffield Academic Press.
Davies, Stevan L. 1995. *Jesus the Healer: Possession, Trance and the Origins of Christianity*. London: SCM.
Dawson, Anne. 2000. *Freedom as Liberating Power: A Socio-political Reading of the Exousia Texts in the Gospel of Mark*. Novum testamentum et orbis antiquus 44. Freiburg: Universitätsverlag.
De Ste. Croix, G. E. M. 1981. *The Class Struggle in the Ancient Greek World from the Archaic Age to the Arab Conquests*. London: Duckworth.
Deissmann, Adolf. 1901. *Bible Studies: Contributions Chiefly from Papyri and Inscriptions to the History of the Language, the Literature, and the Religion of Hellenistic Judaism and Primitive Christianity*. Translated by Alexander Grieve. Edinburgh: T&T Clark. Repr., Peabody, Mass.: Hendrickson, 1988.
———. 1910. *Light from the Ancient East: The New Testament Illustrated by Recently Discovered Texts of the Graeco-Roman World*. Translated by Lionel R. M. Strachan. London: Hodder & Stoughton. Repr., Grand Rapids: Baker, 1978.
Derow, Peter Sidney. 2003a. census. Page 308 in *Oxford Classical Dictionary*. Edited by Simon Hornblower and Antony Spawforth. 3rd ed. Oxford: Oxford University Press.
———. 2003b. imperium. Pages 751–52 in *Oxford Classical Dictionary*. Edited by Simon Hornblower and Antony Spawforth. 3rd ed. Oxford: Oxford University Press.

Derrett, J. Duncan M. 1970. *Law in the New Testament.* London: Darton, Longman & Todd.

———. 1971. Law in the New Testament: The Palm Sunday Colt. *Novum Testamentum* 13:241–58.

———. 1979. Contributions to the Study of the Gerasene Demoniac. *Journal for the Study of the New Testament* 3:2–17.

Derrida, Jacques. 1981. *Dissemination.* Chicago: University of Chicago Press.

———. 1982. *Margins of Philosophy.* Chicago: University of Chicago Press.

———. 1993. *Aporias.* Translated by Thomas Dutoit. Stanford: Stanford University Press.

———. 1997. *Of Grammatology.* Translated by Gayatri Chakravorty Spivak. Baltimore: Johns Hopkins University Press

———. 1998. Faith and Knowledge: The Two Sources of "Religion" at the Limits of Reason Alone. Pages 1–78 in *Religion.* Edited by Jacques Derrida and Gianni Vattimo. Cambridge: Polity.

———. 2002. Des Tours des Babel. Pages 102–34 in *Acts of Religion.* Edited by Gil Anidjar. New York: Routledge.

Dewey, Joanna. 2001. "Let Them Renounce Themselves and Take up Their Cross": A Feminist Reading of Mark 8:34 in Mark's Social and Narrative World. Pages 23–36 in *A Feminist Companion to Mark.* Edited by Amy-Jill Levine with Marianne Blickenstaff. Feminist Companion to the New Testament and Early Christian Writings 2. Sheffield: Sheffield Academic Press.

———. 2004. The Survival of Mark's Gospel: A Good Story? *Journal of Biblical Literature* 123:495–507.

———. 2008. The Gospel of Mark as Oral Hermeneutic. Pages 71–87 in *Jesus, the Voice, and the Text: Beyond the Oral and Written Gospel.* Edited by Tom Thatcher. Waco, Tex.: Baylor University Press.

Dittenberger, W., ed. 1903–1905. *Orientis graeci inscriptiones selectae.* 2 vols. Leipzig: Hirzel.

Donahue, John R., and Daniel J. Harrington. 2002. *The Gospel of Mark.* Sacra Pagina 2. Collegeville, Minn.: Liturgical Press.

Donaldson, Laura E. 1996a. Postcolonialism and Biblical Reading: An Introduction. *Semeia* 75:1–14.

———, ed. 1996b. *Postcolonialism and Scriptural Reading.* Semeia 75. Atlanta: Society of Biblical Literature.

———. 2005. Gospel Hauntings: The Postcolonial Demons of New Testament Criticism. Pages 97–113 in *Postcolonial Biblical Criticism: Inter-*

disciplinary Intersections. Edited by Stephen D. Moore and Fernando F. Segovia. Edinburgh: T&T Clark.

Donaldson, Laura E., and Kwok Pui-lan. 2002. *Postcolonialism, Feminism, and Religious Discourse*. London: Routledge.

Dormandy, Richard. 2000. The Expulsion of Legion: A Political Reading of Mark 5:1–20. *Expository Times* 111:335–37.

Draper, Jonathan A., ed. 2004a. *Orality, Literacy, and Colonialism in Antiquity*. Semeia Studies 47. Leiden: Brill.

———. 2004b. Orality, Literacy, and Colonialism in Antiquity. Pages 1–6 in *Orality, Literacy, and Colonialism in Antiquity*. Edited by Jonathan A. Draper. Leiden: Brill.

Dronsch, Kristina, and Annette Weissenrieder. 2010. A Theory of the Message for New Testament Writings or Communicating the Words of Jesus: From Angelos to Euangelion. Pages 205–35 in *The Interface of Orality and Writing: Speaking, Seeing, Writing in the Shaping of New Genres*. Edited by Annette Weissenrieder and Robert B. Coote. Wissenschaftliche Untersuchungen zum Neuen Testament 260. Tübingen: Mohr Siebeck.

Dube, Musa W. 1997. Toward a Postcolonial Feminist Interpretation of the Bible. *Semeia* 78:11–26.

———. 2000. *Postcolonial Feminist Interpretation of the Bible*. St. Louis: Chalice.

Dube, Musa W., and Jeffrey Lloyd Staley. 2002. *John and Postcolonialism: Travel, Space and Power*. Bible and Postcolonialism 7. London: Continuum.

Duff, Paul Brooks. 1992. The March of the Divine Warrior and the Advent of the Greco-Roman King: Mark's Account of Jesus' Entry into Jerusalem. *Journal of Biblical Literature* 111:55–71.

Duling, Dennis C. 2005. Empire: Theories, Methods, Models. Pages 49–74 in *The Gospel of Matthew in Its Roman Imperial Context*. Edited by John Riches and David C. Sim. London: T&T Clark.

Duran, Nicole Wilkinson, Teresa Okure, and Daniel Patte, eds. 2011. *Mark*. Texts @ Contexts. Minneapolis: Fortress.

Edmondson, Jonathan. 2010. Cities and Urban Life in the Western Provinces of the Roman Empire, 30 B.C.E.–250 C.E. Pages 250–80 in *A Companion to the Roman Empire*. Edited by David Stone Potter. Malden, Mass.: Blackwell.

Edwards, Catharine. 1993. *The Politics of Immorality in Ancient Rome*. Cambridge: Cambridge University Press.

Ehrenberg, Victor, and A. H. M. Jones. 1949. *Documents Illustrating the Reigns of Augustus and Tiberius*. Oxford: Clarendon.

Ehrman, Bart D. 1991. The Text of Mark in the Hands of the Orthodox. *Lutheran Quarterly* 5:143–56.

———. 1993. *The Orthodox Corruption of Scripture: The Effect of Early Christological Controversies on the Text of the New Testament*. New York: Oxford University Press.

Eitrem, S. 1966. *Some Notes on the Demonology in the New Testament*. Symbolae Osloenses Fasciculi suppletorii 20. Oslo: Universitetsforlaget.

Ekman, E. J. 1893. *Illustrerad missionshistoria efter nyaste källor*. 2 vols. Stockholm: Ekman.

Elliott, J. K. 1992. *Essays and Studies in New Testament Textual Criticism*. Estudios de Filologia Neotestamentaria 3. Cordoba: Ediciones el Almendro.

———. 2000. Mark 1.1–3—A Later Addition to the Gospel? *New Testament Studies* 46:584–88.

Elliott, John Hall. 1986. Social-scientific Criticism of the New Testament: More on Methods and Models. *Semeia* 35:1–33.

Elliott, Neil. 1995. *Liberating Paul: The Justice of God and the Politics of the Apostle*. Biblical Seminar 27. Sheffield: Sheffield Academic Press.

———. 2008. *The Arrogance of Nations: Reading Romans in the Shadow of Empire*. Paul in Critical Contexts. Minneapolis: Fortress.

Encyclopaedia Britannica. 1910–1911. 29 vols. 11th ed. Cambridge: Cambridge University Press.

Encyclopædia Britannica. 1969. 24 vols. 14th ed. Chicago: W. Benton.

Engberg-Pedersen, Troels, ed. 2001. *Paul beyond the Judaism/Hellenism Divide*. Louisville: Westminster John Knox Press.

———. 2003. Review of Richard Horlsey, *Hearing the Whole Story: The Politics of Plot in Mark's Gospel*. *Journal of Theological Studies* 54:230–45.

Epp, Eldon Jay. 1997. The Codex and Literacy in Early Christianity and at Oxyrhunchus: Issues Raised by Harry Y. Gamble's *Books and Readers in the Early Church*. *Critical Review of Books in Religion* 10:15–37.

Evans, Craig A. 2000a. *Mark 8:27–16:20*. Word Biblical Commentary 34B. Nashville: Nelson.

———. 2000b. Mark's Incipit and the Priene Calendar Inscription: From Jewish Gospel to Greco-Roman Gospel. *Journal of Greco-Roman Christianity and Judaism* 1:67–81.

Eve, Eric. 2008. Spit in Your Eye: The Blind Man of Bethsaida and the Blind Man of Alexandria. *New Testament Studies* 54:1–17.

Fanon, Frantz. 1967. *Black Skin, White Masks.* Translated by Charles Lam Markmann. New York: Grove.
———. 2004. *The Wretched of the Earth.* Translated by Richard Philcox. New York: Grove Press.
Feldman, Louis H. 1993. *Jew and Gentile in the Ancient World: Attitudes and Interactions from Alexander to Justinian.* Princeton: Princeton University Press.
Ferguson, Christopher. 2012. The Church and Empire. Pages 86–92 in *Challenging Empire: God, Faithfulness and Resistance.* Edited by Naim Ateek, Cedar Duaybis, and Maureen Tobin. Jerusalem: Sabeel Ecumenical Liberation Theology Center.
Fitzgerald, William. 2007. *Martial: The World of the Epigram.* Chicago: University of Chicago Press.
Fleming, Daniel E., and E. Badian. 1993. Tribute and Taxation. Pages 779–82 in *The Oxford Companion to the Bible.* Edited by Bruce M. Metzger and Michael D. Coogan. New York: Oxford University Press.
Forward, Martin. 2005. Paganism. Pages 7–10 in vol. 4 of *The Encyclopedia of Christianity.* Edited by Erwin Fahlbusch et al. Translated and edited by Geoffrey W. Bromiley. 5 vols. Grand Rapids: Eerdmans, 1999–2008.
Foucault, Michel. 1984. What Is an Author? Pages 101–20 in *The Foucault Reader.* Edited by Paul Rabinow. New York: Pantheon.
Fowler, Robert M. 1991. *Let the Reader Understand: Reader-Response Criticism and the Gospel of Mark.* Minneapolis: Fortress.
Fox, Kenneth A. 2003. Review of Troels Engberg-Pedersen, ed., *Paul beyond the Judaism/Hellenism Divide. Novum Testamentum* 45:80–83.
France, Richard Thomas. 2002. *The Gospel of Mark: A Commentary on the Greek Text.* New International Greek Testament Commentary. Grand Rapids: Eerdmans.
Frankfurter, David. 2010. Traditional Cult. Pages 543–64 in *A Companion to the Roman Empire.* Edited by David Stone Potter. Malden, Mass.: Blackwell.
Fredrickson, George M. 2002. *Racism: A Short History.* Princeton Princeton University Press.
Freedman, David Noel, ed. 1992. *Anchor Bible Dictionary.* 6 vols. New York: Doubleday.
Freeman, Philip. 1996. British Imperialism and the Roman Empire. Pages 19–34 in *Roman Imperialism: Post-colonial Perspectives.* Edited by Jane Webster and Nicholas J. Cooper. Leicester: School of Archaeological Studies, University of Leicester.

Friedrich, Gerhard. 1964. εὐαγγελίζομαι, κτλ. Pages 707–37 in vol. 2 of *Theological Dictionary of the New Testament*. Edited by Gerhard Kittel and Gerhard Friedrich. Translated by Geoffrey W. Bromiley. 10 vols. Grand Rapids: Eerdmans, 1964–1976.

Friesen, Steven J. 2004. Poverty in Pauline Studies: Beyond the So-called New Consensus. *Journal for the Study of the New Testament* 26:323–61.

Frostin, Per. 1994. *Luther's Two Kingdoms Doctrine: A Critical Study*. Studia Theologica Lundensia 48. Lund: Lund University Press.

Gallagher, Susan Vanzanten, ed. 1994a. *Postcolonial Literature and the Biblical Call for Justice*. Jackson: University Press of Mississippi.

———. 1994b. Introduction: New Conversations on Postcolonial Literature. Pages 3–33 in *Postcolonial Literature and the Biblical Call for Justice*. Edited by Susan Vanzanten Gallagher. Jackson: University Press of Mississippi.

Gamble, Harry Y. 1995. *Books and Readers in the Early Church: A History of Early Christian Texts*. New Haven: Yale University Press.

Gandhi, Leela. 1998. *Postcolonial Theory: A Critical Introduction*. Edinburgh: Edinburgh University Press.

Garnsey, Peter, and Richard Saller. 1997. Patronal Power Relations. Pages 96–103 in *Paul and Empire: Religion and Power in Roman Imperial Society*. Edited by Richard A. Horsley. Harrisburg, Pa.: Trinity Press International.

Garroway, Joshua. 2009. The Invasion of a Mustard Seed: A Reading of Mark 5.1–20. *Journal for the Study of the New Testament* 32:57–75.

Genette, Gérard. 1995. *Mimologics*. Translated by Thaïs E. Morgan. Lincoln: University of Nebraska.

Gerdmar, Anders. 2001. *Rethinking the Judaism-Hellenism Dichotomy: A Historiographical Case Study of Second Peter and Jude*. Coniectanea biblica: New Testament Series 36. Stockholm: Almqvist & Wiksell International.

———. 2005. Review of Troels Engberg-Pedersen, ed., *Paul beyond the Judaism/Hellenism Divide*. *Biblical Interpretation* 13:80–83.

Gibbon, Edward. 1776–1789. *The History of the Decline and Fall of the Roman Empire*. 6 vols. London: Strahan.

Gilfillan Upton, Bridget. 2006. *Hearing Mark's Endings: Listening to Ancient Popular Texts through Speech Act Theory*. Biblical Interpretation Series 79. Leiden: Brill.

Gish, Steven D. 2004. *Desmond Tutu: A Biography*. Greenwood Biographies. Westport, Conn.: Greenwood.

Glancy, Jennifer A. 2002. *Slavery in Early Christianity*. New York: Oxford University Press.

Gleason, Maud W. 1995. *Making Men: Sophist and Self-presentation in Ancient Rome*. Princeton: Princeton University Press.

———. 2003. By Whose Gender Standards (If Anybody's) Was Jesus a Real Man? Pages 325–27 in *New Testament Masculinities*. Edited by Stephen D. Moore and Janice Capel Anderson. Atlanta: Society of Biblical Literature.

Globe, Alexander. 1982. The Ceasarean Omission of the Phrase "son of God" in Mark 1:1. *Harvard Theological Review* 75:209–18.

Gnilka, Joachim. 1978. *Das Evangelium nach Markus (Mk 1–8,26)*. Evangelisch-katholischer Kommentar zum Neuen Testament 2.1. Zurich: Benziger.

———. 1979. *Das Evangelium nach Markus (Mk 8,27–16,20)*. Evangelisch-katholischer Kommentar zum Neuen Testament 2.2. Zurich: Benziger.

Godard, Barbara. 1993. Intertextuality. In *Encyclopedia of Contemporary Literary Theory: Approaches, Scholars, Terms*. Edited by Irena R. Makaryk. Toronto: University of Toronto Press.

Goldschmid, Léopold. 1897. Les impots et droits de douane en Judée sous les Romains. *Revue des études juives* 34:192–217.

Goodblatt, David M. 2006. *Elements of Ancient Jewish Nationalism*. Cambridge: Cambridge University Press.

Goodman, Martin. 1991. Opponents of Rome: Jews and Others. Pages 222–38 in *Images of Empire*. Edited by Loveday Alexander. Journal for the Study of the Old Testament Supplement Series 122. Sheffield: Sheffield Academic Press.

Göteborgs stads stadsledningskontor. 2010. Göteborgsbladet 2010: områdesfakta. Published annually by Samhällsanalys och Statistik. Online: http://www4.goteborg.se/prod/G-info/statistik.nsf/3a1ad610 2b0c4f0ac1256cdf004881c0/838ccf75c7addfafc12578d1004ce939 /$FILE/SDN%20131%20Angered%20+%20PRI%202010.pdf.

Göteborgsposten, Ledarredaktionen. 2004. "Driv inte politik i kyrkans namn!" *GöteborgsPosten*, May 13.

Gould, Ezra P. 1896. *A Critical and Exegetical Commentary on the Gospel According to St. Mark*. International Critical Commentary. New York: Scribner's.

Gradel, Ittai. 2002. *Emperor Worship and Roman Religion*. Oxford Classical Monographs. Oxford: Clarendon.

Gramsci, Antonio. 2001. *Selections from the Prison Notebooks of Antonio Gramsci*. London: Electric Book. Online: http://site.ebrary.com/lib/gubselibrary/Doc?id=10015105.

Green, Joel B., and Scot McKnight, eds. 1992. *Dictionary of Jesus and the Gospels*. Downers Grove, Ill.: InterVarsity Press.

Grenfell, B. P., et al. 1898–2010. *The Oxyrhynchus Papyri*. London: Egypt Exploration Society in Graeco-Roman Memoirs.

Griffin, Miriam. 1991. Urbs Roma, Plebs and Princeps. Pages 19–46 in *Images of Empire*. Edited by Loveday Alexander. Journal for the Study of the Old Testament Supplement Series 122. Sheffield: Sheffield Academic Press.

Griffiths, Gareth. 2005. Popular Imperial Adventure Fiction and the Discource of Missionary Texts. Pages 51–66 in *Mixed Messages: Materiality, Textuality, and Missions*. Edited by Jamie S. Scott and Gareth Griffiths. New York: Palgrave Macmillan.

Gruen, Erich S. 1984. *The Hellenistic World and the Coming of Rome*. Vol. 1 of. 2 vols. Berkeley: University of California Press.

Guelich, Robert A. 1989. *Mark 1–8:26*. Word Biblical Commentary 34A. Dallas: Word Books.

Gundry, Robert H. 1993. *Mark: A Commentary on His Apology for the Cross*. Grand Rapids: Eerdmans.

———. 2003. Richard A. Horsley's *Hearing the Whole Story*: A Critical Review of Its Postcolonial Slant. *Journal for the Study of the New Testament* 26:131–49.

Haines-Eitzen, Kim. 2000. *Guardians of Letters: Literacy, Power, and the Transmitters of Early Christian Literature*. New York: Oxford University Press.

Hall, Stuart. 1996. When Was "the Post-Colonial"? Thinking at the Limit. Pages 242–60 in *The Post-colonial Question: Common Skies, Divided Horizons*. Edited by Iain Chambers and Lidia Curti. New York: Routledge.

Hamerton-Kelly, Robert. 1994. *The Gospel and the Sacred: Poetics of Violence in Mark*. Minneapolis: Fortress.

Han, Jin Hee. 2005. Homi K. Bhabha and the Mixed Blessing of Hybridity in Biblical Hermeneutics. *The Bible and Critical Theory* 1, no. 4:37.1–12.

Hansen, Holger Bernt. 2002. The Colonial State's Policy towards Foreign Missions in Uganda. Pages 157–75 in *Christian Missionaries and the*

State in the Third World. Edited by Holger Bernt Hansen and Michael Twaddle. Oxford: James Currey.

Hansen, Thorkild. 2000. *Det lyckliga Arabien: En forskningsfärd 1761–1767.* Translated by Olof Hoffsten. Stockholm: En bok för alla.

Hanson, Paul D. 1992. Apocalypses and Apocalypticism: The Genre. Pages 279–80 in vol. 1 of *Anchor Bible Dictionary.* Edited by David Noel Freedman. 6 vols. New York: Doubleday.

Hanson, W. S. 1997. Forces of Change and Methods of Control. In *Dialogues in Roman Imperialism: Power Discourse, and Discrepant Experience in the Roman Empire.* Edited by D. J. Mattingly. Portsmouth, R.I.: JRA.

Harrington, Daniel J. 1998. Catholic Interpretation of Scripture. Pages 29–59 in *The Bible in the Churches: How Various Christians Interpret the Scriptures.* Edited by Kenneth Hagen. Milwaukee: Marquette University Press.

———. 1993. The Gospel According to Mark. Pages 596–629 in *The New Jerome Biblical Commentary.* Edited by Raymond E. Brown, Joseph A. Fitzmyer, and Roland E. Murphy. London: Chapman.

Harris, William V. 1989. *Ancient Literacy.* Cambridge: Harvard University Press.

Harrison, Dick. 2010. Irland. *Nationalencyklopedin.* Online: http://www.ne.se.ezproxy.ub.gu.se/lang/irland/213284.

Hartman, Lars. 2004. *Markusevangeliet 1:1–8:26.* Kommentar till Nya testamentet 2A. Stockholm: EFS-förlaget.

———. 2005. *Markusevangeliet 8:27–16:20.* Kommentar till Nya testamentet 2B. Stockholm: EFS-förlaget.

Head, Ivan. 2004. Mark as a Roman Document from the Year 69: Testing Martin Hengel's Thesis. *Journal of Religious History* 28:240–59.

Head, Peter M. 1991. A Text-Critical Study of Mark 1:1: "The Beginning of the Gospel of Jesus Christ." *New Testament Studies* 37:621–29.

Hearon, Holly E. 2006. The Implications of Orality for Studies of the Biblical Text. Pages 3–20 in *Performing the Gospel: Orality, Memory, and Mark.* Edited by Richard A. Horsley, Jonathan A. Draper, and John Miles Foley. Minneapolis: Fortress.

———. 2008. Storytelling in Oral and Written Media Contexts of the Ancient Mediterranean World. Pages 89–110 in *Jesus, the Voice, and the Text: Beyond the Oral and Written Gospel.* Edited by Tom Thatcher. Waco, Tex.: Baylor University Press.

Hengel, Martin. 1971. *Was Jesus a Revolutionist?* Translated by William Klassen. Facet Books, Biblical Series 28. Philadelphia: Fortress.

———. 1977. *Crucifixion in the Ancient World and the Folly of the Message of the Cross.* London: SCM.

———. 1981. *Judaism and Hellenism: Studies in Their Encounter in Palestine during the Early Hellenistic Period.* London: SCM.

———. 1985. *Studies in the Gospel of Mark.* London: SCM.

———. 1986. *The Cross of the Son of God: Containing The Son of God, Crucifixion, The Atonement.* London: SCM.

———. 1989. *The Zealots: Investigations into the Jewish Freedom Movement in the Period from Herod I until 70 A.D.* Translated by David Smith. Edinburgh: T&T Clark.

———. 2000. *The Four Gospels and the One Gospel of Jesus Christ: An Investigation of the Collection and Origin of the Canonical Gospels.* Harrisburg, Pa.: Trinity Press International.

Herzog II, William R. 1994. Dissembling, A Weapon of the Weak: The Case of Christ and Caesar in Mark 12:13–17 and Romans 13:1–7. *Perspectives in Religious Studies* 21:339–60.

Hess, Jonathan M. 2000. Johann David Michaelis and the Colonial Imaginary: Orientalism and the Emergence of Racial Antisemitism in Eighteenth-Century Germany. *Jewish Social Studies* 6, no. 2:56–101.

Hidal, Sten. 1979. *Bibeltro och bibelkritik: Studier kring den historisk-kritiska bibelsynens genombrott i Sverige 1877–1910 med särskild hänsyn till Gamla testamentet.* Lund: Verbum.

Hingley, Richard. 1996. The "Legacy" of Rome: The Rise, Decline, and Fall of the Theory of Romanization. Pages 35–48 in *Roman Imperialism: Post-colonial Perspectives.* Edited by Jane Webster and Nicholas J. Cooper. Leicester: School of Archaeological Studies, University of Leicester.

Hodgkins, Christopher. 2002. *Reforming Empire: Protestant Colonialism and Conscience in British Literature.* Columbia: University of Missouri Press.

Hoelzl, Michael, and Graham Ward. 2008. Introduction. Pages 1–11 in *The New Visibility of Religion: Studies in Religion and Cultural Hermeneutics.* Edited by Michael Hoelzl and Graham Ward. London: Continuum.

Hollenbach, Paul W. 1981. Jesus, Demoniacs, and Public Authorities: A Socio-historical Study. *Journal of the American Academy of Religion* 49:567–88.

Holmberg, Bengt. 1990. *Sociology and the New Testament: An Appraisal.* Minneapolis: Fortress.
Holtzmann, Heinrich Julius. 1892. *Die Synoptiker. Die Apostelgeschichte.* Vol. 1 of *Hand-Commentar zum Neuen Testament.* Freiburg-im-Breisgau: Mohr.
Hooker, Morna D. 1991. *A Commentary on the Gospel According to St Mark.* Black's New Testament Commentaries. London: Black.
Hopkinson, Michael. 2009. Parnell, Charles Stewart. *The Oxford Companion to British History,* http://www.oxfordreference.com.ezproxy.ub.gu.se/views/ENTRY.html?subview=Main&entry=t110.e3285.
Hornblower, Simon, and Antony Spawforth, eds. 2003. *Oxford Classical Dictionary.* 3rd ed. rev. Oxford: Oxford University Press.
Horrell, David. 2003. Review of Troels Engberg-Pedersen, ed., *Paul beyond the Judaism/Hellenism Divide. Journal of Theological Studies* 54:717–20.
Horsley, G. H. R. 1981. *New Documents Illustrating Early Christianity: A Review of Greek Inscriptions and Papyri Published in 1976.* Sydney: Macquarie University Press.
———. 1983. *New Documents Illustrating Early Christianity: A Review of the Greek Inscriptions and Papyri Published in 1978.* North Ryde: Macquarie University.
Horsley, Richard A. 1993. *Jesus and the Spiral of Violence: Popular Jewish Resistance in Roman Palestine.* San Francisco: Harper & Row, 1987. Repr., Minneapolis: Fortress.
———. 1997. *Paul and Empire: Religion and Power in Roman Imperial Society.* Harrisburg, Pa.: Trinity Press International.
———. 2001. *Hearing the Whole Story: The Politics of Plot in Mark's Gospel.* Louisville: Westminster John Knox.
———. 2003a. *Jesus and Empire: The Kingdom of God and the New World Disorder.* Minneapolis: Fortress.
———. 2003b. Subverting Disciplines: The Possibilities and Limitations of Postcolonial Theory for New Testament Studies. Pages 90–105 in *Toward a New Heaven and a New Earth.* Maryknoll, N.Y.: Orbis.
———. 2006. A Prophet like Moses and Elijah: Popular Memory and Cultural Patterns in Mark. Pages 166–92 in *Performing the Gospel: Orality, Memory, and Mark.* Edited by Richard A. Horsley, Jonathan A. Draper, and John Miles Foley. Minneapolis: Fortress.
———. 2008. Oral Performance and Mark: Some Implications of The Oral and the Written Gospel, Twenty Years Later. Pages 45–70 in *Jesus, the*

Voice, and the Text: Beyond the Oral and Written Gospel. Edited by Tom Thatcher. Waco, Tex.: Baylor University Press.

Horsley, Richard A., Jonathan A. Draper, and John Miles Foley, eds. 2006. *Performing the Gospel: Orality, Memory, and Mark.* Minneapolis: Fortress.

Howard-Brook, Wes, and Anthony Gwyther. 1999. *Unveiling Empire: Reading Revelation Then and Now.* Maryknoll, N.Y.: Orbis.

Huddart, David. 2006. *Homi K. Bhabha.* Routledge Critical Thinkers. London: Routledge.

Hulme, Peter. 1985. Polytropic Man: Tropes of Sexuality and Mobility in Early Colonial Discourse. Pages 17–32 in vol. 2 of *Europe and Its Others.* Edited by Francis Barker, Peter Hulme, Margaret Iversen, and Diana Loxley. 2 vols. Colchester: University of Essex.

Iersel, Bas van. 1998. *Mark: A Reader-Response Commentary.* Journal for the Study of the New Testament Supplement Series 164. Sheffield: Sheffield Academic Press.

Incigneri, Brian J. 2003. *The Gospel to the Romans: The Setting and Rhetoric of Mark's Gospel.* Biblical Interpretation Series 65. Leiden: Brill.

Jacobson, David M. 1999. Palestine and Israel. *Bulletin of the American Schools of Oriental Research* 313:65–74.

Jastrow, Marcus. 1992. *A Dictionary of the Targumim, the Talmud Babli and Yerushalmi, and the Midrashic Literature.* New York: Putnam, 1903. Repr., New York: Judaica.

Johnson, Earl S. 1987. Is Mark 15:39 the Key to Mark's Christology? *Journal for the Study of the New Testament* 31:3–22.

Jørgensen, Marianne, and Louise J. Phillips. 2002. *Discourse Analysis as Theory and Method.* London: Sage.

Joy, David. 2008. *Mark and Its Subalterns: A Hermeneutical Paradigm for a Postcolonial Context.* Bible World. London: Equinox.

Judge, E. A. 1981. The Regional *kanon* for Requisitioned Transport. Pages 36–45 in *New Documents Illustrating Early Christianity: A Review of Greek Inscriptions and Papyri Published in 1976.* Edited by G. H. R. Horsley. Sydney: Macquarie University Press.

Kahl, Brigitte. 2010. *Galatians Re-imagined: Reading with the Eyes of the Vanquished.* Paul in Critical Contexts. Minneapolis: Fortress.

Kautsky, John H. 1982. *The Politics of Aristocratic Empires.* Chapel Hill: University of North Carolina Press.

Keck, Leander E. 1966. Introduction to Mark's Gospel. *New Testament Studies* 12:352–70.

Kee, Howard Clark. 1983. *Community of the New Age: Studies in Mark's Gospel.* Macon, Ga.: Mercer University Press.
Kelber, Werner H. 1979. *Mark's Story of Jesus.* Philadelphia: Fortress.
———. 1997. *The Oral and the Written Gospel: The Hermeneutics of Speaking and Writing in the Synoptic Tradition, Mark, Paul, and Q.* Philadelphia: Fortress, 1983. Repr., Voices in Performance and Text. Bloomington: Indiana University Press.
———. 2004. Roman Imperialism and Early Christian Scribality. Pages 135–54 in *Orality, Literacy, and Colonialism in Antiquity.* Edited by Jonathan A. Draper. Leiden: Brill.
Kelber, Werner H., and Samuel Byrskog, eds. 2009. *Jesus in Memory: Traditions in Oral and Scribal Perspectives.* Waco, Tex.: Baylor University Press.
Kelley, Shawn. 2002. *Racializing Jesus: Race, Ideology, and the Formation of Modern Biblical Scholarship.* Biblical limits. London: Routledge.
Kennedy, David. 1992. Roman Army. Pages 789–98 in vol. 5 of *Anchor Bible Dictionary.* Edited by David Noel Freedman. 6 vols. New York: Doubleday.
Kenyon, Frederic George. 1949. Books, Greek and Latin. Pages 141–43 in *Oxford Classical Dictionary.* Edited by M. Cary et al. 2nd ed. Oxford: Clarendon.
Kim, Tae Hun. 1998. The Anarthrous υἱὸς θεοῦ in Mark 15,39 and the Roman Imperial Cult. *Biblica* 79:221–41.
Kinman, Brent. 1999. Parousia, Jesus' "A-Triumphal" Entry, and the Fate of Jerusalem (Luke 19:28–44). *Journal of Biblical Literature* 118:279–94.
Kittel, Gerhard, and Gerhard Friedrich, eds. 1964–1976. *Theological Dictionary of the New Testament.* Translated by G. W. Bromiley. 10 vols. Grand Rapids: Eerdmans.
Klausner, Joseph. 1925. *Jesus of Nazareth: His Life, Times, and Teaching.* Translated by Herbert Danby. London: Allen & Unwin.
Klein, Ernest David. 1987. *A Comprehensive Etymological Dictionary of the Hebrew Language for Readers of English.* New York: Macmillan.
Klink, Edward W. 2004. The Gospel Community Debate: State of the Question. *Currents in Biblical Research* 3:60–85.
———. 2010a. Conclusion: The Origin and Function of the Gospels in Early Christianity. Pages 153–66 in *The Audience of the Gospels: The Origin and Function of the Gospels in Early Christianity.* Edited by Edward W. Klink. London: T&T Clark.

———. 2010b. Gospel Audience and Origin: The Current Debate. Pages 1–26 in *The Audience of the Gospels: The Origin and Function of the Gospels in Early Christianity*. Edited by Edward W. Klink. London: T&T Clark.

Kloppenborg, John S. 2005. Evocatio deorum and the Date of Mark. *Journal of Biblical Literature* 124:419–50.

Klostermann, August. 1867. *Das Markusevangelium nach seinem Quellenwerthe für die evangelische Geschichte*. Göttingen: Vandenhoeck & Ruprecht.

Koester, Helmut. 1990. *Ancient Christian Gospels: Their History and Development*. London: SCM.

König, Jason, and Tim Whitmarsh, eds. 2007. *Ordering Knowledge in the Roman Empire*. Cambridge: Cambridge University Press.

Kumar, Amitava. 1997. Catachresis Is Her Middle Name: The Cautionary Claims of Gayatri C. Spivak. *Cultural Studies* 11:176–79.

Kümmel, Werner Georg. 1972. *The New Testament: The History of the Investigation of Its Problems*. Nashville: Abingdon.

———. 1975. *Introduction to the New Testament*. London: SCM.

Kwok Pui-lan, 1995. *Discovering the Bible in the Non-biblical World*. Bible and Liberation. Maryknoll, N.Y.: Orbis.

———. 1998a. Jesus/The Native: Biblical Studies from a Postcolonial Perspective. Pages 69–85 in *Teaching the Bible: The Discourses and Politics of Biblical Pedagogy*. Edited by Fernando F. Segovia and Mary Ann Tolbert. Maryknoll, N.Y.: Orbis.

———. 1998b. On Color-Coding Jesus: An Interview with Kwok Pui-lan. Pages 176–88 in *The Postcolonial Bible*. Edited by R. S. Sugirtharajah. Sheffield: Sheffield Academic Press.

———. 2005. *Postcolonial Imagination and Feminist Theology*. London: SCM.

———. 2006. Making the Connections: Postcolonial Studies and Feminist Biblical Interpretation. Pages 45–63 in *The Postcolonial Biblical Reader*. Edited by R. S. Sugirtharajah. Malden, Mass.: Blackwell.

Laclau, Ernesto. 1990. *New Reflections on the Revolution of Our Time*. London: Verso.

———. 1993. Power and Representation. Pages 277–96 in *Politics, Theory, and Contemporary Culture*. Edited by Mark Poster. New York: Columbia University Press.

Laclau, Ernesto, and Chantal Mouffe. 1987. Post-Marxism without Apologies. *New Left Review* 166:79–106.

———. 2001. *Hegemony and Socialist Strategy: Towards a Radical Democratic Politics*. London: Verso.
Lampe, Peter. 2003. *From Paul to Valentinus: Christians at Rome in the First Two Centuries*. London: T&T Clark.
Landgren, Lars. 1871. *Öfversigt af de Protestaniska missionernes uppkomst och närmare tillstånd*. Vol. 1 of. 2 vols. Hudiksvall: Fam. Hellströms förlag.
Lane, William L. 1974. *The Gospel according to Mark: The English Text with Introduction, Exposition, and Notes*. New International Commentary on the New Testament. Grand Rapids: Eerdmans.
Lange, Johann Peter. 1857. *Das Evangelium nach Matthäus*. Theologisch-homiletisches Bibelwerk. Die Heilige Schrift. Des Neuen Testamentes 1. Bielefeld: Velhagen und Klasing.
———. 1858. *Das Evangelium nach Markus*. Theologisch-homiletisches Bibelwerk. Die Heilige Schrift. Des Neuen Testamentes 2. Bielefeld: Velhagen und Klasing.
———. 1865. *The Gospel According to Matthew*. Translated by Philip Schaff. Commentary on the Holy Scriptures: Critical, Doctrinal and Homiletical 1A. New York: Scribner's.
———. 1866. *The Gospel According to Mark*. Translated by William Shedd. Commentary on the Holy Scriptures: Critical, Doctrinal and Homiletical 2. New York: Scribner's.
Lange, N. R. M. de. 1978. Jewish Attitudes to the Roman Empire. Pages 255–81 in *Imperialism in the Ancient World*. Edited by Peter Garnsey and Charles Richard Whittaker. Cambridge: Cambridge University Press.
Lau, M. 2007. Die Legio X Fretensis und der Besessene von Gerasa. Anmerkungen zur Zahlenangabe "ungefähr Zweitausend" (Mk 5,13). *Biblica* 88:351–64.
Leander, Hans. 2010. With Homi Bhabha at the Jerusalem City Gates: A Postcolonial Reading of the "Triumphant" Entry (Mark 11:1–11). *Journal for the Study of the New Testament* 32:309–35.
Lefkowitz, Mary R., and Guy MacLean Rogers. 1996. *Black Athena Revisited*. Chapel Hill: University of North Carolina Press.
Lenski, Gerhard E. 1966. *Power and Privilege: A Theory of Social Stratification*. McGraw-Hill Series in Sociology. New York: McGraw-Hill.
Leslie, James B. 1911. *Armagh Clergy and Parishes: Being an Account of the Clergy of the Church of Ireland in the Diocese of Armagh, from the*

Earilest Period, with Historical Notices of the Several Parishes, Churches, &c. Dundalk: William Tempest.

Levine, Amy-Jill. 1993. Gentile. Pages 249–50 in *The Oxford Companion to the Bible*. Edited by Bruce M. Metzger and Michael D. Coogan. New York: Oxford University Press.

Lewis, I. M. 2003. *Ecstatic Religion: A Study of Shamanism and Spirit Possession*. London: Routledge.

Liddell, H. G., and R. Scott. 1972. *An Intermediate Greek-English Lexicon*. Repr., Oxford: Clarendon.

Liddell, H. G., R. Scott, and H. S. Jones, eds. 1996. *A Greek-English Lexicon*. 9th ed. With a revised supplement edited by P. G. W. Glare. Oxford: Clarendon.

Liew, Tat-siong Benny. 1999a. *Politics of Parousia: Reading Mark Inter(con)textually*. Biblical Interpretation Series 42. Leiden: Brill.

———. 1999b. Tyranny, Boundary and Might: Colonial Mimicry in Mark's Gospel. *Journal for the Study of the New Testament* 73:7–31.

———. 2008. Postcolonial Criticism: Echoes of a Subaltern's Contribution and Exclusion. Pages 211–31 in *Mark and Method: New Approaches in Biblical Studies*. Edited by Janice Capel Anderson and Stephen D. Moore. Minneapolis: Fortress.

———. 2005. *Colonialism/Postcolonialism*. New Critical Idiom. 2nd ed. London: Routledge.

———. 2007. Mark. Pages 105–32 in *A Postcolonial Commentary on the New Testament Writings*. Edited by Fernando F. Segovia and R. S. Sugirtharajah. London: T&T Clark.Linder, N., ed. 1876–1899. *Nordisk familjebok*. 20 vols. Stockholm: Expeditionen af Nordisk familjebok. Online: http://runeberg.org/nfaa/.

Linderski, Jerzy. 2003. Lustration. Page 893 in *Oxford Classical Dictionary*. Edited by Simon Hornblower and Antony Spawforth. 3rd ed. rev. Oxford: Oxford University Press.

Longenecker, Bruce W. 2009. Exposing the Economic Middle: A Revised Economy Scale for the Study of Early Urban Christianity. *Journal for the Study of the New Testament* 31:243–78.

Loomba, Ania. 2005. *Colonialism/Postcolonialism*. New Critical Idiom. London: Routledge.

Lopez, Davina C. 2008. *Apostle to the Conquered: Reimagining Paul's Mission*. Paul in Critical Contexts. Minneapolis: Fortress.

Lorenzoni, Patricia. 2007. *Att färdas under dödens tecken: Frazer, imperiet

och den försvinnande vilden. Göteborg: Göteborgs universitet, Institutionen för idéhistoriaoch vetenskapsteori.
Luckock, Herbert Mortimer. 1902. *Footprints of the Son of Man as Traced by Saint Mark: Being Eighty Portions for Private Study, Family Reading, and Instructions in Church.* London: Longmans, Green.
Lundqvist, Johanna. 2011. Kyrkan ska hålla sig borta från partipolitik. *Kyrkans tidning* June 22. Online: http://www.kyrkanstidning.se/nyhet/kyrkan-ska-halla-sig-borta-fran-partipolitik.
Luther, Martin. 1983. Second Sunday in Lent (Reminiscere). Pages 148–54 in vol. 2 of *Sermons of Martin Luther.* Edited by John Nicholas Lenker. 8 vols. Repr., Grand Rapids: Baker.
Macfie, A. L. 2002. *Orientalism.* London: Longman.
Maclear, G. F. 1883. *The Gospel According to St Mark, with Maps, Notes and Introduction.* Cambridge Greek Testament for Schools and Colleges. Cambridge: Cambridge University Press.
MacMullen, Ramsay. 1963. *Soldier and Civilian in the Later Roman Empire.* Harvard Historical Monographs 52. Cambridge: Harvard University Press.
———. 2000. *Romanization in the Time of Augustus.* New Haven: Yale University Press.
Majeke, Nosipho. 1952. *The Role of the Missionaries in Conquest.* Johannesburg: Society of Young Africa.
Makaryk, Irena R., ed. 1993. *Encyclopedia of Contemporary Literary Theory: Approaches, Scholars, Terms.* Toronto: University of Toronto Press.
Malbon, Elizabeth Struthers. 2008. Narrative Criticism: How Does the Story Mean? Pages 29–57 in *Mark and Method: New Approaches in Biblical Studies.* Edited by Janice Capel Anderson and Stephen D. Moore. Minneapolis: Fortress.
Malherbe, Abraham J. 1983. *Social Aspects of Early Christianity.* Philadelphia: Fortress.
Malina, Bruce J. 2001. *The Social Gospel of Jesus: The Kingdom of God in Mediterranean Perspective.* Minneapolis: Fortress.
Malina, Bruce J., and Richard L. Rohrbaugh. 1992. *Social Science Commentary on the Synoptic Gospels.* Minneapolis: Fortress.
Marchal, Joseph A. 2006. Imperial Intersections and Initial Inquiries: Toward a Feminist, Postcolonial Analysis of Philippians. *Journal of Feminist Studies in Religion* 22, no. 2:5–32.

———. 2008. *The Politics of Heaven*. Paul in Critical Contexts. Minneapolis: Fortress.

Marchand, Suzanne L. 2009. *German Orientalism in the Age of Empire: Religion, Race, and Scholarship*. Cambridge: Cambridge University Press.

Marcus, Joel. 1992. The Jewish War and the Sitz im Leben of Mark. *Journal of Biblical Literature* 111:441–62.

———. 2000. *Mark 1–8: A New Translation with Introduction and Commentary*. Anchor Bible 27. New York: Doubleday.

———. 2009. *Mark 8–16: A New Translation with Introduction and Commentary*. Anchor Yale Bible 27A. New Haven: Yale University Press.

Marrow, Stanley B. 2002. Review of Troels Engberg-Pedersen, ed., *Paul beyond the Judaism/Hellenism Divide*. *Catholic Biblical Quarterly* 64:799–801.

Marshall, Henrietta Elizabeth. 1920. *An Island Story: A History of England for Boys and Girls*. New York: Stokes.

Marxsen, Willi. 1969. *Mark the Evangelist: Studies on the Redaction History of the Gospel*. Translated by James Boyce, Donald Juel, and William Poehlmann, with Roy A. Harrisville. Nashville: Abingdon.

Matera, Frank J. 1988. The Prologue as the Interpretative Key to Mark's Gospel. *Journal for the Study of the New Testament* 34:3–20.

Matthews, John. 2010. Roman Law and Roman History. Pages 477–91 in *A Companion to the Roman Empire*. Edited by David Stone Potter. Malden, Mass.: Blackwell.

Mattingly, David J. 1996. From One Colonialism to Another: Imperialism and the Maghreb. Pages 49–70 in *Roman Imperialism: Post-colonial Perspectives*. Edited by Jane Webster and Nicholas J. Cooper. Leicester: School of Archaeological Studies, University of Leicester.

———. 1997. Introduction: Dialogues of Power and Experience in the Roman Empire. Pages 7–24 in *Dialogues in Roman Imperialism: Power, Discourse, and Discrepant Experience in the Roman Empire*. Edited by D. J. Mattingly. Portsmouth, R.I.: JRA.

McClintock, Anne. 1995. *Imperial Leather: Race, Gender and Sexuality in the Colonial Contest*. London: Routledge.

McDowell, R. B. 1975. *The Church of Ireland 1869–1969*. Studies in Irish History, Second Series. London: Routledge & Kegan Paul.

McHoul, Alec, and Wendy Grace. 1995. *A Foucault Primer: Discourse, Power, and the Subject*. Melbourne: Melbourne University Press, 1993. Repr., London: UCL Press.

McLaren, James S. 2005. A Reluctant Provincial: Josephus and the Roman Empire in Jewish War. Pages 34–48 in *The Gospel of Matthew in Its Roman Imperial Context*. Edited by John Riches and David C. Sim. London: T&T Clark.

McLuhan, Marshall. 1964. *Understanding Media: The Extensions of Man*. London: Routledge & Kegan Paul.

McRay, John. 1992. Gerasenes. Pages 991–92 in vol. 2 of *Anchor Bible Dictionary*. Edited by David Noel Freedman. 6 vols. New York: Doubleday.

Meeks, Wayne A. 1983. *The First Urban Christians: The Social World of the Apostle Paul*. New Haven: Yale University Press.

Menzies, Allan. 1901. *The Earliest Gospel: A Historical Study of the Gospel According to Mark*. London: Macmillan.

Meyer, Heinrich August Wilhelm. 1832. *Kritisch exegetisches Handbuch über die Evangelien des Matthäus, Markus und Lukas*. Göttingen: Vandenhoeck & Ruprecht.

———. 1858. *Das Neue Testament Griechisch, das Evangelium des Matthäus*. Göttingen: Vandenhoeck & Ruprecht.

———. 1867. *Kritisch exegetisches Handbuch über die Evangelien des Markus und Lukas*. Göttingen: Vandenhoeck & Ruprecht.

———. 1880–1881. *Critical and Exegetical Handbook to the Gospel of Matthew*. Translated by Peter Christie. 2 vols. Critical and Exegetical Commentary on the New Testament. Edinburgh: T&T Clark.

———. 1884. *Critical and Exegetical Handbook to the Gospels of Mark and Luke*. Translated by Robert Ernest Wallis. Critical and Exegetical Commentary on the New Testament. New York: Funk & Wagnalls.

Meyers, Carol. 1992. Temple, Jerusalem. Pages 350–69 in vol. 6 of *Anchor Bible Dictionary*. Edited by David Noel Freedman. 6 vols. New York: Doubleday.

Michel, Otto. 1965. κύων, κυνάριον. Pages 1101–4 in vol. 3 of *Theological Dictionary of the New Testament*. Edited by Gerhard Kittel and Gerhard Friedrich. Translated by Geoffrey W. Bromiley. 10 vols. Grand Rapids: Eerdmans, 1964–1976.

Michaelis, Johann David. 1782. Recensionen. Ueber die burgerliche Verbesserung der Juden von Christian Wilhelm Dohm. Pages 1–40 in vol. 19 of *Orientalische und exegetische Bibliothek*. Frankfurt am Mayn: Johann Gottlieb Garbe.

———. 1793. *Mosaisches Recht*. Vol. 1 of 6. 2nd ed. Reutlingen: Johannes Grözinger, 1788–1793.

Millard, Alan Ralph. 2000. *Reading and Writing in the Time of Jesus*. New York: New York University Press.

Miller, Robert J. 1991. A Reordering of Power: A Socio-political Reading of Mark's Gospel. *Catholic Biblical Quarterly* 53:352–54.

Mitchell, M. M. 2005. Patristic Counter-evidence to the Claim That "The Gospels Were Written for All Christians." *New Testament Studies* 51:36–79.

Mitternacht, Dieter, and Anders Runesson, eds. 2007. *Jesus och de första kristna: Inledning till Nya testamentet*. Stockholm: Verbum.

Moltmann, Jürgen. 1967. *Theology of Hope: On the Ground and the Implications of a Christian Eschatology*. London: SCM.

Mommsen, Theodor. 1854–1856. *Römische Geschichte*. 3 vols. Berlin: Weidmann.

Moore, Stephen D. 1989. *Literary Criticism and the Gospels: The Theoretical Challenge*. New Haven: Yale University Press.

———. 1994. *Poststructuralism and the New Testament: Derrida and Foucault at the Foot of the Cross*. Minneapolis: Fortress.

———. 1997. History after Theory? Biblical Studies and the New Historicism. *Biblical Interpretation* 5:288–98.

———. 2005. Questions of Biblical Ambivalence and Authority under a Tree outside Delhi; or, the Postcolonial and the Postmodern. Pages 79–96 in *Postcolonial Biblical Criticism: Interdisciplinary Intersections*. Edited by Stephen D. Moore and Fernando F. Segovia. Edinburgh: T&T Clark.

———. 2006. *Empire and Apocalypse: Postcolonialism and the New Testament*. Bible in the Modern World. Sheffield: Sheffield Phoenix Press.

———. 2008. Deconstructive Criticism: Turning Mark Inside-Out. Pages 95–110 in *Mark and Method: New Approaches in Biblical Studies*. Edited by Janice Capel Anderson and Stephen D. Moore. Minneapolis: Fortress.

Moore, Stephen D., and Fernando F. Segovia. 2005. Postcolonial Biblical Criticism: Beginnings, Trajectories, Intersections. Pages 1–22 in *Postcolonial Biblical Criticism: Interdisciplinary Intersections*. Edited by Stephen D. Moore and Fernando F. Segovia. London: T&T Clark.

Moore, Stephen D., and Yvonne Sherwood. 2011. *The Invention of the Biblical Scholar: A Critical Manifesto*. Minneapolis: Fortress.

Moore, Stephen D., and Janice Capel Anderson. 1998. Taking It Like a Man: Masculinity in 4 Maccabees. *Journal of Biblical Literature* 117:249–73.

Moore-Gilbert, Bart J. 1997. *Postcolonial Theory: Contexts, Practices, Politics*. London: Verso.
Morison, James. 1873. *Mark's Memoirs of Jesus Christ: A Commentary on the Gospel According to Mark*. London: Hamilton and Adams.
Moxnes, Halvor. 2012. *Jesus and the Rise of Nationalism: A New Quest for the Nineteenth-century Historical Jesus*. London: Tauris.
Myers, Ched. 1988. *Binding the Strong Man: A Political Reading of Mark's Story of Jesus*. Maryknoll, N.Y.: Orbis.
Naess, Arne. 1974. *Gandhi and Group Conflict: An Exploration of Satyagraha. Theoretical Background*. Oslo: Universitetsforlaget.
Neill, Stephen, and Tom Wright. 1988. *The Interpretation of the New Testament 1861–1986*. Oxford: Oxford University Press.
Neville, David J. 2007. Toward a Teleology of Peace: Contesting Matthew's Violent Eschatology. *Journal for the Study of the New Testament* 30:131–61.
———. 2008. Moral Vision and Eschatology in Mark's Gospel: Coherence or Conflict? *Journal of Biblical Literature* 127:359–84.
New Encyclopædia Britannica. 1985. 15th ed. 32 vols. Chicago: Encyclopædia Britannica.
Newheart, Michael W. 2004. *"My Name Is Legion": The Story and Soul of the Gerasene Demoniac*. Collegeville, Minn.: Liturgical Press.
Neyrey, Jerome H. 1991. *The Social World of Luke-Acts: Models for Interpretation*. Peabody, Mass.: Hendrickson.
Niebuhr, Carsten. 1772. *Beschreibung von Arabien. Aus eigenen Beobachtungen und im Lande selbst gesammelten Nachrichten abgefasset von Carsten Niebuhr*. Copenhagen: Möller.
———. 1774–1778. *C. Niebuhrs Reisebeschreibung nach Arabien und anderen umliegenden Ländern*. 2 vols. Copenhagen: Möller.
Nilsson, Bengt. 2010. Irland. *Nationalencyklopedin*. Online: http://www.ne.se.ezproxy.ub.gu.se/lang/irland/213284.
Oakes, Peter. 2003. Christian Attitudes to Rome at the Time of Paul's Letter. *Review and Expositor* 100:103–11.
O'Collins, Gerald G. 1992. Crucifixion. Pages 1207–10 in vol. 1 of *Anchor Bible Dictionary*. Edited by David Noel Freedman. 6 vols. New York: Doubleday.
Odén, Robert. 2012. *Wåra swarta bröder: Representationer av religioner och människor i Evangeliska fosterlandsstiftelsens Missions-Tidning, 1877–1890*. Studia Missionalia Svecana 111. Uppsala: Uppsala Universitet.

Oepke, Albrecht. 1967. παρουσία, πάρειμι. Pages 858–71 in vol. 5 of *Theological Dictionary of the New Testament*. Edited by Gerhard Kittel and Gerhard Friedrich. Translated by Geoffrey W. Bromiley. 10 vols. Grand Rapids: Eerdmans, 1964–1976.

Olshausen, Hermann. 1833. *Biblischer Commentar über sammtliche Schriften des Neuen Testaments*. 2nd ed. Vol. 1. Königsberg: August Wilhelm Unzer.

———. 1847. *Biblical Commentary on the Gospels, Adapted Especially for Preachers and Students*. Translated by Sergius Loewe. Vol. 1. Edinburgh: T&T Clark.

Olsson, Birger. 2006. Tolkningstyper och tolkningskriterier. Pages 147–60 in *Vad, hur och varför? Reflektioner om bibelvetenskap: Festskrift till Inger Ljung*. Edited by Lars Hartman, Lina Sjöberg, and Mikael Sjöberg. Uppsala: Acta Universitatis Upsaliensis.

Olsson, Maria. 2009. Den talande tystnaden: Om kvinnornas tystnad i Markusevangeliets slut. *Svensk exegetisk årsbok* 74:81–101.

Ong, Walter J. 1977. *Interfaces of the Word: Studies in the Evolution of Consciousness and Culture*. Ithaca: Cornell University Press.

———. 1987. Text as Interpretation: Mark and After. *Semeia* 39:7–26.

Onions, C. T., ed. 1966. *The Oxford Dictionary of English Etymology*. Oxford: Oxford University Press.

Overduin, Nick. 2002. Hearing the Whole Story: The Politics of Plot in Mark's Gospel. *Calvin Theological Journal* 37:348–51.

Oxford English Dictionary. 1989. Prepared by J. A. Simpson and E. S. C. Weiner. 2nd ed. 20 vols. Oxford: Clarendon.

Palmberg, Mai. 2009. The Nordic Colonial Mind. Pages 35–50 in *Complying with Colonialism: Gender, Race and Ethnicity in the Nordic Region*. Edited by Suvi Keskinen, Salla Tuori, Sari Irni, and Diana Mulinari. Surrey: Ashgate.

Patte, Daniel. 1985. Review of Werner Kelber, *The Oral and the Written Gospel*. *Journal of the American Academy of Religion* 53:136–37.

———. 2011. Contextual Reading of Mark and North Atlantic Scholarship. Pages 197–213 in *Mark*. Edited by Nicole Wilkinson Duran, Teresa Okure, and Daniel Patte. Texts @ Contexts. Minneapolis: Fortress.

Peckham, Brian. 1992. Phoenicia, History of. Pages 349–57 in vol. 5 of *Anchor Bible Dictionary*. Edited by David Noel Freedman. 6 vols. New York: Doubleday.

Pecora, Vincent P. 2010. Review of Ananda Abeysekara, *The Politics of*

Postsecular Religion: Mourning Secular Futures. Journal of the American Academy of Religion 78:858–62.
Perkins, Pheme. 1984. Taxes in the New Testament. *Journal of Religious Ethics* 12:182–200.
———. 1995. The Gospel of Mark. Pages 507–734 in vol. 8 of *The New Interpreter's Bible*. Edited by Leander E. Keck. Nashville: Abingdon.
Perkinson, Jim. 1996. A Canaanitic Word in the Logos of Christ; or the Difference the Syro-Phoenician Woman Makes to Jesus. *Semeia* 75:61–85.
Peterson, Dwight N. 2000. *The Origins of Mark: The Markan Community in Current Debate*. Biblical Interpretation Series 48. Leiden: Brill.
Pettersson, Per. 2009. The Nordic Paradox—Simultaneously Most Secularised and Most Religious. Pages 79–92 in *Europe: Secular or Post-Secular?* Edited by Hans-Georg Ziebertz and Ulrich Riegel. Berlin: Lit.
Pfohl, Gerhard. 1965. *Griechische Inschriften als Zeugnisse des privaten und öffentlichen Lebens*. Tusculum-Bücherei. Munich: Heimeran.
Pilch, John J. 1995. Death with Honor: The Mediterranean Style Death of Jesus in Mark. *Biblical Theology Bulletin* 25:65–70.
Pippin, Tina. 2005. The Heroine and the Whore: The Apocalypse of John in Feminist Perspective. Pages 127–45 in *From Every People and Nation: The Book of Revelation in Intercultural Perspective*. Edited by David M. Rhoads. Minneapolis: AugsburgFortress.
Plumptre, E. H. 1897. The Gospel According to St. Matthew, St. Mark, and St. Luke. In *A New Testament Commentary for English Readers by Various Writers*. Edited by Charles John Ellicott. New York: Dutton.
Pope, Marvin H. 1992. Hosanna. Pages 290–91 in vol. 3 of *Anchor Bible Dictionary*. Edited by David Noel Freedman. 6 vols. New York: Doubleday.
Porter, Stanley E., and Jeffrey T. Reed, eds. 1999. *Discourse Analysis and the New Testament: Approaches and Results*. Sheffield: Sheffield Academic Press.
Powell, Mark Allan. 1990. *What Is Narrative Criticism?* Minneapolis: Fortress.
Prakash, Gyan. 1992. Postcolonial Criticism and Indian Historiography. *Social Text* 31/32:8–19.
———. 1995. Introduction: After Colonialism. Pages 3–17 in *After Colonialism: Imperial Histories and Postcolonial Displacements*. Edited by Gyan Prakash. Princeton: Princeton University Press.

Pratt, Mary Louise. 1992. *Imperial Eyes: Travel Writing and Transculturation*. London: Routledge.
Preisker, H. 1967. λεγιών. Pages 68–69 in vol. 4 of *Theological Dictionary of the New Testament*. Edited by Gerhard Kittel and Gerhard Friedrich. Translated by Geoffrey W. Bromiley. 10 vols. Grand Rapids: Eerdmans, 1964–1976.
Price, Simon R. F. 1984. *Rituals and Power: The Roman Imperial Cult in Asia Minor*. Cambridge: Cambridge University Press.
Prior, Michael. 1997. *The Bible and Colonialism: A Moral Critique*. Biblical Seminar 48. Sheffield: Sheffield Academic Press.
Punt, Jeremy. 2008. Intersections in Queer Theory and Postcolonial Theory, and Hermeneutical Spin-offs. *Bible and Critical Theory* 4, no. 2:24.1–16.
Radl, W. 1993. παρουσία. Pages 43–44 in vol. 3 of *Exegetical Dictionary of the New Testament*. Edited by Horst Balz and Gerhard Schneider. 3 vols. Grand Rapids: Eerdmans, 1990–1993.
Räisänen, Heikki. 2000a. Biblical Critics in the Global Village. Pages 9–28 in Heikki Räisänen et al., *Reading the Bible in the Global Village*. Atlanta: Society of Biblical Literature.
———. 2000b. På väg mot en etisk bibelkritik. *Svensk exegetisk årsbok* 65:227–42.
———. 2010. *The Rise of Christian Beliefs: The Thought World of Early Christians*. Minneapolis: Fortress.
Rajkumar, Peniel Jesudason Rufus. 2007. A Dalithos Reading of a Markan Exorcism: Mark 5:1–20. *Expository Times* 118:428–35.
Rebera, Ranjini Wickramaratne. 2001. The Syrophoenician Woman: A South Asian Feminist Perspective. Pages 101–10 in *A Feminist Companion to Mark*. Edited by Amy-Jill Levine with Marianne Blickenstaff. Feminist Companion to the New Testament and Early Christian Writings 2. Sheffield: Sheffield Academic Press.
Regul, Jürgen. 1969. *Die antimarcionitischen Evangelienprologe*. Vetus Latina. Aus der Geschichte der lateinischen Bibel 6. Freiburg: Herder.
Reimarus, Hermann Samuel. 1970. *The Goal of Jesus and His Disciples*. Leiden: Brill.
———. 1778. *Von dem Zwecke Jesu und seiner Jünger: Noch ein Fragment des Wolfenbüttelschen Ungenannten*. Braunschweig: Lessing.
Reinach, Théodore. 1903. Mon nom est Légion. *Revue des études juives* 47:172–78.

Remus, Harold. 2002. Persecution. Pages 431–52 in *Handbook of Early Christianity: Social Science Approaches*. Edited by Anthony J. Blasi, Paul-André Turcotte, and Jean Duhaime. Walnut Creek, Calif.: AltaMira.
Renan, Ernest. 1958. *Œuvres complètes*. Vol. 8 of 10 vols. Paris: Calmann-Lévy, 1947–1961.
Resseguie, James L. 2005. *Narrative Criticism of the New Testament: An Introduction*. Grand Rapids: Baker.
Rey-Coquais, Jean-Paul. 1992. Decapolis. Pages 116–21 in vol. 2 of *Anchor Bible Dictionary*. Edited by David Noel Freedman. 6 vols. New York: Doubleday.
Rhoads, David M. 1991. Review of Ched Myers, *Binding the Strong Man: A Political Reading of Mark's Story of Jesus*. *Catholic Biblical Quarterly* 53:336–38.
Rhoads, David, Joanna Dewey, and Donald Michie. 1999. *Mark as Story: An Introduction to the Narrative of a Gospel*. 2nd ed. Minneapolis: Fortress.
Riches, John Kenneth. 1993. *A Century of New Testament Study*. Cambridge: Lutterworth.
Riddle, Matthew B. 1879. The Gospel of Mark. Pages 246–336 in *A Popular Commentary on the New Testament. By English and American Scholars of Various Evangelical Denominations*. Edited by Philip Schaff. New York: Scribner's.
Rives, James B. 2007. *Religion in the Roman Empire*. Blackwell Ancient Religions. Malden, Mass.: Blackwell.
Robbins, Vernon K. 1991. A Reordering of Power: A Socio-political Reading of Mark's Gospel. *Religious Studies Review* 17:16–22.
———. 1996. *The Tapestry of Early Christian Discourse: Rhetoric, Society, and Ideology*. London: Routledge.
Roberts, Colin H., and T. C. Skeat. 1983. *The Birth of the Codex*. London: Oxford University Press.
Rogers, Guy MacLean. 1996. Multiculturalism and the Foundations of Western Civilization. Pages 428–43 in *Black Athena Revisited*. Edited by Mary R. Lefkowitz and Guy MacLean Rogers. Chapel Hill: University of North Carolina Press.
Rohrbaugh, Richard L. 1993. The Social Location of the Marcan Audience. *Biblical Theology Bulletin* 23:114–27.

Roskam, Hendrika Nicoline. 2004. *The Purpose of the Gospel of Mark in Its Historical and Social Context*. Supplements to Novum Testamentum 114. Leiden: Brill.

Rostovtzeff, Michael Ivanovitch. 1957. *The Social and Economic History of the Roman Empire*. 2nd ed. Revised by P. M. Fraser. 2 vols. Oxford: Clarendon.

Runesson, Anna. 2006. Kontextuell exegetik i en postkolonial värld: Bibeltolkning i dagens indien. Pages 122–49 in *Varför ser ni mot himlen? Utmaningar från den kontextuella teologin*. Edited by Anders Runesson and Torbjörn Sjöholm. Stockholm: Verbum; Institutet för kontextuell teologi.

———. 2007. "Legion heter jag, för vi är många": En postkolonial läsning av Mark 5:1–20. Pages 475–81 in *Jesus och de första kristna: Inledning till Nya testamentet*. Edited by Dieter Mitternacht and Anders Runesson. Stockholm: Verbum.

———. 2011. *Exegesis in the Making: Postcolonialism and New Testament Studies*. Biblical Interpretation Series 103. Leiden: Brill.

Runions, Erin. 2001a. Called to Do Justice? A Bhabhian Reading of Micah 5 and 6:1–8. Pages 153–64 in *Postmodern Interpretations of the Bible: A Reader*. Edited by A. K. M. Adam. St. Louis: Chalice.

———. 2001b. *Changing Subjects: Gender, Nation and Future in Micah*. Playing the Texts. London: Sheffield Academic Press.

Said, Edward W. 1979. *Orientalism*. New York: Vintage.

———. 1993. *Culture and Imperialism*. New York: Vintage.

———. 1994. Afterword. Pages 329–52 in *Orientalism*. Repr., with a new afterword. New York: Vintage.

———. 1996. Orientalism and After. Pages 65–88 in *A Critical Sense: Interviews with Intellectuals*. Edited by Peter Osborne. London: Routledge.

Salmon, E. T. 1969. *Roman Colonization under the Republic*. Aspects of Greek and Roman Life. London: Thames & Hudson.

Samuel, Simon. 2002. The Beginning of Mark: A Colonial/Postcolonial Conundrum. *Biblical Interpretation* 10:405–19.

———. 2007. *A Postcolonial Reading of Mark's Story of Jesus*. Library of New Testament Studies 340. London: T&T Clark.

Sanneh, Lamin O. 1989. *Translating the Message: The Missionary Impact on Culture*. American Society of Missiology Series 13. Maryknoll, N.Y.: Orbis.

Sardar, Ziauddin. 1999. *Orientalism*. Concepts in the Social Sciences. Buckingham: Open University Press.

Schäfer, Peter. 1997. *Judeophobia: Attitudes toward the Jews in the Ancient World*. Cambridge: Harvard University Press.
Schanz, Paul. 1881. *Commentar über das Evangelium des heiligen Marcus*. Frieburg im Breisbau: Herder.
Schildgen, Brenda Deen. 1999. *Power and Prejudice: The Reception of the Gospel of Mark*. Detroit: Wayne State University Press.
Schlatter, Adolf. 1925. *Geschichte Israels von Alexander dem Grossen bis Hadrian*. 3rd ed. Stuttgart: Calwer.
Schoedel, William R. 1985. *Ignatius of Antioch: A Commentary on the Letters of Ignatius of Antioch*. Hermeneia. Philadelphia: Fortress.
Schubart, W., et al., eds. 1895–2005. *Aegyptische Urkunden aus den Königlichen* (later *Staatlichen*) *Museen zu Berlin, Griechische Urkunden*. 19 vols. Berlin: Weidmann.
Schürer, Emil. 1979. *The History of the Jewish People in the Age of Jesus Christ*. Vol. 2. Edited and revised by Geza Vermes and Fergus Millar. 3 vols. in 4. Edinburgh: T&T Clark, 1973–1987.
Schüssler Fiorenza, Elisabeth. 1983. *In Memory of Her: A Feminist Theological Reconstruction of Christian Origins*. New York: Crossroad.
———. 1992. *But She Said: Feminist Practices of Biblical Interpretation*. Boston: Beacon.
———. 2007. *The Power of the Word: Scripture and the Rhetoric of Empire*. Minneapolis: Fortress.
Schweitzer, Albert. 2000. *The Quest of the Historical Jesus*. Translated by John Bowden. London: SCM.
Seager, Robin. 2005. Introduction. Pages xvii–xlvi in *Plutarch: Fall of the Roman Republic*. London: Penguin.
Seeley, David. 1993. Jesus' Temple Act. *Catholic Biblical Quarterly* 55:263–83.
Segovia, Fernando F. 2000. *Decolonizing Biblical Studies: A View from the Margins*. New York: Orbis.
———. 2005. Mapping the Postcolonial Optic in Biblical Criticism: Meaning and Scope. Pages 23–78 in *Postcolonial Biblical Criticism: Interdisciplinary Intersections*. Edited by Stephen D. Moore and Fernando F. Segovia. Edinburgh: T&T Clark.
———. 2006. Biblical Criticism and Postcolonial Studies: Toward a Postcolonial Optic. Pages 33–44 in *Postcolonial Biblical Reader*. Edited by R. S. Sugirtharajah. Oxford: Blackwell.

Segovia, Fernando F., and Mary Ann Tolbert, eds. 1995. *Reading from This Place: Social Location and Biblical Interpretation in Global Perspective.* 2 vols. Minneapolis: Fortress.

Segovia, Fernando F., and R. S. Sugirtharajah, eds. 2007. *A Postcolonial Commentary on the New Testament Writings.* Bible and Postcolonialism 13. London: T&T Clark.

Senior, Donald. 1984. *The Passion of Jesus in the Gospel of Mark.* Passion Series 2. Wilmington, Del.: Glazier.

Shaffer, Elinor S. 1975. *"Kubla Khan" and The Fall of Jerusalem: The Mythological School in Biblical Criticism and Secular Literature, 1770–1880.* Cambridge: Cambridge University Press.

Sharp, Gene. 1979. *Gandhi as a Political Strategist: With Essays on Ethics and Politics.* Boston: Porter Sargent.

Sharpe, Jenny. 1993. *Allegories of Empire: The Figure of Woman in the Colonial Text.* Minneapolis: University of Minnesota Press.

Shea, Victor. 1993. New Historicism. Pages 124–30 in *Encyclopedia of Contemporary Literary Theory: Approaches, Scholars, Terms.* Edited by Irena R. Makaryk. Toronto: University of Toronto Press.

Shiell, William David. 2004. *Reading Acts: The Lector and the Early Christian Audience.* Biblical Interpretation Series 70. Boston: Brill.

Shiner, Whitney. 2000. The Ambiguous Pronouncement of the Centurion and the Shrouding of Meaning in Mark. *Journal for the Study of the New Testament* 78:3–22.

———. 2003. *Proclaiming the Gospel: First-century Performance of Mark.* Harrisburg, Pa.: Trinity Press International.

Sigurdson, Ola. 2009. *Det postsekulära tillståndet: Religion, modernitet, politik.* Göteborg: Glänta produktion.

Sjöberg, Erik. 1953. *Exegeterna om kvinnliga präster.* Stockholm: Svenska kyrkans diakonistyrelses bokförlag.

Slemon, Stephen, and Helen Tiffin. 1989. Introduction. Pages ix–xxiii in *After Europe: Critical Theory and Post-colonial Writing.* Edited by Stephen Slemon and Helen Tiffin. Sydney: Dangaroo.

Smallwood, Mary E. 1976. *The Jews under Roman Rule.* Studies in Judaism in Late Antiquity 20. Leiden: Brill.

Smend, Rudolf. 1987. Johann David Michaelis und Johann Gottfried Eichhorn: Zwei Orientalisten am Rande der Theologie. Pages 58–81 in *Theologie in Göttingen.* Edited by Bernd Moeller. Göttingen: Vandenhoeck & Ruprecht.

Smith, Dennis E. 1990. Narrative Beginnings in Ancient Literature and Theory. *Semeia* 52:1–9.
Smith, George. 1863. Pages 191–95 in *The Missionary Magazine and Chronicle*. London: London Missionary Society.
Smith, Morton. 1999. The Gentiles in Judaism 125 BCE–CE 66. Pages 192–249 in *The Early Roman Period*. Vol. 3 of *The Cambridge History of Judaism*. Edited by William Horbury, W. D. Davies, and John Sturdy. Cambridge: Cambridge University Press.
Soares-Prabhu, George M. 1994. Two Mission Commands: An Interpretation of Matthew 28:16–20 in the Light of a Buddhist Text. *Biblical Interpretation* 2:264–82.
Söderling, Fredrik. 2012. Lilla Hjärtat "uppenbart rasistisk" enligt forskare. In *Dagens Nyheter* Nov. 22. Online: http://www.dn.se/dnbok/lilla-hjartat-uppenbart-rasistisk-enligt-forskare.
Sokoloff, Michael. 2002. *A Dictionary of Jewish Palestinian Aramaic*. Dictionaries of Talmud, Midrash and Targum. Ramat-Gan: Bar Ilan University Press.
Sörberg, B. 1887. Missionen ett såningsarbete. *Missions-Tidning, under inseende af Svenska Kyrkans Missions-Styrelse* 21, no. 2: 33–36.
Spencer, Richard A. 2000. Tax. Pages 1277–78 in *Eerdman's Dictionary of the Bible*. Edited by David Noel Freedman. Grand Rapids: Eerdmans.
Spivak, Gayatri Chakravorty. 1988a. Can the Subaltern Speak? Pages 271–313 in *Marxism and the Interpretation of Culture*. Edited by Cary Nelson and Lawrence Grossberg. Urbana: University of Illinois Press.
———. 1988b. A Literary Representation of the Subaltern. Pages 241–68 in *In Other Worlds: Essays in Cultural Politics*. New York: Routledge.
———. 1990. Poststructuralism, Marginality, Post-coloniality and Value. Pages 219–44 in *Literary Theory Today*. Edited by Peter Collier and Helga Geyer-Ryan. Cambridge: Polity.
———. 1993. *Outside in the Teaching Machine*. New York: Routledge.
———. 1999. *A Critique of Postcolonial Reason: Toward a History of the Vanishing Present*. Cambridge: Harvard University Press.
Spivak, Gayatri Chakravorty, and Sarah Harasym. 1990. *The Post-colonial Critic: Interviews, Strategies, Dialogues*. New York: Routledge.
Spurr, David. 1993. *The Rhetoric of Empire: Colonial Discourse in Journalism, Travel Writing, and Imperial Administration*. Post-Contemporary Interventions. Durham, N.C.: Duke University Press.
Staley, Jeffrey L. 2006. "Clothed and in Her Right Mind": Mark 5:1–20 and Postcolonial Discourse. Pages 319–27 in *Voices from the Margin: Inter-*

preting the Bible in the Third World. Edited by R. S. Sugirtharajah. 3rd ed. Maryknoll, N.Y.: Orbis.

Stanley, Christopher D. 1996. "Neither Jew nor Greek": Ethnic Conflict in Graeco-Roman Society. *Journal for the Study of the New Testament* 64:101–24.

Stanton, Graham. 1997. The Fourfold Gospel. *New Testament Studies* 43:317–46.

———. 2004. *Jesus and Gospel.* Cambridge: Cambridge University Press.

Starr, Raymond J. 1987. The Circulation of Texts in the Roman World. *Classical Quarterly* 37:213–23.

Stauffer, Ethelbert. 1956. Messias oder Menschensohn. *Novum Testamentum* 1:81–102.

Stegemann, Ekkehard W., and Wolfgang Stegemann. 1999. *The Jesus Movement: A Social History of Its First Century.* Translated by O. C. Dean. Edinburgh: T&T Clark.

Stemberger, Günter, and Markus Bockmuehl. 1996. *Introduction to the Talmud and Midrash.* Edinburgh: T&T Clark.

Stenström, Hanna. 2005. Historical-critical Approaches and the Emancipation of Women: Unfulfilled Promises and Remaining Possibilities. Pages 31–45 in *Her Master's Tools? Feminist and Postcolonial Engagements of Historical-critical Discourse.* Edited by Caroline Vander Stichele and Todd Penner. Atlanta: Society of Biblical Literature.

Stern, Menahem. 1974–1984. *Greek and Latin Authors on Jews and Judaism.* 3 vols. Jerusalem: Israel Academy of Sciences and Humanities.

Strauss, David Friedrich. 1835. *Das Leben Jesu kritisch bearbeitet.* 2 vols. Tübingen: Osiander.

———. 1860. *The Life of Jesus Critically Examined.* 2 vols. New York: Blanchard.

———. 1879. *The Life of Jesus for the People.* 2nd ed. 2 vols. London: Williams & Norgate.

Strecker, Christian. 2002. Jesus and the Demoniacs. Pages 117–33 in *The Social Setting of Jesus and the Gospels.* Edited by Wolfgang Stegemann, Bruce J. Malina, and Gerd Theissen. Minneapolis: Fortress.

Strecker, Georg. 1991. εὐαγγέλιον. Pages 70–74 in vol. 2 of *Exegetical Dictionary of the New Testament.* Edited by Horst Balz and Gerhard Schneider. 3 vols. Grand Rapids: Eerdmans, 1990–1993.

Stuart, Doug. 2002. Convert or Convicts? The Gospel of Liberation and Subordination in Early Nineteenth-century South Africa. Pages 66–75 in *Christian Missionaries and the State in the Third World*. Edited by Holger Bernt Hansen and Michael Twaddle. Oxford: James Currey.

Stuhlmacher, Peter. 1991. The Theme: The Gospel and the Gospels. Pages 1–25 in *The Gospel and the Gospels*. Edited by Peter Stuhlmacher. Grand Rapids: Eerdmans.

Sugirtharajah, R. S., ed. 1991. *Voices from the Margin: Interpreting the Bible in the Third World*. Maryknoll, N.Y.: Orbis.

———, ed. 1998a. *The Postcolonial Bible*. Bible and Postcolonialism 1. Sheffield: Sheffield Academic Press.

———. 1998b. A Postcolonial Exploration of Collusion and Contruction in Biblical Interpretation. Pages 91–116 in *The Postcolonial Bible*. Edited by R. S. Sugirtharajah. Sheffield: Sheffield Academic Press.

———. 1999a. A Brief Memorandum on Postcolonialism and Biblical Studies. *Journal for the Study of the New Testament* 73:3–5.

———. 1999b. Imperial Critical Commentaries: Christian Discourse and Commentarial Writings in Colonial India. *Journal for the Study of the New Testament* 73:82–112.

———. 1999c. *Asian Biblical Hermeneutics and Postcolonialism: Contesting the Interpretations*. Sheffield: Sheffield Academic Press.

———. 2002. *Postcolonial Criticism and Biblical Interpretation*. Oxford: Oxford University Press.

———. 2006. Introduction: Theoretical Practices. Pages 5–6 in *The Postcolonial Biblical Reader*. Edited by R. S. Sugirtharajah. Oxford: Blackwell.

———, ed. 2008. *Still at the Margins: Biblical Scholarship Fifteen Years after Voices from the Margin*. London: T&T Clark.

Swete, Henry Barclay. 1898. *The Gospel according to St Mark*. London: Macmillan.

———. 1909. *The Gospel According to St Mark*. 3rd ed. London: Macmillan.

Taylor, Vincent. 1953. *The Gospel According to St. Mark*. London: Macmillan.

———. 1961. *The Text of the New Testament*. London: St. Martin's.

Telford, William R. 1980. *The Barren Temple and the Withered Tree: A Redaction-critical Analysis of the Cursing of the Fig-tree Pericope in Mark's Gospel and Its Relation to the Cleansing of the Temple Tradition*. Journal for the Study of the New Testament Supplement Series 1. Sheffield: JSOT Press.

———. 1995. *Mark*. New Testament Guides. Sheffield: Sheffield Academic Press.

Tellbe, Mikael. 2001. *Paul between Synagogue and State: Christians, Jews and Civic Authorities in 1 Thessalonians, Romans, and Philippians*. Coniectanea biblica: New Testament Series 34. Stockholm: Almqvist & Wiksell.

Thatcher, Tom. 2008a. Beyond Texts and Traditions: Werner Kelber's Media History of Christian Origins. Pages 1–26 in *Jesus, the Voice, and the Text: Beyond the Oral and Written Gospel*. Edited by Tom Thatcher. Waco, Tex.: Baylor University Press.

———, ed. 2008b. *Jesus, the Voice, and the Text: Beyond the Oral and Written Gospel*. Waco, Tex.: Baylor University Press.

Theissen, Gerd. 1978. *Sociology of Early Palestinian Christianity*. Philadelphia: Fortress.

———. 1983. *The Miracle Stories of the Early Christian Tradition*. Translated by Francis McDonagh. Edinburgh: T&T Clark.

———. 1992. *The Gospels in Context: Social and Political History in the Synoptic Tradition*. Edinburgh: T&T Clark.

———. 2001. *Gospel Writing and Church Politics: A Socio-rhetorical Approach*. Chuen King Lecture Series 3. Hong Kong: Theology Division of Chung Chi College, Chinese University of Hong Kong.

———. 2002. The Political Dimension of Jesus' Activities. Pages 225–50 in *Social Setting of Jesus and the Gospels*. Edited by Wolfgang Stegemann, Bruce J. Malina, and Gerd Theissen. Minneapolis: Fortress.

Thiselton, Anthony C. 1992. *New Horizons in Hermeneutics*. Grand Rapids: Zondervan.

———. 2009. *Hermeneutics: An Introduction*. Grand Rapids: Eerdmans.

Thomas, Alan, with Ben Crow et al. 1994. *Third World Atlas*. 2nd ed. Buckingham, U.K.: Open University Press.

Thompson, Michael B. 1998. The Hole Internet: Communication between Churches in the First Christian Generation. Pages 49–70 in *The Gospels for All Christians: Rethinking the Gospel Audience*. Edited by Richard Bauckham. Edinburgh: T&T Clark.

Thomson, J. E. H. 1915. Apocalyptic Literature. In *International Standard Bible Encyclopaedia*. Edited by James Orr. 5 vols. Chicago: Howard-Severance.

Thurman, Eric. 2003. Looking for a Few Good Men: Mark and Masculinity. Pages 137–61 in *New Testament Masculinities*. Edited by Stephen D. Moore and Janice Capel Anderson. Atlanta: Society of Biblical Literature.

———. 2007. Novel Men: Masculinity and Empire in Mark's Gospel and Xenophon's An Ephesian Tale. Pages 185–229 in *Mapping Gender in Ancient Religious Discourses*. Edited by Todd Penner and Caroline Vander Stichele. Boston: Leiden.
Tolbert, Mary Ann, ed. 1983. *The Bible and Feminist Hermeneutics*. Semeia 28. Chico, Calif.: Scholars Press.
———. 1989. *Sowing the Gospel: Mark's World in Literary-Historical Perspective*. Minneapolis: Fortress.
Toorn, Karel van der, Bob Becking, and Pieter W. van der Horst, eds. 1999. *Dictionary of Deities and Demons in the Bible*. 2nd ed. Leiden: Brill.
Tosh, John. 2002. *The Pursuit of History: Aims, Methods and New Directions in the Study of Modern History*. Harlow: Longman.
Tottie, H. W. 1884. Något om missionssaken i London. *Missions-Tidning, under inseende af Svenska Kyrkans Missions-Styrelse* 9, no. 5:107–19.
———. 1885. De kristnas förpligtelser i fråga om missionsarbetet ibland hedningarne (2 Mos. 17:8–13). *Missions-Tidning, under inseende af Svenska Kyrkans Missions-Styrelse* 10, no. 3:61–69.
Townsend, John T. 1986. Missionary Journeys in Acts and European Missionary Societies. *Anglican Theological Review* 68:99–104.
Trench, Richard Chenevix. 1850. *Notes on the Miracles of Our Lord*. New York: Appleton.
Tuckett, C. M. 1992. Messianic Secret. Pages 797–800 in vol. 4 of *Anchor Bible Dictionary*. Edited by David Noel Freedman. 6 vols. New York: Doubleday.
Ussing, Henry. 1902. *Evangeliets segertåg genom världen: Historisk öfversikt af den evangeliska missionens utveckling*. Lund: Gleerup.
Vaan, Michiel de. 2008. *Etymological Dictionary of Latin and the Other Italic Languages*. Leiden Indo-European Etymological Dictionary Series 7. Leiden: Brill.
Van Oyen, Geert. 2003. Irony as Propaganda in Mark 15:39? Pages 125–42 in *Persuasion and Dissuasion in Early Christianity, Ancient Judaism, and Hellenism*. Edited by Pieter W. van der Horst et al. Leuven: Peeters.
Vander Stichele, Caroline, and Todd Penner, eds. 2005a. *Her Master's Tools? Feminist and Postcolonial Engagements of Historical-critical Discourse*. Atlanta: Society of Biblical Literature.
———. 2005b. Mastering the Tools or Retooling the Masters? The Legacy of Historical-Critical Discourse. Pages 1–29 in *Her Master's Tools? Feminist and Postcolonial Engagements of Historical-critical Discourse*.

Edited by Caroline Vander Stichele and Todd Penner. Atlanta: Society of Biblical Literature.

———. 2007. *Mapping Gender in Ancient Religious Discourses*. Biblical Interpretation Series 84. Leiden: Brill.

———. 2009. *Contextualizing Gender in Early Christian Discourse: Thinking beyond Thecla*. London: T&T Clark.

Verbrugge, Verlyn D. 2007. Review of William Shiell, *Reading Acts: The Lector and the Early Christian Audience*. Online: *Review of Biblical Literature*.

Versnel, Hendrik Simon. 1970. *Triumphus: An Inquiry into the Origin, Development and Meaning of the Roman Triumph*. Leiden: Brill.

Via, Dan O. 2002. *What Is New Testament Theology?* Guides to Biblical Scholarship. Minneapolis: Fortress.

Volkmar, Gustaf. 1857. *Die Religion Jesu und ihre erste Entwickelung nach dem gegenwärtigen Stande der Wissenschaft*. Leipzig: Brockhaus.

Vos, Howard F. 1982. Gerasa. Pages 447–48 in vol. 2 of *The International Standard Bible Encyclopedia*. Edited by Geoffrey W. Bromiley. 4 vols. Grand Rapids: Eerdmans, 1979–1988.

Waetjen, Herman C. 1989. *A Reordering of Power: A Sociopolitical Reading of Mark's Gospel*. Minneapolis: Fortress.

Wallace-Hadrill, Andrew, ed. 1989. *Patronage in Ancient Society*. Leicester-Nottingham Studies in Ancient Society 1. London: Routledge.

Wanke, Joachim. 1990. Ἕλλην, Ἑλληνίς. Pages 435–36 in vol. 1 of *Exegetical Dictionary of the New Testament*. Edited by Horst Balz and Gerhard Schneider. 3 vols. Grand Rapids: Eerdmans, 1990–1993.

Ward, Graham. 2000. *Cities of God*. Radical Orthodoxy. London: Routledge.

Warneck, Gustav. 1876. *Die apostolische und die moderne Mission*. Gütersloh: Bertelsmann.

———. 1881. *Hvarför är det nittonde århundradet ett missionsårhundrade?* Translated by C. Strömberg. Stockholm: Evangeliska Fosterlands-stiftelsen.

———. 1884. *De protestantiska missionernas historia från reformationen till nuvarande tid*. Stockholm: Fosterlands-stiftelsen.

———. 1898. *Abrik einer Geschichte der protestantischen Missionen von der Reformation bis auf die Gegenwart*. Berlin: Warneck.

———. 1901. *Outline of a History of Protestant Missions: From the Reformation to the Present Time*. New York: Revell.

———. 1903. *De protestantiska missionernas historia från reformationen till nuvarande tid: Ett bidrag till den nyare tidens kyrkohistoria*. Translated by Adolf Kolmodin. Stockholm: Evangeliska Fosterlands-stiftelsen.
Warrior, Robert Allen. 1991. A Native American Perspective: Canaanites, Cowboys, and Indians. Pages 287–95 in *Voices from the Margin: Interpreting the Bible in the Third World*. Edited by R. S. Sugirtharajah. Maryknoll, N.Y.: OrbisWasserman, Tommy. 2007. Fönster mot handskriftsvärlden. *Svensk Teologisk Kvartalskrift* 83:75–84.
———. 2011. The "Son of God" Was in the Beginning (Mark 1:1). *Journal of Theological Studies* 62:20–50.
Watson, Duane F. 1992. Babylon in the NT. Pages 565–66 in vol. 1 of *Anchor Bible Dictionary*. Edited by David Noel Freedman. 6 vols. New York: Doubleday.
Webster, Jane. 1996. Roman Imperialism and the "Post Imperial Age." Pages 1–17 in *Roman Imperialism: Post-colonial Perspectives*. Edited by Jane Webster and Nicholas J. Cooper. Leicester: School of Archaeological Studies, University of Leicester.
Weiss, Bernhard. 1872. *Das Marcusevangelium und seine synoptischen Parallelen*. Berlin: Hertz.
Weissenrieder, Annette. 2010. The Didactics of Images: The Fig Tree in Mark 11:12–14 and 20–21. Pages 260–82 in *The Interface of Orality and Writing: Speaking, Seeing, Writing in the Shaping of New Genres*. Edited by Annette Weissenrieder and Robert B. Coote. Wissenschaftliche Untersuchungen zum Neuen Testament 260. Tübingen: Mohr Siebeck.
Weissenrieder, Annette, and Robert B. Coote, eds. 2010. *The Interface of Orality and Writing: Speaking, Seeing, Writing in the Shaping of New Genres*. Wissenschaftliche Untersuchungen zum Neuen Testament 260.Tübingen: Mohr Siebeck.
Welborn, Laurence L. 2005. *Paul, the Fool of Christ: A Study of I Corinthians 1–4 in the Comic-philosophic Tradition*. Journal for the Study of the New Testament Supplement Series 293. London: T&T Clark.
———. 2009. "Extraction from the Mortal Site": Badiou on the Resurrection in Paul. *New Testament Studies* 55:295–314.
Wengst, Klaus. 1987. *Pax Romana and the Peace of Christ*. Translated by John Bowden. London: SCM.
Westcott, Brook Foss, and Fenton John Anthony Hort. 1882. *The New Testament in the Original Greek: Introduction, Appendix*. Cambridge: Macmillan.

Windisch, Hans. 1964. Ἕλλην, κτλ. Pages 504–16 in vol. 2 of *Theological Dictionary of the New Testament*. Edited by Gerhard Kittel and Gerhard Friedrich. Translated by Geoffrey W. Bromiley. 10 vols. Grand Rapids: Eerdmans, 1964–1976.

Wink, Walter. 1984. *Naming the Powers: The Language of Power in the New Testament*. Vol. 1 of *The Powers*. 3 vols. Philadelphia: Fortress, 1984–1992.

———. 1986. *Unmasking the Powers: The Invisible Forces that Determine Human Existence*. Vol. 2 of *The Powers*. 3 vols. Philadelphia: Fortress, 1984–1992.

———. 1992a. Beyond Just War and Pacifism: Jesus' Nonviolent Way. *Review and Expositor* 89:197–214.

———. 1992b. *Engaging the Powers: Discernment and Resistance in a World of Domination*. Vol. 3 of *The Powers*. 3 vols. Minneapolis: Fortress, 1984–1992.

Winn, Adam. 2008. *The Purpose of Mark's Gospel: An Early Christian Response to Roman Imperial Propaganda*. Wissenschaftliche Untersuchungen zum Neuen Testament 2/245. Tübingen: Mohr Siebeck.

Winter, Paul. 1961. *On the Trial of Jesus*. Berlin: de Gruyter.

Witherington, Ben, III. 2001. *The Gospel of Mark: A Socio-rhetorical Commentary*. Grand Rapids: Eerdmans.

Wolfreys, Julian. 2004. *Critical Keywords in Literary and Cultural Theory*. New York: Palgrave Macmillan.

World Encyclopedia. 2008. Oxford: Oxford University Press. Online: http://www.oxfordreference.com.ezproxy.ub.gu.se/views/BOOK_SEARCH.html?book=t142&subview=BookHomePages.

Wrede, William. 1901. *Das Messiasgeheimnis in den Evangelien: Zugleich ein Beitrag zum Verständnis des Markusevangeliums*. Göttingen: Vandenhoeck & Ruprecht.

Wright, N. T. 1996. *Jesus and the Victory of God*. Christian Origins and the Question of God 2. London: SPCK.

Yoder, John Howard. 1972. *The Politics of Jesus: Vicit Agnus Noster*. Grand Rapids: Eerdmans.

Young, Robert J. C. 2001. *Postcolonialism: An Historical Introduction*. Oxford: Blackwell.

Zanker, Paul. 1988. *The Power of Images in the Age of Augustus*. Jerome Lectures. Ann Arbor: University of Michigan Press.

Index of Ancient Sources

Biblical Writings

Genesis
- 1:26–27 — 135
- 3:14 — 279
- 9:6 — 135
- 32:22ff. — 113
- 49:8–12 — 259

Deuteronomy
- 21:23 — 248
- 28:25–68 — 266

Psalms
- 2:7 — 90

Isaiah
- 40:9 — 188
- 42:1 — 90
- 42:17–19 — 223
- 43:8–9 — 223
- 52:7 — 188
- 60:6 — 188
- 61:1 — 188

Ezekiel
- 17:23 — 211
- 31:6 — 211

Daniel
- 2:44 — 250
- 4:10–12 — 211
- 4:20–21 — 211
- 7 — 249
- 7:13–27 — 251
- 7:14 — 250
- 7:27 — 250

Micah
- 7:16 — 223

Zechariah
- 9:9 — 259

Matthew
- 2:23 — 164
- 3:13–17 — 89
- 5:41 — 261
- 5:47 — 225
- 6:7 — 225
- 8 — 140
- 8:5–13 — 288
- 8:28 — 212
- 8:28–34 — 97
- 10:16 — 134
- 26:73 — 174
- 13:32 — 211
- 14:1 — 231
- 15:21–28 — 221
- 17:25 — 277
- 18:17 — 225
- 22:17 — 131
- 22:19 — 277, 278
- 25:31–46 — 120, 240
- 25:32 — 120
- 27:32 — 261
- 27:54 — 139

Mark

1:1	1, 9, 87–94, 185–99, 244, 291–92, 296, 311, 312
1:4–11	231
1:9	297
1:9–11	286
1:11	87, 88, 89
1:12–13	210, 298
1:12–16:8	22
1:14	231, 298
1:14–15	192, 210, 218
1:14–8:21	9, 192, 298
1:15	251
1:16	243
1:16–20	210
1:24	286, 87
1:30	234
1:21–28	192
1:21–22	210
1:23–24	210
1:25–26	210
1:28	235
1:29–31	223
1:29–34	192
1:30–34	210
1:34	286
1:35–39	210
1:40–42	210
1:40–45	192
1:45	210
2:1–12	192, 210
2:4	210
2:4–12	224
2:6	210
2:13	174, 278, 313
2:16	210
2:22	184
2:24	210
3:1–5	214
3:1–6	192
3:5	210
3:6	210
3:7	174
3:7–10	210
3:10	235
3:11	87, 210, 286
3:13–19	210, 230
3:15	192
3:16	243
3:20–27	192
3:21–22	210
3:22	174
3:22–23	243
3:23–27	210, 265
3:25	265
3:35	232
4:1	174
4:1–20	251
4:1–34	211, 218, 298
4:5	211, 218, 298
4:14	237
4:16	211, 218, 298
4:17;	197
4:21	224
4:30–32	211, 218, 298
4:30–34	251
4:35	212, 218
4:38–39	212
4:39	174
4:41	174, 235
5:1	174, 212
5:1–20	9, 95–108, 192, 201–219, 223, 230, 262, 288, 290, 311, 314
5:3–4	214
5:6	216
5:7	216, 286
5:8	215
5:9	87, 201–219, 298
5:9–13	214
5:10	206, 213, 216
5:11	206
5:13	174, 206, 207
5:14–15	216
5:15	214, 216, 235
5:17	214, 216, 273
5:19	98, 260, 262
5:19–20	216
5:20	235
5:21	174, 230
5:21–24	192, 223

INDEX OF ANCIENT SOURCES

5:21–43	230	8:27	242
5:24	230	8:27–33	243, 244, 273, 300
5:24–34	233	8:27–10:45	242
5:25–34	192	8:29	214, 242, 244
5:27	235	8:31	174, 242, 244
5:33	233	8:31–9:1	9, 117–21, 239–253, 311
5:35–43	192, 223	8:31–32	242
5:41	175	8:32–33	213
6:5	192	8:33	243, 245
6:7	192	8:34	233, 241, 248, 300
6:7–13	230	8:34–9:1	245, 273
6:14–29	231, 273	8:35	48, 249
6:30	231	8:35–37	249
6:30–44	237, 300	8:36	249
6:31	230	8:37	249
6:32–44	232	8:38	249, 251
6:41	232	8:38–9:1	252, 264, 301
6:47–49	174	9:1	118, 252
6:52	232	9:2–8	118, 252
6:53–56	192, 230	9:2–9	242, 286
6:55	224	9:7	87
6:56	235	9:10	242, 286
7:1	174	9:10–13	231
7:1–13	231	9:14–29	192
7:14–23	231, 299	9:30–37	243
7:24–30	9, 109–15, 192, 221–38, 245, 273, 274, 299, 300, 311, 312, 313	9:31	242
		9:32	242, 286
		9:33	242
7:24	109, 222, 235, 315	9:34	242
7:25	235	10:13–16	251
7:26	175, 221, 225–30, 314, 316	10:17	242
7:1–23	124	10:23	248
7:26	110	10:30;	197
7:27–28	232, 238, 300	10:32	242
7:28	235, 237	10:32–45	243
7:29	235, 237, 300	10:33	174
7:30	224	10:33–34	242
7:31–37	192, 223	10:42	288
7:34	175	10:42–44	262
7:36	235	10:45	233
8:1–10	232, 237, 300	10:46	242
8:6	232	10:46–52	192, 242
8:17–21	232	10:52	242
8:22–26	192, 214, 242	11:1–11	9, 123–29, 219, 253, 255, 257, 273, 301, 312
8:22–10:52	9, 242, 300		

Mark (cont.)

11:1–22	9, 255–267, 311
11:1–16:8	9, 301
11:2	259, 260
11:3	154, 260, 262, 302
11:5	260
11:6	260
11:8	128, 257
11:9	257
11:9–10	263–234
11:10	126
11:11	258, 259, 302
11:12–14	265, 302
11:12–22	265–267, 273
11:15–19	302
11:16	265
11:18	174
11:20–22	265, 302
11:23	265
11:27	174
11:27–33	231, 273
12:1–12	240, 273
12:6–7	286
12:8	273
12:9	240
12:12	274
12:13	274
12:13–17	6, 9, 22, 107, 123, 131–38, 236, 255, 269–84, 302, 311, 312, 318
12:14	131, 274, 275, 276, 277, 281, 282, 313
12:15	274
12:16	274
12:17	131, 134, 269, 272, 274, 282, 284, 302
12:18–27	237
12:27–33	237
12:35–37	286
12:28–34	174, 251
12:38–40	174
12:41–44	241, 265
12:42	233
13:1–2	265
13:1–37	241
13:10	119
13:19	197
13:24	197
13:24–27	249, 252
13:26	118, 241, 264
14:1–2	174
14:3–9	233, 241
14:22	232, 237
14:22–25	237, 300
14:36	289
14:43	174
14:43–52	237
14:53	174
14:61–62	249, 286
14:62	118, 241, 252, 264
14:66–72	174, 213
15:1–5	174
15:1–15	197, 282, 288
15:1–39	274
15:15	237
15:16–20	288
15:17, 20	237
15:18	287
15:19	237
15:19	237
15:17–19	237
15:20	289
15:21	237, 261
15:21–22	142
15:29	289
15:29–32	289
15:31	174, 289
15:32	289
15:33	289
15:33–39	252
15:35–36	231
15:38	289
15:39	9, 139–44, 193, 199, 232, 285–93, 303, 311, 312, 315
15:40–41	290
15:40–16:8	233, 299
15:44–45	288
16:1–7	234
16:1–8	192, 290
16:8	234

INDEX OF ANCIENT SOURCES

Luke		Romans	
1:26	164	1:4	91
7:1–10	288	1:5	228
9:7	231	1:13	228
19:2–8	276	1:14	227, 228
19:28–44	258	1:16	227, 228
20:22	278	1:22	227
23:1–25	197	2:9	228
23:34	141	2:10	228
23:46	141	2:14	228
23:47	141	2:24	228
		3:9	228
John		3:29–30	228
7:35	226	11:17–24	221
12:20	226	13:1	284
13:36	170	13:1–7	196, 284, 303
19:20	226		
21:18–19	170	1 Corinthians	
		1:17–18	247
Acts		1:22	227
2:5–13	175	1:22–24	228
4:13	170	7:17–24	248
4:25–27	227	11:2–16	248
5:29	271	11:7	135
5:37	281	14:33–36	248
6:1	175, 226	15:20–28	240
7:19	237	15:23	249
9:29	175, 227	15:24–25	251
10	140		
14:1–2	227	2 Corinthians	
17:4	227	11:26	237
18:4–6	227		
11:20	227	Galatians	
12:12	169	1:14	237
12:25	169	2:3	227
13:5	169	3:28	228, 238, 248
13:13	169	4:4	91
15:37	169	5:11	247
15:39	169	6:12–14	247
17:5	196	6:14	248
17:6–7	185, 196		
17:1–9	196	Ephesians	
21:37	227	2:16	247

Philippians
- 3:2 — 238
- 3:5 — 237
- 3:18 — 247

Colossians
- 1:20 — 247
- 2:14 — 247
- 3:11 — 227, 238
- 4:10 — 169
- 4:11 — 227
- 4:14 — 227

1 Thessalonians
- 2:19 — 249
- 3:13 — 249
- 4:15 — 249
- 5:23 — 249

2 Thessalonians
- 2:1 — 249
- 2:8 — 249

2 Timothy
- 4:11 — 169
- 4:13 — 180

Philemon
- 24 — 169

Hebrews
- 12:2 — 240

James
- 3:9 — 135

1 Peter
- 1 Peter — 5
- 2:9 — 237
- 5:12–13 — 168
- 5:13 — 170, 172
- 2:13–17 — 192

2 Peter
- 3 — 118

3 John
- 1:7 — 225

Revelation
- 12:9 — 211
- 17:18 — 192
- 17–18 — 196
- 20:2 — 211

Apocrypha, Pseudepigrapha, and Early Jewish Writings

1 Maccabees
- 1:1 — 226
- 1:4 — 275
- 1:11 — 226
- 1:13 — 226
- 1:14 — 226
- 1:10 — 226
- 8:4 — 276
- 8:18 — 226
- 10:86 — 256
- 11:60 — 256
- 13:43–48 — 256
- 14:7 — 256

2 Maccabees
- 4:10 — 226
- 4:17 — 226
- 4:21–22 — 257
- 11:2 — 226
- 4:36 — 225
- 6:4 — 226
- 8:5 — 226
- 8:9 — 226
- 8:16 — 226
- 10:4 — 226

3 Baruch — 250

4 Ezra — 250
- 11:40–45 — 162
- 13 — 249

INDEX OF ANCIENT SOURCES

1 Enoch		2.258–263	263
6:1–8	211	2.402	277
10:1–8	211	2.433–434	257
46–48	249	2.284–292	233
91:12–17	251	2.433	281
93	250	2.433–434	188
		2.499–506	207
Wisdom		3.8	214
1–6	249	3.340–408	163
		4.488	214
Qumran		4.596	192
1QM 1	162	4.618	190, 214
1QM 1:14–15	211	4.657	187
4Q286	211	5.322	187
4Q246 II 1–8	250	5.446–459	247
		5.563	192
Sibylline Oracles		6.312–313	188, 190, 214
5:162–173	162	7.29	188
5:256	225	7.132–157	256
		7.253	281

Philo, *On the Special Laws*

2.92–95	282
3.159–163	282

Ancient Christian Writings

Acts of Peter

37:8	170

Josephus, *Jewish Antiquities*

10.210	163
11.332–336	256
15.361	231
16.12–15	256
16.60	187
17.354–18.2	280
17.271–281	188
18.3–4	280
18.85–87	263
18.116–119	231
20.97–98	263
20.102	281
20.168–171	263

Aristides of Athens, *Apology*

2	46

Augustine, *De consensu evangelistarum*

1.2.4	1

1 Clement

5:4	170

Diognetus

1	237

Eusebius, *Historia ecclesia*

3.1	170
3.39.4	178
3.39.15	168
5.1.29–31	197
6.14.5–7	168

Josephus, *Jewish War*

1.154	276
1.304	267
2.118	281
2.233	281
2.258–260	188

Irenaeus, *Adversus haereses*
3.1.1 — 168

Martyrdom of Polycarp
3:2 — 237
17:1 — 237

Tertullian, *Ad nationes*
1.8 — 237

Tertullian, *Scorpiace*
15 — 170

Greek and Latin Writings

Aelius Aristides, *Roman Oratio*
58–71 — 165
61 — 165
104–105, 109 — 156

Athenaeus of Naucratis, *Deipnosophistae*
6.253 c — 256

Augustus, *Res Gestae Divi Augusti*
1.1 — 156

Caesar, *De bello gallico*
1.1 — 156
4.1–5 — 156
6.11–29 — 156

Cicero, *Epistulae ad Quintum fratrem*
1.16 — 160
1.1.34 — 276
1.16 — 275

Cicero, *De haruspicum responso.*
19 — 156

Cicero, *Pro Flacco*
67 — 161
28.69 — 276

Cicero, *De provinciis consularibus*
10 — 238

Cicero, *Pro Rabirio Perduellionis Reo*
16 — 246

Dio Cassius
52.19.6 — 165
65.8.1 — 214
51.20.2–4 — 257
56.46 — 289

Diodorus Siculus
26.5. — 205
37.26 — 256

Dionysius of Halicarnassus, *Antiquitates romanae*
1.5.1 — 161
2.56 — 289
6.42 — 206

Epictetus, *Diatribai*
4.1.79 — 261

Horace, *Ars poetica*
386–90 — 180

Horace, *Carmina*
1.3.30 — 207

Horace, *Satirae*
1.3.80–83 — 247
2.3.1–2 — 180

Juvenal, *Satirae*
14.96–106 — 162

Livy
pref. 7 — 156
9.16.19–19.17 — 160
29 — 279
36.17.5 — 238

INDEX OF ANCIENT SOURCES

Martial, *Epigrams*
- no verse — 182
- 14.184–192 — 180
- 1.2 — 180

Nicolaus of Damascus, *Vita Caesaris*
- 31 — 206

Pausanias, *Graeciae description*
- 10.4.1 — 164

Persius, *Satirae*
- 3.10–11 — 180

Pliny the Elder, *Naturalis historia*
- 2.189–190 — 156
- 5.66–70 — 6
- 5.75–76 — 224
- 7.95–117 — 156
- 25.16 — 166

Pliny the Younger, *Epistulae*
- 10.96–97 — 197

Plutarch, *Antonius*
- 24.3–4 — 256

Plutarch, *Aristides*
- 7.5 — 166

Plutarch, *Moralia*
- 554 — 247

Plutarch, *Otho*
- 12 — 206

Plutarch, *Romulus*
- 13 — 205
- 20 — 206
- 27.6–7 — 289

Polybius
- 16.25.1–9 — 256

Quintilian, *Institutio oratoria*
- 3.31 — 180
- 5 — 166
- 2.21.16 — 166
- 10.3.32 — 180
- 11.3.142 — 178

Sallust, *Bellum catalinae*
- 11.5 — 160

Seneca, *De clementia*
- 1.1.2. — 156

Strabo, *Geographica*
- 3.3.8 — 206

Suetonius, *Divus Augustus*
- 7 — 214
- 94 — 211

Suetonius, *Divus Julius*
- 1.56.6 — 180

Suetonius, *Nero*
- 25.1–3 — 256

Suetonius, *Vespasianus*
- 1 — 190
- 7 — 192, 214

Tacitus, *Agr.*
- 30 — 159
- 32 — 158

Tacitus, *Annales*
- 15.44 — 197
- 13.50–51 — 282

Tacitus, *Germania* — 156–57

Tacitus, *Historiae*
- 5.2–13 — 162
- 1.2 — 190
- 5.13 — 190
- 4.81 — 192

Varro   162

Virgil, *Aeneid*
  1.254–296   156

Rabbinic Writings

b. 'Abodah Zarah
  2b   163

b. Shabbat
  33b   163

Genesis Rabbah
  20:1   279
  65:1   162

Leviticus Rabbah
  13:5   162

Inscriptions and Papyri

Dittenberger 1903–1905 (*OGIS*)
  540, 15–18   205
  548, 9   205
  643, 7   205
  716, 4   205

Ehrenberg and Jones 1949
  98   189

Grenfell et al. 1898–2010 (P.Oxy.)
  276, 9   205
  2760, 8–9   205
  3111, 5–6   205

Schubart et al. 1895–2005 (BGU)
  272, 1   205
  802, XIV, 25   205
  1108, 3   205

Index of Subjects

agency xi, 27, 33, 37–41, 44–48, 191, 250, 266, 283–84, 303
apocalyptic notions
   as response to imperial domination 234, 249–50, 279
   in Mark's Gospel 188–192, 211, 241, 251–53, 264–66, 301
   Roman appropriation of 190–91
Alexander the Great 160, 225, 256, 275
anachronism 13–15
angareia (forced labor), alluded to in Mark's Gospel 260–62
aporia 239, 245, 286, 288, 291, 300, 311
apotheosis 289–291, 303
Augustus (Octavian) 92, 153, 156, 157, 189–90, 191, 211, 257, 261–62, 276, 279, 280, 288, 289, 297
Babylon 170, 172
Bible and colonialism 27–30
biblical studies
   colonial heritage of 8, 61, 72, 76, 115, 147–48
   nineteenth century 78–83
   ongoing transition of 2–6
   origin of discipline 64–71, 295, 305–21
   postcolonial critique of 2–4, 16–17, 60–72
catachresis 37, 40–41, 183, 203–7, 245–49, 275, 278, 298, 304, 310–11, 312. *See also* Spivak, Gayatri
center and periphery 7, 14, 31, 60–64, 71, 117, 152, 156–57, 170, 172, 228–29, 266, 296, 313, 314, 316, 317, 318–19

Christian mission ix, 16–17, 57–58, 60, 75–83, 96–102, 106–7, 109–15, 118–21, 125–28, 131, 145–48, 256, 307, 312, 317
Church of Sweden vii, xiii
   female ministers 4
codex as literary medium 179–84, 186–88, 296–97
colonial ambivalence 41, 44–46, 48, 159, 161–64, 192–99, 230, 238, 259, 265–67, 273, 285, 291–93, 295, 297, 302, 303, 312. *See also* Bhahba, Homi
colonial heritage x, 8, 31, 61, 72, 76, 115, 147, 148, 295, 305–16, 317, 319, 321
cross (*stauros*) viii, 139, 142, 199, 237, 240–41, 244, 245–49, 251, 261, 285, 289, 291, 300, 301, 315
culture 48, 53, 57–59, 62, 77, 110, 112, 114, 115, 136, 141, 152, 155, 156, 165, 172, 177, 278. *See also* discourse
cultural diversity 46
Diaspora 151, 162, 163, 226, 319
différance xi, 238, 300
disciples 125, 126, 139, 210, 212, 230, 231, 232, 242–43, 248, 251, 260, 262, 265, 290, 291, 292, 300, 321
   gender of 233–36, 238, 299–300
discourse
   analysis 10–13, 34–37
   colonial 11
   definition of 10
   European colonial 34–37, 40, 41, 44–45
   Roman imperial 151–66. *See also* Roman Empire

discourse (cont.)
  theory   10–13, 43
emperors
  and Jesus   215, 288–91, 298
  and masculinity   298
  and taxation   283
  as divinized   156, 189, 191, 271, 288, 289
  as ruler of the world   215, 290, 298
  as Son of God   273, 288–291
eschatology   xi, 20, 21, 117–21, 167, 239–53, 264, 301
ethnicity 5, 31, 38, 39, 46, 109, 114, 156, 157, 162, 175, 183, 221–38, 248, 296, 299, 300, 312, 315, 316
European colonialism   34–37, 40, 41, 44–45. *See also* center and periphery
exegesis 4, 6, 185. *See also* biblical studies
  as opposite of eisegesis   5
Exegetdeklarationen (the exegetical declaration)   4
feminist criticism   5, 17, 43, 52–54, 223
Flavian dynasty   163, 188–92, 213–15, 218, 262, 288, 297, 298
Galilee 6, 9, 18, 19, 20, 109, 166, 168, 170, 173, 192, 222, 224, 233, 234, 237, 299
gender 5, 22. *See also* masculinity and feminist criticism
  in biblical scholarship   63
  in colonial discourse and Mark commentaries   27–29, 102–7, 109–13
  in Mark's Gospel   215, 221–24, 230–38, 41–245, 290, 299–300, 312, 321
  in postcolonial criticism   22, 31, 52–54
  in Roman imperial discourse   157, 158–59, 162, 233, 237
  in the Church of Sweden   4
Gentile 89, 91, 94, 109–15, 139–44, 152, 161, 217–18, 222, 223, 225–230, 295, 299, 312, 314–16. *See also* heathen and pagan
Gospel, in relation to Roman imperial discourse   188–92, 297

Gospel community debate   171–72
Greek/Jew dichotomy
  and orientalism   80, 87–94, 113–15, 120, 126, 133, 139, 143–44, 145–48
  in contemporary scholarship   151–53
Greeks and Jews in the Roman Empire   159–64
heathen   ix, 14, 57, 58, 67, 77, 81–83, 95–102, 106, 108, 109–13, 139–43, 145–48, 162, 202, 217, 225, 311–16. *See also* pagan *and* gentile
hegemony   35, 42, 158, 321
Herod   230–31, 244, 257, 266, 273,
Hinduism   33
Historical criticism. *See* biblical studies
Hosanna cries in Mark's Gospel   263–64
hybridity 41, 46–48, 160, 161, 221, 222, 229, 230, 295, 312. *See also* Bhahba, Homi
ideology   12
identity   7, 11–13, 41–48
imperial cult   288
interpellation   11–13
Ireland and British colonialism   134–38
Islam   33
Jerusalem 9, 123–29, 214, 226, 265–67, 276, 301
  in relation to Galilee in Mark   9, 20, 174, 210, 231, 242–43, 255–67, 301
Jerusalem temple   124, 129, 162, 167, 172, 231, 257, 258, 265–67, 273–74, 282, 289, 302, 304
Jewish revolt 118, 167–68, 177, 188–92, 250, 252, 297, 299, 304
Jews. *See also* Greek/Jew dichotomy *and* Greeks and Jews in the Roman Empire
  and European colonialism 16, 69–70, 80, 87–94, 113–15, 120, 126, 133, 139–40, 143–44, 145–48
  in antiquity 18, 19, 20, 152–53, 159–64, 166, 173, 175, 190–92, 196, 202, 225–30, 231, 233, 238, 263, 266, 273, 276, 279–81, 287, 295, 299
John the Baptist   188, 192, 210, 231–32, 273, 297

INDEX OF SUBJECTS

kyrios (Lord) in Mark's Gospel 260–62
legion 165
  in Mark 5:9 as denoting the Roman army 107–8, 201–19, 230, 298
liberation theology ix, 19, 37, 50–51, 64, 209, 223, 239–40, 247–48, 250, 256, 263
Lord. *See kyrios*
Mark's Gospel 45–46, 48
  as based on Peter's memories 1, 168–72, 278, 296
  as collective representation in its initial circulation 13, 22, 41, 45, 151–304
  choice of passages in current study 9
  contemporary interest in 1–2
  John the Baptist in 188, 192, 210, 231–32, 273, 297
  in its ancient imperial setting 151–304
  narrative crisis 222, 230–38, 241–45
  neglected character of 1–2
  nineteenth-century reception of 87–148
  plot 173, 210–13, 218, 222, 230–38, 241–45, 273, 297–304, 312–13
  primary audience 166–75
  provenance 167–70
  scholarship on 17–23
  significance of urban/rural division for 167–75, 210, 231, 242–43, 255–67, 301
  structure 9, 242
Marxism 10, 12, 13, 19, 33, 34, 35, 38, 42, 43, 50, 58, 117, 154, 155–58, 209, 244
masculinity 77, 157, 160, 161, 210, 215, 237, 262, 289, 298, 303. *See also* gender
material density 247
metonymic gap 275–81
might is right, ideology of 21, 117–21, 132–38, 148
mimicry 41, 44–46, 160–62, 172, 211, 240, 256, 258–67, 273, 283–84, 291, 295, 301–4, 312, 321. *See also* Bhahba, Homi
mourning 310–311

multiculturalism 46
narrative criticism 1, 3, 9, 20, 187, 196, 221–38, 239, 242, 243, 245, 252–53, 264–65, 285–88, 291–93, 295–304
nationalism 16
negotiation in relation to imperial power 6, 21–22, 36, 41, 44, 46–48, 160, 197, 198–99, 267, 281–84, 285, 292, 293, 295, 297, 303, 308, 310, 321. *See also* Bhahba, Homi
new visibility of religion vii
oral medium 172–78, 183, 187, 198, 278, 292, 296. *See also* written medium
orientalism (*See also* Said, Edward) 8, 17, 34–37, 55–60, 78, 80, 81, 89–94, 114, 145, 148
overdetermination 12
pagan 152, 161, 166, 225, 229, 314–16. *See also* heathen *and* gentile
parousia 21, 117–21, 128, 239–53, 256, 259, 260, 264–65, 301
past and present 6–10, 13–15, 62–63
Paul 4, 16–17, 91, 111, 157, 166–67, 173, 174–75, 221, 226, 227–29, 238, 240, 248, 249, 283, 303
pedagogical and performative 263–64, 302. *See also* Bhahba, Homi
persecution 18, 197–98
pharmakon 37, 40–41, 239, 251–52, 301, 310, 312. *See also* Spivak, Gayatri
place, significance of 134–38
plot 173, 210–13, 218, 222, 230–38, 241–45, 273, 297–304, 312–13
postcolonial criticism
  and Sweden viii–xi
  as research field 31–34
  in biblical studies 49–72
  meaning of "post" 30–31
  secularist tendency of 55–60, 310
  theory 27–48
post-Marxism 10, 43–44
postsecular vii, viii, 10, 23, 245, 307, 308, 309–11, 313, 321
poststructuralism 2, 11, 21, 31–34, 37–38, 43, 50, 61–63, 65

power   ix, 10–15, 18, 20, 21, 22,
    31–48, 53, 117–22, 126, 128–29, 154,
    158, 165, 186, 192, 239–53, 255–67,
    275–76, 283–84, 291–93, 295–304.
    See also resistance
Priene   189
race, racism   ix, 16, 37, 46–48, 57, 69,
    80, 89, 93–94, 96, 102–8, 112–13, 143,
    147, 155, 315
religion and politics   vii–viii
representation   11–13. *See also* identity
resistance   19–20, 21–23, 33, 36, 38, 40–
    41, 44–48, 128–29, 134–38, 154, 158,
    160, 167, 174, 244, 247, 250, 270, 271,
    275, 278, 280–84, 313, 317
return of religion   vii
Roman Empire   153–66. *See also*
    discourse: Roman imperial
    center and periphery in   152, 156–57,
        170, 172, 228–29, 266, 296
    forced labor (*angareia*)   157, 260–62
    Greeks and Jews in   159–64
    Mark's audience in   166–75
    Mark's stance vis-à-vis   185–304
    taxation   154, 157, 164–65, 269,
        275–84
    urban/rural division   164–166
Rome
    as center in the Roman Empire   165
    as location of Mark's provenance
        168–72
Romulus   205, 289–91, 303
sea, use of in Mark   169, 174, 278
social-scientific criticism   11, 19, 20, 50,
    51, 170, 207–10
sociorhetorical criticism   11
Son of God
    in contemporary scholarship   151–53
    in Mark's Gospel   192–99, 214, 232,
        262, 285–93, 297, 303, 313
    in nineteenth-century commentaries
        87–94, 139–44
spiritual/worldly dichotomy   17, 118,
    123–29, 131–34, 137, 145–48, 255–56,
    269, 273, 312, 313
    as resistance   128–129
subaltern   37–40, 221, 233–38. *See also*
    Spivak, Gayatri
Sweden   vii–x
    and the postcolonial   viii–xi
taxation
    in Mark's Gospel   269, 273–84
    in the Roman Empire   154, 157,
        164–65
    interpretations of the tribute episode
        (Mark 12:13–17)   131–38, 147–48,
        270–73
textual criticism   192–99
third space   41, 46–48, 263,
    265, 267, 285–93, 303–4, 312. *See also*
    Bhahba, Homi
triumphal entry
    in Roman imperial discourse   158,
        161, 218, 256–58
    in Mark's Gospel   258–65, 273, 298,
        301, 302
uninheriting   310, 319
Vespasian. *See* Flavian dynasty
written medium, significance of   7, 13,
    165, 169, 172–74, 175–84, 187, 198,
    296–97. *See also* oral medium and
    codex

Index of Authors

Abeysekara, Ananda   307, 309–11, 319
Aland, Barbara   179, 181
Aland, Kurt   179, 181
Alexander, Lovedale   183
Althusser, Louis   12
Anderson, Janice Capel   215, 237
Annen, Franz   203, 204
Asad, Talal   309
Ashcroft, Bill   31
Barton, John   5
Bauckham, Richard   171
Belo, Fernando   19
Betz, Hans Dieter   204
Bhabha, Homi   22, 25, 29, 30, 32, 37, 41–48, 199, 211, 230, 235, 240, 255–267, 285–93, 295, 301, 302, 309, 311, 312
Bøe, Sverre   247
Boer, Roland   50
Borg, Annika   5–6
Borg, Marcus   52
Boring, Eugene   185, 187
Botha, P. J. J.   165, 173, 195, 196
Bowersock, G. W.   237, 289
Brandon, S. G. F.   18, 19, 52, 247, 255
Broadbent, Ralph   17
Buell, Denise   46, 307, 315, 320
Byrskog, Samuel   xiii, 168–70, 176
Cameron, Averil   149
Carter, Warren   20
Catchpole, David   255, 256, 257, 258
Cavallo, Guglielmo   179, 182
Chadwick, George A.   85, 95–97, 113, 118, 128–29, 134–38, 147
Chakrabarty, Dipesh   309–10, 319

Clark, Elisabeth   62–63
Collins, Adela Y.   152, 193, 194, 257, 258, 259, 260, 290, 292
Collins, John   3, 162, 188, 250
Conrad, Joseph   3, 29
Cranfield, C. E. B.   186, 193, 235, 242, 255, 271, 286, 315
Crossan, John Dominic   51, 52, 207–8
Crossley, James   167
Culpepper, Alan   287
Dalman, Gustaf   91–94
De Ste. Croix, G. E. M.   154, 155, 164, 165, 166
Deissmann, Adolf   92
Derrett, Duncan   201, 206, 260, 261, 262, 277
Derrida, Jacques   32, 37–41, 239, 241, 251, 286, 291–93, 310, 316
Dewey, Joanna   1, 177, 178, 198, 245
Donahue, John   186, 193, 242, 271, 286
Donaldson, Laura   49, 50, 52, 109, 209, 215, 222, 317
Draper, Jonathan   165
Dronsch, Kristina   187
Dube, Musa   8, 50, 52, 53, 63, 70, 96, 109
Duff, Paul B.   256, 257, 258
Edwards, Catharine   160, 161
Ehrman, Bart   194, 195, 196
Elliott, J.K.   181, 194, 198
Elliott, John   19
Elliott, Neil   50, 283, 315
Engberg-Pedersen, Troels   152
Epp, Eldon   181, 183
Evans, Craig   185, 189, 272
Fanon, Frantz   32, 41, 44, 207–10

Fitzgerald, William 182
Forward, Martin 316
Foucault, Michel 10, 11, 14, 15, 32–40, 65, 117, 154, 172
Fowler, Robert 286, 289
France, Richard 271
Friesen, Steven 175
Gallagher, Susan 49, 50, 317
Gamble, Harry 169, 179–81
Gandhi, Mohandas 32–33
Garroway, Joshua 204–5, 212–13, 216–18
Gerdmar, Anders 152
Gnilka, Joachim 201, 271
Gramsci, Antonio 34, 35, 39, 59, 158
Griffiths, Gareth 31
Grinell, Klas xiii
Guelich, Robert 169, 186, 225
Gundry, Robert 107, 204, 213
Gutiérrez, Gustavo 51
Gwyther, Anthony 50
Haines-Eitzen, Kim 194–96
Hall, Stuart x
Hanson, Paul 249, 250
Harrington, Daniel 167, 186, 193, 242, 271, 286, 316
Harris, WIlliam 165
Hartman, Lars 152, 186, 194, 225, 226, 260, 271, 274, 316
Head, Ivan 167, 168
Head, Peter 193, 194
Hearon, Holly 176, 177
Hengel, Martin 151–52, 168, 169, 246, 314
Hess, Jonathan 16
Hodge, Caroline Johnson 315
Hodgkins, Christopher 82
Hollenbach, Paul 201, 207–10, 216
Holmberg, Bengt 11
Hooker, Morna 169, 186, 225–28, 242, 263, 271
Horsley, Richard 19–20, 42–43, 50, 51, 123, 170, 172–73, 207–8, 210, 222, 244, 256, 263, 307
Hort, F. J. A. 84, 194
Howard-Brook, Wes 50
Iersel, Bas van 168, 225, 242, 272
Incigneri, Brian 167, 168, 170, 171, 197
Jobling, David 13
Johnson, Earl 287, 288, 289
Joy, David 202, 217
Judge, E.A. 261
Kautsky, John 155, 156
Keck, Leander 185
Kelber, Werner 2, 171, 172–74, 176–78, 201
Kelley, Shawn 16
Kim, Tae Hun 152, 288
Kinman, Brent 253, 256, 257, 258
Kloppenborg, John 167
Kümmel, Werner G. 66–67, 69, 168
Kwok Pui-lan 2, 16, 52, 53, 61, 63–64, 109, 111
Lacan, Jacques 32, 44–48
Laclau, Ernesto 10, 12
Lane, William 204, 271, 286
Lau, M. 202, 206
Leander, Hans 255
Lenski, Gerhard 155, 156
Levine, Amy-Jill 315
Liew, Tat-siong Benny 1, 8, 21, 22, 50, 70, 117–21, 233, 239–41, 249–252
Longenecker, Bruce 175
Loomba, Ania 10, 14, 22, 32, 33
Lopez, Davina 52, 157–159, 161
Lundahl, Mikela xiii
Malbon, Elizabeth 239, 285, 287
Malherbe, Abraham 174, 175
Malina, Bruce 52
Marchal, Joseph 52
Marchand, Suzanne 17, 36, 56, 78, 81
Marcus, Joel 167, 169, 186, 187, 188, 193–194, 202, 203, 216, 221, 223, 225, 231, 234, 242, 252, 270, 271, 274, 277
Matera, Frank 185
Mattingly, D. J. 153–154, 158
Meeks, Wayne 166, 174–175
Meyers, Carol 266
Michaelis, Johann David 16, 55–56, 66–70

INDEX OF AUTHORS

Michie, Donald 2
Moore, Stephen xiii, 2, 31, 34, 41, 46, 49–54, 65–71, 139, 201, 202, 215, 217, 237, 240–41, 245, 266, 285, 286, 289
Moore-Gilbert, Bart 30
Mouffe, Chantal 10
Moxnes, Halvor 16
Myers, Ched xiii, 19–20, 52, 169, 170, 171, 192, 201, 210, 214, 223, 231, 244, 253, 255, 264–66, 270, 272
Oepke, Albrecht 253
Olsson, Birger 5
Olsson, Maria 234
Ong, Walter 169
Patte, Daniel 3
Penner, Todd 52, 64–66, 70–71
Perkins, Pheme 260, 271, 282
Perkinson, Jim 109, 222, 235, 236
Peterson, Dwight 171
Pilch, John 237
Pope, Marvin 263
Powell, Mark 285
Preisker, H. 203, 204
Price, Simon 15, 157
Prior, Michael 51
Punt, Jeremy 52,
Räisänen, Heikki 64–71
Ranke, Leopold von 61–62
Reimarus, Hermann Samuel 18
Renan, Ernest 80, 93–94, 147
Resseguie, James 285, 287
Rhoads, David 1, 287
Robbins, Vernon 11
Rohrbaugh, Richard 166, 173, 201,
Roskam, Hendrika 18
Rostovtzeff, Michael 165–66
Runesson, Anna ix, xiii, 61, 202, 216
Runions, Erin 50
Said, Edward 8, 17, 30, 31, 32, 34–37, 38, 41, 48, 55–60, 71, 76, 77, 81, 89–94, 148, 309, 312
Samuel, Simon 21–22, 153, 160, 161, 185, 192, 240
Schildgen, Brenda Deen 1, 2, 16, 320
Schürer, Emil 214

Schüssler Fiorenza, Elisabeth 52, 53, 223
Schweitzer, Albert 16
Schweitzer, Albert 3
Segovia, Fernando 14–15, 49–54, 63, 81, 320
Semler, Johann Salomo 66–69, 79
Sharpe, Jenny 27–29
Sherwood, Yvonne 65–71
Shiell, William 178
Shiner, Whitney 169, 178, 287
Smallwood, Mary 192, 214
Smith, Dennis 185
Soares-Prabhu, George 61, 63
Spivak, Gayatri xi, 30, 32, 37–41, 48, 183, 207, 221–38, 251–52, 295, 298, 309, 310–11, 312, 319
Stanley, Christopher 162, 316
Stanton, Graham 1, 179–84, 187
Starr, Raymond 182, 183
Stegemann, Ekkehard 155, 156, 173
Stegemann, Wolfgang 155, 156, 173
Stenström, Hanna xiii
Strauss, David F. 73, 75–76, 99, 102, 125
Strecker, Christian 209
Strecker, Georg 188
Stuhlmacher, Peter 188
Sugirtharajah, R. S 17, 21, 49, 50, 60, 63, 81, 202, 320
Swete, Henry Barclay 84–86, 100, 107, 118, 123–24, 126, 136, 143–44
Taylor, Vincent 186, 198, 225, 229–30, 252, 255, 260, 263, 269, 271
Telford, William 167, 168, 265
Thatcher, Tom 176, 177
Theissen, Gerd 52, 169, 173, 174, 202, 210, 224
Thörn, Lennart xi
Thurman, Eric 161, 211, 233, 289
Tiffin, Helen 31
Tolbert, Mary Ann 50, 53, 223
Tosh, John 61–62
Townsend, John 16–17
Tutu, Desmond 307, 317
Van Oyen, Geert 287

Vander Stichele, Caroline   52, 64–66, 70–71
Waetjen, Herman   19, 20, 169, 170, 173, 201, 202, 207, 223
Ward, Graham   vii, 237
Wasserman, Tommy   xiii, 186, 194
Weissenrieder, Annette   176, 187, 265
Welborn, Laurence   246–47
Wengst, Klaus   201, 204
Westcott, B.F.   84, 194
Windisch, Hans   225–30
Wink, Walter   52, 261
Winn, Adam   20–21, 185, 192
Witherington, Ben   271
Yoder, John H.   52
Young, Robert   33
Zanker, Paul   157
Zetterholm, Magnus   xiii

www.ingramcontent.com/pod-product-compliance
Lightning Source LLC
Chambersburg PA
CBHW021351290426
44108CB00010B/197